To friendship between

ISRAEL AT FIFTY Scotland

& Israel

Mark Rance

ISRAEL AT FIFTY

Five Decades of Struggle for Peace
A Diplomat's Narrative

Moshe Raviv

Weidenfeld & Nicolson
LONDON

To Hana and our children
Orna, Ilan and Yuval

First published in Great Britain in 1998
by Weidenfeld & Nicolson

Second impression 1998

© 1998 Moshe Raviv

A CIP catalogue record for this book is available
from the British Library.

ISBN 0 297 81851 1

Printed in Great Britain by
Butler & Tanner Ltd, Frome and London

Weidenfeld & Nicolson
The Orion Publishing Group Ltd
Orion House
5 Upper Saint Martin's Lane
London, WC2H 9EA

Contents

involvement in Syria and Egypt, the War of Attrition along the Suez; the Rogers Plan, and its rejection by both sides; Nasser's death – Sadat becomes President of Egypt; the deep-penetration raids in Egypt, and their consequences; terror in the air; 'Black September' – confrontation between King Hussein and the Palestinians in Jordan; Syrian troops threaten the Hashemite Kingdom; King Hussein turns to Israel – IDF units are mobilized – the Syrians retreat; the proposal for an interim Suez Canal agreement, and its failure; the second Rogers initiative for a cease-fire, and its acceptance by Israel and Egypt; Begin leaves the National Unity Government

THE FIFTH DECADE, 1988–98

Acknowledgements

The genesis of this volume can be traced back to one of many friendly conversations with Lord Weidenfeld in early 1995. It was his enthusiasm and encouragement, and my sense that the fiftieth year of the State of Israel would be a time both of immense pride and intense introspection which should be expressed, that gave me the impetus to write. I am immensely grateful to him.

A special debt of gratitude goes to my editor, Elsbeth Lindner. Her erudite advice, professionalism and patience made my work so much easier. Ravi Mirchandani was also extremely helpful and I am very grateful to him.

Sincere thanks also to the US Ambassador Alfred (Roy) Atherton for his comments on the chapter dealing with the attempts to reach a partial Suez Canal agreement with Egypt; to Brigadier-General Arye Shalev, of the Jaffee Center for Strategic Studies at Tel Aviv University, for his comments on the Six Day War and the Yom Kippur War chapters; and to Ambassador Eytan Ruppin for his suggestions for the chapter dealing with the relations between Israel and Germany.

The volumes of selected documents on Israel's foreign relations edited by Meron Medzini were invaluable in my work. My appreciation and gratitude to him.

Many of the pictures in the book are the work of two photographers, Sydney Harris and John R. Rifkin. My sincere thanks to both of them.

Above all, many of the ideas in the book resulted from endless discussions with my colleagues in the Ministry of Foreign Affairs during the past forty years. Their talent and creative thinking helped me shape my opinions. I am grateful to them all.

Moshe Raviv
Jerusalem
May 1998

Biographical Note

Since October 1993 I have served as ambassador to the Court of St James's. By the time this book appears I will have completed more than forty years in the Israeli diplomatic service, including fourteen years in three separate tours of duty in London and six years in our Embassy in Washington DC.

I arrived in Israel in October 1948, a few months after the state was proclaimed, and a mere six months after my bar mitzvah, having spent the war years in the Ukraine. My parents made their way to Israel separately, with a stopover in the camps in Cyprus, courtesy of the British mandatory authorities. In 1956, after the completion of high school and army service, I joined the Ministry of Foreign Affairs, while continuing my university studies in international relations at the Hebrew University in Jerusalem and at London University.

In March 1958 I was assigned to London, as head of the Embassy archive, and in 1961, I was promoted to the diplomatic service with the rank of attaché; and later second secretary, responsible for dealings with the Commonwealth countries.

In July 1964, I was appointed as deputy to the political adviser to Foreign Minister Golda Meir, a position I held until her resignation at the end of 1965.

In January 1966, Abba Eban succeeded Mrs Meir as Foreign Minister, and invited me to become his political secretary. For the next two and a half years I worked in very close association with Eban. The diplomatic activity during the Six Day War and the Security Council debate on Resolution 242 were our foremost challenges during that period.

In June 1968, I was appointed political counsellor to the Israeli Embassy in Washington, serving for five years with ambassador Yitzhak Rabin. After Rabin returned to Israel, I was asked by Abba Eban to remain in my post for another year with his successor, Simcha Dinitz returning to Israel in 1974.

After a short period as director of the East European Department in the Foreign Office, I was appointed, in February 1976, as Head of the North American Department, serving under Foreign Minister Yigal Allon.

In the summer of 1978, I received my first ambassadorial assignment as envoy to the Philippines. From Manila I also covered Hong Kong, and the next three years presented me with a wonderful opportunity to get acquainted with south-east Asia and beyond.

Between 1981 and 1983, I headed the Economic Department of the Foreign Ministry. In mid-1983 I was appointed to the Embassy in London as minister plenipotentiary (deputy chief of mission).

After five years in London I became, in 1988, deputy director-general of the Foreign Ministry in Jerusalem, in charge of information, dealing, amongst other issues, with Israel's information efforts during the Gulf War, the Madrid Peace Conference and launching the multilateral peace negotiations in the Moscow conference.

In October 1993, I returned as ambassador to the Court of St James's.

Throughout my diplomatic career I have been accompanied by my wife Hana, whom I married in 1955. She shared the joys and sorrows, the travels and travails and the heavy responsibility of diplomatic life as a wonderful companion, critic, friend and mother of our three children; our daughter, Orna, who is a journalist with an Israeli daily newspaper, Ilan, who is a banker with a leading bank in Tel Aviv and our son Yuval, currently working in investment banking in the city of London.

Introduction

This narrative is not a scholarly account of Israel's first fifty years. It is a record of close observation and personal analysis by one who was fortunate to be intimately involved in the making and practice of Israel's diplomacy during four decades of this formative period in the history of the Jewish state. This book does not cover, therefore, the whole spectrum of accomplishments and failures during this era but rather concentrates on Israel's foreign relations and its relentless quest for peace.

The State of Israel was proclaimed three years after the end of the Second World War and the terrible tragedy that befell the Jewish people. In a modest hall of the Tel Aviv Museum, David Ben-Gurion read out the Declaration of Independence on 14 May 1948. Conscious of the historic crossroads in the destiny of the Jewish people, the first Prime Minister of Israel referred to the ancient ties between the Jewish people and Israel: 'Here [in the Land of Israel] their spiritual, religious and political identity was shaped. Here they first attained statehood, created cultural values of national and universal significance, and gave the world the Eternal Book of Books.'

A series of historical events profoundly influenced the attitudes of Israel's founding fathers: the Zionist dream of re-establishing in a Jewish sovereignty in Eretz Israel after two thousand years in exile; the deep sense of the loss of six million Jews in the Holocaust; the struggle to terminate the British mandate; and the ongoing battle against the Arabs, who had rejected the Partition Plan and opposed the establishment of Israel. It was to the Arabs that Ben-Gurion addressed himself in the declaration saying, 'We extend our hand to all neighbouring states and their peoples in an offer of peace and good neighbourliness.'

It took thirty-one years for Egypt to reply positively to this historic call by signing a peace treaty with Israel in 1979. The Palestinians procrastinated much longer; the first serious breakthrough was achieved fourteen years later in the negotiation of the Declaration of Principles in Oslo in 1993. The peace treaty with Jordan was signed by Prime Minister Rabin and King Hussein in 1994.

Throughout those years, Israel fought five bitter wars, a continuous chain of terrorist activities, a full-scale War of Attrition in the Sinai and the intifada. Thousands and thousands of gallant soldiers gave their lives in the defence of the young state. Their heroism afforded long periods of relative tranquillity, in which wave after wave of immigration was absorbed; the Israeli Defence Forces were built into a modern and sophisticated fighting army; and the economic and social structure was moulded. Thus Israel could resist the pressures to settle for less than full peace treaties with its neighbours.

To the names of the war heroes we must add those of the martyrs for peace. They are the three leaders who were struck down by Arab and Jewish extremists for making peace: King Abdullah of Jordan, President Sadat of Egypt and the Prime Minister of Israel, Yitzhak Rabin.

At the time of writing, the circle of violence has not ended. Peace treaties with Syria and Lebanon are still needed in order to conclude a comprehensive peace.

During the past fifty years, numerous attempts were made to negotiate peace. Only a few were successful. The relentless quest for peace, together with the need to establish firmly Israel's position in the international community, has dominated Israel's diplomatic efforts and history. It is with these continuous endeavours that this narrative deals.

1

From the British Mandate to Jewish Sovereignty

The history of the creation of Israel as a Jewish state is inseparable from British foreign and colonial policy between 1917 and 1948. Speaking in Parliament in June 1996, Prime Minister John Major correctly asserted that the relationship between Israel and Britain was better than 'in any stage in the history of the State of Israel'. Compared to the bitter controversies, severe tensions and heated passions which characterized the beginning of this relationship, the current state of affairs clearly demonstrates the dramatic improvements since the struggle for Jewish sovereignty reached its climax.

By 1917, as the First World War drew to an end, the Zionist movement, led by Dr Chaim Weizmann and Nachum Sokolov, had grown into a meaningful force. In their conversations with allied statesmen in London and Paris the two leaders articulated the aim of Jewish nationalism – a national home in Palestine. As immigration into Palestine was growing and the Jewish population was becoming more assertive, the British government, under Lloyd George and his Foreign Secretary, Arthur Balfour, realized that a striving Jewish community in Palestine might become an important asset in the British imperial strategy in the Middle East and in the defence of the Suez Canal.

Weizmann could also see the advantages of close collaboration with Britain for achieving the realization of the Zionist dream – the return of the Jewish people to Zion, to the land of Israel. His efforts during 1917 were therefore devoted to achieving a commitment to a Jewish Homeland from the British Cabinet. Weizmann's affinity with Britain, his diplomatic skills and powers of persuasion and Balfour's profound understanding of the Jewish dilemma and the Zionist objectives greatly helped. Speaking to Harold Nicolson in 1917, Balfour said that the 'Jews have been exiled, scattered and oppressed. If we can find them an asylum, a safe home, in their native land, then the full flowering of their genius will burst forth and propagate.'[1] Weizmann and Balfour also developed a personal friendship, and after much collaborative endeavour their efforts came to fruition. The Balfour Declaration, approved by the British Cabinet, was enshrined in a letter of 2 November 1917 to Lord Rothschild, a prominent member of the Jewish community in England. A key sentence in the declaration said that 'His Majesty's Government view with favour the establishment in Palestine of a national home for the Jewish people, and will use their best endeavours to facilitate the achievement of this objective.'

The Balfour Declaration electrified the Jewish world. Wherever there were Jews they rejoiced in new hope. Yet its full realization was years away, years filled with rivers of blood and great anguish. However, support for a British protectorate in Palestine, which was one of the objectives of the declaration, was assured.

At the end of the First World War the British and French agreed to divide between themselves the responsibility for the countries that had formed part of the Turkish Empire. France would assume responsibility for Syria while Britain would have the mandate over Palestine. This arrangement was approved by the Peace Conference in San Remo on 25 April 1920. The Arab population in Palestine at the time amounted to approximately 560,000, while the number of Jews had decreased to 55,000, as many had left during the war because of the hardships that it caused. Clashes between the two communities ensued and the imposition of law and order was one of the first tasks of the new British administration.

Britain, as the mandatory power, intended to ensure the cooperation of Arabs and Jews in the development of Palestine. However, attempts made by the British to work together with both populations were constantly frustrated by the Arabs. The first British High Commissioner, Sir Herbert Samuel, wished to establish an advisory council with the participation of Muslims, Jews and Christians, but extremists among the Arabs subjected the Muslim representatives to heavy pressure and they had to withdraw from the council. The High Commissioner further suggested to the Arabs that they form an agency which would operate in the same manner as the Jewish Agency, the main self-governing Jewish organization, which was authorized by the mandate. However, they refused. It was in line with their consistent rejection of any measure of the self-governing authority that the British High Commissioner accorded the Jews. Arab hostility to the Zionist enterprise was uncompromising and early attempts to reach even limited agreements were unsuccessful. The Zionist leadership, including Ben-Gurion himself, made many attempts to develop a meaningful dialogue with the Arabs, sadly without much success. Whether proposals for cooperation came from the British or the Jews, they ended in failure. Only at the municipal level was there a measure of collaboration.[2]

Despite continuous tensions, British-controlled Palestine developed rapidly. The High Commissioner introduced proper modes of administration, an infrastructure was built, an education system, a judiciary and all the other organs of government began to operate in an orderly manner. The two major points of contention by the Arabs that continuously surfaced were the rate of Jewish immigration and the acquisition of land by Jews. In fact, both communities were growing. The Arab community increased from 600,000 in 1920 to 960,000 by 1935. They benefited from the ordinances and the administrative competence of the mandate, yet Arab nationalism and extremism, led by the Mufti, Haj Amin al-Husseini, the president of the Supreme Muslim Council, was constantly on the rise. Long periods of tranquillity were interrupted by outbreaks of violence against Jews, the most notorious of which erupted in 1929, when sixty Jews were murdered in Hebron. Between 1936 and 1939 the Arab violence was directed against both the British and the Jews, in what became to be known as the Arab Revolt.

As the end of the 1930s approached, the European horizon had become darker and grimmer and war became a real possibility. In Palestine, Arab violence continued and in London there was the fear that in case of war the Arabs might side with the Nazis, as indeed some of them eventually did. In February 1939 Britain decided to convene a round table conference in London in a renewed attempt to reach an understanding between the Jews and Arabs in Palestine. However, the Arabs put forward an uncompromising pre-conference demand – the termination of the British mandate and the establishment of an Arab state in Palestine, which could only lead to the complete failure of the conference. The British government, headed by Neville Chamberlain, then set out its policy in a White Paper on the Palestine question, a document that clearly ignored Jewish concerns and was apparently designed to appease the Arabs. On the key issue of Jewish immigration there were new, severe limitations; only 75,000 Jews were to be allowed into Palestine in the next five years. Rigid restrictions were imposed on the purchase of land and there was stipulation that after ten years a Palestinian state would be established, which under prevailing circumstances would have meant a state dominated by an Arab majority with a Jewish minority. These policies caused deep disappointment to the Yishuv (the Jews living in Palestine) and the Zionist movement and presented a crushing blow to the hopes and dreams of millions of Jews in Europe, who were under imminent peril. The White Paper completely disregarded the threat of Hitler and Nazi Germany, and the fact that the noose was tightening around six million Jews, who had nowhere to flee except to Palestine. It rendered meaningless the promise contained in the Balfour Declaration of 1917, of Palestine becoming a national home for the Jews.

The anger generated by the White Paper was shortly to be overtaken by a much graver agony – the outbreak of the Second World War – in September 1939. Instantly every Jew became an ally of the British in the long and bitter struggle against Nazi Germany. Ben-Gurion as chairman of the Zionist Executive defined this attitude very succinctly: 'We will fight with the British against Hitler as if there were no White Paper; we will fight the White Paper as if there were no war.' To the young and able, the leadership of the Yishuv recommended joining the British forces. This call was heeded by over a hundred thousand volunteers, who served in many branches of the forces. In the latter stages of the war a Jewish Brigade was formed as part of the British Army. It took part in the fight for the liberation of Italy from Mussolini's Fascist dictatorship. Two future presidents of the State of Israel, Herzog and Weizmann, and a considerable number of top officers of the Israel Defence Forces, were among the many Jewish men and women who fought alongside the British forces.

The active struggle against the mandate had to be delayed until the war was over. However, the quest for a better future and the planning of the Zionist leadership for developments in Palestine in the postwar 'world order' continued. It was hoped that close collaboration with the allies during the war would result in a much more sympathetic understanding of the Zionist cause after it. Representatives from the Zionist organizations met in New York in May 1942, in the middle of the war, and issued what became to be known as the Biltmore Programme for the postwar period. Its outline was consistent with the long-term objectives of the Zionist movement: free immigration supervised by the Jewish Agency, the right to develop uncultivated land in Palestine and the 'establishment of a Jewish Commonwealth integrated into the structure of the new demo-cratic world'. The Biltmore Programme became the manifesto of the World Zionist Organization.

At the end of the Second World War, with the overwhelming majority of Jews in east and central Europe wiped out by the Holocaust, the surviving remnants attempted to find a new life in Palestine. They soon realized that the end of the war had brought little respite to their plight. The displaced-persons camps were filled with Jewish survivors. Jewish refugees from eastern Europe, who correctly sensed that the Communist regimes would soon put a stop to emigration, flocked to the same camps, now overflowing with people. The vast majority of the camp dwellers were single-minded in their determination to go to the promised land of Eretz Israel, to Palestine. It seemed that everything had changed as a result of the horrors of the war except the policies set out by Britain in the 1939 White Paper, which blocked immigration into Palestine. The tragic irony was that many Jews perished in the Holocaust because the gates of Palestine had been closed before the war, and now those who survived remained in an untenable situation for the same reason.

In Britain the Labour Party won the 1945 elections. Clement Attlee replaced Winston Churchill as Prime Minister and Ernest Bevin became Foreign Secretary. The Zionist Organization had high hopes of accelerating the termination of the British mandate, especially in light of the Labour Party annual conference resolution of 1944, which advocated a Jewish state in Palestine, but it soon became clear that there was nothing more remote from Bevin's thought than fulfilling that promise. Bevin's concerns now seemed to be centred on how to appease the Arabs so that British interests in the Arab world would be assured, how to protect the oil flow from the Middle East and how to continue the British military presence in the eastern Mediterranean. Another priority was to maintain the goodwill of the American people, Britain's reconstruction being greatly dependent on American economic aid and on the continuation of the special relationship between the US and the UK. The fate of the hundreds of thousands of Jewish refugees in the displaced-persons camps seemed of secondary importance. As far as Bevin was concerned, these people should have resettled in Europe, thus ignoring the fact that parts of Europe had become a gigantic mass grave for Jews. These policies, although expressed by Bevin as Foreign Secretary, reflected the views of the Foreign Office and the army high command, and were supported by Prime Minister Attlee.

Although the British mandate had initially been welcomed by the Zionist Organization and the Yishuv, there was an inherent conflict between the Jewish population, which by the end of the Second World War was approximately half a million, and the mandatory colonial power, Great Britain. At its root was the clash between the desire of the British government to continue its presence in Palestine and the determination of the Jewish people, inside and outside Palestine, to establish a Jewish state. This conflict reached its climax after the Second World War. The Jews now saw the mandate even more clearly as a transient phase, while Britain, under Attlee and Bevin, was not prepared to consider a finite timetable for its termination (and only did so two years later, in 1947).

Faced with this reality, the Zionist organizations had no choice but to embark on a direct collision course with the British government. Their objective was twofold: free immigration and a Jewish state. The means to achieve them were an increase in the Jewish population in Palestine through illegal immigration and the stepping up of the defence capability, which included training of the Hagannah and the Palmach, the underground defence arms of the state to be, as well as the procurement of any and all types of arms. These capabilities were to enable the future Jewish state to protect itself against an Arab onslaught once the mandate had been relinquished. Simultaneously, diplomatic efforts were intensified in order to gain the support of American and British public opinion.

There was a clear consensus in the Zionist movement on the objectives, yet sharp differences on the tactics, expressed in three main viewpoints. The moderates were led by Chaim Weizmann, the president of the World Zionist Organization. He believed that British public opinion would turn the tide and favoured patience and perseverance. The activists, who were led by David Ben-Gurion, chairman of the executive of the Jewish Agency and the leader of the Jews living in Palestine, took a balanced approach favouring a controlled use of force and diplomacy. They did not exclude a limited use of force against material objects such as the blowing up of bridges, but they opposed the killing of British soldiers and wanted to avoid an outright confrontation with the British at all costs. The militant approach was led by the Revisionist Party headed by Menachem Begin, who advocated the use of force, and built Etzel as their military wing. A more extreme splinter group – known as Lehi – was later formed, headed by Yair Stern and then by Yitzhak Shamir. Etzel and Lechi did not accept the discipline of the Yishuv leadership, although during certain stages of the struggle there was cooperation between the three. As all shades of the Zionist movement fought for a common goal, they all contributed in various degrees to its attainment.

By 1946, it became clear that it was extremely difficult to reconcile the Jewish hopes and aspirations with Arab demands. Already the Arabs adopted a policy of 'all or nothing', which blocked any attempt to find a solution acceptable to both sides. They demanded an Arab state in the whole of Palestine. It was this negative, but unfortunately consistent, approach that then and in later years stood in the way of all attempts to resolve the Arab–Israeli conflict. Not until fifty years later, half a dozen wars and much blood of Jews and Arabs alike, did the Arabs accept the fundamental principles of compromise.

In December 1946 the first postwar Zionist Congress convened in Geneva, and the various approaches to the struggle against the British mandate were tested and voted upon. As a result, Dr Weizmann stepped down as president of the Zionist Organization and Ben-Gurion took his place. It was clear that diplomacy alone would not persuade the Attlee government to relinquish the mandate. An element of resistance was also required, and Ben-Gurion, who commanded widespread support in the Yishuv, was the right man to lead the conclusive Zionist drive. However, Dr Chaim Weizmann remained a prominent leader, and was very helpful in the diplomatic efforts to win a Jewish state. He became the first President of the State of Israel in 1948.

Illegal immigration into Palestine intensified in spite of attempts by the British Navy to block it. The confrontations between destitute refugees and British naval ships received worldwide publicity and caused considerable embarrassment to the Attlee government. Some ships, like the *Exodus*, were returned to their port of embarkation; pictures of women and children being dragged off ships by British soldiers caused consternation. American public opinion became enraged, and eventually President Truman felt that he had to press London to allow a larger number of Jews into Palestine.

The rift between the United States' views of the issue and the Bevin approach grew wider. Besides his innate anticolonialist inclination, President Truman was also concerned with the human aspects of the problem – with the plight of the survivors. Two American initiatives were of significance in the process: the establishment of the Anglo-American Committee of Inquiry at the beginning of 1946, a development which the Attlee government did not like but could not reject, and the Truman Declaration in the autumn of 1946.

After months of deliberations, the Anglo-American Committee submitted, on 1 May 1946, a unanimous set of recommendations of which two were particularly significant: the British should allow the immediate immigration of 100,000 Jewish survivors of Nazi persecution into Palestine, and the eventual establishment of a bi-national state. President Truman endorsed the first recommendation on the day that the committee's report was published. He rightly chose to ignore its proposal of a bi-national state. The reaction of the British government was less positive. Soon after the release of the report Attlee made clear his disapproval of it and voiced in the House of Commons a most unrealistic demand – that 'Jews and Arabs in Palestine alike must disarm immediately.'

Richard Crossman, a prominent Labour Member of Parliament and one of the six British members of the Anglo-American Committee wrote to the Prime Minister. Expressing his distress at Attlee's feeling that the report was 'grossly unfair to Great Britain', he went on to expose the historic reversal of Labour policy on Palestine. In Crossman's words:

> I believe that morally we are bound to rescue those Jews in Europe, and let them go to the only place which will welcome them, the National Home. I believe that militarily this can be done with the minimum risk of bloodshed if we are firm and show the Arabs that we mean business. But equally I am convinced that the Labour government, which has consistently supported Zionism and denounced the White Paper, cannot go back on its word in the face of this unanimous report without causing the very bloodshed you are so anxious to avoid, and also performing what must be a deeply dishonourable action.[3]

Although Foreign Secretary Bevin had announced that he would accept the Anglo-American report if it were unanimous, its recommendations were rejected, and the idea of a bi-national state lost ground. So did other options for a solution, like 'provincial autonomy'. At the same time the notion of the partition of Palestine into a Jewish state and an Arab state gained momentum in the United States. This idea was convincingly expounded by Dr Nahum Goldman, the president of the World Jewish Congress, who travelled to Washington and, in a series of conversations with top American officials, convinced them that partition was the only viable solution to the Palestine question. They, in turn, persuaded President Truman of its merits.

On 4 October 1946, the eve of the most important Jewish holy day, Yom Kippur, President Truman published the Truman Declaration along with the customary greetings to the American Jewish community. As a courtesy to its ally, Great Britain, the President had sent a copy of his declaration a day earlier to Attlee, who asked Truman to postpone its publication. Truman refused and the declaration was published as planned.

The Truman Declaration of 4 October 1946, which advocated 'the creation of a viable Jewish state in control of its own immigration and economic policies in an adequate area of Palestine, instead of the whole of Palestine', ranks second only to the Balfour Declaration in the annals of Zionism and in the history of Israel. It greatly advanced the idea of partition as the only feasible option. Attlee's reaction to the statement was fury; he wrote to Truman complaining that he had not had even a 'few hours' grace from the President' so that he could acquaint himself with the actual situation and the probable results.[4] At the end of 1946, the gulf between Britain and the United States on the subject of Palestine was wider than ever before.

At the beginning of 1947, informal talks between a Jewish Agency delegation led by Ben-Gurion and the Foreign and Colonial Secretaries were held in London. This was the last attempt by the British government to persuade the Zionist Organization to consider the one-state option before they relinquished the mandate over Palestine. For their part, Ben-Gurion and his colleagues used this opportunity to prompt the British government to accept the notion of partition. In the first conference, on 29 January 1946, Ben-Gurion explained that his delegation had two aims in mind; to assure Jewish national sovereignty and Jewish–British friendship. There was no meeting of minds on a basis for a solution. The theme of Jewish–British friendship was further expanded in a private conversation between Ben-Gurion and Bevin on 12 February 1947. It was a remarkable attempt to find, at the eleventh hour, some common ground. It was at Ben-Gurion's request that they met, with only the top Middle East expert in the Foreign Office, Harold Beely, present. Bevin told Ben-Gurion that if it were proved that a compromise between Jews and Arabs was impossible, Britain would leave Palestine. Bevin added that Britain 'does not have to carry the burden alone, and it has no interest in Palestine'. Ben-Gurion was apparently surprised that after such a fierce fight against Zionist policy in Palestine, Bevin would suddenly assert that Britain had no interest in Palestine. He said:

> You know better the British interest and if you think that you have no interest
> in Palestine, I shall not take it upon myself to tell you that you have. I shall

tell you why we are interested that England maintains its position in the world and in this part of the world. It is not out of gratitude for the Balfour Declaration – there are more profound reasons than that. For us, this is a partnership of interests and ideals. Although it is impertinent when a tiny people speak of a partnership with a world power ... We shall remain a small people but a European people.

Bevin replied that he did not want Britain to conduct a policy of a world power and that he believed in peace and equality.

The conversation is recorded in its entirety in Ben-Gurion's memoirs, and it is interesting in that even amidst such a difficult struggle, Ben-Gurion avoided confrontation with Britain. On the contrary, he pointed out the Jews' affinity and respect for Anglo-Saxon ideals of liberalism, freedom and tolerance. He went beyond idealism to strategy, and made it clear to Bevin that if there was an interest in maintaining British forces in the Negev it would not be impossible. In that conversation Ben-Gurion also expressed the agreement of the Zionist Organization to the partition of Palestine, the plan he had outlined in detail to Harold Beely the day before. Although it may not have been the ideal solution, Ben-Gurion and many of his colleagues in leadership positions believed that partition held the best promise for an independent Jewish state.

It seems that by then Bevin had already decided to relinquish the British mandate on Palestine. The confrontation with the Yishuv and the illegal immigrants was costly and humiliating. One hundred thousand British troops were stationed in Palestine in order to protect a lost cause, and the cost of maintaining troops reached an expenditure of £30–40 million a year, which could scarcely be afforded at a time when Britain was suffering severe economic hardships. Also, the rift with the US over this issue was widening and public opinion both in Britain and across the Atlantic was critical of the Bevin policies. At last the British government recognized the futility of its struggle as well as the impossibility of reconciling the determined drive for a Jewish state with Arab nationalism. Two days after Bevin's conversation with Ben-Gurion, on 14 February 1947, the British government decided to transfer the issue of Palestine to the United Nations, without any recommendation or suggestion as to how to proceed. A few days later Bevin, weary and frustrated, announced the decision to Parliament.

With this decision, the long and difficult struggle against the British mandate saw its closing stages. On 29 November 1947 the General Assembly of the UN approved the resolution on the partition of Palestine. Seven months later, on 14 May 1948, the State of Israel was proclaimed.

As for Bevin's role on Palestine, it is instructive to read the view of Lord Jenkins: 'What were his mistakes? Palestine is clearly a strong candidate.

Here he was both stubborn and provocative ... he showed a lack of imagination in his failure to appreciate the force of the Jewish determination to establish a state in Palestine.'[5]

Even with fifty years of hindsight it is hard to understand Bevin's actions. How had he failed to see the impact that the Second World War and the Holocaust had had on the Jewish people and on British and world public opinion? How he did not comprehend that, after such a change in the fortunes of the Jewish people, the White Paper policy of 1939 could under no circumstances be carried forward. How could he not find a way to balance the British interest in the Arab world with a more forthcoming attitude to the historic return of the Jews to Zion? Although his policy was sanctioned by Attlee and supported and at times initiated by Harold Beely and his colleagues in the Foreign Office, Bevin was the driving force, the advocate of these policies and he bears the major responsibility for making an initially friendly Jewish population in Palestine hostile to Britain. Immense resources were squandered in a lost cause, and the suffering of hundreds of thousands of war refugees was unnecessarily prolonged. History will record that many British political leaders, not least Winston Churchill, opposed Bevin's policies on Palestine. However, in our pantheon of anti-Zionists Bevin will for ever rank high.

During my service as ambassador to London I was interested whether, after almost five decades, now that the State of Israel is flourishing, people who had worked with Bevin would entertain second thoughts on the 1945–7 mandatory policy and perhaps admit that things could have been different. I found that Sir Harold Beely was still alive and well, and invited him for a drink at the Atheneum in July 1996. I said to Sir Harold that a diplomat who does not possess a sense of history is, in my view, not a good diplomat. This is why I was interested to meet him as the surviving chief adviser to Bevin on the Middle East. I asked Sir Harold whether, looking back over a period of fifty years, he still thought that the Bevin policy on Palestine was right. I emphasized that we were talking about the years 1945–8, immediately after the end of the Second World War and the Holocaust. Was there a need to create such a rift between Great Britain and the Jews? Beely replied that at the time he had supported Bevin's judgement on the Palestine issue. Bevin had a plan of his own for solving the Palestine question, which was a bi-national state; Beely was putting Bevin's thoughts in the right language, but the plan did not work.

I was not able to detect any sense of regret in Beely's words. Recalling that he was the secretary to the Anglo-American Committee of Inquiry I asked Beely whether Richard Crossman's accusation, that Bevin went back on his promise to accept the recommendations of the committee if they were unanimous, was correct. Beely made the point that he was not a member of the committee, just its secretary, and that Crossman had been his friend. He believed that Crossman was right in his assertion – Bevin had given such a promise, although he used 'loose and not exact' language.

In Israel, bitterness over recent policy was soon replaced by appreciation for the positive influence which the British system of government had on the administration of the state and on its democracy. The shared values and friendship of which Ben-Gurion spoke to Bevin became the dominant sentiment.

In my years of service in Britain I detected few scars left from the conflicts and controversy during the mandate. As minister in the Embassy in the 1980s, when I prepared, together with the ambassador, Yehuda Avner, the visit of Prime Minister Shamir to London, I came across conversations and press articles which recalled that he had headed the militant anti-British group Lehi; in another instance, in May 1996, a Foreign Office official unwisely inserted a reference to the British mandate in a speech of the Foreign Secretary. On her first visit to Israel as Prime Minister, Mrs Thatcher had wondered how, 'in the light of past experience', people would receive her. She later wrote in her autobiography that there was no cause to worry. The British Prime Minister was warmly welcomed by the government and by cheering crowds, and so was John Major when he visited Israel in 1995.

Of the former territories of the British Empire, Israel continues to be one of the more friendly towards Britain. It remains a unique fact of history that when the Jewish people came to the end of an epic era, which spread over two thousand years of exile, and inaugurated a new chapter of independence and sovereignty, their fate was intertwined with Britain's post-colonial history.

2

The Partition of Palestine

The decision by the British government to relinquish the mandate and to transfer the issue of Palestine to the United Nations was far from identical to granting statehood to the Jewish inhabitants in Palestine. Another fifteen months of tireless struggle and diplomatic ingenuity were required until this aim was achieved. However, it was a turning-point that allowed the United States, which was much more sympathetic to the Jewish quest for a sovereign state, to take the lead in finding a solution. It enabled the Jewish Agency (the central Jewish political body which negotiated with the British government on Palestine) and the Zionist organizations to mobilize the support of many governments, in one of the most energetic and successful diplomatic campaigns carried out by a non-state.

The leadership of the Zionist organizations had concluded for quite some time that the preferred solution acceptable by the majority, but not by all Zionists, was the partition of Palestine into separate Jewish and Arab states. Weizmann and Ben-Gurion were in complete agreement on this point, but still lacking was an international legal basis for the implementation of such a plan. In his announcement to Parliament on 18 February 1947, Bevin made it clear that in his view the British government had 'no power under the terms of the mandate' to partition the country between the Arabs and Jews, and it therefore submitted the problem 'to the judgement of the UN'.

Faced with the responsibility for finding a solution on Palestine, the United Nations General Assembly, which convened in April 1947, decided to form a Special Committee, chaired by a representative from Sweden and composed of eleven states, which would travel to the Middle East and then suggest a solution. This committee, which became known as UNSCOP (United Nations Special Committee On Palestine), invited the parties to appoint liaison officers to travel and work with it. The Arabs refused to cooperate. The Jewish Agency appointed two able officers, David Horowitz and a brilliant and creative young diplomat, Abba Eban, to fill these positions. Although they enjoyed no official standing and were just liaison officers, the two representatives made every possible effort to persuade the members of UNSCOP of the merits of the partition plan.

They also apprised the leader of the Jewish Agency, Ben-Gurion, and its chief spokesman on foreign affairs, Moshe (Shertock) Sharett, later the first Foreign Minister of Israel, of the progress achieved, as well as of the 'deficiencies' which they detected in the attitudes of the committee members, so that their work could be supplemented by the necessary efforts in the respective capitals.

The United Nations Special Committee on Palestine published two reports on 1 September 1947. The majority, seven representatives, voted for the partition of Palestine, proposing complete Israeli sovereignty in a Jewish area, including the Negev. Jerusalem was to remain a *corpus separatum*. The minority of three supported the impractical option of a bi-national federal state. Australia declined to express an opinion. With the positive recommendations of the UNSCOP Report, the struggle for statehood took a tremendous leap forward; however the report still had to be ratified by a two-thirds majority of the United Nations General Assembly. Three months of vigorous diplomatic activity ensued, literally around the globe, in order to achieve this majority. The UN at the time was composed of fifty-seven states, including five Arab nations. The British position was against partition, and British officials doubted that the plan would be widely supported in the UN.

The key to attaining broad support was, of course, the attitude of the United States. At this point the US commitment to partition, which was given personally by President Truman to Weizmann, was firm. So was the Soviet position. The historic vote, in the General Assembly of the United Nations, took place on 29 November 1947. Thirty-three states voted for partition, thirteen voted against and ten abstained. One was absent. A majority of the international community clearly favoured the establishment of a Jewish state.

The adoption of the partition resolution by the United Nations was another crucial landmark. Yet between November 1947 and the actual end of the mandate in May 1948, five long months remained for Arab pressure and other attempts to thwart its implementation. The Arabs rejected partition and mounted a fierce campaign against a Jewish state; violence in Palestine continued and threats to the continuation of the supply of Arab oil to the West surfaced. Abba Eban wrote in his memoirs of that period that 'the charter of Jewish freedom was also a signal for a savage war'.

In Washington some officials became apprehensive of partition and feared that US interests in the Middle East would be adversely affected. The State Department suggested that if the UN were unable to implement the Partition Resolution peacefully, a Special General Assembly of the UN should appoint a 'trustee' for Palestine. On 19 March 1948 Warren Austin, the US ambassador in the Security Council, announced in the council a new American initiative, to replace partition by an international trusteeship for Palestine. The State Department wrongly believed that trusteeship would stop the violence and that it would be in force until a peaceful understanding between Jews and Arabs in Palestine was reached. This point of view ignored the numerous attempts by the British to work out a peaceful understanding, all of which had ended in complete failure.

This reversal of American policy on such a key issue, barely two months before the State of Israel was to be proclaimed, was an unwelcome surprise for the Yishuv, the Jewish Agency and the American Jewish community. The diplomatic efforts by Dr Weizmann, Sharett, Eban and their colleagues in the American Zionist Organization were echoed by a wave of public criticism of the American policy change. Before long President Truman distanced himself from the trusteeship proposal. The day after ambassador Austin's announcement, the President called in his assistant Clark Clifford and told him that he failed to understand what had happened on the Palestine issue. He saw Dr Weizmann and told him that the United States was for partition and would stick to it. He must think that the President was 'a plain liar'.[1]

On 22 March 1948 the American Secretary of State, George Marshall, wrote to Charles E. Bohlen, later to be appointed the American ambassador to Paris (and to Moscow), casting some light on the President's attitude. In his discussion on Palestine with the President, wrote Marshall, Truman said 'that the reason he was so much exercised in the matter was the fact that Austin made his statement without the President having been advised that he was going to make it at that particular time. He had agreed to the statement, but said that if he had known when it was going to be made, he could have taken certain measures to have avoided the political blast of the press.' On 25 March, the President told a press conference that the US had not reversed its position on partition, and that the notion of trusteeship was proposed as a temporary measure to stop bloodshed. It is this conflicting testimony that might serve to reveal how torn President Truman was between his clear commitment to Weizmann to support the partition of Palestine and the pressures which his Secretary of State and State Department officials brought to bear on him in favour of the sterile (even if temporary) proposition of a trusteeship.

The vacillation of the US position in the pre-state weeks was not confined to the UN and to public diplomacy. Ten days before Israel was proclaimed, Moshe Sharett flew to Washington to confer with the Secretary of State. Meeting George Marshall and under-secretary Robert Lowett, Sharett reported he was cautioned that 'if the Jews persisted in their course, they must not seek the help of the US in the event of an Arab invasion'. Marshall further added that by establishing a Jewish state 'you are undertaking a grave responsibility'. Against the background of British hostility and wavering American support, the pre-state diplomacy had formidable obstacles and an uphill struggle to traverse, in order to achieve the end goal: Jewish sovereignty. The partition resolution was not altered and the moment of decision arrived. With biblical resolve Ben-Gurion seized it and proclaimed the State of Israel.

THE FIRST DECADE

1948–58

3

Independence and War

The fourteenth of May 1948 will for ever remain engraved in the Jewish calendar as one of the most significant dates after the destruction of the Second Temple by the Romans in the year AD 70. As the last governor, Sir Alan Cunningham, sailed away from Palestine's shores that day, the British mandate saw its final hours and David Ben-Gurion proclaimed the State of Israel. This historic act could not take place in Jerusalem, the city which was to be the capital of Israel, for it was under heavy siege by Arab forces. Thirty-seven representatives from all the political parties in the Yishuv therefore solemnly gathered in the Tel Aviv Museum to sign the declaration. Fifty years later it is hard to recapture the mood of that moment, the combination of excitement and emotion that overwhelmed the Jewish world, as more than eighteen hundred years of exile, dispersion, pogroms and holocaust, came to an end, and a new Jewish national identity was born – independent and sovereign Israel. History records no other instance of a people, scattered to all corners of the globe, that returned to its ancient homeland, the land where the first Hebrews set foot four thousand years ago, still adhering to the same heritage, respecting the same biblical traditions and speaking the same language as its forefathers.

The spontaneous rejoicing was subdued because of the fears over future developments and the fact that thousands of young people were manning army posts. The members of the Provisional Government led by Ben-Gurion shared the elation of the hour, but uneasily, sensing the awesome responsibility upon their shoulders. They had experienced last-minute pressures to postpone the declaration of the state. They knew that the Arab armies were poised to invade Israel, and that they faced the daunting task of defending the country while building a new and democratic administration. They were also aware that the British, the Americans and the international community, represented by the United Nations, had spared no effort in trying to reach a compromise acceptable to both Arabs and Jews. All these attempts had been met with cast-iron Arab intransigence. Ben-Gurion and his colleagues, along with the six hundred and fifty thousand Jews living in Palestine, knew that there was no alternative left but to fight. Thus the provisional government, ignoring the diplomatic constraints and braving the imminent military dangers, made the momentous decision and declared independence.

Within hours of midnight of 14 May, a column of some 10,000 Egyptian troops crossed the border of former Palestine, advanced towards Gaza, and continued straight on to Ashdod, situated only about thirty kilometres south of Tel Aviv. They eventually succeeded in cutting off the Negev in the south from central and northern Israel. Egyptian military aircraft bombed Tel Aviv, Syrian mortars opened fire on the kibbutzim in the Galilee, and Jordanian troops advanced towards Jerusalem. This combined assault by the regular Arab armies came in addition to the ongoing attacks by irregular troops of Palestinian Arabs. The War of Independence broke out on several fronts while the Israel Defence Forces (IDF) were in their initial, formative stage, ill-equipped and with few weapons, without artillery, tanks or aeroplanes. But the Declaration of Independence would have been rendered completely meaningless had the IDF failed to defend the newly born state against the combined assault of the Arab armies.

Six days after Independence, on 20 May 1948, with the war raging on all fronts, the UN Security Council called for a cease-fire and nominated Count Folke Bernadotte of Sweden as a special mediator. This proposed truce was accepted by Israel but, not unexpectedly, rejected by the Arabs.

Outnumbering the Jews by forty to one, the Arabs believed that they could overcome Israel by sheer force of arms, and the Arab High Command called upon Palestinian Arabs to leave Palestine in order to return shortly with the triumphant Arab armies. Thousands of Palestinian Arabs heeded this call and thousands more were driven out in the heat of the fierce fighting. Together they created the Arab refugee tragedy. The exodus of thousands of Arabs from Haifa was an illustration of the prevailing mood among the Palestinian Arabs. Three weeks before the state was proclaimed, the mayor of Haifa had met representatives of the Arab community and asked them to remain in the city. In replying, the Arabs said that they wished to consult their 'higher committee' in Beirut. The Mufti and the Arab League decreed that Arabs would not live under Jewish rule. Subsequently many thousands of Arabs left Haifa.[1] The total number of Palestinian Arabs who left before and during the War of Independence is estimated at about half a million.

While fighting continued on all fronts, the gates of Zion opened wide for Jewish immigration. Holocaust survivors from the camps in Europe who were eagerly awaiting this moment of redemption, and the 'illegal' immigrants detained by the British in special camps in Cyprus, were the first to arrive. Simultaneously, a gigantic effort was under way to acquire arms; every rifle, machine-gun or piece of artillery which arrived was immediately dispatched to the front line. The IDF, strengthened by the new arms, went on the offensive. In the north they pushed back the Syrian army and the irregular Arab forces who held parts of the Galilee, including Nazareth. In the central plain they fought against Iraqi forces. In Jerusalem the Jordanian Arab Legion under a British commander, General Sir John Glubb, succeeded in capturing the Old City, which remained under Jordanian rule until 1967. The western parts of the city were freed in a number of heroic battles, which remain enshrined in the military annals of the IDF. A young Palmach commander, Yitzhak Rabin, was one of the gallant fighters for the liberation of Jerusalem. A great part of the Negev in the south was cut off by the Egyptian army, in command of a strategic line which stretched from Al-Auja to Be'er Sheva and on to Hebron. The commanding officer in the south was the former Palmach commander, General Yigal Allon, who succeeded after a series of fierce battles in driving the Egyptian troops back into the Sinai. The battles for the liberation of the Negev eventually came to an end in January 1949. Within seven months of independence, Israel enjoyed a completely different geographic configuration, but at the heavy cost of 6,600 soldiers who fell in battle and many more who were injured. The number killed represented 1 per cent of the total Jewish population living in Israel when the state was established, and it was a huge loss by any standard. Neither the UN nor any outside power had prevented the invasion of the Arab armies or rushed to the assistance of the newly born Jewish state.

The War of Independence was a supreme military test in which Israel prevailed thanks to great courage, high motivation and the readiness for sacrifice of its defenders. The new border lines which resulted from the War of Independence were closer to the mandatory borders and afforded Israel a more defensible and sustainable geographic cohesion. It is a fact of history that the map of Israel which existed between 1948 and 1967 was drawn in the blood of its defenders. Israelis with a handful of Jewish volunteers from abroad stood in isolation against the onslaught of the Arab armies, and triumphed.

The results of the battlefield influenced Arab thinking and decision making, and the military setbacks, coupled with an unprecedented exodus of Arab refugees, began to make the Arabs more receptive to UN cease-fire proposals. Eventually, in November 1948, they decided to accept the Security Council call for a cease-fire and agreed to enter negotiations on an armistice.

This was part of a major diplomatic effort during the latter part of 1948 and the beginning of 1949 to negotiate armistice agreements with Egypt, Jordan, Syria and Lebanon. Dr Ralph Bunch, an American diplomat, assumed the role of UN mediator and the island of Rhodes was the agreed site for the discussions. The Israeli delegation was led by the director-general of the Ministry of Foreign Affairs, Dr Walter Eytan, and Colonel Yigal Yadin, the head of operations of the IDF. The delegation to the talks with Jordan was headed by Lieutenant-Colonel Moshe Dayan and Reuven Shiloah. Between February and April 1949, agreements were concluded with Egypt, Jordan and Lebanon. The negotiations with Syria were difficult and lasted longer. Having been in the forefront of the Arab struggle against the partition of Palestine, and Damascus serving as the headquarters of the 'Supreme Arab Committee' for the Palestinians, which organized the irregular forces fighting against the Jewish state, Syria displayed great hostility and stubbornness. Syrian troops were also entrenched in strategically important positions, which she gave up in return for Israel's agreement to demilitarize certain areas. Only in July 1949 was the Israel–Syria armistice agreement signed.[2]

The armistice agreements were the first accords ever reached between Israel and the Arab countries and as such they had a number of interesting features. For example, Egypt was the leading Arab state to sign the agreement. The other Arab countries followed her example. The same was true thirty years later when President Sadat of Egypt and Prime Minister Begin signed a full-fledged peace treaty between Israel and Egypt, the first such agreement with an Arab country. Syria was the last Arab country to engage in negotiations, and the last to sign an armistice agreement; it will also be the last to sign a peace treaty, as upon this writing peace negotiations with Syria are at an impasse. This time, unlike 1949, Damascus will not allow Lebanon to conclude an agreement with Israel before it does.

The real negotiations with Jordan were not conducted at Rhodes. It was the monarch himself, the late King Abdullah, who met Israeli representatives secretly, among them Mrs Golda Meir, at his summer palace at Shuneh in Jordan, and worked out the details of the accord. They were then transmitted to the official Jordanian delegation at Rhodes, which put its formal signature to the agreement. The same practice was followed forty-five years later by the grandson of King Abdullah, King Hussein. Negotiations with Jordan on a peace treaty were held at Madrid and in Washington but the main points of the treaty were hammered out directly by Prime Minister Rabin and H.M. King Hussein, who together signed the agreement in October 1994.

Back in 1949, the Palestinian Arabs were represented by Jordan; had they accepted the partition scheme, they could have negotiated an armistice on their own behalf, but in the prevailing circumstances they had no official standing. The Israeli leadership hoped that the armistice agreements would be a precursor to permanent peace; the first article started by saying, 'with a view of promoting the return of permanent peace in Palestine'. However, thirty years and five wars passed before the first peace agreement was signed. In the absence of anything better, the armistice regime fulfilled its role and until 1967 served as a point of reference in the relations between Israel and its neighbours, yet belligerence, terror and economic boycott against Israel continued. Nevertheless the armistice agreements represented the first diplomatic encounter between Israel and its Arab neighbours and were recognized as an important diplomatic achievement. The UN mediator, Dr Ralph Bunch, received the Nobel Prize for mediating them.

One of the very first tests of Israeli diplomacy was to assure the widest possible international recognition of the state and to liaise with the UN on the Security Council resolutions for cease-fire arrangements. The Foreign Ministry, like most other government departments, was in its infancy. Foreign Minister Moshe Sharett, assisted by the young and able director-general, Dr Walter Eytan, assembled a small group of people, which included Arthur Lourie, later ambassador to Britain, Gideon Raphael, later ambassador to the UN and to Britain, Aryeh Levavi, later director-general of the ministry, and Shmuel Bentzur, who became ambassador to Vienna and Switzerland. Together with a handful of other officials who trained in a special seminar for diplomats for a year before independence, they mastered the diplomatic challenges facing the new state. Some of the foundations of diplomatic practice, established by Walter Eytan, have served Israeli diplomacy well for fifty years and will continue to do so for a long time to come. Israel's UN front was led by the first ambassador to the United Nations, thirty-two-year-old Abba Eban. In Washington, Israel was at first represented by Eliyahu Elath and later by Eban, who became ambassador to the United States on top of his UN responsibility.

The first country to recognize Israel was the United States. Within hours of the Proclamation of Independence President Truman recognized Israel de facto. Immediate recognition by the most important world power was of crucial importance in the efforts to establish legitimacy; more so since it was known that Secretary of State George Marshall did not support Israel's Declaration of Independence. The important act of recognition was achieved, to a large extent, thanks to the personal dialogue between Dr Chaim Weizmann and President Truman. The American President's commitment to the partition plan and his agreement to include the Negev in the future Jewish state were also a result of the profound influence of Weizmann on Truman's view of the unfolding drama in Palestine. Two days later, on 17 May, the Soviet Union accorded *de jure* recognition to Israel. It took somewhat longer for the former mandatory power to recognize the new state; it was only on 30 January 1949, eight months after independence and after the first elections to the Israeli Parliament, that the United Kingdom recognized Israel de facto. Some countries made their decision earlier, others procrastinated for the next forty-three years; India and China, with sizeable Muslim minorities, established full diplomatic relations with Israel only after the Madrid Peace Conference in 1991.

Membership of the UN, which in retrospect seemed so natural, took a full year to realize. Israel submitted its request for membership in November 1948. According to the UN procedure the Security Council must approve new members. In the first vote on Israel's membership, it was split, with five countries voting for Israeli membership, and six against. Despite the support of the United States and Soviet Union, Israel failed to achieve the necessary majority of seven votes. Only in May 1949 did the General Assembly accept Israel as a full member of the United Nations.

Even the question of how to address the representative of the state in the Security Council was hotly debated, and when the president of the council invited Abba Eban as 'the representative of the State of Israel' there were objections; in the ensuing debate it was decided to put the question to a vote. Five members of the Security Council voted against Eban being officially called the representative of Israel. Two of them, Syria and China, were known opposers, but disappointingly for Israel they were joined by Britain and Belgium, who also voted against. Seven members of the council raised their hands in favour of the representative of Israel. In retrospect the semantics surrounding a title might seem a trivial issue but in 1948 it was a vivid illustration of the difficult struggle for legitimacy which Israel had to wage.

One of the traumatic experiences of the first six months of Jewish statehood, with severe international implications, was the assassination in September 1948 of the UN mediator Count Bernadotte, gunned down while travelling in Jerusalem by the Jewish dissident group Lehi.

The relations between the government of Israel and Count Bernadotte had been difficult and complex, and his initiatives often bewildered the Israeli leadership. His proposals ignored the partition resolution of the General Assembly, suggesting a union between Israel and Jordan. Most unacceptable to Israel were his notions on how to deal with the question of Jerusalem, first suggesting that the holy city be part of the Arab area and later that it be under an international regime. He also suggested that the Negev in the south be ceded to the Arabs. Although the government rejected Bernadotte's proposals, he was treated with due respect and hospitality as a citizen of a friendly country, Sweden, and an emissary of the highest international body. Bernadotte also played an important role in the cease-fire arrangements and their supervision.

But when the details of the Bernadotte proposals were published, there was an enormous public outcry in Israel; appallingly, this resulted in his assassination. It created a wave of shock in Israel and hardened Ben-Gurion's resolve to rein in all the dissident groups under the wing of the IDF to achieve a single disciplined defence force in the country. The only relic of the Bernadotte report to be incorporated in a General Assembly

Resolution in December 1948 was the establishment of a conciliation commission to assist the parties in the negotiations of a permanent settlement. The commission, consisting of representatives from the United States, France and Turkey, met in Lausanne, Switzerland, for about six months and produced no results. The attempt to create a forum for direct negotiations failed because the Arab countries had hoped that they would be able to reverse the course of history by force. Their refusal to negotiate directly with Israeli representatives to the conciliation commission, their reluctance to sit around the same table or even to be in the same room with Israelis made any serious negotiations completely impractical.

The quest for a real and permanent peace with the Arab countries was constant and formed an inseparable part of the platform of every Israeli government. It was pursued through many channels and was articulated clearly and unequivocally in numerous public statements of Israeli leaders. In outlining the basic principles of the first Knesset, on 8 March 1949, Ben-Gurion emphasized the need 'to achieve a (peace) pact between Jews and Arabs' and pledged 'support for all steps designed to strengthen peace and ensure equality between peoples'.[3] One of the most detailed peace proposals was delivered by the ambassador to the UN, Abba Eban, as early as 1 December 1952. In a speech to the political committee of the United Nations, Eban suggested replacing the armistice agreements by peace treaties between Israel and the Arab countries. They should be achieved in direct negotiation, without preconditions, and cover the questions of borders, security, refugees and economic cooperation. '... Israel is prepared to make the attainment of peace in its region a primary theme of its national policy, and to bring all its resources of thought and effort to bear upon that task,' Eban asserted, but there was no affirmative Arab response to his passionate call.

The most practical and realistic of all Israel's partners in the early fifties was King Abdullah of Jordan. A forward-looking statesman, he rightly perceived Israel as a permanent reality in the Middle East and recognized that the basic interests of the two countries converged more than they diverged, and that cooperation and good neighbourly relations would serve both Jordan and Israel well. Like the Israeli leaders, he had a keen interest in blocking any possibility of Jerusalem becoming an international city. Despite the hostility towards Israel in the Arab world, he continued to negotiate with Israeli representatives for a peace treaty for eleven months after the armistice was signed. A draft was prepared and even initialled. The Arab League, when it learned of the king's efforts, convened and promptly decided to expel any member state which negotiated peace with Israel. In addition to the Arab pressures, King Abdullah was advised by the British to refrain from a settlement with Israel. During a conference of British ambassadors to the Middle East, which took place in London in July 1949, the British envoy to Jordan, Sir Alec Kirkbride, stated that 'King Abdullah was personally anxious to come to agreement with Israel and in fact it was our restraining influence which had so far prevented him from doing so.'[4] Listening to this advice and sensing the growing volatility in the region, the king halted the negotiations in March 1950. The extremists were not satisfied, and on 20 July 1951, upon entering the mosque in Jerusalem, King Abdullah was assassinated by a Muslim fanatic, his young grandson, Prince Hussein, later HM King Hussein, witnessed the atrocity.[5]

An astounding early initiative to build bridges between Israel and Egypt came from the British Foreign Secretary Ernest Bevin. In the spring of 1951, Bevin invited himself for lunch at the residence of the Israeli envoy to London, Eliyahu Elath. Only the two of them were present and Elath's record of the conversation describes how Bevin defined the lunch as most secret and asked him to transmit the content of the talk directly to Ben-Gurion, but not in letter or cable form. Elath was to fly to Israel and give the Israeli Prime Minister a verbal account. Ben-Gurion's reply should be conveyed directly to himself or to the permanent under-secretary of the Foreign Office, Sir William Strang. Simultaneously, said Bevin, the Egyptian ambassador was flying that same evening to Cairo, to deliver a similar message to his Prime Minister, Nahas Pasha.

Bevin asserted that the Middle East was one of the regions on which the peace of the world depended. The Arabs had been defeated by Israel but Israel's victory did not bring her peace with its neighbours and she continued to live under threat. This situation would prevent Israel from devoting its human and material resources to building an economic and social infrastructure as a foundation for its political independence. The Arabs were also impeded from finding constructive solutions to their problems, for both sides were rearming for the next confrontation. As the British Foreign Secretary, and as a person who always attempted to promote understanding, Bevin wanted to pave the way to peace between Israel and its neighbours. The key to the attainment of that objective was peace between Israel and Egypt. Both parties would have to compromise. Bevin had no specific proposals on the shape of the final settlement, and thought that these would crystallize in the negotiations between the parties; he would be willing to assist with 'advice and mediation'. The Labour Party and the British government, he said, were to help the inhabitants of the Middle East not as rulers but as partners; the results would be helpful to Britain, which was protecting the area against external dangers. He relied on Ben-Gurion's vision and political acumen to appreciate what he was trying to achieve. Bevin's final remark, according to Elath was: 'I have done enough for the Arabs for them to accept my proposal.'

Elath flew to Israel and reported his conversation with Bevin in a meeting with Ben-Gurion and Foreign Minister Sharett. The Prime Minister suggested that Elath should have told Bevin that the Israeli government had no trust in his intentions as far as Israel was concerned and, that it could not rely on his impartiality on a subject connected with the relations between Israel and the Arabs. Analysing Bevin's motives in proposing his initiative, the participants in the meeting concluded that Bevin must have been concerned with the difficulties between Britain and Egypt on the stationing of British troops in the Suez Canal Zone and had hoped to ease some of the tensions by promoting peace between Israel and Egypt. Failing to persuade the British government to evacuate its troops from Egypt, Cairo had taken its case to the UN as far back as July 1947, but without results. Hence it had become a very contentious issue between Britain and Egypt.

Upon his return to London, Elath reported to Sir William Strang the Israeli attitude towards the Bevin initiative, and Strang asserted that the Egyptian response was also negative. Shortly after that Bevin resigned as Foreign Secretary; a few weeks later he passed away.[6]

Ben-Gurion's judgement in rejecting the Bevin proposal was based not only on the bitterness and distrust which Bevin's policies had generated during the latter years of the British mandate, but also on the anti-Israel attitude of the Attlee government after the decision to relinquish the mandate. The British abstained in the UN vote on the partition plan; they gave their support to the trusteeship proposal; and they tried to convince the Americans that the State of Israel might become a Communist satellite. According to a report that the US Embassy in London sent to the State Department on 22 August 1948, the British view was that Israel might become a Communist state within five years.[7] This idea was based on the assumption that many Jewish immigrants to Israel had arrived from Eastern Europe. It demonstrated little understanding of the psychology of people who fled from Communist regimes and who, from their terrible personal experience, knew what it was like to live under a totalitarian system and would never support Communism in Israel. In the fifty years of statehood there was always a tiny Communist party in the Israeli Parliament, but they hardly touched the 5 per cent mark and were never part of an Israeli government.

The most antagonistic British action during the first years of Israeli independence centred on attempts to sever the Negev from Israel and hand it to the Arabs, to form a land corridor between Jordan and Egypt. Attlee and Bevin pursued this point with such vigour that they dispatched the British ambassador to the United States, Sir Oliver Franks, to see President Truman on the subject. Truman received Sir Oliver on 13 January 1949. When the ambassador explained the strategic importance of maintaining 'an uninterrupted and compact piece of Arab territory in the southern Negev', the President replied that 'he was not prepared to make a point of the Negev. It was a small area and not worth differing over.'[8]

The Negev is about a third of Israel's total territory, it affords Israel direct access to the Red Sea and consequently to Africa and Asia; Bevin's efforts to strip Israel of this link were therefore fiercely resisted by the Israeli government. Bevin was so frustrated that his short-sighted policy on Palestine and Israel did not materialize that he blamed the Americans. In a letter to Sir Oliver Franks of 3 February 1949 he wrote:

> The fact that the Americans have so consistently favoured one party to the dispute, namely the Jews, has made it necessary for us to bear the whole burden of trying to keep the balance, which is in our joint interest, and to lean or appear to lean further on the other side than would otherwise have been the case. This has inevitably placed a strain on Anglo-American relations. But an even greater strain has been placed on them by the fact that the Americans have repeatedly agreed with us on a common line and then have let us down.[9]

With such an enormous clash of outlook and policy, Ben-Gurion could not have accepted Bevin's mediation effort. Bevin's policies in the first years of Israel cast a long shadow over the possibility of a genuine British mediation role. His unfriendly legacy was unfortunately inherited in later years by many officials who also adopted an anti-Israel attitude. Bevin viewed the Balfour Declaration as a historic mistake and not as a far-sighted act which had helped the return of the Jews to Zion. Until the late eighties the Foreign Office attempted to block the participation of senior Cabinet members in the annual Balfour commemoration dinner in Israel. In January 1949, Winston Churchill said that Bevin's policies in Palestine had led to '... vast waste of money, the repeated loss of British lives, to humiliation of every kind'.[10] It was not only Conservative politicians who distanced themselves from Bevin's policies; within his own party, Labour leaders like Hugh Gaitskell and Hugh Dalton criticized him over his attitude towards Israel.

Israel always recognized that Egypt, the most highly populated Arab country, with an ancient history and culture, and holding a position of leadership in the Arab world, must be instrumental in any movement towards peace. The July 1952 revolution in Egypt, which deposed King Farouk and led to the ascendancy of two officers, General Mohammed Naguib and Colonel Gamal Abdal Nasser, to the leadership, provided a faint glimmer of hope that a change in the relationship between the two countries might be possible. Naguib's assertion that he and many of his colleagues in the army were opposed to Egypt's invasion of Israel in 1948 reinforced this hope. Ben-Gurion, speaking in the Knesset on 18 August

1952, referred positively to the events in Egypt, emphasizing that 'there never was nor is there now any reason for political, economic or territorial conflict between the two neighbours'.

The new military leadership was, however, absorbed in domestic problems and inter-Arab relationships. Before long General Naguib was removed from his position and Nasser became the head of state. In Israel Ben-Gurion retired temporarily and at the beginning of 1954 Moshe Sharett became Israel's second Prime Minister. He was very keen to communicate directly with Nasser in order to promote a long-term understanding but also, more immediately, to bring relief to a group of Jews who were imprisoned in Cairo, caught after trying to blow up some Egyptian institutions and accused of spying for Israel. It was one of the more notorious débâcles of Israeli intelligence in the first years of statehood. Verbal messages were exchanged via a personal representative of Nasser in Paris. At some point a message by Sharett, on 21 December 1954, was put on paper: Sharett stressed how much Israel was looking forward to 'tangible evidence that you and your friends are preparing the ground for an eventual settlement with Israel'. He then went on to stress the importance of free passage of Israeli shipping through the Suez Canal and expressed the hope that there would be no death sentence in the trial of the Jews held in Cairo.

On 31 December 1954, Nasser acknowledged Sharett's communication in writing, adding that his special emissary would transmit verbal answers to the points raised. According to the Israeli envoy, Gideon Raphael, Nasser's emissary declined any notion of conducting the dialogue at a higher level. He insisted that before discussing free passage for Israeli ships through the Suez Canal tensions between the two countries must be reduced. Nor was Nasser forthcoming on the fate of the defendants at the Cairo trial. He articulated his policy towards Israel in a speech on 8 September 1954, saying that 'sooner or later Israel will have to cede the Negev to the Arabs.' At the same time he courted the Soviet Union as a potential supplier of arms to Egypt, and aided and abetted terrorist incursion into Israel by Palestinians – fedayeen – trained and assisted by Egyptian intelligence.[11] The peace overtures by Sharett were rebuffed by Nasser.

The growing strains between Israel and Egypt, were mainly due to continuous terrorist activity from the fedayeen headquarters in Gaza. Israeli retaliation and the massive supply of arms from Czechoslovakia to Egypt, caused serious concern not only in Israel but in Washington and Western capitals. The United States attempted to mediate a limited understanding between Jerusalem and Cairo on the de-escalation of border clashes, without success. The mounting dangers to peace in the early and mid fifties were great, and the US administration was constantly looking for ways to lower the tensions and promote understanding.

One of the most serious attempts to defuse the tension between the two countries was the mission of an American special presidential envoy. In January 1956, Robert Anderson, a former secretary of the navy and a close friend of President Eisenhower, was dispatched in great secrecy to Jerusalem and Cairo to try and arrange a meeting between Ben-Gurion and Nasser, to explore the possibility of an accommodation. Israel welcomed the Anderson mission, yet was disinclined to accept a prolonged American mediation effort. Knowing that Dulles would not hesitate to recommend territorial concessions by Israel in the Negev, Ben-Gurion was not keen to create a new source of conflict with the United States. The talks with the high-level envoy were conducted personally by the Prime Minister and Foreign Minister, thus assuring secrecy. Ben-Gurion intimated to Anderson that if he and Nasser were to meet he would have constructive suggestions to make.

Nasser's attitude was in sharp contrast to Ben-Gurion's; he refused a meeting, maintaining that direct negotiations with Israel were impossible. He insisted that in any future settlement there must be a land connection between Egypt and Jordan, which meant that Israel would have to give up a substantial part of the Negev. On halting the ongoing border clashes, Nasser refused to give an undertaking that Egypt would respect the armistice agreement and observe a cease-fire. He denied Israel freedom of passage through the Suez Canal. After two months of shuttling between Washington, Jerusalem and Cairo a disappointed Robert Anderson returned to the United States.

The only dividend of this serious diplomatic effort was a somewhat better understanding in Washington of Nasser's thinking and of the danger he posed to Israel and to stability in the Middle East.[12] Nasser appeared as a champion of Arab nationalism, yet in reality he used nationalism as a vehicle for a much broader and far-reaching pan-Arab policy, which was expansionist and aimed at attaining Egyptian hegemony in the Arab world, while simultaneously downgrading the standing of the United States and the West in the Middle East. He needed the land corridor to Jordan in order to extend his volatile influence to Aman and from there to Iraq. Unfortunately for him Israel stood in his way.

The impact of the Cold War on Israel and the Middle East was most negative and impeded many attempts to bring peace closer. The pro-Israel attitude displayed by the Soviet Union during the 1947 debate on partition and in 1948, after the state was established, soon changed. The Soviet Union realized in the early fifties that by its philosophy, ethos and the nature of its democracy, Israel would always be part of the Western outlook and, as such, would ferociously reject Communism. As the young Jewish state rekindled the latent yearning for Zion in the hearts of the three million Jews living in the Soviet empire, Stalin and his followers feared that their ties with Israel might unravel the closed totalitarian Communist system; consequently, Moscow embarked on a bloody anti-Semitic campaign which included persecution, imprisonment and the deportation of Jews to labour camps.

Viewing the Middle East as a strategic area in 'close proximity' to their southern borders, the Soviet Union and their satellite regimes in Eastern Europe decided to penetrate the Arab world and spread their influence in this torn region. They knew that Islam and Communism had very little in common, and that they would have to find another common denominator with the Arabs. The method they used for the advancing of their aims was the exploitation of the Israeli–Arab conflict by offering political and military support to the Arabs. The result of this Soviet drive was an assured veto for pro-Israel resolutions in the Security Council and huge supplies of modern weapons, mostly on a grant basis, flowing to Egypt and later to Syria as well. The Soviet support strengthened Arab obduracy in refusing to engage in direct negotiations with Israel and fed the illusion that, despite setbacks in wars, with Soviet support they would be able to overcome Israel by force.

Two diplomatic initiatives in the fifties, which historically were of little consequence but in their time had a resonance, were the Tripartite Declaration and the Baghdad Pact. Both were concerted Western efforts designed to promote stability in the Middle East. In the Tripartite Declaration, which was signed in May 1950, the United States, Britain and France pledged themselves to act 'both within and outside the United Nations to stop any threatened action to violate frontiers and armistice lines.' But the declaration hardly featured in the many crises in future years; as the Soviet Union did not directly attack any Middle Eastern country, it was not put to the test. In 1956 Britain and France initiated the Suez operation against Egypt, which made it irrelevant in this case; and in the regional context of the Arab–Israeli conflict it could not prevent cross-border terrorism or the deadly threat which Israel faced in 1967 when Egyptian troops amassed in the Sinai.

In striving to contain Soviet expansion and bolster pro-Western regimes, Britain and the United States encouraged the establishment of the Baghdad Pact. This was an agreement between Iraq and Turkey, signed on 24 February 1955, designed 'to ensure the internal stability and security in the Middle East'. Britain, Pakistan and Iran joined the pact, which became known as 'The Northern Tier'. The United States supported this new alignment but, sensing the rivalries in the Arab world, preferred not to join formally. Nasser viewed the Baghdad Pact as an anti-Egyptian move, and the Soviet Union clearly saw the anti-Soviet motivation of its founders.

Israel was excluded from this new venture. Barred from the pro-Western regional security arrangement, it had to face the Soviet–Egyptian military build-up in isolation. Middle Eastern states belonging to the Baghdad Pact benefited from the supply of arms from the West, and those belonging to the Soviet–Egyptian axis were flooded with arms from the East. The only exception was the one country which was in serious peril, Israel, which pleaded with the Eisenhower administration for arms.

On 27 September 1955, Nasser announced the conclusion of a far-reaching arms deal with Czechoslovakia, including the supply of tanks, guns, fighter planes and submarines. Two days later Cairo radio, following up this new and threatening development, proclaimed, 'the day of Israel's destruction is coming nearer. There will be no peace on the borders, for we demand revenge and revenge means the destruction of Israel!' The British reaction to the Czech arms deal was voiced by the Prime Minister, Anthony Eden. Speaking at the annual Lord Mayor's Banquet at the Guildhall on 9 November, Eden stressed the 'new element of danger' which the massive arms supply to Egypt injected into the Middle East situation. He put the responsibility squarely on the Soviet Union, saying that it was impossible 'to reconcile this Soviet action with protestations that they wish to end the Cold War'. He then suggested that a compromise between the partition lines of 1947 and the armistice lines agreed in 1949 should be found and that Israel should hand over the 'excess' territory to the Arabs; once again a veiled reference to Israel giving up part of the Negev. Eden's Guildhall proposal, its content and timing, was received with deep disappointment by the Israeli government and Ben-Gurion reacted by describing it as a 'reward to aggressors'. In later years Eden himself regretted his Guildhall proposal; in his memoirs he stated that once the Russians began to supply Egypt with such 'formidable quantities' of arms 'it was unwise to raise the issue of frontiers'.[13]

In the first decade of its existence Israel faced: an uninterrupted chain of fedayeen terrorist attacks, which killed and injured 153 people in the first nine months of 1955 alone; an economic boycott imposed by the Arab League; a blockade of its shipping through the Suez Canal decreed by Egypt; hostility from the Soviet Union and the Communist countries; and considerable pressures from the Western powers. Under these dire circumstances priority had to be given to security considerations. Israel could not then, and cannot now, afford to lose a single war, for it would mean the end of the hard-earned Jewish sovereignty. In this struggle for survival, the political and military leadership had to develop a strategy which would prepare the army for the next round of fighting and deter the frequent terrorist attacks on innocent civilians. In the absence of any other viable means of preventing the terrorist attacks, the strategy of reprisals was adopted, a strategy developed by the IDF headed by Moshe Dayan as Chief of Staff. This was seen as the only available response to the fedayeen, who came in small units, attacked, injured and killed people, and then found refuge in the neighbouring countries. Egypt, Jordan, Syria and Lebanon not only allowed these terrorist groups to operate from their territories, but also provided them with shelter, weapons and intelligence, which meant that whenever Israel decided to hit back, its troops had to cross the armistice lines into the Arab country from which the atrocity originated and attack army installations.

The policy was based on the concept of deterrence: any country which aided and abetted the killing of innocent civilians, including children, would have to pay a high price. It was an answer to immediate security imperatives rather than to the strategic problems of the Arab–Israeli conflict. It obviously had its shortcomings: it increased Arab bitterness, and frequently brought Israel into conflict with the international community and the United Nations. It sharpened the domestic political debate, mainly between Ben-Gurion and Sharett, leading eventually to the resignation of Sharett. It also put a serious strain on Israel's diplomatic efforts, which had to defend the strategy of retaliation and reprisal vis-à-vis the Great Powers and the international community. Israeli diplomacy was always looking for ways to de-escalate the conflict, to narrow the divide and to build bridges of understanding. Continuous warfare made this task very difficult, yet the primary responsibility of the government was to defend its citizens, and there was no alternative to an active, punishing defence.

4

The Suez War and the Sinai Operation

D uring 1956 two distinctly separate and profoundly negative sets of circumstances developed in the Middle East. The instigator of both was the President of Egypt, Colonel Gamal Abdal Nasser. Encouraged by the generous shipments of arms from Czechoslovakia and emboldened by Soviet political support, he nationalized the Suez Canal, intensifying his pressure on Israel and embarking on a fierce confrontation with Britain and France. Israel monitored closely the concentration of Egyptian troops in the Sinai and was acutely aware of Nasser's fervent ambition to lead the Arab world. It therefore had to give serious weight to the possibility that he might initiate a full-scale war against the Jewish state. Considering Nasser's policies, his rhetoric and his euphoric mood, a preventive strike against the Egyptian military build-up in the Sinai had become an operative option in Israeli military planning from the middle of 1955. Of immediate concern to the Israeli General Staff was the intensified terrorist activity originating from the El-Arish and Gaza areas, which were under Egyptian control. The fedayeen terror incursions became bolder, indiscriminately killing and injuring soldiers and civilians, sometimes within ten miles of Tel Aviv. The reprisal and retaliation policy which Israel had followed did not have the expected deterrent effect. The large-scale Israeli attack in Gaza in February 1955, which left scores of Egyptian soldiers dead or injured, did not curb the overall terrorist activity. A more effective strategy had to be devised to contain terrorism. As the Suez Canal was blocked to the transit of Israeli vessels, Ben-Gurion's long-term objective was to open to Israeli shipping the navigation route from Eilat to the Indian Ocean. This could be achieved only by controlling the Straits of Tiran at the southern tip of the Gulf of Eilat. In view of Nasser's hostility, there was little hope of attaining these important goals except by a military operation.

The Czech arms deal with Egypt or, as it was called at the time, the 'cotton-for-arms agreement' (Egypt was to pay for the arms in cotton), represented a major turning-point in the fortunes of the Middle East.[1] It was an ominous development for the West and it had new and serious dangers for Israel. The existing military balance between Israel and the Arab countries, precarious in any case, had changed to the detriment of

Israel, which was now confronted by an Egypt armed with modern weapons and supported by the Soviet Union.

Concern about Nasser and his designs was not confined to Israel. The mood of foreboding was shared by the United States, Britain and France. On 8 March 1956, President Eisenhower noted in his diary: 'We have reached the point where it looks as if Egypt, under Nasser, is going to make no move whatsoever to meet the Israelites in an effort to settle outstanding differences. Moreover, the Arabs, absorbing major consignments of arms from the Soviets, are daily growing more arrogant and disregarding the interests of Western Europe and of the United States in the Middle East region.'[2] Subsequently the President instructed his Secretary of State, John Foster Dulles, to make it clear to Nasser that he could not have it both ways, cooperate with the Soviet Union and at the same time enjoy preferential treatment by the United States. Eisenhower's stance impacted directly on Egypt's outstanding request for a $1.3 billion loan to finance the Aswan Dam.

Sir Anthony Eden had made a very similar assessment of Egypt under Nasser. In preparing for his first conference with President Eisenhower in February 1956, soon after he became Prime Minister, Eden described the Middle East situation as 'more immediately dangerous'. He explained why: 'Soviet arms continued to flow into Egypt from Czechoslovakia, and Moscow was showing an increasing determination to intrude into Middle Eastern affairs ... The consequences could be very grave.'[3]

Paris shared the same point of view, and the French had additional reasons for detesting Nasser's policies, as he supported and fuelled the anti-French revolt in Algeria. Yet, despite the unvaried perception among the Western allies of the serious dangers inherent in the developments in Egypt, there was no unified plan of action on how to counter them. Nasser's quest for hegemony in the Arab world was reinforced by his drive to oust Western influence from the Middle East, and although the governments in Baghdad and Aman may have had their reservations, the Arab masses applauded him. Persevering with his volatile rhetoric, Nasser made another anti-American move in May 1956 when he recognized the People's Republic of China. The sense of dismay in the Eisenhower administration and in Congress grew to such an extent that substantial US financing of the Aswan Dam became impossible.

On 19 July 1956 the US Secretary of State Dulles informed the Egyptian ambassador in Washington that the United States would not grant the loan for the building of the High Dam. The Egyptian envoy came to the meeting equipped with a reply, which he relayed to Dulles: Cairo had a Soviet offer to assist in the construction of the Aswan Dam. The next day the British Cabinet also decided to withdraw from participation in the financing of the dam.

Seven days later, on 26 July 1956, Nasser gave his defiant reaction. In a fiery speech he announced the nationalization of the Suez Canal, the revenues from which would be used to replace the American and British funding of the dam. He described his decision to breach a long-standing international contract, the Constantinopol Convention of 1888, which fully guaranteed freedom of passage through the canal, as a battle against imperialism and 'a battle against Israel, the vanguard of imperialism'. He followed up his speech by ordering the seizure of the assets of the Suez Canal Company, which was jointly owned by France and Britain.

In Europe the shock waves were immediate and considerable, as Western Europe depended heavily on Middle Eastern oil, about fifty per cent of which passed through the Suez Canal, more than seventy million tons in 1955 alone. The British Prime Minister immediately consulted senior Cabinet colleagues and the Chiefs of Staff. The Cabinet which convened in the wake of the new challenge posed by Nasser concluded, according to Eden, that if the Suez Canal did not remain an international waterway, it would lead to 'the loss one by one of all our interests and assets in the Middle East, and even if Her Majesty's Government had to act alone they could not stop short of using force to protect their position'.[4] This was a clear and unequivocal assessment, which was, at the time, supported by the opposition and in the newspapers. On 27 July Eden communicated the considered opinion of the British Cabinet to President Eisenhower. After discussing economic and political pressure on Nasser, Eden wrote: 'My colleagues and I are convinced that we must be ready, in the last resort, to use force to bring Nasser to his senses. For our part we are prepared to do so.' Eden also suggested immediate consultation between Britain, France and the United States.

The French government viewed the situation with similar gravity. Apprehensive of the adverse impact that Nasser's provocation would have on their position in north Africa, they were as determined as the British to confront him, if everything else failed, by force.

In Israel the nationalization of the Suez Canal was regarded as an ominous and daring act by Nasser. For years the Egyptian President had blatantly violated the Constantinopol Convention, and an explicit Security Council Resolution, by barring Israeli ships from the canal. His new act of defiance enhanced his standing in Egypt and in the region. If he detected weakness in the Western reaction, his next move might be against Israel. Moreover, it was hard to imagine that Nasser had engaged in such a confrontation without receiving the blessing of the Soviet Union. Although Israel did not suffer a direct loss from the nationalization of the canal, any strengthening of Nasser's position heightened the level of danger it faced. By this time the close cooperation between Israel and France in defence and intelligence, which was shaped by Shimon Peres and his colleagues in the Ministry of Defence during 1955, was bearing fruit: Israel was expecting shipments of arms from France. On the morrow of Nasser's proclamation, the French notified Israel that Foreign Minister Christian Pineau was due to leave for London shortly for consultations with Britain and the United States. In preparation, they asked for a report on Egyptian troop deployment and added that Israel should be ready to fulfil its part, if asked to.[5]

In the new circumstances the reaction of the United States was of cardinal importance. The State Department issued a statement on 27 July, saying that the nationalization carried 'far-reaching implications' for the maritime powers and the countries owning the Suez Canal Company.[6] After conferring with his advisers, Eisenhower dispatched the deputy under secretary of state, Robert Murphy, to participate in the tripartite consultations taking place in London at the beginning of August. His instructions to Murphy illustrate the reserved and cautious stance which he had adopted from the beginning of the Suez crisis. Murphy's brief was more of a catalogue of what not do than a directive for action: not to join the British and French in hasty action; to prevent the French from tying the Suez crisis with the Arab–Israeli conflict; and to prefer action by all the maritime powers rather than by Britain, France and the United States. The State Department view was that Nasser might have had a legal basis for nationalizing the Suez. However, the Joint Chiefs of Staff were of a different opinion, which they conveyed to the Secretary of Defence: that Nasser's action was 'so detrimental to the interests of the United States that Eisenhower should consider the desirability of taking military action in support of Britain, France and others as appropriate'. Admiral Burke told the President that the Joint Chiefs of Staff were of the opinion that 'Nasser must be broken.'[7]

This was not, however, Eisenhower's view. He did not think that the Suez Canal was a vital American interest which merited the involvement of US troops. The American dependence on the canal for its shipping was less than that of the Europeans and despite the very low esteem he entertained for Nasser, he believed, somewhat naïvely, that it might be possible to work out a solution to the crisis through negotiation. Moreover, Eisenhower was determined to prevent the British and French from using force, because he was not sure of the Soviet reaction and its possible implications for the United States. Above all, he was concerned with his re-election to a second term of office which was only three months away, and preferred not to have his campaign overshadowed by a war. Some believe that there was also a streak of an anti-colonialist view shaping his adamant position. When Murphy reported from London the British and French determination to confront Nasser, if necessary by force, the President instructed Secretary Dulles to fly to London to convey to the allies his opposition to their plan for military intervention. On 31 July 1956 Eisenhower wrote a personal letter to Eden, which Dulles carried to London. The key sentence in it read: 'I have given you my personal conviction, as well as that of my associates, as to the [un]wisdom even of contemplating the use of military force at this moment.'[8] The President sent a message in similar terms to the French Prime Minister, Guy Mollet.

Eden and Mollet were convinced that negotiations with Nasser would not produce results and if he remained in power his ability to continue with aggression would be considerable. Therefore their unspoken objective, which was not shared by Eisenhower, was to unseat Nasser as a by-product of the military operation.

British and French military planning continued; reserve troops were called to duty and naval forces were moved to the Mediterranean theatre. In the tripartite consultations in London, Dulles spoke of making Nasser 'disgorge' what he had swallowed, while pressing for a diplomatic initiative to solve the crisis. Faced with American pressure, Britain and France agreed to call a wider conference on 16 August, with the participation of twenty-four maritime countries including Egypt. Nasser refused to attend the London Conference, maintaining that its purpose was to interfere in the domestic affairs of his country. He rejected any notion of international control of the Suez Canal. The only concession he was prepared to make was to attempt to find a solution within the framework of the United Nations, where he had a guaranteed Soviet veto, and to give a limited promise to uphold the freedom of passage for all ships, except Israeli vessels.

The London Conference convened with the participation of twenty-two out of the twenty-four invited states; Egypt and Greece did not attend. After lengthy deliberations, in which the Russians played a less than constructive role, eighteen members agreed on a joint declaration, which was published on 23 August 1956. Its essence was that an international board would be responsible for the operation of the canal and the sovereign rights of Egypt would be recognized. The Soviet Union, India, Indonesia and Ceylon dissented. They favoured an international advisory board. A small committee headed by the Prime Minister of Australia, Robert Menzies, travelled to Cairo to present the recommendations of the London Conference to Colonel Nasser. Menzies, an experienced and well-respected statesman, used all his diplomatic skills to try and persuade Nasser to accept the proposals of the London Conference. However, Nasser rejected them, maintaining that an international board was tantamount to 'the restoration of collective colonialism'.[9] A major diplomatic effort with the participation of the three major Western powers thus ended in failure. Nasser had gained precious time, and the consensus in Britain in favour of a military operation began to crumble, with the Labour Party insisting that the use of force had to be sanctioned by the United Nations. Given the Soviet veto in the Security Council, their suggestion was a non-option, as no resolution against Egypt would be adopted there. American pressure on Britain and France to refrain from using force continued, in private messages from Eisenhower to Eden, in diplomatic exchanges and in public. In a press conference on 11 September, the President was asked whether the US would support Britain and France if they should use force. Eisenhower included in his reply the following sentence: '... this country will not go to war ever while I am occupying my present post unless the Congress is called into session and Congress declares such a war'.[10] It was obvious that Congress would never declare war for a cause that was not defined as a vital interest of the United States. Nasser could only derive satisfaction from this position, and so did the Soviet Union, because the Western alliance was clearly split on the handling of the Suez crisis.

Two additional diplomatic attempts were made to find a peaceful solution to the Suez crisis. In early September the United States suggested the establishment of an association of canal users, better known as the 'Users' Club'. Its purpose was to re-establish the 'rights of passage' under the Constantinopol Convention of 1888, which stipulated that 'at all times and for all powers the free use of the Suez Maritime Canal' should be guaranteed. The French were extremely sceptical of the American proposal, and believed that its sole purpose was to delay military action. Eden, wishing to exhaust every possible diplomatic avenue before going to war, persuaded the Cabinet to accept the new idea and the eighteen nations forming the Users' Club were invited to a second London Conference, to discuss its structure and functions. It was a futile exercise, for Nasser did not show the slightest inclination to accept the idea. On 15 September he denounced the Users' Club as an 'association for waging war'.

Equally frustrating was the subsequent attempt to pass an operative resolution in the UN Security Council to assure free and uninterrupted passage through the Suez Canal. On 13 October 1956 the Soviet Union vetoed the resolution and another diplomatic initiative was therefore blocked.

Israeli intelligence watched these developments closely, strongly convinced that the real issue was not just the freedom of navigation in the Suez Canal, but Nasser himself, his aggressive policies, his militancy, his inflammatory statements and his attempts to undermine the moderate regimes in the Arab world. Israel was convinced that if Nasser succeeded in nationalizing Suez, his capacity to attack her would be enhanced. Moreover, he would undermine the regimes in Jordan and Iraq and strive to nationalize the oil reserves in the Arab world. This assessment was close to Eden's point of view. While Western diplomatic efforts were under way, the build-up of Soviet arms in Egypt was greatly reinforced. The Egyptian concentration of troops in the Sinai, coupled with Nasser's rhetoric, and the incendiary language used in the media, had to be taken seriously. Radio Cairo, for instance, asserted that 'the day of Israel's destruction is coming closer ... revenge means the death of Israel'.[11] Ben Gurion and the Israeli government saw the gathering clouds and viewed the confrontation with Nasser as a battle for the survival of the Jewish state.

The close relations between Israel and France during 1955 matured in the first part of 1956. The first accord on a substantial supply of arms from France was worked out in June 1956 in a secret conference at Vermars. Israel was represented by Shimon Peres, the director-general of the Ministry of Defence, and by the Chief of Staff, General Moshe Dayan.[12] One day after the nationalization of the Suez, on 27 July, Peres was invited to meet the French Defence Minister, Maurice Bourgès-Maunoury. In the conversation, Bourgès-Maunoury asked him how long it would take the Israeli Defence Forces to cross the Sinai Peninsula and reach the Suez. Peres believed that it would require a fortnight, while the French estimate was that three weeks would be needed. Bourgès-Maunoury further asked whether Israel would be prepared to participate in a tripartite military operation against Egypt, and Peres replied that under certain circumstances it would.[13] Evidently, an intimate and unique relationship between Israel and France in defence and intelligence had been developed, which grew closer as the Suez crisis unfolded.

In August the French asked for details of Israel's ports and airfields. From this request, as well as from other conversations, it became clear that although France preferred to keep the war against Nasser as a confrontation between the West and Egypt, and not as another clash in the Arab–Israeli conflict, they seriously contemplated close cooperation with Israel. Ben-Gurion ordered the French to be provided with the information and to be treated 'as brothers'.

At the end of August the French sought Israel's official permission for eight fighter planes to land at an Israeli military airfield for refuelling and to allow the French pilots to be based in Israel during the operation; approval was granted. Some days later the French passed on to Israel the Anglo-French plan for 'Operation Musketeer' and suggested that Israel be invited to join the operation seven days after D-Day. Ben-Gurion agreed to cooperate and suggested dispatching Chief of Staff Dayan to Paris to discuss details. However, the operation was stopped when the British and French reluctantly agreed to Dulles's proposal to form the Users' Club. Bourgès-Maunoury, in a private letter to Ben-Gurion congratulating him on his seventieth birthday, referred to the French interest in the region, stating that both countries should do 'something' together in order to protect their interests *vis-à-vis* Egypt. Ben-Gurion replied expressing Israel's readiness to cooperate. The French were dismayed and disappointed by the delays after the second London Conference, and their Cabinet decided to authorize the military command to discuss a joint operation with Israel.[14]

At this stage the dialogue on the Suez operation had to involve ministers as well as defence and military experts. A high-level Israeli delegation headed by the Foreign Minister, Golda Meir, arrived in Paris on 29 September. It included the transport minister, Moshe Carmel, the director-general of the Ministry of Defence, Shimon Peres, and the Chief of Staff, General Moshe Dayan. The talks were shrouded in secrecy and were held in a private home. The French were represented by the Foreign Minister, Christian Pineau, Abel Thomas, the director-general of the Ministry of Defence, Louis Mangin, adviser to Bourgès-Maunoury and the deputy chief of staff, General Maurice Challe.

The instructions which the departing delegation received from Ben-Gurion, after discussion in the Cabinet, were as follows: the Israeli objectives were to open the route to Eilat, and not to fight Jordan unless the latter tried to help Egypt, or Iraqi troops entered Jordan. Ben-Gurion was still very suspicious of Britain and was afraid that Britain might involve herself in fighting Israel because of her treaty commitments to Jordan; he wanted the delegation to emphasize that Israel would not act against other Arab countries as long as they did not come to Egypt's assistance. He also expected the French to obtain at least tacit agreement from the United States, and a promise that Washington would not impose sanctions or an embargo on Israel. Ben-Gurion added another penetrating thought in his instruction to Golda Meir: 'It is imperative that the French understand the difference between Israel's situation and theirs in case of failure. For them it would be a political or military setback that would not affect their country but only their prestige. For Israel failure might be a disaster.'[15]

In the discussions with the Israeli delegation to Paris, Pineau stated that after the nationalization of the Suez, the French had reached the conclusion that only a military operation could reverse Nasser's action. The United States was opposed to a military move and the Soviet Union was exploiting this stance. As far as Britain was concerned, there was uncertainty, for although Eden was an activist, the Foreign Office was following a wait-and-see attitude. He therefore wanted to explore the possibility of a joint French–Israeli operation. Each country would act in its own best interest and France would provide Israel with military assistance and with political support in the Security Council, including an unreserved veto. According to the treaty of 1955 between the United Kingdom and Egypt, Britain could seize the Suez Canal by force if there were a war.

The Israeli delegation made it clear that it too did not believe that a diplomatic solution was possible. Israel was prepared to cooperate with

France but would have liked to know more about the British attitude and the American and Soviet positions. The French estimate was that the Russians would not send troops to intervene; they would, however, continue with their military assistance to Nasser. Pineau suggested that neither France nor Israel should raise the issue with the United States. A definitive answer from London was expected by mid October. If Israel started the operation, Britain would join. The military experts then discussed operational questions and the supply of arms to Israel. It was agreed that a French delegation headed by General Challe would join the Israeli delegation on their return trip to look closely at airfields and airforce facilities.

The Israelis were most intrigued by the ambivalent British attitude towards the joint operation. On the one hand, Britain did not want to fight in collaboration with Israel against an Arab country, yet it wanted Israel to open hostilities in order to provide them with an excuse to join the war and appear as if coming to the rescue of Egypt. This they wished to accomplish by French mediation, without meeting Israeli leaders or military chiefs, so that they would not be accused of acting in concert with Israel. At some point Eden gave the French a signed statement to be transmitted to Israel. It stated that Britain and France would require both Israel and Egypt to withdraw from the Suez Canal zone. If one or both parties would not comply, British and French troops would intervene to assure the smooth functioning of the canal; Britain would not come to the assistance of Egypt in the case of a war between Israel and Egypt. This commitment did not apply to Jordan, which had a defence pact with the United Kingdom.

French and Israeli joint planning continued during October. Diplomatic initiatives faltered one after the other, elections in Jordan gave the pro-Nasser party, led by Suleiman Nabulsi, a majority. Jordan promptly aborted its agreement with Iraq and planned to join the unified command with Egypt and Syria, as Nabulsi stated that he considered Colonel Nasser 'the saviour of Arab national interests and welfare'.[16] French public opinion was enraged when a ship loaded with arms from Egypt destined for Algiers was intercepted by their navy. Both developments illustrated the new reality; Nasser continued to plot and therefore war against Egypt became highly probable. Ben-Gurion and Guy Mollet felt that at such an advanced stage of planning, a meeting with the British was inevitable. Mollet took the initiative. Ben-Gurion and Selwyn Lloyd, with a handful of their advisors, were invited to a top-secret conference at Sèvres. The Israeli delegation included Dayan and Peres, and Dayan's aide de camp, Colonel M. Baron; Selwyn Lloyd invited his close advisor, Sir Donald Logan, to travel with him. Mollet, Pineau and Bourgès-Maunoury met the Israeli Prime Minister on 22 October 1956. Pineau explained that Eden genuinely wanted Britain to join in the military operation but had problems in

Parliament, in his own party and even in Cabinet. Any delay would weaken him further. The Soviet Union was absorbed with problems in Poland and Hungary. As to America, it was important to start the operation before the elections, which were due for November 1956, and which might have had a restraining effect on Eisenhower's reaction. The next day the British Foreign Secretary joined the talks. When Lloyd reiterated the proposal that Israel should start the war and provide the pretext, Ben-Gurion replied that Israel did not want to be branded as an aggressor. The Israeli delegation was struck by the very reserved attitude of the British Foreign Secretary, which sharply contrasted with the openness of the French. Lloyd mentioned that he had been holding talks with the Egyptian Foreign Minister, Fawzi, in search of a peaceful solution to the crisis, and that some progress had been made. He insisted that the British and French make their move forty-eight hours after the Israeli operation started and that Israel's attack should be a major warlike act and not just a reprisal, so that it would justify the British–French intervention.

Ben-Gurion had great difficulty with both demands. The first would put Israel in the forefront of the whole Suez war and would invite much condemnation; the latter demand was even more dangerous because it meant that for forty-eight hours Israel would fight alone, with Israeli population centres exposed to attacks by the Egyptian air force. The sooner the British and French came in and disabled Egyptian airfields and her air force, the more lives would be saved. His initial reaction was therefore negative. Yet Ben-Gurion was acutely aware of the fact that if further delays occurred, the whole operation might be called off and Israel would, in all likelihood, have to fight Nasser alone under even more difficult circumstances. After long deliberation Dayan proposed a compromise – that the two Western powers would make their move twelve hours after Israel started the war. Selwyn Lloyd took the compromise suggestion to Eden in London. Pineau, who had little confidence in the British Foreign Secretary, followed him to London to talk to Eden himself. The French Foreign Minister returned the next day to Sèvres with Eden's approval for the new plan. Selwyn Lloyd remained in London and Eden dispatched to Sèvres an assistant under-secretary in the Foreign Office, Patrick Dean, who, together with Donald Logan, represented Britain.

The Sèvres Protocol, which set out the plan for the Suez operation, was formulated and signed on 24 October 1956 by Ben-Gurion, Pineau and Patrick Dean for Britain. Only three copies, in French, were available, one for each representative. Eden ordered the British copy to be destroyed, a strange practice in a democracy, motivated by a naïve belief that a joint decision, taken by three democratic governments, could be concealed for ever. Be that as it may, no copy of the protocol was found in British archives. Pineau produced the substance of the protocol in his book *1956-*

Suez. An exact text has not yet been discovered in France. Ben-Gurion slipped his copy into his pocket and deposited it later in the State Archive. Its publication was authorized in 1996 and herewith is the full text.

The results of the conversations which took place at Sèvres from 22 to 24 October 1956 between the representatives of the Governments of the United Kingdom, the State of Israel and France are as follows:

1. In the evening of 29 October 1956, the Israeli forces launch an extensive operation against the Egyptian forces with the aim of reaching the Canal Zone the next day.

2. On being informed of these events, the British and French Governments, during the day of the 30 October 1956, respectively and simultaneously make the two appeals to the Egyptian Government and Israeli Government, complying with the following guidelines:

A. *To the Egyptian Government*

a) Halt all acts of war.

b) Withdraw all the troops to a distance of ten miles from the Canal.

c) Accept temporary occupation of key positions along the Canal by the Anglo-French forces, in order to ensure freedom of passage along the Canal for vessels of all nations, until a permanent settlement.

B. *To the Israeli Government*

a) Halt all acts of war.

b) Withdraw all the troops to a distance of ten miles east of the Canal.

In addition, the Israeli Government will be informed that the French and British Governments have demanded that the Egyptian Government accept the temporary occupation of the key positions along the Canal by the Anglo-French forces.

It is agreed that if one of the two Governments refuses or does not agree within a time limit of twelve hours, the Anglo-French forces will intervene, using the necessary means to ensure that their demands are accepted.

C. The representatives of the three governments agree that the Israeli Government will not be obliged to accept the clauses in the appeal which are addressed to it if the Egyptian Government does not accept the clauses in the appeal which are addressed to it.

3. In the event that the Egyptian Government does not agree to the clauses in the appeal which apply to it within the stipulated time limit, the Anglo-French forces will launch military operations against the Egyptian forces in the early hours of the morning of 31 October.

4. The Israeli Government will send forces with the aim of occupying the west coast of the Gulf of Aqaba and the group of islands of Tiran and Sanafir, to ensure freedom of navigation in the Gulf of Aqaba.

5. Israel undertakes not to attack Jordan during the period of operations against Egypt. But, if during the same period, Jordan attacks Israel, the British Government undertakes not to go to the aid of Jordan.

6. The arrangements in this protocol must remain strictly secret.

7. They will come into effect after the three governments have agreed.

Signed: C. Pineau, Patrick Dean, D. Ben-Gurion

The agreement has two annexes; one is a French–Israeli protocol, in which France commits itself to send French fighter planes and naval ships to Israel for defence purposes in the period 29–31 October (this document was kept secret from the British). The second was the following letter from Prime Minister Guy Mollet to David Ben-Gurion:

25.10.1956

Dear Prime Minister,

I hereby confirm to you the agreement of the French Government regarding the outcome of the Sèvres discussions and the terms of the final protocol.

Moreover, I have received a letter from Sir Anthony Eden in which he confirms to me the agreement of the British Government. For your personal information, I have enclosed a photocopy of this letter.

Yours sincerely,
Guy Mollet

Eden's letter to Mollet said: 'Her Majesty's Government have been informed of the course of the conversations held at Sèvres on October 22–24. They confirm that in the situation there envisaged they will take the action described.'[17]

During the Suez War, I was a sergeant in an armoured brigade fighting in the Sinai. My younger brother Yechiel was among the first soldiers who parachuted into the Mitle Pass, close to the Suez Canal, at the very beginning of the war on 29 October 1956.

Neither I nor my comrades doubted the necessity of destroying the fedayeen infrastructure in Gaza and the huge concentrations of Egyptian troops in the Sinai in order to prevent the continuation of terrorism and a possible assault on Israel. There was no joy in going to war, and the swift victories which we obtained were overshadowed by the sadness of the casualties we suffered. The troops knew from the military grapevine that French pilots and aeroplanes were in Israel, and were relieved that we were not alone. We knew little of the political and diplomatic efforts which preceded the operation – Israel's second war.

Later, while working in the Foreign Ministry, I learned more about this historic chapter. In London, I found that of the three British participants at the Sèvres Conference – Selwyn Lloyd, Sir Patrick Dean and Sir Donald Logan – only Logan was still alive. He was the only British official who participated in both sessions at Sèvres (in the first with Lloyd and in the second with Dean). On 15 November 1996 I lunched with him, and we had a long and comprehensive discussion on Suez. After a forty-year interval, Sir Donald was no longer bound by secrecy, and had strong and perceptive opinions on the Sèvres encounter.

One of my first questions to him concerned the British attitude towards Israel at the time. Given that the two democratic countries, with a coincidence of interests and a common enemy (Nasser), were trying to act together, was there a need for Eden to adopt such an indirect attitude? Why not confront the plain truth and act upon it?

Logan explained that only eight years after the British relinquished the mandate on Palestine, feelings towards Israel were still raw; there was no way Eden could persuade British public opinion to back a joint action with Israel against an Arab country. He accepted my assertion that, British public opinion aside, Eden was also concerned with the way the Arab countries would perceive the events and that too influenced his thinking.

According to Sir Donald, Selwyn Lloyd 'was desperately against' the Suez War, for he believed in a diplomatic solution on which he was working with Fawzi. At the same time he felt that he must fulfil the instructions of his Prime Minister. It was later in life that Lloyd wondered whether he should have resigned at that stage. Patrick Dean was taken by complete surprise when he was asked by Eden to go to Sèvres; he did not know the content of Eden's conversations with Guy Mollet and Pineau, nor of the correspondence between them; his only instructions were to make clear to the French and the Israelis that nothing would happen unless there was a clear threat to the Suez Canal. The 'threat' was of course to be provided by Israel.

Regarding Eisenhower's opposition to war against Nasser, which he communicated directly to Eden, Sir Donald said that the Americans never explicitly told Britain not to go to war. The ambivalent language employed by Dulles, as well as the belief by Eden and Macmillan that Ike would do no harm to his ally, led to scepticism about Eisenhower's intentions. In view of Eisenhower's personal letter to Eden of 31 July 1956, and in the light of his public statements, it is arguable whether the scepticism was justified.

Logan said that Eden was surprised when Patrick Dean and he returned to Britain with the Sèvres Protocol, as he did not expect a written document to be produced. The following day (25 October) Eden instructed them to return to Paris and ask the French to destroy their copy of the document. However Pineau refused Eden's request, for Israel had its copy and Ben-Gurion would certainly not agree to destroy such an important document. The French probably saw the need for secrecy as a temporary requirement and did not feel any remorse or regret about cooperating with Israel. Their interests in the Arab world did not suffer serious setbacks as a result of Suez; indeed the French were the first to break the secrecy of the diplomatic activity which preceded the Suez War.

Eden's view of Israel at the time, and his inability to accept it as a serious and genuine ally and partner against an extreme pro-Soviet dictator, was at the heart of his efforts to conceal any association with the Jewish state in fighting Nasser. It led to his insistence on a wobbly and unbelievable pretext. This in turn caused him to be less than candid with his colleagues, with Parliament and with the British public. In his research on Suez, Keith Kyle asserted that the British Cabinet 'was deceived about the extent of collusion with the Israelis'.[18] Despite the Sèvres agreement and the British insistence that the Israeli attack must pose a serious threat to the Suez Canal, Eden wrote to Eisenhower, a week after the Sèvres conference, on 31 October: 'We would not wish to support or even condone the action of Israel.'[19] Before long it became clear that there was a discrepancy between the 'story' and the unfolding Suez War. Once the notion that the British Prime Minister was misleading the country crept into the public perception, Eden had great difficulty in persuading Parliament and the media that the operation was justified and served the British interest.

Did Eden believe in the first instance that he could get away with it? According to Logan, the Prime Minister was confident that he could handle the situation in a very secretive manner – if only it were left to him. In Eden's untruthfulness about Suez it is possible to see the genesis of the failure of the Anglo-French operation in 1956, and eventually his own political downfall. Sir Donald Logan stressed that nevertheless Israel did not expose the truth for many years, in order not to embarrass a former British leader.

As agreed at Sèvres, the campaign started in the late afternoon of 29 October with Israeli paratroopers parachuting in approximately forty-five miles east of the Suez. Twenty-four hours later Britain and France submitted the agreed 'appeal' or rather ultimatum to Israel and Egypt. As envisaged at the Sèvres discussions, Israel accepted the terms of the ultimatum while Egypt rejected it. To the consternation of the Israeli government, the Anglo-French military operation and more importantly, the planned bombing of military airfields in Egypt, was delayed for about twelve hours, and commenced only on the evening of 31 October. During these first crucial two days Israel carried the burden of the war alone, exposed to the danger of Egyptian air raids.

The Israeli General Staff, aware that time was a critical factor because of the political pressures which would build up, encouraged the field commanders to advance swiftly. The war aims were clear: to destroy the fedayeen terrorist infrastructure in the El Arish and Gaza areas; to eliminate the potential threat to Israel from the Egyptian divisions amassed in the Sinai; and to capture Sharm el-Seikh, which controls the Straits of Tiran, at the entrance to the Gulf of Aqaba.

By 5 November, within seven days, these objectives had been attained, but hundreds of Israeli soldiers fell in the Sinai campaign, many more were injured and one Israeli soldier was a prisoner of war in the hands of the Egyptians. Israel held six thousand Egyptian officers and soldiers, and had seized a considerable amount of Egyptian military equipment. The end of the war led to a bitter struggle to translate the military gains into long-term political assets.

The United States had had ample intelligence reports about the possibility of the armed confrontation, but the outbreak of war just a few days before the American elections enraged President Eisenhower. On 30 October, the Security Council convened at the request of the United States with its chief representative, Henry Cabot Lodge, demanding a cease-fire and the immediate withdrawal of Israeli forces behind the armistice lines. In case any doubt remained, Lodge emphasized that 'nothing less will suffice'. A draft resolution containing the above elements was put to a vote. As promised, Britain and France vetoed the resolution. This was the first time that the United Kingdom cast its veto in the Security Council, and ironically it was in favour of an Israeli position.[20]

On 31 October the Security Council convened again. By that time Israeli troops were racing westwards in the Sinai, but true to the original planning of the operation and to the acceptance of the Anglo-French ultimatum, did not get close to the Suez Canal. On that evening the British and French started to bomb Egyptian airfields. However, the British representative in the council maintained that the United Kingdom 'did not support Israeli intentions to capture Egyptian territories'.[21] It was nevertheless obvious that Security Council action would be blocked by a double veto by the British and French. The General Assembly of the United Nations was thus convened under the 'Uniting for Peace' procedure which was adopted during the Korean War in 1951, to circumvent the Soviet veto and allow the Assembly to act on 'Security Council' matters. The resolutions passed in the assembly accorded the Secretary-General of the UN, Dag Hammarskjöld, an active role in the crisis. He exercised his duties with a legalistic, narrow approach which often angered Jerusalem and did little to make the Sinai campaign a stepping-stone to a future peace. A more useful contribution from the General Assembly was the acceptance of a proposal by the Canadian representative, Lester Pearson, to establish the United Nations Emergency Force (UNEF), which played a significant role in de-escalating the conflict.

Political pressure on Israel was exerted by the two superpowers, the United States and the Soviet Union, couched in firm but friendly terms in private and public discourse with Eisenhower and Dulles, and communicated in hostile and threatening language by the Russians. In his letter to Ben-Gurion of 5 November 1956, Bulganin maintained that the Sinai operation 'cannot but affect the future of Israel and will place a question [mark] upon the very existence of Israel as a state'. Moscow consequently recalled the Soviet ambassador from Tel Aviv. In a second note, of 15 November, Bulganin demanded immediate withdrawal of Israeli forces from Egyptian territory and compensation for war damages.[22] This intimidating pressure on Israel took place as the Soviet military was crushing the Hungarian uprising with brutal force, completely ignoring all UN resolutions on the subject.

It became obvious to Ben-Gurion and the Israeli government that under the circumstances it would be impossible to exchange the occupation of the Sinai for a fully fledged peace treaty with Egypt, which would include the cessation of terror, the end to economic boycott and free shipping through the Suez Canal. The policy was therefore to gain time, in order to enlist the support of public opinion for Israeli objectives in the United States and the Western world, and to insist on a joint UN–Israeli administration in Gaza, to ensure that it would not again serve as a base for terror and to secure free passage through the Straits of Tiran.

Abba Eban, as ambassador to the US and to the UN, had to cope with the pressures of the US administration and to persuade public opinion that Israel's war was justified in view of the threat from Nasser's Egypt. His speeches at the UN and his very effective television and radio broadcasts helped to create a more favourable atmosphere towards Israel. In the diplomatic struggle, Eban suggested to the government a formula that would remove UN pressure and gain time; it made 'satisfactory arrangements with UN forces' a condition for the withdrawal of Israeli troops. Ben-Gurion approved this approach. As it was clear that the key to any solution to the Suez crisis lay in Washington, Eban negotiated directly with Dulles and, after months of strenuous effort, an agreement was reached, embodied in a policy statement by the Israeli Foreign Minister Golda Meir, and the crisis was brought to an end. It was classic diplomacy at its very best. At the Embassy in Washington Eban was assisted by his deputy chief of mission, Reuven Shiloah, and at the Israeli Mission to the UN by Ambassador Mordechai (Regi) Kidron.[23]

The statement, given on 1 March 1957 by Golda Meir in the General Assembly of the UN, announced Israel's readiness to withdraw completely from the two remaining areas occupied during the Sinai campaign, Sharm el-Seikh and the Gaza Strip, conforming to the 'assumptions and expectations' that were agreed upon with the United States. These stipulated that the Gulf of Aqaba 'comprehends international waters in which the right of free and innocent passage exists'. The US and other maritime powers endorsed this in the General Assembly. It was further agreed that a UN Emergency Force would be stationed at the Straits of Tiran and that it would prevent 'belligerent acts' and remain there 'until peaceful conditions were assured'. On Gaza, it was agreed that the UN would be responsible for the civil administration until a peace settlement was reached.

For the next ten years, until 1967, Israeli and foreign ships sailed through the Gulf of Aqaba to and from Eilat, which became an important commercial port, crucial in the development of Israel's trade with countries in Asia and Africa. A special pipeline from Eilat to Ashkelon carried Iranian oil and the city of Eilat flourished as a major tourist centre. The developments in Gaza were less satisfactory. Ten days after Golda Meir's statement, the Egyptians announced the return of their civil administration to Gaza. In reply to Israel's protestations the US underlined Nasser's unreliability but did nothing to reverse his violation of the agreement. The main achievement, however, was that no terrorist incursions from Gaza occurred for the next decade.

Moreover, the Middle East landscape after the Suez War was very different. Nasser's hold on Egypt was still considerable, yet his galloping radical advance was somewhat slowed, his hero image tarnished and his self-confidence shaken. The imminent perils facing Israel were temporarily lifted and its deterrent capacity was enhanced. For the second time in its eight years of existence, Israel emerged victorious from a military confrontation with Egypt, and this time an Egypt well armed and backed by the Soviet Union.

The Eisenhower administration missed an important opportunity to progress from the armistice agreement to, at least, a non-belligerency pact between Israel and Egypt. The Russians were absorbed with the unrest in Poland and Hungary, and a constructive American policy fully backed by Britain and France with Israeli troops still in the Sinai might have produced a better agreement and reduced Soviet penetration into the Middle East. Instead Eisenhower exerted pressure on Israel to withdraw. Broadcasting to the American people on 20 February 1957, he implied that if Israel did not accept the Dulles proposals, which called for withdrawal, the 'US would have to adopt measures which might have far-reaching effects on Israel's relations throughout the world'. No Israeli government could ignore such pressure from its most important ally. Eisenhower maintained that his policy was based on the principle that conflicts should not be solved by war, and by a need to safeguard the integrity of the United Nations. He failed to understand Nasser's designs and the dangers which the Israeli government had had to pre-empt. All the deliberations in Washington which preceded and followed the Suez War lacked practical suggestions on how to deal with the Arab–Israeli conflict and reduce the perils which Israel faced. The assurances which Israel received from the US were phrased in vague and elusive language: 'I believe that Israel will have no cause to regret' its decisions, the President wrote to Ben-Gurion.[24] This expectation was put to a severe test only ten years later, in 1967.

Eisenhower's attitude was also harsh towards the British and French. Wartime alliances and camaraderie were overtaken by anger and by a sense of betrayal, ignoring the serious efforts that were made for a peaceful solution to the Suez crisis. The President put considerable political and economic pressure on both countries.

The Anglo-French bombing on 31 October was followed by the landing of forces at Port Said on 6 November, with the intention of occupying a twenty-mile strip along the Suez Canal and holding it until a satisfactory arrangement was achieved for the control of the Canal. The six-day interval between the bombings and the landings were detrimental to the operation. By 6 November the Israeli operation was over. Hammarskjöld, with the full support of the US and Soviet Union, was working around the clock to impose a cease-fire. Eisenhower and American officials subjected Eden to intense pressure to accept an immediate cessation of hostilities. The press and the Labour Party fiercely attacked the government; senior members of the British Cabinet, among them Butler and Macmillan, opposed the continuation of the fighting. Eden, worn out, agreed to stop the fighting at midnight on 6 November. The French wanted to continue to advance towards Suez, but in view of Eden's insistence they followed the British lead. Nasser, glad that the two superpowers were doing the work for him, could afford to negotiate toughly with Hammarskjöld on the terms of the stationing of the UN Emergency Force in the canal zone. Eventually UNEF took over the canal zone on 21 November, and the Anglo-French troops withdrew. Ironically, when Selwyn Lloyd and the British ambassador in Washington, Harold Caccia, visited Dulles in hospital on 17 November, the latter asked the Foreign Secretary: 'Selwyn, why did you stop? Why didn't you go through with it and get Nasser down?'[25]

Eisenhower did not, however, shirk, the deterrence of Soviet intervention. When Bulganin wrote to the President in early November suggesting that Soviet and American troops should intervene in Egypt, Eisenhower strongly objected to any force which was not under a United Nations mandate entering the area. This policy was backed up by public warnings, by a heightened state of alert in the American forces and by suitable movements of the Sixth Fleet. Furthermore, this strong anti-Soviet posture was at the root of Eisenhower's message to Congress of 5 January 1957, in which he proposed joint action by the executive and legislature to meet the dangers from 'international communism', expressing readiness to assist every country in the Middle East which might be threatened. This proposal was ratified by Congress in March, authorizing the deployment of US forces to counter 'international communism' and became known as the 'Eisenhower Doctrine'. Its impact on the solution of the Arab–Israeli conflict was hardly noticeable, yet it allowed for the landings of American marines in Lebanon in 1958 after Egypt and Syria united temporarily under the banner of the United Arab Republic, and posed a threat to the pro-Western regime in Lebanon.

The aftermath of Suez subjected Eden to concentrated domestic pressure to explain the relation between the Suez War and the Sinai campaign. Not only did Labour leaders persist in their questions to the Prime Minister on the subject, Tory Members of Parliament joined them. Eden could have come out with a resounding defence of an action in which he deeply believed. Instead, he told Parliament on 20 December 1956: 'I want to say this on the question of foreknowledge and to say it quite bluntly to the House that there was not foreknowledge that Israel would attack Egypt – there was not.'[26] On 9 January 1957 Anthony Eden resigned as Prime Minister. His failing health was a major factor in his decision, with the handling of the Suez crisis weighing heavily on him. In May 1957 Guy Mollet's government stepped down in France and a year later de Gaulle returned to power.

5

Israel Celebrates Its Tenth Anniversary

As the first decade drew to a close and Israel celebrated its tenth anniversary in 1958, the country could take pride in a wide range of achievements. It was a decade of rapid and dynamic growth that would hardly be surpassed in future years. Close to a million new immigrants had arrived from countries far apart, with the largest waves coming from Iraq, Romania, Yemen, north Africa, Bulgaria and Poland. Their integration into the social and cultural fabric of Israeli society was one of the foremost challenges that the first Israeli governments faced. An extensive programme of land settlement was initiated, with desolate areas in northern Israel and in the Negev receiving priority. Hundreds of new settlements and townships were built and cities like Kiryat Shemona and Demona were established.

Defence had to be given preferential consideration in view of the dangers which Israel was to meet, and universal conscription was introduced, at first thirty months for men and two years for women. The length of service for men was later extended to three years. The Israeli defence forces fulfilled a dual purpose: while building a well-trained, strong and modern fighting force, they simultaneously served as a social melting-pot for the young conscripts, who came from a great variety of backgrounds.

Education also received a very high priority and hundreds of new schools were built as well as two new universities, the Tel Aviv University and Bar-Ilan. Infrastructure projects – roads, water conduits, electricity-generating facilities, hospitals – were constructed. Great efforts were invested by two leading economic ministers, Levi Eshkol and Pinchas Sapir, to build a modern export-oriented industrial base, with considerable success.

Israel's democratic structure, based on proportional representation, sailed through a number of political tempests, of which the most notable were: the controversy over relations with Germany; the Lavon Affair, which failed to establish who gave the authority to mount a rogue intelligence operation in Cairo; and the resignation of Foreign Minister Moshe Sharett in June 1956 because of differences of opinion with Ben-Gurion on the defence strategy and especially on the policy of retaliation for terrorist attacks in Israel.

As Prime Minister and Minister of Defence, Ben-Gurion was responsible for security, and for giving the country confidence that the constant terrorist assaults could be handled. Sharett was more aware of the diplomatic consequences of reprisals, but was unable to suggest any alternative. Both aimed at the same objectives and cooperated for many years in the struggle for independence and sovereignty, but the Prime Minister did not believe that outside powers could bring the Arabs to the negotiating table if they were unwilling to come. Eisenhower tried and was unsuccessful (the Anderson Mission). Ben-Gurion suspected Eden and the British of wanting to sever the Negev from Israel as the price of a doubtful compromise. Eden's Guildhall speech of November 1955 proved how right he was. The French did not have the necessary influence in the Middle East and the Soviet Union was totally behind the Arabs. Under the circumstances Ben-Gurion reached the conclusion by mid-1956 that a confrontation with Nasser's Egypt was inevitable and, believing that Sharett might stand in the way, he forced his resignation. For the Labour Party and for Sharett personally it was a painful and traumatic departure.

Debates between secular and religious ministers accompanied all the negotiations for coalition governments after elections. Nevertheless Ben-Gurion, and Sharett when he was Prime Minister, preferred to have religious parties in the government. It helped to build consensus and preserved unity. Although Ben-Gurion was for separation of religion from state, he agreed to what become known as the status quo on religious matters, which exempted yeshiva (religious seminary) students from military service, established a separate network of religious schools and sanctioned the non-recognition of the reform movement in Israel. At the same time Ben-Gurion wrote in 1958 to one of his most revered religious leaders, Rabbi Maimon, cautioning against attempts to legislate religious laws which would lead to fierce controversies and might pose a danger to the state.[1]

By the end of the fifties Israel's international standing was already well established as one of the family of democratic, forward-looking states. Its relation with the Jewish communities in the diaspora was enhanced and communities in the United States, Western Europe and Latin America contributed generously to funds to assist immigrant absorption.

My wife Hana and I celebrated the tenth anniversary in our Embassy in London, shortly after our arrival on our first diplomatic mission. I felt a profound sense of gratitude for the way our first ten years in Israel had passed, with our parents having employment, me and my two brothers, Yechiel and Efraim, having benefited from a good education and a reasonably satisfactory army service, with Hana, who arrived in Israel on the same boat with me in October 1948, having graduated as a teacher and both of us, as a young married couple, looking forward to an exciting diplomatic service. It was an illustration of the challenge and opportunity that the State of Israel offered its newcomers.

RELATIONS BETWEEN ISRAEL AND GERMANY

6

Special Relations

On 6 May 1995, I accompanied the Israeli President, Ezer Weizman, and Mrs Weizman to a banquet in the London Guildhall, hosted by the Lord Mayor of the City of London, to mark the fiftieth anniversary of Victory in Europe day. The keynote speaker was Her Majesty the Queen. Others present were Prime Minister John Major, senior Cabinet Ministers, the leader of the opposition Tony Blair, and fifty heads of states and governments and their ambassadors. President Weizman, one of three heads of state present who had served in the British forces during the war, represented both the Jewish people, who had been subjected to boundless suffering from Nazi Germany, and the State of Israel.

During the dinner, President Weizman, seated opposite me, engaged in lively conversation with Air Chief Marshal Sir Michael Graydon, commander of the Royal Air Force, leaving me time for thought. I looked around the glittering hall, and recalled how as a child of six I had been deported with my parents from a little town in Bukovina, Romania, by Romanian collaborators with Nazi Germany to a ghetto in the Ukraine. It was there, in Moghilov, on the banks of the river Dniester, that we spent the war years and all, luckily, survived.

Israel and the Jewish people owe a great deal to the British, who had fought valiantly alone against Nazi Germany until they were joined by the United States and the other allies. The mere thought of what might have been the fate of the tiny Jewish population in Palestine, had not Field Marshal Montgomery and the Eighth Army halted the advance of Rommel's armies at El-Alamein, is frightening. They might well have ended up in the gas chambers, as did much of European Jewry. Those few hundred thousand Jews in Palestine founded the State of Israel in 1948. Thoughts of the distance Israel had travelled in the past fifty years, and the personal travail of myself and my family during the same period, filled me with a sense of profound gratitude.

In her after-dinner address the Queen said, 'We can never forget the untold number of casualties suffered in these six long years, by servicemen and women and civilians alike, on all sides, nor the sacrifices and suffering of so many innocent victims – in particular the Jews in Europe – before peace could be achieved.' This was the only reference to the Holocaust in an evening, whose theme was peace and reconciliation. Among the heads of state present was the President of Germany, and Chancellor Helmut Kohl. The Queen emphasized that 'former enemies have become staunch allies'. Yet although former enemies may achieve peace and reconciliation, the Nazi genocide of the Jews in Europe belongs to a different category and will for ever remain an underlying factor in the relationship between Israel and Germany.

This relationship is different from any other set of bilateral relations which Israel has established with countries around the globe and will for ever be overshadowed by the Holocaust. As the relationship contains elements of tension and drama, any attempt to describe it as 'normal' ignores the inherent complexity and the deep emotions which dominate it. There is a challenge which leaders and intellectuals in both countries face, which is to strengthen understanding between the two peoples and develop broad cooperation and dialogue. At the heart of the matter is the Germans' need to be truthful about the past and to ensure that the lessons of the Holocaust and its inhuman atrocities are remembered and adequately taught. For Israelis and Jews there is the need to overcome the pain and anguish, remember one of the most devastating chapters in Jewish history and be convinced that the new Germany is vastly different from the Nazi regime. Both will have to accept that as long as human civilization endures, questions about why and how the Holocaust could happen will remain unanswered.

Both Israel and Germany were fortunate in having, in the early postwar years, leaders with vision and courage to lay the foundation of the post-Holocaust relationship: Israel's first Prime Minister, David Ben-Gurion, and West Germany's first Chancellor Dr Konrad Adenauer. The courage demonstrated by the Jewish leader, attempting to chart a course of rapprochement with Germany only six years after the end of the Second World War, was remarkable. The loss of six million Jews in the Holocaust, was so fresh in our minds that any mention of Germany invoked infinite agony.

The proclamation of an independent and sovereign Jewish state, a mere three years after the end of the Second World War, was in itself a huge historic accomplishment. 'Israel has risen from the ashes of the Holocaust' was a truism repeated again and again. Thousands of survivors flocked into the country. The original 650,000 Jews in Israel, while waging the War of Independence with the Arabs, were also struggling to absorb wave after wave of immigration.

The Israeli government under Ben-Gurion set out its priorities, which were not difficult to define – to build a strong defence force so that Israel could withstand and, if possible, deter any Arab onslaught; and to integrate hundreds of thousands of new immigrants into the fabric of the country.

The question of funding these two major efforts, while meeting the other needs of the new state, became the primary concern of the government. Reparations from Germany were a possible source of finance, especially considering that many of the new immigrants were Holocaust survivors.

Ben-Gurion also realized that before long West Germany would regain its influence in Europe. Moreover, it was clear that in the new postwar, Cold War reality Germany would side with the free world against the Soviet Union. Thus Ben-Gurion favoured the exchanges which Dr Nahum Goldman, the President of the World Jewish Congress, had established with the West German Chancellor, Dr Adenauer, on the subject.

The German Chancellor never underestimated the magnitude of the tragedy that Nazi Germany had inflicted on the Jewish people. He correctly sensed that without the assumption of responsibility for the Holocaust, Germany would find it hard to regain respectability among the family of nations and come to terms with its own criminal past. Adenauer's religious beliefs and strong moral convictions added motivation to the dialogue with Jewish leaders, and to his attitude to reparations. Yet a formal denunciation of the Nazi crimes against the Jewish people was not immediately forthcoming.

Influential German intellectuals found it incomprehensible that, six years after the end of the war, Germany had not yet admitted formal responsibility for the Holocaust. This view was succinctly articulated by Dr Rudolf Kustermeier, who wrote, in an article in *Die Welt* at the beginning of September 1951: '... after so much of the most inhuman inhumanity, we want to be human, that means upright and honest ...' As the public debate on the issue in Germany became intense, Adenauer finally felt that the time was ripe to make a formal declaration in the German Parliament.

Words alone could not produce a change of attitude where such a deep chasm and justified bitterness existed. It was clear that admittance of guilt by Germany must also be expressed in material terms, in compensation for the loss of property and wealth by the Jewish victims of the Holocaust.

The claim that Germany should pay reparations to the Jewish people was advanced shortly after the war ended. In September 1945, Dr Chaim Weizmann, the head of the World Zionist Organization, wrote to the allied powers on the subject. The official request for reparations by the State of Israel was submitted on 12 March 1951, in a note from Foreign Minister Moshe Sharett to the four occupying powers of Germany – the US, USSR, Great Britain and France. The sum requested was US $1 billion from West Germany, and $500 million from East Germany. The sum was based on the costs of absorbing half a million survivors from countries which were under Nazi occupation. However, Foreign Minister Sharett made it perfectly clear that a crime of such 'vast and fearful dimensions' as the Holocaust could not be erased by material compensation. The United

States, Britain and France supported Israel's request. The Soviet Union did not reply. This was a clear indication that nothing should be expected from East Germany.

Recognizing fully public sensitivity, Ben-Gurion would not bring the issue formally before the Knesset until two additional requirements had been fulfilled: the public assumption of responsibility for the Holocaust by Dr Adenauer and an indication as to whether West Germany would meet the requested amount of reparations.

After considerable drafting and redrafting, Dr Adenauer made a statement in the Bundestag on 27 September 1951. He attempted to set a 'new and healthy basis' for the attitude of Jews towards Germany. Emphasizing that not all Germans had participated in the Nazi atrocities, he admitted that 'indescribable crimes were committed in the name of the German people'. In other words, in the name of all Germans. Therefore 'moral and material reparations' were due. He declared that his government was prepared to work out the material reparations with representatives of Jewish organizations and with the State of Israel, which had absorbed so many homeless refugees. He also recognized the obligation of the German government to pay restitution to individual claimants. There was overwhelming support in the Bundestag for Adenauer's declaration and the session ended with a minute's silence.

With the passage of time and the unfolding of a vast volume of testimony and documentation, not the least during the Eichmann trial, it became clear that many more Germans than was admitted by the Adenauer government actively participated in the Holocaust. In his autobiography, Lord Weidenfeld quotes a top German intelligence officer, General Lahousen, who told him, 'Whatever you may hear now, all of us in senior positions knew ... Don't let anyone tell you that the general staff was ignorant of the "Final Solution".' The overwhelming feeling in Israel and of the Jewish people everywhere was that without the active participation and passive acquiescence of a great many Germans, the Holocaust would not have been possible. Still, the Chancellor's basic acceptance of responsibility, and his indication to Dr Goldman that he was prepared to negotiate on the basis of the amount of reparations requested by Israel, convinced Ben-Gurion that the issue could be placed before the Israeli Parliament.

The debate in the Knesset took place on 7–9 January 1952. It was heated and extremely emotional and was accompanied by stormy street demonstrations. Ben-Gurion asked the Knesset to approve the beginning of negotiations with West Germany. He was fiercely opposed by the leader of the right-wing party Herut, Menachem Begin. Addressing an anti-reparation demonstration in Jerusalem, Begin announced that 'this will be a war of life and death'. He spoke in similar terms in the Knesset and as a result was suspended from a number of sessions.

The public demonstrations became violent, compelling Ben-Gurion to order the army to protect the Knesset. Resistance to negotiations with Germany did not come only from the right of the political spectrum: the left-wing Mapam party and the Communists also expressed strong opposition. However, the government carried the vote by a majority of sixty-one to fifty. The Knesset decided to authorize the Foreign Affairs and Defence Committee to decide what action should be taken, which gave the government the go-ahead to open negotiations with Germany.

On 21 March 1952, two months later, the talks commenced in Wassenaar near the Hague. The Israeli delegation was headed by Dr Giora Yosephtal and Dr Felix Shinnar. Twenty-two Jewish organizations which came together under the 'Claims Conference' were represented by Moses Leavitt and Dr Alex Easterman. The German delegation was led by Professor Franz Bohm, the Dean of the Goethe University in Frankfurt. The negotiations were not crisis free. Some German ministers sought to link the negotiations with Israel and the Jewish organizations to the outcome of the London Conference on German external debts, which was involved in negotiations on all Germany's war debts. The concept of linkage was chiefly held by Hermann Abs, a German banker, who was head of the delegation to the London Conference, but he was supported by other officials in Bonn.

The mere equation of the Holocaust survivors with 'other claims' was in itself deeply offensive. Moreover, the Germans were not prepared to indicate the level of reparations they would pay. Deploring this lack of sensitivity, the Israeli delegation was instructed by the government to suspend negotiations. Dr Adenauer now intervened personally. Sensing that some of his ministers were reluctant to accept responsibility towards Israel and the Jewish people, he threatened to resign from the Cabinet.

Talks soon resumed, and agreement was finally reached and embodied in the Luxembourg Treaty, signed on 10 September 1952 by Foreign Minister Sharett and Dr Adenauer. This was the first international treaty that the Federal Republic of Germany had signed. In a brief statement, Sharett recognized the historic stand by Dr Adenauer, yet he also pointed out the impossibility of atonement for the lives of the millions of Jews who had perished.

The Luxembourg agreement stipulated that the Federal Republic of Germany would pay Israel the sum of three billion DM (about $715 million), the payments to be made in essential goods over a period of twelve years. In addition, 450 million DM would be paid to the Claims Conference of Jewish organizations for the rehabilitation of Nazi victims not living in Israel. The Federal Republic also undertook to enact legislation for the restitution of individual Nazi victims.

With the resolution of the reparations issue, the first barrier in a complex relationship was surmounted. However, Arab criticism of Germany now began to mount and, to Israel's great astonishment, some politicians in Germany delayed ratification. A full six months were required before both houses of the German parliament ratified the Luxembourg Treaty, on 19 and 20 March 1953. This was an early example of the constant opposition which Dr Adenauer encountered to his policy of building sustainable bridges between Germany and Israel. He was supported by his office, by the Social Democrats and by sections in his own party. Yet opposition was also clearly evident. On the question of reparations, the outcome was ultimately satisfactory. However, on the establishment of diplomatic relations with Israel he proved less successful.

In the postwar years, the Federal Republic made great efforts to achieve economic recovery. These were linked to a ceaseless drive to develop export markets, in the Arab countries as well as elsewhere. Had the German government, from the very beginning, made it unequivocally plain that its attitude towards Israel would in no way be influenced by Arab pressure, the Arabs would have had to accept this position, as they had a considerable interest in good relations with Germany.

Germany implemented fully its commitments under the Luxembourg Treaty. The German goods which started to arrive in Israel in July 1953 contributed immensely to the infrastructure network of Israel, especially in areas such as communications, shipping and the development of modern industry in the young state. To deal with the shipments of goods, the Israeli purchasing mission in Cologne was established under Dr Felix Shinnar. It became the precursor to the Israeli Embassy in Bonn.

The next important stage in the relations between Israel and the Federal Republic should have been the establishment of diplomatic ties between the two countries. Dr Adenauer wanted very much to crown his efforts to forge a new rapport with Israel and the Jewish people with the exchange of ambassadors. However, this decision was delayed for another twelve years, and only implemented by Dr Adenauer's successor, Dr Ludwig Erhard, in May 1965. The delay was not caused by Israel. It was due mainly to the self-entrapment of German foreign policy and its subordination to the 'Hallstein Doctrine'. The unification of Germany was a cornerstone of West German policy. It therefore followed that recognition of East German sovereignty must be prevented. In September 1955 the German under secretary of state, Dr Walter Hallstein, outlined a policy which stated that diplomatic relations between a third country and East Germany (DDR) would be regarded as an 'unfriendly act calculated to aggravate the division of Germany'. This was known as the 'Hallstein Doctrine'.

No state or group of states made better use of this policy than the Arab countries. Arab pressures on Germany, which intensified after the

Luxembourg agreement, now turned into outright blackmail. The Arab countries made it clear to the Federal Republic that if it wished them to abstain from establishing diplomatic relations with the DDR, Bonn must refrain from setting up diplomatic ties with Israel.

Under these circumstances, the German Foreign Ministers, Heinrich von Brentano and afterwards Dr Gerhard Schroeder, blocked any progress towards diplomatic relations, and persuaded Dr Adenauer not to pursue the subject. So much so that when the first historic meeting between Ben-Gurion and Dr Adenauer took place, in 1960 in New York, it was agreed beforehand that the question of diplomatic relations would not be raised. Nevertheless the importance of the first encounter of the two leaders and the symbolism of their public handshake can hardly be overstated. In New York the German Chancellor agreed to Ben-Gurion's request for a long-term economic-development loan. The sum was later set at a much lower level than the 500 million DM per annum (for a period of ten years) which Ben-Gurion had requested. However, these loans, which continued over the years, gave a further impetus to the development of economic and trade relations between the two countries, and ranked second only to the American aid which Israel received.

As a result of the reparations, the economic links between Israel and Germany developed rapidly, supplemented by a great variety of exchanges and dialogues between teachers, trade unions, youth groups, politicians and ordinary tourists. The role of education, and the need to include Holocaust studies in a meaningful way in the school curriculum, was the subject of many seminars between Israeli and German teachers. Intellectuals were grappling with the need to answer the complex questions arising from the appalling breakdown of humanity and morality.

Against this background, two events in the early sixties were of special significance: the Eichmann trial and the contribution of German scientists to the Egyptian war machine.

On 23 May 1960, Prime Minister David Ben-Gurion announced in the Knesset that Adolf Eichmann had been apprehended by the Israeli security services and was to be tried under the Nazi and Nazi Collaboration Punishment Law, 1950. Eichmann had been one of the chief architects of the extermination of Jews. After continuous attempts by the Israeli security services, and by Simon Wiesenthal, to track him down, he was discovered in Argentina, hiding under a false identity, and was apprehended by Israeli Mossad agents and flown to Israel. He was charged with crimes against the Jewish people and against humanity, and his trial started on 11 April 1961, in Jerusalem. Millions in Germany and in other countries followed it daily. The Israeli government paid for a well-known German lawyer, Dr Robert Servatius, to act for Eichmann in court. Eichmann's main defence was that he had followed orders. The chief prosecutor was the Israeli

Attorney-General Dr Gideon Hausner, and a panel of three distinguished Supreme Court justices sat in judgement. Israelis of all walks of life identified with the resounding words of Dr Hausner in his opening statement, when he said, 'As I stand before you, judges of Israel, I do not stand alone. With me, at this place and at this hour, stand six million accusers.'

Day after day the most gruesome evidence unfolded. Survivors recounted their ordeals, and documents amassed from many countries reinforced their accounts. The trial lasted for eight months, at the end of which Eichmann was found guilty. The verdict was handed down on 11 December 1961; the sentence was death. After his appeal to the Supreme Court was rejected, Eichmann was executed on 31 May 1962. This is still the sole case of the death sentence being carried out in Israel in the first fifty years of its statehood.

The impact of the Eichmann trial in Germany was very considerable. Its widespread coverage by the media enhanced understanding of the Holocaust and generated sympathy for the Jewish state. In his memoirs, Shimon Peres recounts a conversation with Dr Adenauer on the subject. The Chancellor told him that the Eichmann trial revealed to him the tragedy of the Holocaust in all its depth and shocked him anew.

During the same period, the activities of German scientists in Egypt had become a point of conflict and a considerable irritant to Israeli–German relations. In the early sixties, Israeli intelligence learned that German scientists were actively assisting the Egyptian war machine. Egypt had developed a rocket which it claimed was for 'meteorological purposes', but which in reality was a military weapon to enhance its offensive capability. German rocket scientists, among them experts from the Stuttgart rocket institute, had been engaged in this enterprise.

The Israeli government repeatedly raised the matter with Bonn. Those scientists who were working in the Stuttgart rocket institute before they went to Egypt were dismissed by the institute. However, work on the project continued, and the Egyptians succeeded in developing a rocket capable of hitting targets at a distance of up to two hundred miles. The German government maintained that legal constraints prevented it from acting against German citizens working abroad. The Israeli government and public were astounded. Could the Germans assist a war effort which undermined Israel's security so soon after the Holocaust?

The issue became a source of tension between Israel and Germany as well as a cause of domestic disagreement. The chief of Mossad at the time, Isser Harel, favoured intensified action against the German scientists. He was supported by Israel's Foreign Minister, Golda Meir. Ben-Gurion on the other hand, who had devoted so much time and effort to building up relations with Germany, was hesitant. He might have believed that in the end the German government would find a way to stop these activities by its scientists. Indeed, a few years later, Germany did what they should have done years before and persuaded the scientists to leave Egypt by offering them attractive opportunities in Germany.

The military relationship between Israel and Germany was intricate and fraught with difficulties. Germany was in the process of becoming an important source of weapons supply for Israel. Ben-Gurion did not want to endanger this relationship. The arguments among Israeli Cabinet Ministers on how best to handle the German scientists issue became very emotional and, some maintain, influenced Ben-Gurion's decision to retire from politics in 1963, the year in which Dr Adenauer also stepped down. The scientists issue faded away, but it left its scars.

Unfortunately, the work of German scientists in Egypt was not the only instance in which Germans were involved in a weapons production effort endangering Israel. Years later, in June 1996, the German magazine *Stern* reported that a huge chemical weapons plant had been built in Aleppo, Syria, and that a German firm headed by Hans Joachim Rose was instrumental in the notorious enterprise. The same firm was also involved in the building of a similar plant in Libya. Fifty years after the end of the Second World War the conscience and the moral judgement of some Germans is again severely called into question.

In 1964, Dr Adenauer, by then retired, visited Israel to receive an honorary doctorate from the Weizmann Institute. He met Ben-Gurion in his Negev retreat at Sdei-Boker. It was an emotional encounter between two old warriors. People present recounted that Adenauer's eyes were filled with tears.

Two years later, in April 1966, I accompanied Foreign Minister Abba Eban as political secretary to represent Israel at Dr Adenauer's funeral. The Israeli delegation was headed by David Ben-Gurion. This was my first visit to Bonn. When we landed in Cologne airport, we were met by a guard of honour like all the other official delegations, and I vividly remember the shock I felt when the German soldiers saluted us. To all of us in the delegation, it was clear that Adenauer and Ben-Gurion had left an indelible mark on relations between Israel and Germany.

As part of the Cold War rivalry, the Soviet Union intensified its arms supply to the Arab countries. Israel's military industry was in its infancy, and the United States declined, during those formative years, to supply it with the weapons essential for its defence. As a result Israel was constantly looking to the European markets to buy arms. France, and to some extent Great Britain, were major suppliers. However, Shimon Peres, who was the director-general of the Ministry of Defence, decided to explore the possibility of acquiring arms from the Federal Republic of Germany.

In 1957, Peres secretly met the German Minister of Defence, Franz-

Joseph Strauss. As the leader of the Christian Democratic Union, Strauss was considered a right-wing politician, but he understood well that Israel, although not a member of NATO, was part of the Western defence against the Soviet drive for expansion. Peres obtained his agreement to supply Israel with German surplus weapons on a favourable basis. Adenauer agreed to Strauss's approach to Israel on condition of total secrecy.

At Strauss's suggestion, Peres also met the leaders of the three main political parties in Germany, in order to smooth the way to parliamentary acquiescence to the arms supply to Israel. As a result, Israel received planes and helicopters, anti-aircraft guns and many other essential items during the next few years.

The major test of the Israeli–German defence relationship came in 1964. News leaked to the press that there were secret arms deals between Israel and Germany. At the time, Israel was expecting the supply of American Patton tanks stationed in Germany. The news reports angered the Arabs, who once again threatened to establish diplomatic relations with East Germany.

Politicians in the Free Democrat and Social Democrat parties condemned the arms deal. It seemed that never had so few tanks – fifteen Pattons – caused such a political furore. Nasser retaliated by inviting Walter Ulbricht, the President of East Germany, to visit Egypt.

Israel expected a firm stand on the part of the German government, believing that in view of the dangers that Israel faced from the Arab rearmament by the Soviet Union, Germany could defend the supply of the tanks to the Jewish state. The German Chancellor, Dr Ludwig Erhardt, did not think so. In February 1964, the German government announced that it would stop the supply of further weapons to non-NATO countries – Israel. It also cautioned Egypt that a visit by Ulbricht to Cairo would be considered a hostile act. This warning failed to impress President Nasser, and ten days later Ulbricht landed in Cairo.

The Bonn government could not but view the Egyptian decision as a contravention of the Hallstein Doctrine. Erhardt saw the invitation to Ulbricht as a de facto recognition of East Germany. As a result, the German government decided, at last, to establish diplomatic relations with Israel. Dr Erhardt asked a prominent businessman and close friend of his, Dr Kurt Birrnbach, to undertake a special mission to Israel, in order to negotiate both outstanding issues: the non-supply of tanks to Israel and the modalities of the establishment of diplomatic relations.

Dr Birrnbach paid three visits to Israel between 7 March and 14 April 1965. Mrs Golda Meir, who was serving her last year as Foreign Minister, was unwell, and the Prime Minister, Levi Eshkol, asked his deputy Abba Eban to head the delegation to the talks. Shimon Peres participated as deputy defence minister and architect of the defence relationship with

Germany. Eban was joined by two able Foreign Ministry officials, Jochanan Meroz, who later became ambassador to Bonn, and Holocaust survivor Zeev Sheck, later ambassador in Austria and Italy.

During the Birrnbach mission, I was working in the office of Foreign Minister Golda Meir, as deputy to her political advisor, Simcha Dinitz. I remember Mrs Meir's agony in having to negotiate with Dr Birrnbach. Her attitude towards Germany was very emotional, and although she accepted and supported the reparations from Germany, the setbacks which the relationship had endured since, and especially the work of the German scientists in Egypt, moved her deeply. It came therefore as no surprise to me that the negotiations with Birrnbach were mainly conducted by Deputy Prime Minister Abba Eban.

Another intriguing aspect was how a Holocaust survivor, a victim of the death camp Terezienstadt, could negotiate with Germans. As I was quite friendly with Zeev Sheck – we had served together in the Israeli Embassy in London in the late fifties – I put the question to him. Sheck replied that he felt great satisfaction in being a member of the negotiating team. The Germans, he said, had wanted to annihilate the Jewish people, and now he was proudly negotiating, on behalf of the sovereign Jewish State of Israel, the establishment of diplomatic relations between Israel and Germany.

The outcome of the Birrnbach negotiations was a package which consisted of the establishment of diplomatic relations and the supply of the arms which Israel needed so badly, to be sent by the United States and paid for by Germany. In addition, Dr Birrnbach promised that the German government would make every effort to persuade the German scientists who were still in Cairo to leave Egypt. The agreement was ratified by the government. On 12 March 1965, Abba Eban presented it to the Knesset, which approved the establishment of diplomatic relations with Germany. On the exchange of the official letters between Prime Minister Eshkol and Chancellor Erhardt, ten Arab countries severed relations with West Germany.

The diplomatic ties between Israel and Germany were accepted by the majority of Israelis in a mood of profound reflection, rather than with the negative attitude which had characterized the debate on the reparations in earlier years, although the arrival of the first German ambassador to Israel, Dr Rolf Pauls, was greeted with demonstrations. Twelve years of close cooperation on economic issues, trade, science and the supply of military equipment brought thousands of Israelis into contact with their counterparts in the Federal Republic. By the mid 1960s, an intensive network of two-way interactions was taking place. Israelis and Germans saw the benefit and the symbolism in diplomatic links between Jerusalem and Bonn. Yet the political dialogue did not lack friction and conflict.

In the first decade after the conclusion of the Luxembourg Treaty, the relations between the two countries were defined as 'special relations', a term borrowed from the close alliance between the United States and Great Britain during the Second World War. In the case of Israel and Germany, this definition merely implied that because of the Holocaust, the relations had a unique dimension.

Some German politicians were of the opinion that, with the payment of reparations and the establishment of diplomatic relations, the relationship between the two countries should no longer be defined as 'special' but rather as 'normal'. Although these are only code words, the change implied that henceforth Israel should be treated like any other country.

For Israelis and politicians like Golda Meir, Yigal Alon, Abba Eban and others, this suggestion was astounding. It demonstrated a lack of sensitivity, and a failure, or reluctance, to understand that the Holocaust was not a transient event, but a national tragedy that would remain deeply ingrained in the consciousness of the Jewish people. Israel expected that the Holocaust would stay equally deeply rooted in the consciousness of the German people, for the past could not be altered.

Hence the definition 'special relations'. Statements voiced by German politicians, like that of the Foreign Minister, Walter Scheel, who said that 'our relations with Israel are as our relations with other countries', were a source of serious disappointment to Israelis.

Against this background, the first two ambassadors assumed office, Dr Rolf Pauls representing Germany in Israel, and Asher Ben-Nathan as Israel's envoy to Bonn. The relationship received a new impetus, and as the dialogue intensified and covered new areas of activity and interest, cooperation grew and mutual understanding was enhanced. Both men were very able and experienced, and made an important contribution towards setting the relationship on a firm basis.

By the late 1960s, the European Economic Community had developed into an influential body. As the greater part of Israeli export and import trade was transacted with Western Europe, Israel was interested in concluding a preferential agreement with the EEC. Germany took a supportive and helpful role in achieving this objective, as well as subsequent agreements with the EEC.

Relations between countries are seldom conducted on an even plateau. More often than not, they traverse hilly ground, influenced by unpredictable events and by the statesmen who inspire and direct them. In the five decades since 1951, Israeli–German relations have had their share of difficult moments. For Israel it was hard to accept that in times of great danger, for example during the Six Day War in 1967 and, even more, during the Yom Kippur War in 1973, Germany adhered strictly to a policy of neutrality.

In 1973, as the war was being waged, the United States prepared to rush badly needed military supplies to Israel. It was clear that any delay in providing armaments would cost the lives of Israeli soldiers. The negative German attitude to facilitating the shipment of arms to Israel was expressed in a statement in Bonn on 25 October 1973: 'Germany's strict neutrality forbids any deliveries of weapons using West German territory or installations.' True, Germany was greatly dependent on Arab oil yet, in the prevailing circumstances and with the Arab threat to Israel's existence, Israel had expected far more.

Another instance of aggravation was the release of the three Arab terrorists accused of the murderous attack on eleven Israeli Olympic athletes in Munich in 1972. The kidnapping and killing of the athletes by Palestinian terrorists was profoundly traumatic for Israel. Three of the terrorists were apprehended and jailed by German police, but in October 1972 a German airliner was hijacked, and the three terrorists were released to procure its safety. To Israel, a country which has to confront terrorism continuously, the German decision was incomprehensible. Prime Minister Meir described the release as shocking, and the Israeli ambassador to Bonn was recalled for consultations.

The insistence of West Germany's Foreign Minister, Walter Scheel, on 'even-handedness' towards the 1973 Arab–Israeli conflict was understandably disliked in Jerusalem and caused much ill-feeling, and although Chancellor Brandt was personally committed to Israel, formal German policy remained much the same during his tenure. Brandt's government constantly emphasized its desire for a friendly relationship with the Arabs and took great care in balancing pro-Israeli by pro-Arab rhetoric. It was Brandt who defined the relations between Germany and Israel as 'normal relations with a special character'. However, in the Socialist International – a conference of socialist parties – Brandt developed a friendly relationship with Shimon Peres which served both countries well, and possibly bridged some gulfs. Brandt's kneeling in prayer for forgiveness at the Warsaw ghetto was a valuable demonstration of his attitude towards the Shoah.

In the seventies and eighties, the Palestinian problem often became a focal point of difference between the two countries. The meeting of Foreign Minister Gerhard Schroeder with Yasir Arafat in Damascus as far back as 1974, was a case in point. The divergence of views on the Palestinian question erupted into a heated public confrontation between Prime Minister Begin and Chancellor Helmut Schmidt. During a visit to Saudi Arabia, Schmidt expressed support for a Palestinian state, and later on he voiced reservations on Israel's settlements policy. Begin reacted with great ferocity to Schmidt's Saudi Arabia statement, terming it 'most callous'. He also attacked Schmidt personally, reminding him of his service in the German army during the war. Schmidt reiterated, on 7 May 1981 that he was aware of the 'special moral and historical quality of German–Israeli relations'.

In 1970, the first official visit of an Israeli Foreign Minister to Germany took place when Abba Eban visited Bonn. Yitzhak Rabin paid the first official prime ministerial visit in 1975. Chancellor Brandt and German Foreign Ministers visited Israel as part of the ongoing high-level relationship. German economic development aid continued to be granted to Israel on a yearly basis, and individual restitutions were paid in full compliance with the Luxembourg Treaty.

Helmut Kohl became Chancellor in 1984, and it soon became clear that here was a leader with a thorough understanding of the Nazi past and its lessons for the future. He also entertained feelings of friendship and understanding towards the State of Israel and the Jewish people. Speaking in Bergen-Belsen in April 1985, he said, 'This darkest chapter of our history must always serve as a reminder to us – not because we ask the question why those who risked their lives in opposing the terror ultimately failed in their efforts. The decisive question is, rather, why so many people remained apathetic, did not listen properly, closed their eyes to the facts.'

Israeli–German relations became closer after the 1991 Gulf War. German companies, like other European companies, had helped considerably the Iraqi drive to acquire unconventional arms. Soon after Iraq started to bombard Israel with Scud missiles, the German Foreign Minister Hans Dietrich Genscher arrived in Jerusalem and witnessed the damage. In his talks with government ministers he offered Germany's assistance. In response, Defence Minister Moshe Arens requested a renewal of arms supplies from Germany to Israel, which had been stopped in 1965. Genscher agreed to discuss the issue, and an Israeli delegation promptly left for Bonn.

Chancellor Kohl himself took charge of the negotiations. He decided that the Israeli request should be met and that Germany would build three submarines for the Israeli navy, two of which would be paid for by Germany.

With the evolution of a common foreign policy by the European community, various EEC initiatives which were supported by Germany were opposed by Israel, for instance the Venice Declaration and, later, the sanctions which were applied to Israel in the wake of the war with Lebanon in 1982.

In many other instances Germany under Kohl demonstrated understanding towards Israel's policy. Germany was helpful in the negotiation and conclusion of the new agreement between Israel and the European Union in December 1995. Similarly, Bonn supported the agreement for cooperation in science and technology between Israel and the EU.

One of Kohl's first visits abroad as Chancellor was to Israel in 1984. Since then he has visited Israel several times, in 1995 representing Germany at the funeral of Prime Minister Rabin, and later in the same year to receive a honorary doctorate at the Be'er Sheva University. During his tenure, the official visits to Germany of Prime Minister Peres and Presidents Chaim Herzog and Ezer Weizman took place.

Kohl's stated objectives are to promote reconciliation and cooperation and, in his words, 'to help safeguard Israel's future and maintain its viability'. Israel's relations with Germany in the eighties and nineties benefited considerably from the work of two top Israeli ambassadors to Bonn – Benjamin Navon and Avi Primor. However, they were also greatly aided by a changed international environment – the unification of Germany and the Arab–Israeli peace process.

East Germany never accepted responsibility for the Holocaust, nor did it pay reparations to Nazi victims. Throughout the years it displayed a hostile attitude towards Israel. Moreover, it became a base for Palestinian terror, the terrorists received training, intelligence and weapons there. Until 1989, it was totally dominated by Soviet influence, and followed the Soviet anti-Israel policies. When the Berlin Wall collapsed on 11 November 1989, some politicians in Berlin thought that East Germany might stay independent. After the first free elections in the German Democratic Republic were held, the Peoples' Chamber, their parliament, convened, and on 12 April 1990, it assumed responsibility on behalf of the citizens of East Germany for the humiliation, expulsion and murder of Jewish women, men and children during the Nazi regime. The chamber asked Jews around the world for forgiveness for the hypocrisy and hostility of the Communist policies towards Israel. The East German government in Berlin initiated talks with Israel on setting up diplomatic relations, and established contacts with Jewish leaders in the United States.

After ensuring that Genscher and the West German government would have no objections to Israel's contacts with East Germany, Michael Shilo, later Israeli ambassador to Norway, was sent to Copenhagen for talks with East German officials. Between January and May 1990, three meetings took place. By May it became clear that Germany would be united and therefore the exchanges were stopped. In July 1990, the monetary union between the two Germanies was affected and in December 1990 the first elections were held in the reunited Germany.

The challenge of unifying Germany was historic and indeed remarkable for Chancellor Kohl. Two aspects were of concern to Israel: first, there was apprehension that a strong and united Germany might be too dominant. This notion was expressed by Israeli Prime Minister Shamir, as it was voiced by Mrs Thatcher in London. More directly, officials in Israel were wondering whether seventeen million Germans, born and bred in a Communist environment hostile to Israel, would influence adversely the friendship and cooperation with Bonn which Israel had nurtured so carefully.

In the first meeting of the all-German Bundestag, Chancellor Kohl asserted that Germans would never forget or suppress the crimes committed by the Nazis. The memory of the Holocaust, the unparalleled genocide of European Jews, would be kept alive, he promised.

Israel decided to intensify its activity in the new Länder and opened a consulate in Berlin. Nearly a decade later it is clear that, as the East Germans adapted rapidly to freedom and freedom of information, they were more influenced by the West German outlook on Israel than the other way round. Yet manifestations of anti-Semitism, racism and xenophobia are still more prevalent in the eastern parts of Germany. The struggle to combat these irrational and harmful trends is a constant and primary challenge for the Bonn government.

By the time Chancellor Kohl took office, Israel was at peace with Egypt. In 1993 the historic breakthrough with the Palestinians occurred and in 1994 the peace treaty with Jordan was signed. The whole Middle East scene was changing. Arab pressures on Germany and Europe faded as oil turned into a sellers' market. The Arab boycott began to disappear, and many causes of friction with Israel became history. Kohl follows a consistent policy of support for the Middle East peace process, and Germany is assisting the economic development in the Palestinian areas as well as in Jordan.

A current issue of contention between Jerusalem and Bonn is the soft German attitude towards Iran. The scramble of the present regime in Iran to acquire nuclear weapons, its opposition to the peace process in the Middle East and its championing of terror remains a source of danger and concern for Israel and for many of the neighbouring Arab countries in the Middle East and the Persian Gulf. Germany strongly supports the European Union policy of a 'critical dialogue' with Iran, whereas Israel views this exchange with much doubt. This is an area where Israeli–German relations allow for a different perspective to be discussed openly.

It is a fact of history that in addition to the convergence of interest between Israel and Germany, expressed by the policies of Ben-Gurion and Adenauer, the rapprochement between the two countries was aided by the fact that the Israel of the fifties was very European in outlook, values and culture. Continuous bitterness towards Germany would only have widened the gap and deprived the state of an important ally. Moreover, German and Austrian Jews, who arrived in Israel as refugees in the thirties, were well educated, and contributed greatly to public life. Some of them, like Dr Felix Shinnar and Asher Ben-Nathan, played key roles in developing the links with the new Germany. They illustrate how much richer Jewish and Israeli life would have been if the Jews in Germany, Austria and the rest of Europe had not perished.

On a more personal level, once my family built its new life in Israel, our bookshelves were filled again with German books as well as Hebrew literature, and my late father, David Herstig, compiled and published the first German–Hebrew, Hebrew–German dictionary after the war.

From Adenauer to Kohl, and from Ben-Gurion to Shimon Peres, Israeli–German relations have overcome great difficulties and have registered many achievements. More than fifty years after the end of the Second World War, however, we still hear the recurring themes, hardly influenced by the passage of time. Speaking in Washington in May 1996, the German Foreign Minister, Klaus Kinkel, came back to Adenauer's basic ideas of denying collective guilt while underlining the German responsibility 'for the horrors that have happened'.

As for the future, what are Israel's expectations of the relationship with Germany? To state these broadly, responsibility for the past carries an intrinsic obligation to recognize the uniqueness of the relations between the two countries. At times, clashes of interests may occur. In such cases we would expect that judgements would not be made on the basis of a narrow definition of German self-interest. Decisions might rather be qualified by moral considerations inherent in this very special relationship, for this is a relationship which transcends the traditional patterns of interaction between states and of foreign-policy decision making. Similarly, given German history, we would expect a continuous effort to combat anti-Semitism and racism. Helmut Kohl, who complements his discourse with Israel by an ongoing German–Jewish dialogue with distinguished Jewish leaders, understands these imperatives, and also that such a particular approach to Israeli–German ties is, in the final analysis, compatible with long-term German interests.

THE SECOND DECADE
1958–68

7

A Decade of Progress

The late fifties and early sixties saw a turbulent and unstable Middle East. A violent and bloody revolution in Iraq in 1958 led to the assassination of King Faisel and the pro-Western Prime Minister Nuri Said. In Lebanon civil war broke out and its President invited American assistance. President Eisenhower acceded to the request and US marines landed in Beirut. Jordan too was apprehensive of Egyptian and Syrian intentions under their temporary merger in the United Arab Republic and asked for a Western troop presence. British paratroopers rushed to Amman after receiving permission to overfly Israel. In Syria there were frequent *coups d'état*. Not one of all these revolutions led to an attempt to introduce democracy to an Arab country; one military officer merely unseated the other and the totalitarian systems of government were perpetuated.

In this stormy environment Israel was less exposed to impending military threats by the Arab countries. Anti-Israel rhetoric was virulent and was employed to gain popularity among the Arab masses, yet the reality was that the Sinai campaign had left Egypt militarily weak, and Syria and Jordan would not attack Israel alone. However, terrorist activity from Jordan and clashes with Syria in the demilitarized zone continued. This situation of relative tranquillity afforded Israel a decade of consolidation and allowed her to concentrate on domestic priorities. The 1959 general elections gave the Labour Party a handsome majority of forty-seven members in the Knesset (out of 120), among them three young parliamentarians who were to play a prominent role in future Israeli politics: Abba Eban, Moshe Dayan and Shimon Peres. There was an increase in immigration, and many Jews who had left Egypt in 1957 and Hungary during the anti-Soviet revolution arrived in Israel, while the inflow of people from Morocco, Tunis and Algiers continued. By the end of its second decade the Jewish population in Israel was approaching 2.4 million.

The harnessing of every drop of water and the planning of the water supply system was of crucial importance to the future development of the country. A series of projects were undertaken to put in place a water infrastructure, including the transfer of water from Israel's only sweet-water lake, the Kinneret, to the south. The completion of the Jordan Valley Project was in many ways the linchpin of this endeavour and there were a number of Syrian attempts to stop the work on it, targeting the construction sites in northern Israel, but unsuccessfully. The National Water Carrier was completed and one of the results of an improved water supply system was that Israel became more than self-sufficient in the production of food. The surplus in fruit, vegetables and dairy produce was exported, while cereals and meat were in short supply and had to be imported. In a short few years Israel moved from food rationing to self-reliance in many products.

An important improvement in the quality of education was achieved in the sixties with the introduction of educational television, by courtesy of the Rothschild Memorial Fund. It allowed children, teachers and parents in remote settlements and townships to benefit from high-quality programmes, and accelerated their Hebrew studies and their integration into Israeli society. The same fund was responsible for the building of the Knesset and, in recent years, the Supreme Court building in Jerusalem.

With the election of President Kennedy in 1960 came a marked improvement in relations between Israel and the United States. The damage to the relationship left by the Sinai campaign was dissipating and the Israeli government felt that the new President understood the dangers that the country faced. Foreign Minister Golda Meir travelled to the US in 1962, and met the President in Florida. In her memoirs she recorded a very emotional exchange, telling the President: 'What is written on the wall for us is: Beware of losing your sovereignty again, for this time you may lose it for ever.' The President reassured her that he understood this – 'nothing will happen to Israel.'[1] A State Department record of this conversation describes the President's commitment in these words: 'The United States ... has a special relationship with Israel in the Middle East really comparable only to that which it has with Britain over a wide range of world affairs ... we are in a position then to make clear to the Arabs that we will maintain our friendship with Israel and our security guarantees ... In case of an [Arab] invasion the United States would come to the support of Israel.'[2] Kennedy followed up on his commitment by writing to Prime Minister Eshkol in October 1963 (soon after Ben-Gurion's resignation) affirming US capability and preparedness to safeguard Israel.[3] This was the strongest recognition of United States responsibility for the security of Israel and, together with the President's decision to sell Israel Hawk missiles, it represented a welcome change of policy.

The tormenting questions surrounding the relations between the Jewish state and Germany were much in the forefront of public interest in the early sixties. Ben-Gurion's announcement in the Knesset in May 1960 that one of the chief architects of the Holocaust, Adolf Eichmann, had been apprehended by Israeli agents (in the Argentine) and his subsequent trial revived the memories of one of the darkest periods in modern history.

The supply of German arms to Israel and the work of German scientists in Egypt assisting in the development of missiles preoccupied the governments and parliaments in both countries. Intense exchanges eventually led to the establishment of diplomatic relations between Israel and Germany in May 1965. A year later the retired German Chancellor Konrad Adenauer visited Israel and received an honorary doctorate from the Weizmann Institute. However, his visit was not problem free. At a dinner at the Prime Minister's residence, the host proposed a toast and remarked that '... the Jewish people continued to look to testimony that Germany recognized the burden of the past and sought a new path for herself in the comity of nations'.[4] Eshkol was reflecting the prevailing mood and thinking in Israel; however, Adenauer took offence and interpreted the words as criticism of the German government. He refused to raise his glass during the toast to Israeli–German understanding. The president of the World Jewish Congress, Dr Nahum Goldman, who was present at the dinner, calmed the eighty-eight-year-old statesman.

Israel followed the formation of the European Economic Community with a great deal of interest. It envisaged that this huge market, composed of friendly countries, would absorb an important part of its exports. It therefore sought an agreement on preferential tariffs with the EEC. The first such agreement, leading to the reduction of tariffs on a number of Israeli products, was concluded in 1960 and was renewed for another five years in 1967.

The close ties with France, forged during the Suez War, continued for a number of years. The manufacturers of defence equipment and of aeroplanes displayed a continuing interest in the Israeli market and they were rewarded with lucrative contracts. However, as the war in Algeria ended, France began to look for ways to restore its traditional ties with – and influence in – the Arab world, and a cooling of relations with Israel resulted. The visit of Prime Minister Eshkol to Paris in 1964 and his conversation with de Gaulle did not basically change this French policy trend despite the fact that the French President referred to Israel as 'our friend and ally'. Friendly statements were also voiced in London both during the Eshkol–Wilson meeting in 1964 and in Parliament, where Harold Wilson stated in April 1965 that Britain would not sacrifice her ties with Israel in order to achieve better relations with Egypt.[5]

Israel's foreign relations during this decade were also characterized by an unprecedented drive to develop close ties with the emerging nations in Asia and Africa. The opening of the sea route through Sharm el-Sheikh facilitated this initiative. While success in bringing the Asian countries closer was limited, as states with large Muslim populations, like India, Indonesia and others, were reluctant to establish diplomatic relations with Israel, the outcome in Africa was fruitful. Many African countries drew an analogy between their own struggle for independence and Israel's fortunes, admiring its rapid economic growth and the way the country had handled social and labour problems, and believing that the Israeli experience could be applied in their lands. Israel, surrounded by hostile countries, considered its relations with Africa as a way to bypass its isolation in the Middle East, and welcomed the challenge of extending a helping hand to the African states that were seeking its friendship. In return it expected understanding, goodwill and political support in the United Nations. In later years the extension programmes, specifically designed for the requirements of developing countries, also included trainees from Latin America. Special institutes were established for this purpose, such as the Afro-Asian Institute for Labour Studies and an agricultural extension group which dealt with training and assistance in agriculture and irrigation. The group was coordinated jointly by the Ministry of Agriculture and the Ministry of Foreign Affairs. Israeli doctors, agronomists, social and community workers, irrigation experts, trade union leaders and, in some instances, police and military instructors, worked with their counterparts in many countries in Africa.[6] This effort received the wholehearted support of Foreign Minister Golda Meir, who took a personal interest in Israel's work in Africa and was emotionally involved in it. Mrs Meir felt that this was an area where Israel had something to offer and could be genuinely helpful to other peoples. She visited countries in east and west Africa in order to see first-hand the results of this drive which was led by the Ministry of Foreign Affairs. The only limitation was the shortage of manpower and budgets that could be allocated for this purpose, and more often than not requests for assistance had to be turned down, causing disappointment. In this pioneering endeavour the Foreign Ministry was greatly assisted by the deputy director-general, Ehud Avriel, later ambassador to Italy, and by the head of the Department for International Cooperation, Aharon Remez, later ambassador to Great Britain. But many initiatives came from the envoys in African capitals; Hannan Yavor in Ghana and Nigeria, Shlomo Hillel, ambassador to Guinea and director of the African Department (later Speaker of the Knesset and a Cabinet Minister), and Shimeon Amir, as well as many other colleagues in the Foreign Office and in other capitals.

An interesting feature of this effort was the participation of about two hundred trainees a year from Iran in a variety of programmes, some in agriculture and urban development. In 1960 the Shah declared that Iran recognized Israel de facto and from then until the advent of Ayatollah Khomeini in 1979, Israel built up a strategic relationship with Iran which was beneficial to both countries. Israel's cooperation with developing countries continued in later years and by the time of writing more than forty-five thousand people from the 'Third World' had received instruction in Israel. After the conclusion of the Oslo Agreement with the Palestinians, hundreds of Palestinians received their training in institutions created by the Center for International Cooperation of the Ministry of Foreign Affairs.

While serving in the Embassy in London in the early sixties I was directly involved in developing our ties with countries in east and west Africa. This was the era of frequent African constitutional conferences on independence in Britain in which the top leadership participated. Being in charge of Commonwealth affairs in the Embassy, I used the opportunity of their visits to meet leaders like Jomo Kenyata and Tom M'Boya of Kenya, Obote, later President of Uganda, Dr Azikiwe of Nigeria, and many others, and interested them in our work in Africa. Some of them would visit Israel on their way back home, others would ask for Israeli experts in various fields. In one case I was asked to give a legal opinion on a constitutional draft. I consulted the ministry and a top constitutional lawyer was sent from Israel. The drawing-room in our flat became the site of complicated legal deliberations. Arthur Lourie, who headed the Embassy, was very supportive of these efforts and would always be available for meetings with African personalities. In later years we were obviously disappointed to see anti-Israel statements made by some of the leaders we had met, who had earlier displayed friendship and understanding, but at least I knew that we had done our best to put the Israeli point of view across to them. Whenever the Arab–Israeli conflict became volatile, the majority of the African states would adopt an unfriendly attitude to Israel following the radical line of the Third World block of countries. Yet there were also encouraging incidents, like the response of the President of Tanzania to Arab criticism of its ties with Israel: he told the Arabs that Tanzania 'will not allow its friends to determine who our enemies shall be'.

The most remarkable feature of Israeli domestic politics of the early sixties was the end of the Ben-Gurion era. Shortly after the fifteenth anniversary of independence, on 16 June 1963, Ben-Gurion made the stunning announcement that for personal reasons he was resigning as Prime Minister. He had intended to resign from the government on the morrow of the Independence Day celebrations; however, the federation between Egypt, Syria and Iraq, which was established in April 1963 and which he viewed as a new and serious danger to Israel, made him delay the announcement. Ben-Gurion's concern emanated from the stated goal of this new and hostile coalition, which was 'the establishment of a military unity [of the three states] capable of liberating the Arab homelands from the dangers of Zionism'.[7] He therefore reacted angrily in the Knesset when the Lord Privy Seal, Edward Heath, on being asked about the federation, told Parliament that the British government had no reason to believe that the Arab states were 'contemplating an attack on Israel'. Ben-Gurion felt that the Heath statement of 1 May 1963 was in contradiction to the declared aims of the new union and as Prime Minister and Minister of Defence he wanted to alert the major powers to the added dangers confronting Israel. Indeed one of his last acts in office was a personal letter to the heads of states of the US, Great Britain and France on the subject.

According to Israeli law Ben-Gurion should have remained as head of the government until a new Cabinet was formed. However, he requested that his resignation become effective immediately and suggested to President Shazar that he nominate the Finance Minister, Levi Eshkol, as the new Prime Minister. Within a week Eshkol presented his new Cabinet for Knesset approval. Constitutionally the transition could not have been smoother, yet it represented a marked change in Israel's political establishment. Ben-Gurion, the founding father of the state, possessed unique qualities of character, vision and leadership, and except for a brief period in which Sharett was Prime Minister, had been at the helm of government since 1948. He set the priorities for the country in its most crucial formative period. Eshkol had worked closely with Ben-Gurion as Minister of Finance and had been given a fairly free hand in planning and leading the economy. He was a dedicated hard-working minister, with a down-to-earth practical approach, a doer rather than an orator. His immediate disadvantage was that he was the successor to such a towering personality as Ben-Gurion. Moreover, before long he found himself in conflict with Ben-Gurion on two issues which at the time were debated with great ferocity. Ben-Gurion demanded the establishment of a judicial committee of inquiry to investigate the Lavon Affair, the security mishap of 1954 in which a rogue intelligence operation in Cairo had led to the arrest of a number of young Jews and the execution of two of them. Eshkol, with the support of the party secretariat, resisted this demand because a committee of seven, which had investigated the case in previous years had exonerated the then Minister of Defence, Pinhas Lavon, from giving the order for the operation. Ben-Gurion had never accepted those findings, because it meant that an army officer was the highest authority responsible for the mishap. Eshkol did not see any benefit in reopening a very acrimonious chapter of years gone by, and thought that the revived controversy would only cause damage. Ben-Gurion was so enraged by Eshkol's stance that he demanded his resignation.

In the search for a wider consensus, Eshkol believed that it was important to bring together the socialist parties in the Knesset to work in greater unison. Achdut Ha'avoda was ideologically close to the Labour Party (Mapai), and the Prime Minister worked hard with its leader, Yigal Allon, to create the Alignment (Ma'arach) between the two parties so that they could contest the elections on a joint list. Ben-Gurion objected to this move, claiming that a large party like Labour should not make concessions to a smaller and more militant party. The controversy was fierce and Dayan, who was Minister of Agriculture in Eshkol's Cabinet, and supported

Ben-Gurion, resigned from the government. Ben-Gurion left the central committee of the Labour Party and eventually formed his own splinter party – Rafi. Despite the fact that Dayan and Peres, in loyalty to their revered leader, joined Ben-Gurion, the new party did poorly in the elections, ending up with only ten members in the Knesset. The way Ben-Gurion treated his successor was widely deplored, because it went beyond voicing a discordant note on matters of policy, attacking the Prime Minister personally. For Ben-Gurion, a legendary figure, it was a sad and painful finale to a brilliant political career, as well as an illustration of the shifting fortunes of politics.

Eshkol led the government with a steady and experienced hand. The Alignment, the party he led in the 1965 elections, won forty-nine seats, and he became Prime Minister in his own right. Like Ben-Gurion before him he also held the portfolio of Minister of Defence, and took great pains to ensure that the army had an adequate budget and the most sophisticated equipment, so that it was ready for any confrontation which might occur. He refused to rely on a single major source of arms supply, namely France, and obtained tanks, Hawk anti-aircraft missiles and Skyhawk bombers from the United States. When presenting his new government to the Knesset on 12 January 1966, Eshkol emphasized that 'Israel's central aim in the Near East is the advancement of peace.'

After the elections, Golda Meir, in bad health, decided to resign as Foreign Minister, a post she had held for the past nine years, and become the secretary of the Alignment. At the beginning of 1966 Abba Eban, who had been Deputy Prime Minister and Minister of Education in the previous government, was appointed Foreign Minister. Eban's experience in the highest and most trying diplomatic missions and his unique talents made him a perfect choice. He instilled enthusiasm in the ministry and propelled Israeli diplomacy to much higher intellectual and professional levels. He worked with Eshkol in a congenial and loyal manner and was continuously looking for ways to strengthen Israel's standing globally and for new openings to promote peace regionally.

Shortly before Eban assumed office, Arthur Lourie, with whom I worked closely for four years in the London Embassy, introduced me to him. By then Eban was already a famous personality and I vividly remember my excitement when he invited me to become his political secretary. It was a challenge which I was pleased to accept and thus started an exciting and fulfilling two and a half years in one of the most sensitive positions in the Ministry of Foreign Affairs. In his systematic review of foreign policy, region by region, Eban dwelt on our shallow relationships with the countries in Eastern Europe. These were certainly orchestrated, if not dictated, by Moscow, which followed a clear anti-Israel and pro-Arab policy. The question then addressed was in which of the capitals did we have the best chance of at least probing whether it was possible to improve our relations with that part of the world. We had embassies in all of them yet the Polish Foreign Minister, Adam Rapacki, seemed more suitable than his colleagues in the area, and the most likely to accept a visit by an Israeli Foreign Minister. Still we could not expect an official invitation from him. I, therefore suggested to Eban that our ambassador in Warsaw, Dov Satat, would notify the Polish Foreign Ministry that we were planning a conference of Israeli ambassadors in Eastern Europe to take place in Warsaw, and see their reaction. Within a few days Satat, who on a personal level had very good contacts, cabled back that there was no objection to the conference, and Rapacki had agreed to attend a lunch for the Israeli Foreign Minister at his residence.

In May 1966, Abba Eban, Gideon Rafael and myself travelled to Warsaw and met our colleagues in the region. Our first item on the programme was a visit to the death camp at Auschwitz. It was one of the saddest and most shocking days that I have experienced in my diplomatic travels. As the Polish guide showed us around the camp the gruesome reality engulfed us in a much more vivid way than we had ever imagined. A profound sense of astonishment, disbelief and utter bewilderment of what men could do to their fellow men filled our hearts and our minds. When we all gathered on the ruins of the crematorium in Birkenau and together recited the Kaddish, the mourner's prayer, we were overwhelmed by sorrow and grief. Most of us had family who had perished in the Holocaust. I remember a thought which occurred to me while I was walking among the barracks – of how proud the martyrs of Auschwitz would have been to know that twenty-two years later, the Foreign Minister of an independent and sovereign Israel and the Israeli ambassadors to the various European capitals would pray for them on the very site where they had gone to the gas chambers reciting the Ani Maamin, a reiteration of their faith in the Almighty. As we travelled in our bus back to Cracow, we sank into a pensive silence. Looking out of the window we saw the railway lines and the Polish villagers on the way; they must have known of the tragedy and the horrors that were occurring so close to their own homes.

The ambassadors' report had one common theme – constraints and restrictions on their activity. Only the ambassadors in Bucharest and Belgrade, Eliezer Doron and Avigdor Dagan, had some scope for promoting bilateral relations. The conversation with Rapacki was friendly and animosity towards the Soviet Union was audible behind many of his guarded remarks, yet he had little to offer that could improve our unsatisfactory relations with Eastern Europe. In Warsaw we visited the Jewish Historical Society and saw the ghetto diaries of Dr Ringleman as well as pictures and exhibits of what used to be one of the great Jewish centres in the world. We laid a wreath on Umschlagsplatz, the square in which the Jews of

Warsaw were amassed before they were deported to the concentration camps, and departed with the feeling that we left behind a wall-to-wall graveyard, where one-third of the Jewish people living in Europe had perished.[8] Until the Soviet empire crumbled twenty-five years later, no similar conference of Israeli ambassadors in Eastern Europe was held.

Our major diplomatic endeavour continued to focus on the United States and Western Europe. After the assassination of President Kennedy in 1963, Vice-President Lyndon Johnson assumed the presidency. He was the majority leader in the Senate during the Suez War and developed a friendly and warm attitude towards Israel. The Israeli ambassador in Washington, Avraham Harman, a dedicated and conscientious diplomat, and Minister Efraim Evron, continued the cordial relationship with him and with his close aides, ties which Abba Eban had developed during his tenure in the US. In 1964 Eshkol became the first Israeli Prime Minister to be invited officially to Washington. In his conversation with Johnson he received assurances of arms supplys and political support to block Syrian attempts to frustrate the construction of the National Water Carrier. In this context Johnson reiterated President Kennedy's commitment of 8 May 1963, that 'In the event of direct or indirect aggression we would support appropriate courses of action in the United Nations or on our own to put a stop to such aggression.'[9]

This commitment was very important because Israel viewed any attempt to interfere with its national water scheme as a *casus belli*, a reason for war. On its part, Israel gave a commitment to draw water within the limits of the Regional Unified Plan which specified the following allocation of the Jordan water: the Kingdom of Jordan, forty-seven per cent; Israel, thirty-eight per cent; Syria, twelve per cent; and Lebanon, 2 per cent. This plan was agreed in the fifties by experts from Israel, Jordan, Lebanon and Syria in their discussions with the American special envoy, Eric Johnston. However, political considerations by Syria stifled regional cooperation in a field vital to all four countries, as Johnston himself recorded: 'In October 1955, it [the Jordan Valley development plan] was rejected by Syria because it would benefit Israel as well as the Arab countries.'[10]

Syrian efforts to deny Israel the Jordan waters intensified in the sixties. Having failed to stop the work on the project, they now attempted to cut off the headwaters of the river originating in Syria. The Congress of the ruling Ba'th party decided in 1963 that Israel's work on the Jordan–Negev conduit and its diversion of the waters 'must be prevented by force'.[11] Determined to undermine the completion of Israel's National Water Carrier, it solicited the help of other Arab governments and, at the first Arab summit conference held in Cairo in January 1964, Syria raised a battle-cry calling for an immediate war on Israel. However, President Nasser was not ready for immediate war and so the Arab heads of state agreed to finance the diversion of the headwaters of the Jordan, with some to flow into the Mediterranean, utterly wasted. Prime Minister Eshkol and Foreign Minister Golda Meir reacted strongly to the Syrian threats by declaring that any attempt to divert the Jordan headwaters would be viewed as an act of aggression. However, the Syrian government did not heed these warnings and built up a concentration of heavy equipment on their diversion site. Israel attacked the site in March 1965, destroying the piled-up earth-moving equipment and putting an end to Syrian attempts to divert the Jordan tributaries – the Hazbani and the Banias.

The January 1964 Arab summit also agreed to establish a joint military command and a Palestinian army as well as a Palestinian political organization. The PLO was subsequently established at the First Arab Palestine Congress in Jerusalem and its charter, the National Covenant, was published on 28 May 1964.

Syria's belligerent attitude towards Israel was persistent; it was evident before and during the union with Egypt, under the banner of the United Arab Republic (UAR), and continued after the break-up of this fragile merger in 1961. Syria's hostility was not influenced by the frequent changes of government in Damascus and military clashes between Israel and Syria were not confined to controversy over the diversion of the Jordan waters. Syrian troops shot at Israeli farmers and at fishermen on Lake Kinneret, and planted road mines. Retaliation by Israel earned it swift condemnation at the Security Council, while Syrian violence was sanctioned by the Soviet Union and protected by its veto in the council. The statements of the Ba'th Arab Socialist Party spoke openly about the 'elimination of Israel' and of the need of the Arab armies 'to enter the struggle'. This incitement to war was supplemented by their training and dispatching Palestinian terrorist groups, either directly or via Jordan and Lebanon, to cause havoc in Israel; 1966 was consequently a year marked by continuous violence emanating from Syria. The clashes escalated and, following serious shelling of Israeli villages, the air force was called in. In the ensuing air battle, on 7 April 1966, six Syrian MiG fighter planes were shot down, two of them over Damascus, the capital of Syria.

Syria had the capacity to provoke incidents and aggravate the situation, but its leaders knew that it could not face the Israeli military response alone, and thus it intensified its efforts to draw Egypt into war with Israel. At first Nasser was hesitant, sending a military delegation to Syria, which insisted that Israel should not be allowed to prescribe the timing of war. At that point the Soviet Union, fearing that Israeli reaction to the Syrian terror and intimidation campaign might topple the Syrian government, engaged in one of their more sinister campaigns of disinformation: they reported to the Syrians that Israel was building up a remarkable concentration of troops on its northern border, they even 'knew' how many divisions were involved, eleven to thirteen, all with the aim of attacking Syria. These Soviet reports were completely false, and Israel informed the American and French ambassadors that they were utterly unfounded. Eshkol even invited the Russian ambassador to accompany him to the northern border and witness for himself the absence of any concentration of forces. However, the truth did not fit Soviet strategy – to thrive on conflict – and so the fires of war were duly fuelled. During his trial following the Six Day War, the Egyptian defence minister, Badran, admitted that the offensive deployment of Egyptian troops in the Sinai was the result of 'false Soviet reports'.[12] Soviet intelligence knew that the information they conveyed to Cairo was baseless. The Egyptian government had many opportunities to verify the facts – through the UN, their own intelligence and through third countries – yet no effort was made by Nasser to establish the real facts; for him as well the truth did not fit his aggressive designs.

8

The Six Day War

On the morning of 15 May 1967, Israel's nineteenth anniversary of independence, a few hours before the annual military parade was to commence, the Chief of Staff, General Yitzhak Rabin, informed Prime Minister Eshkol that the Egyptian army was in a high state of readiness. Some hours later came the first reports of Egyptian troops moving into the Sinai.

Like thousands of Israelis, I was watching the parade in Jerusalem totally unaware that we were only days away from a major war. As political secretary to the Foreign Minister I would have known if any major development had been anticipated. However, nothing so extraordinary as a massive offensive deployment of the Egyptian army was expected, nor were Israeli initiatives under way. Upon returning home from the parade, I received a Foreign Office courier with a top-secret cable from our Embassy in Washington reporting that the United States government had informed them of the Egyptian troop movements across the Suez Canal. I immediately called Abba Eban, giving him the news. He asked me to come straight to his residence and, after reading the cable, called the Prime Minister and informed him of the report from Washington. Eshkol replied that he had received similar information from the Chief of Staff. Both men were pondering the meaning of the troop movements. A few hours later I accompanied the Foreign Minister to Eshkol's residence for the first high-level consultation on the steps taken by Egypt. We were all puzzled by Nasser's decision to move his troops in broad daylight, ruling out the possibility of a surprise attack. He clearly felt no need for secrecy. Some capitals, and even some Israelis, initially interpreted the troop movement as posturing and therefore less threatening. However, the government could not afford to underestimate the dangers inherent in the new developments. It was obvious that Nasser was displaying his boldness, which, to a large extent, was due to the Soviet's backing of his brinkmanship and to their supply of modern arms. He was also testing Israel's resolve.

The next day, 16 May, Nasser moved on the diplomatic front by sending an official notification to the commander of the United Nations Emergency Force, asking that those UN forces which were stationed in the Sinai be removed and transferred to Sharm el-Sheikh and Gaza. It was the first serious violation of an arrangement which had existed for ten years and was part of the agreement ending the Israeli occupation of the Sinai following the Suez War. The Secretary-General of the United Nations, U Thant, decided not to allow the Egyptian President to dictate the deployment of UN forces and insisted that they stay in all their positions, or otherwise they would be totally withdrawn. With bravado, Nasser replied that in that case all the UN forces must be withdrawn and U Thant complied, cautioning the Egyptian Foreign Minister that the UNEF withdrawal 'may have grave implications for peace'.[1] The government of Israel was surprised, because it had assumed that U Thant would not act hastily, without consulting the Security Council, whose member states were aware of the November 1956 agreement between Hammarskjöld and Nasser on the stationing of the UN force. It is a matter for historians to decide whether, with a different approach by the Secretary-General the Six Day War could have been avoided. One finds it hard to believe that it would have made much difference as long as Nasser intended to escalate the tensions and assumed that Soviet support would deter Israel from reacting; it might have caused some delay, but little more. The decision to evacuate the UN Emergency Force and the continuous advances of Egyptian tanks, artillery and troops into the Sinai were a clear indication of offensive intentions. They warranted precautionary military countermeasures by Israel, accompanied by diplomatic initiatives. Lest there should be any doubts about Nasser's intentions, Radio Cairo clarified them. It declared on 16 May that 'the existence of Israel has continued too long ... the battle has come in which we shall destroy Israel'.[2]

Israeli ambassadors were instructed to convey to their host governments that the Egyptian contention that Israel planned to attack Syria was totally unfounded. A message to this effect was also conveyed to the UN, which in turn transmitted it to Damascus and Cairo. In a report to the Security Council of 19 May the Secretary-General stressed that UN observers 'have verified the absence' of Israeli troop concentrations on the northern border. Moreover, the Egyptian army checked the Soviet information on troop concentrations. On 14 May the Chief of Staff, General Fawzi, accompanied by intelligence officers, flew to Damascus for talks with their Syrian counterparts. Upon his return to Cairo he reported that neither Syrian nor Egyptian military intelligence could confirm massive Israeli troop deployments in the north.[3]

Abba Eban met the ambassadors of the three Western powers, the United States, Britain and France, and expressed Israel's misgivings on the withdrawal of UNEF, stressing that it represented a change in the status quo and recalling that according to the 1957 understandings only the United Nations General Assembly could decide on the evacuation of the

UN force. Of particular importance was Eban's meeting with the US ambassador, Walworth Barbour, on 18 May, to which he invited the chief of military intelligence, General Yariv, to assess the Egyptian troop deployment in the Sinai; three infantry divisions, six hundred tanks and a build-up of artillery – and the flow of troops was continuing. Some were stationed only twenty kilometres from the Israeli border. Eban stressed that Nasser's demand that the United Nations force be withdrawn meant that he wanted to clear the way for an attack on Israel. There was an urgent need for de-escalation, for a reduction of troops in the Sinai, for a clear signal to the Soviet Union that if Israel were compelled to act, the US would support it.

Between 19 and 22 May Eshkol informed the Western powers that if Egypt did not attack Israel 'we will not take action against Egyptian forces at Sharm el-Sheikh – until and unless they close the Straits of Tiran to free navigation by Israel'.[4] In his reply to Eshkol the British Prime Minister, Harold Wilson, reiterated the view of Her Majesty's Government that 'the Straits of Tiran constitute an international waterway which should remain open to the ships of all nations'. The Israeli government left no one in doubt that a blockade of the straits would compel Israel to take military measures in order to defend its right of free passage in the Gulf of Aqaba.

On 22 May Eshkol reported to the Knesset on the gravity of the situation, informing it that the Egyptian military deployment had gone up from 35,000 troops on 14 May to 80,000. He refuted the allegations of Israeli troop concentrations and expressed Israel's 'readiness to participate in an effort to reinforce stability and advance peace in our region'. This was a serious attempt to de-escalate the build-up to war.

During these tense days we were monitoring the situation hour by hour, studying carefully the assessments from the main capitals and supplementing the official conferences with small informal meetings in which Eban; Rabin; the chief of intelligence, General Aharon Yariv; Rabin's chief of Cabinet, Colonel Efrat and myself, exchanged views on military and diplomatic developments. One of these sessions took place on 21 May. With Nasser's rhetoric growing more volatile and Egyptian troop reinforcement in the Sinai continuing, we felt that war was hardly avoidable. The possibility that Nasser's next move might be the closure of the Straits of Tiran was thoroughly examined. Time was of the essence in any military action and Rabin asked the Foreign Minister how long the army would have before the Security Council exerted pressure to stop a military operation. Eban estimated that we would have from twenty-four to seventy-two hours.

The key of course, was Washington, but neither the United States nor any other friendly country had much to offer except to counsel restraint. It became obvious that Israel would have to confront the crisis alone. Rabin did not waste time but began preparing the army for every contingency. As Prime Minister Eshkol was also the Minister of Defence and had to run the government, deal with the unfolding political pressures and make sure that all the civilian aspects of the emergency were properly addressed, Rabin was more than just a Chief of Staff. He continuously briefed and advised the Cabinet and the Foreign Affairs and Defence Committee of the Knesset, and in many regards had to fulfil ministerial responsibilities in addition to commanding the army. With war imminent, this was a heavy and daunting task.

Less than forty-eight hours after our meeting, on 23 May, Gamal Abdal Nasser gave his reply to Eshkol's call for an effort to advance peace. In a fiery and belligerent speech to a group of officers in the Sinai, he announced that the Straits of Tiran had been closed to Israeli ships and to strategic cargoes, namely oil, carried by other ships to Israel. He warned that should Israeli ships attempt to sail through, they would be fired upon. He asserted that on 13 May Cairo had received 'definite information' of 'huge' Israeli troop concentrations on the Syrian border, and added, 'Under no circumstances can we permit the Israeli flag to pass through the Gulf of Aqaba. The Jews threaten war. We say they are welcome to war.'[5] In an atmosphere fraught with tension, both the announcement of the blockade and the rhetoric were highly provocative, indeed the speech itself was an act of aggression. Nasser was not unaware of the consequences. Israel had warned him publicly and through the United States. Messages of caution were sent to Cairo from other capitals as well, but he chose to ignore them. Apparently Syria had received the same 'definite information' from the Soviets of non-existent Israeli troop concentrations, because on the very day which Nasser mentioned, 13 May, Syria sent a message to the members of the Security Council saying that the intended aggression of the 'Zionist circles' would meet not with Syrian opposition alone – it would be opposed by all the progressive Arab states. Similar language was used in official Syrian statements.

The 'definite information' on Israeli troop concentrations mentioned by Nasser was one of the foremost triggers of the Six Day War. How it unfolded became apparent in later years in the evidence of Soviet and Egyptian officials. Georgiy Kornienko, chief of the American department in the Soviet Foreign Ministry in 1967, chronicled the false Soviet warning in *The Cold War: Testimony of a Participant*.[6] He writes: 'On May 13 the KGB representative in Cairo, in line with standing practice of an exchange of information with Egyptian intelligence, transmitted to the Egyptians a communication received by him from Moscow on the existence of information concerning an Israeli troop concentration (ten to twelve brigades) on the Syrian frontier.' Kornienko referred to the conversation that the station chief of Soviet intelligence in Cairo, Sergei, had with Salah

Nasr, director of intelligence in Egypt. He further claimed that the transfer of this information was approved by the 'leadership of Soviet intelligence' but not by the political leadership. Similar information was conveyed on the very same day by the Soviet ambassador in Cairo, Pojidaev, to the under-secretary in the Egyptian Foreign Ministry, ambassador Ahmed Hassan al-Feki and to the Speaker of Parliament, Anwar Sadat, during his visit to Moscow.[7] This Soviet game of brinkmanship, of playing with fire, is now well documented. However, its motives are still unclear. By the time Nasser declared the closure of the straits he knew that the Soviet information was false, yet it did not change his march to war.

At 5 a.m. on 23 May the telephone rang at my home. The Foreign Minister was on the line. Eban told me that he had received a call from army headquarters with the news that Nasser had closed the Straits of Tiran to Israeli shipping. Our fears had not been unfounded. The minister asked me to invite the top officials of the ministry to his residence at 6 a.m., adding that he would telephone the ambassadors of the United States, Britain and France, and convey to them the grave news. We gathered in Eban's home in the early hours of the morning. The mood was full of foreboding. After reviewing the first reports of Nasser's speech and the information received during the night from our embassies, we left for a special session of the Cabinet Defence Committee in Tel Aviv.

Nasser's defiant blockade following the evacuation of UNEF revealed that the assurances which Israel had received in 1957 from the United States and France were completely ineffective. For Abba Eban, who had negotiated these assurances in good faith with Dulles and with the French Foreign Minister Pineau and his ambassador in Washington, Hervé Alphand, it was a very painful moment. The key sentences in Dulles's *aide-mémoire* of 11 February 1957 were very much on his mind: 'The United States believes that the gulf [of Aqaba] comprehends international waters and that no nation has the right to prevent free and innocent passage in the gulf and through the straits giving access thereto.' This firm statement was repeated by US Ambassador Lodge before the General Assembly of the United Nations. We pondered what America would do now to enforce this policy. Would she, France and the United Kingdom accept that Israel had the right to apply Article 51 of the UN Charter and act in self-defence, in order to break the blockade? This was a leading assumption which Washington and Paris had accepted in 1957. Was General de Gaulle's aloofness towards the security of Israel similar to Guy Mollet's friendly attitude a decade earlier? Far from it. True, these were not iron-clad bilateral agreements, and after the war some State Department officials drew a distinction between 'statements of policy' and 'commitments', yet the more we discussed these issues, the more convinced we became of the fragility of international guarantees or assurances, and the more determined that henceforward Israel should always be able to rely on herself alone in the event of a crisis.

Israel faced three immediate problems: the terror and sabotage activities emanating from Syria and some perpetrated by the Palestinian El Fatah organization; the heavy Egyptian troop concentration in the Sinai which, at any given moment, could attack; and the blockade of the gateway to the Gulf of Aqaba, the Straits of Tiran. With these issues uppermost in our minds we joined the ministers and the Chief of Staff in the Cabinet Defence Committee meeting on 23 May 1967.

Eban brought to the meeting the latest communication from our deputy chief of mission in Washington, Efraim Evron, reporting a conversation with the under-secretary of state, Eugene Rostow, saying that President Johnson was urging Nasser to reduce the concentration of Egyptian troops and respect the principle of freedom of navigation in the Gulf of Aqaba. Johnson asked Israel not to act unilaterally for forty-eight hours. From all the messages coming from Washington it was clear that the United States wished to be consulted. When one of the ministers suggested that the Israeli Foreign Minister should travel to the United States to meet the President and impress upon him the seriousness of the situation, both Eban and Eshkol welcomed the idea. Eban wanted to test the American commitment of 1957 and find out whether it could be translated into immediate action, and also to secure US support and understanding – not concurrence – in case all efforts to prevent war failed and Israel had to act alone. Rabin did not believe that a delay of forty-eight hours would influence the outcome of the war, although he was concerned at evidence of a fourth Egyptian division entering the Sinai and at information that Syria had reinforced its troops on the Golan Heights. After lengthy deliberations the Cabinet resolved that the blockade of the straits was an act of aggression, that a decision on the Israeli reaction would be postponed for forty-eight hours and that the Prime Minister and Foreign Minister would decide on Eban's trip to meet the US President.

President Johnson reacted strongly to the blockade and issued a statement on 23 May supporting 'all efforts, in and outside the UN ... to reduce tensions and restore stability'. He warned against miscalculations, expressed dismay at the 'hurried withdrawal' of UNEF, deplored the Egyptian troop concentrations and, on the closing of the straits, said that it 'has brought a new and very grave dimension to the crisis. The United States considers the gulf to be an international waterway and feels that a blockade of Israeli shipping is illegal and potentially disastrous to the cause of peace.' The President added that on this last point the US was 'seeking clarification'. These were strong words – yet not strong enough to cause Nasser to lift the blockade or de-escalate the military build-up in the Sinai.

On 26 May, Eshkol received a letter from the Soviet Premier, Kosygin, ignoring the Soviet misinformation about Israeli troop concentrations which had sparked the crisis. He also made no mention of the build-up of the Egyptian army in the Sinai and the closure of the straits, but urged Israel to solve the conflict by 'non-military means' and laid the responsibility on 'that side which will initiate the aggression'. On 1 June Eshkol replied, recalling the terrorist activities coming from Syria and stressing that the removal of UNEF was accompanied by Egypt's declared intention to 'go to war' with Israel. The date of Kosygin's message to Eshkol coincided with mounting concern in the Kremlin that their false information had mushroomed into a serious confrontation and that war was imminent. Between 25 and 28 May an Egyptian delegation headed by the Minister of War, Shams Badran, visited Moscow secretly. The delegation included also the ambassadors Ahmed Hassan al-Feki and Salah Bassiouny. According to information now available, Badran told Kosygin of Nasser's intention to launch a pre-emptive strike and asked for Soviet support and arms. Kosygin opposed the idea, arguing that if Egypt initiated an attack it would be branded as an aggressor. He expressed his confidence that if war were to break out, Egypt would win.[8] Similar information was provided by Bassiouny. He maintained that during the Moscow talks the 'request to de-escalate' and allow oil shipments destined for Israel to pass through the straits had been a recurring theme for the Soviets. Moreover, the first deputy foreign minister, Vladimir Semeonov, invited Feki to his dacha for dinner on 26 May, trying to convince him of the need to prevent war. However, a different line was adopted by the new Soviet Defence Minister, Marshal Grechko, in his talks with Badran. Reportedly he told Badran, when he saw him off at Moscow airport, that the Russians would 'fill all Egypt's requests for arms' and that 'the Soviet Union would enter the war on Egypt's side if the United States entered the war' and that 'if something happens and you need us, just send us a signal'.[9] Bassiouny recounted that when he was writing the report on the Moscow talks, Badran asked him to change the conclusions on the basis of his conversations with Grechko.

This account illustrates the full gravity of the peril which Israel faced. Nasser, emboldened by his own military advisers, especially Field Marshal Abd al-Hakim Amr and Badran, who wanted war, was prepared to launch a pre-emptive attack. He was further encouraged to do so by the highest authority in the Soviet military, promising overall support. The Soviet government emerges as less monolithic than was assumed at the time, with Kosygin engaged in efforts to prevent war and Grechko doing the opposite. It is not clear what line Breznev took. The effect of the Badran report on his Moscow talks in Cairo is documented in 'Battle Order No.

2', from the deputy supreme commander, Field Marshal Amr, of 2 June 1967 to his troops:

> ... in view of the strong position of the government of the Soviet Union and its readiness to intervene immediately if any big power should go to war against Egypt, it is no longer to be expected under any circumstances that the United States government should join in a military adventure on Israel's side ... Israel will not be able to bear the burden of mobilization for a long time. Mobilization has already brought total paralysis of the Israeli economy ... Accordingly, I have completed my plans and issued my orders for the organization of the operation...[10]

In Jerusalem we were looking at the whole spectrum of Western policy in the crisis. British support for the principle that the Straits of Tiran was an international waterway was reiterated by Lord Caradon in the Security Council. However, most disappointing was the attitude of President de Gaulle. For Israel, which had enjoyed a fairly good relationship with France and was at that stage heavily dependent on French arms, this was to be a serious setback.[11]

After the Defence Cabinet meeting in Tel Aviv on 23 May the domestic and international timetables moved with speed and ferocity. In view of the crisis, Eshkol invited members of the opposition to join the deliberations. They were Menachem Begin of the right-wing Gahal party and Peres and Dayan of Ben-Gurion's party Rafi. This did not prevent members of these parties as well as some people from other parties undermining the Prime Minister and spreading hints that he was not up to handling the complex situation. As for Eban's trip to meet Johnson, some feared that it might restrict Israel's freedom of action, especially if the US President were to veto a military operation. Eshkol dismissed these doubts and I continued with the arrangements for the journey. During the day our ambassador in Paris, Walter Eytan, cabled that there would be a meeting of the Cabinet, after which he might be seeing President de Gaulle. Following consultations with Eshkol, the Foreign Minister suggested to Eytan that we make a stopover in Paris and that he himself would meet the President. At 3.30 a.m. Eban and I took off on a special charter flight for Paris.

My heart was heavy, knowing that the country was fully mobilized. Many of my friends were with their units, Egyptian troop reinforcements were flowing into the Sinai, Nasser's arrogance was increasing by the day, but international support for Israel in its hour of peril was less than forthcoming. There was no way in which the country could maintain such a high state of alert for a lengthy period, because the call-up of reserve units included people from all walks of life and the economy was nearly grinding to a halt. Was this a time for the Foreign Minister to travel and not be at the hub of hour-by-hour decision making I asked myself, while the jet cruised towards Paris. At the same time it was obvious to me that no effort must be spared if there was the slightest chance of avoiding war, and it was imperative to explore whether the three Western powers would act according to their assurances in 1957, break the blockade of the Gulf of Aqaba and put pressure on Nasser to withdraw his troops from the Sinai. The first test was to come soon.

We arrived in Paris in the early morning of 24 May, and were received at the airport by the ambassador, Walter Eytan, one of the most experienced diplomats in the Israeli foreign service. He confirmed the meeting with de Gaulle, briefed us on the thinking in the French government on the crisis and on its reflection in the media. After checking in at an Orly airport hotel, Eban and Eytan left for the Elysée Palace. In my hotel room I received constant updates from Jerusalem and prepared for our next stop – Washington DC. Shortly after our arrival in France I received word from our Embassy in London that Harold Wilson would like to meet the Israeli Foreign Minister if it were possible. After checking the flight schedules and consulting Eban I replied affirmatively.

Eban and Eytan returned from the meeting with the French President and we rushed to catch the flight to London without having time to sit quietly with the ambassador and analyse this historic encounter. On the plane Eban dictated to me a resumé of the conversation while Eytan cabled a detailed report to Jerusalem. The main points were clear: de Gaulle urged Israel not to wage war and at any rate not to shoot first, ignoring the fact that the blockade of the straits by Nasser was tantamount to a declaration of war and that the Egyptian troop concentrations presented an imminent threat which Israel could not ignore. He insisted that the Four Powers be left to resolve the crisis, overlooking the fact that Soviet policies and its misinformation were at the root of the crisis, and that the Russians would gladly capitalize on Nasser's aggression and would not support a solution satisfactory to Israel. For de Gaulle, it was more important to pursue his dream of a united Europe from the Atlantic to the Urals, in which the Soviet Union was to play a prominent role, than to worry about Israel's destiny. He displayed an unfounded confidence in his ability to influence Soviet policies. He did not deny that in 1957 his country had strongly and unequivocally supported the principle of freedom of navigation in the Straits of Tiran, but when Eban recalled these assurances, the general plainly said, '1967 is not 1957,' adding that there were no Western solutions in 1967 and the Soviets must be included in the attempts to resolve the conflict. Translated into the stark reality which we faced, it meant that during the Suez crisis in 1957, when France was interested in Israel's cooperation, its commitment to the principle of freedom of navigation in the Gulf of Aqaba was valid, while only ten years later, when Israel was subjected to an unlawful blockade and to a dire threat, the high principle had evaporated.

The French proposal for a four-power conference was received with little enthusiasm in Washington, and the Soviet Union, believing that Nasser was riding high, rejected it. This did not prevent the French government from issuing a statement on 2 June, conceding that each of the states in the Middle East had 'the right to live', yet declaring that 'the state that would be the first – wherever it might be – to take up arms will not have either her approval and even less her support'. One might assume that de Gaulle was not aware of Battle Order No. 3/67, issued by the Egyptian High Command on 18 May, saying that 'an offensive operation is planned for the cutting off of the southern Negev area and to conquer Eilat', and then outlining the forces which would be allocated for the operation.[12] Even if the detailed order were not known at the time, the French government certainly had enough information to assess the danger which Israel was facing. Yet it did not prevent them from imposing an arms embargo on 3 June, before the first shot was fired.

As a student of international relations and a practising diplomat, I had, up to this time, held General de Gaulle in high esteem. Listening to Eban's account of the conversation with him, I sensed his remoteness, his lack of under-standing of Israel's predicament and his ability to ignore former French assurances when it suited him. It was clear to me that in this crisis the hero of the Second World War was motivated by two considerations: crude self-interest and the game of power politics. His stature diminished in my eyes. For Israel it was a sad and disheartening lesson, which would long be remembered whenever a suggestion of international guarantees came up.

We landed in London and, after an update by Ambassador Aharon Remez and Yeshayahu Anug, drove straight to Downing Street. The Prime Minister received us in the Cabinet room with warmth and friendship, and his concern at the developments was evident. Eban delivered a comprehensive review of the situation and sharpened the choices before us: 'to surrender, to fight alone or to join with others in an international effort to force Nasser's withdrawal from his present course'.[13] Wilson expressed his belief and the consensus in the Cabinet that Nasser should not be allowed to triumph. Britain was firmly supporting freedom of navigation in the Straits of Tiran and was prepared to act in concert with other maritime states in an attempt to open the straits. He was sending the minister of state at the Foreign Office, George Thompson, to Washington to discuss the crisis with the United States.

Wilson's presentation offered support and hope. How different from the cold atmosphere we had found in Paris. It was my first visit to 10 Downing Street and my first meeting with a British Prime Minister. I was impressed by Wilson's attitude, although he offered no tangible assurances, but then we did not ask for anything specific. I came away with a feeling that Wilson understood the dangers which Israel faced and was prepared to help although he had no clear proposal for effective action.

The next day we continued our journey to the United States. Upon our arrival in Washington we received a most urgent cable from the Prime Minister detailing the reinforcement of the Egyptian military build-up in the Sinai and its offensive posture. In view of the massive deployment of troops an attack on Israel could not be ruled out and the question was, if it happened how would the United States react? Could she deter such an offensive? The cable read 'Israel faces a grave danger of general attack by Egypt and Syria. In this situation, implementation of the American commitment is vital in declaration and action immediately, repeat immediately, meaning a declaration by the US government that any attack on Israel is equivalent to an attack on the United States, etc.'[14] Eban was asked to convey the content of the message immediately to the US government. It was entirely clear to us that in Jerusalem the issue of immediate concern was the threat of troop concentrations, with the blockade of the straits coming second. The meeting with President Johnson was to take place the next day; meanwhile the Foreign Minister asked Ambassador Harman to set up an urgent meeting with the Secretary of State, Dean Rusk. This meeting took place shortly after our arrival. Rusk knew that the situation was serious but did not share the Israeli assessment of an imminent attack. He promised to convey the message to the President, adding that the Senate Foreign Relations Committee had discussed the crisis in the Middle East that morning and that the consensus was in support of Israel, provided the US did not act alone. Rusk could not give any commitment of what the US would do and remarked that Eban had raised issues which would involve constitutional decisions. He also cautioned against Israel being the first to open hostilities, saying that if that were to happen, the US would find it difficult to assist.

The discussions continued the same evening at a dinner in the State Department, with top officials taking part, including Eugene Rostow, under-secretary of state for political affairs, Lucius Battle, assistant secretary for Middle East affairs and Joseph Sisco, assistant secretary for United Nations affairs. The Pentagon, too, was represented. All aspects of the crisis were discussed. Although many years have passed since, I cannot forget the calm, matter-of-fact attitude in which the situation was analysed while we sipped our wine, when I knew well and could sense in my bones the tension, the agony and the alertness of our people back home. How on earth could we convey the true crisis to the officials gathered on the seventh floor of the State Department? Eban did brilliantly, but could words alone accomplish such a mammoth task, convey the sense of concern in Israel and the full weight of the responsibility which we felt?

Before the dinner was over, Eban returned to the secretary's office. The US administration was labouring hard for the fullest possible assessment of the situation. In the meantime the Egyptian ambassador was warned sternly that his country must not embark on any offensive. After consulting the President, Rusk was able to give Eban the first outline of possible US action; Eban informed the Israeli government that there would be an attempt to open the straits by the maritime powers. A declaration by these powers expressing their readiness to exercise freedom of navigation would be followed by a naval task force which would sail through the straits.

In Eban's conversation with the Secretary of Defence Robert McNamara and the chairman of the Joint Chiefs of Staff, General Earl Wheeler, it was evident that the US viewed an impending attack by Egypt as less alarming than we did, and they thought that in any eventuality Israel would win the war. Their estimate was that after Nasser had gained the advantage by his latest steps, he would wait for Israel to make the next move.

Contrary to our expectations we were given no time for the meeting between the President and the Foreign Minister. Our suspicions heightened when, on 26 May, Rusk called Eban to ask whether he would remain in Washington for another day. Eban replied that he would have to leave that same day. It became clear to us that the US felt that war was coming and had hoped to gain time, believing that as long as Eban was abroad war would not start and as long as it did not break out, it might still be prevented. Another reason for the delay was Johnson's desire to formulate a line which would reflect US policy, and he needed time to consult. In the meeting with his top advisers, prior to meeting Eban, Johnson expressed his belief that in view of the mood in Congress he would not be able to commit the US to the use of force. McNamara stated his disapproval of the idea of a maritime expedition to unblock the Straits of Tiran and Dean Rusk coined the famous phrase that 'Israel will only be alone if it goes alone.'[15] At Eban's request, Efraim Evron, who had excellent contacts in the White House, went to see Walt Rostow, the President's adviser on national security, to impress upon him the urgency of a meeting. Rostow explained to him that in view of the delicate situation the President wanted to insure that the public statements following a meeting with him would be fully coordinated. Assurances were given and Eban, accompanied by Harman and Evron, then met Johnson.

During Evron's meeting with Rostow, President Johnson invited Evron to his office. An extraordinary step, but as the whole situation was out of the ordinary, it was the more appreciated. It is difficult to gauge the

President's intention in this tête-à-tête. Did he wish to demonstrate his friendship to Israel, aware that he could convey little in the way of a commitment to Eban in the official meeting? Did he intend to sound out Evron on the Israeli view of the emergency? Did he want to make it clear that the US could not get involved in the crisis without congressional approval, which was unlikely because of Vietnam? The sentence from this conversation which stayed in Evron's memory was: 'I, Lyndon Johnson, have to get congressional approval if I want to act as President of the United States. Otherwise I'm just a six-foot-four Texan friend of Israel.'[16]

In his meeting with the President, Eban delivered a full overview of the critical situation. He analysed the issues: freedom of passage in the Gulf of Aqaba and the danger of imminent attack by Egypt with its large troop concentrations. (On the day the meeting took place, 26 May, Nasser spoke to the Arab Trade Unions in Cairo declaring that 'The battle will be a general one and our basic objective will be to destroy Israel.'[17]) Eban recalled the 1957 agreement with the United States, which led to Ben-Gurion's decision to withdraw from the Sinai, and stressed that Israel was determined to resist Nasser's aggression. Considering the messages received from Washington after the blockade was imposed, he wanted to find out whether Israel would have to confront Egypt alone, or whether her resistance 'might take place within the framework of an international effort'.[18] If the United States were to take the initiative there was a possibility that Nasser would back down without war.

President Johnson reiterated his firm stand on the Gulf of Aqaba being an international waterway and promised that the 'best influence' of the US would be employed to open the straits. He suggested that the first attempt to open them must be made by the United Nations. If it failed, it would be 'up to Israel and all of its friends' to break the blockade. He indicated that Britain and Canada were prepared to be helpful and spoke of an international effort – an international task force – believing that it would not take long to construct it. In the meantime Israel should not precipitate matters. Johnson then handed Eban a short *aide-mémoire* which summarized the essential policy lines of the US and included the following text:

Regarding the Straits we plan to pursue vigorously the measures which can be taken by maritime nations to assure that the Straits and the Gulf remain open to free and innocent passage of all nations. I must emphasize the necessity for Israel not to make itself responsible for the initiation of hostilities. Israel will not be alone unless it decides to do it alone. We cannot imagine that Israel will make that decision.[19]

Soon after this conversation we took a flight to New York, heading home. Ambassador Harman was travelling with us so that he could prepare a full record of the conversation with the President during the stop-over at Kennedy airport. Eban used the time to drive to Manhattan for a meeting with the US ambassador to the UN, Arthur Goldberg, who was extremely sceptical about any constructive action coming from the UN and about the feasibility of the naval task-force. He stressed the importance of congressional support for the President's course of action. Upon Eban's return Harman gave us a near verbatim report of the conversation with Johnson, as well as his views of the meeting, and Eban and I departed for Israel. Throughout the long flight I read Harman's report again and again and discussed it with Eban. I felt that emotionally Johnson sensed the huge dilemma which Israel was confronting and that he wanted very much to be helpful. The naval task-force, if it took shape, might solve the problem of the blockade, but not the threat of the Egyptian troop concentrations in the Sinai, which placed Israel in a most vulnerable situation, for the country could hardly endure a prolonged siege without being weakened economically, physically and morally. While waiting for the task-force to be assembled, Israel might be attacked at any moment and her priority was therefore to lift the siege *before* breaking the blockade. Similarly I was acutely aware of the dangers that Nasser might pose to Israel, and beyond, should he win the confrontation without a war. I was not sure that the siege and Nasser's standing as a destructive force were as central to Johnson's thinking as they were to ours. An Egyptian victory without war would surely have enhanced Soviet prestige and influence in the area, with Israel becoming its prime victim and Western interests coming second. At the same time I believed that if we could risk a delay, we should allow Johnson a little more time to test the idea of a naval task-force, so that he could convince himself that every possible avenue had been exhausted before Israel went to war. It was clear to me, as I believe it was to Eban, that with the US deeply embroiled in Vietnam, the President was not in a position to take on new commitments without congressional approval, and the mood in Congress was not favourable to new US military engagements. More and more I felt that, despite all the friendship and expressions of support, in the end Israel would have to rely on herself and make her own decisions.

We arrived at Lod airport late on the evening of Saturday 27 May, and drove straight to the Prime Minister's office in Tel Aviv where the Cabinet had already assembled and been briefed on the latest developments on the military front. The discussion was adjourned briefly to allow for a private meeting between Eban and the Prime Minister. Rabin asked me to join him in an adjacent room to hear my assessment of Johnson's position. I said that the President was friendly but was asking for some more time to prepare the international task-force. Rabin replied that this was going to be very difficult. Eshkol was waiting for Eban's return before granting the green light to the army and now the Americans were demanding additional time. As we talked, the Cabinet resumed its deliberations and Eban invited me to participate in the meeting. With us was also the director-general of the Foreign Ministry, Aryeh Levavi. The army was represented by Rabin; his deputy chief of staff General Haim Barlev; General Ezer Weizman, head of operations; and the chief of intelligence, General Aharon Yariv. It soon became clear that the army was poised to launch an attack the next morning. Eban gave a detailed report of the whirlwind trip to Paris, London and Washington. De Gaulle's pontificating was of little relevance in this hour of decision. Wilson's attitude was encouraging but did not offer any immediate relief. It was the views of President Johnson, and his disposition to take firm action, which became the focus of the Cabinet debate. Eban strongly expressed the view that we should allow some more time to see whether the US could mount the task-force. If these efforts failed at least we would have gained US understanding and support. The powerful argument against this line of thought was that with each passing day more Egyptian forces flowed into the Sinai and built up their strength.

The responsibility on the shoulders of the eighteen ministers was awesome. If we postponed action and the Egyptians attacked first, Israel would win the war but the number of casualties would be very high and the civilian population would be exposed to the danger of air raids. If we engaged immediately, we risked the loss of US support, without which our ability to translate battlefield victories into a new political reality would be greatly weakened. The views around the Cabinet table were vigorously expressed and equally divided; nine ministers supported immediate action and nine were against. Given the late hour, Eshkol decided to continue the discussion the following day.

In the twenty-four hours between 27 and 28 May Eban and I learned of the mounting pressures for war, which had intensified during our trip to the three Western capitals. In the army, the chief of intelligence, General Yariv, who was following the Egyptian troop build-up closely, was deeply concerned at any postponement of the operation. He also reflected the sense of the field commanders who faced the Egyptian build-up. Even more concerned was the head of the general staff, General Ezer Weizman. Victory, and our ability to keep the casualty figures low, depended upon the destruction of the Egyptian air force on the ground in the first hours of the war. The plan to achieve this objective had been perfected during Weizman's eight-year tenure as commander of the air force. General Motty Hod, who had replaced him as air-force chief only a year before, was working to the same plan, in which surprise was an essential factor. The second set of pressures came from politicians, some traditional opponents of the Prime Minister and others who genuinely viewed the delay as a sign of indecision and put pressure on Eshkol to relinquish the Ministry of Defence to Yigal Allon and later to Moshe Dayan, the hero of the Suez War.

Between the two Cabinet meetings, Eshkol received a message from President Johnson reinforcing what he had told Abba Eban in Washington, that Israel should not embark on a pre-emptive strike. He and the Secretary of State, Dean Rusk, stressed that the US and the UK were working on the composition of the naval task-force and that Canada and Holland might join. In the light of these renewed assurances, Eshkol led the Cabinet on 28 May in deciding to allow the US two weeks to explore that option. The vote in Cabinet was seventeen to one. It was not lack of courage which determined the outcome of the vote but rather fidelity to an iron-clad principle of the young Israeli democracy, that war was an act of last resort. At Rabin's suggestion the Prime Minister met the army General Staff and explained the postponement of the war. The generals argued robustly against the decision but Eshkol stood his ground.

In the next few days a series of new developments aggravated the situation. On 29 May Nasser addressed the Egyptian National Assembly: 'The issue today is far more serious than they say. They want to confine the issue to the Straits of Tiran, and UNEF and the right of passage. We demand the full rights of the Palestinian people ... We are not afraid of the United States and its threats, of Britain and its threats, or of the entire Western world and its partiality to Israel.'[20] King Hussein of Jordan, impressed by the euphoria which Nasser inspired and by his speech to the National Assembly widening the conflict to the Palestinian issue, decided to ally himself with the Egyptian dictator. On 30 May he arrived in Cairo and instantly signed a defence pact with Egypt, putting the royal Jordanian forces under Egyptian command. As a result Israel would now have to wage war on three fronts – Egypt, Syria and Jordan.

The reports from across the Atlantic were discouraging. The Security Council deliberation on the crisis did not produce a single ray of hope; the trip of the UN Secretary-General to Cairo on 23–24 May ended in failure. Neither the discussions which the British Foreign Secretary, George Brown, held in Moscow, attempting to convince the Kremlin leaders to work for the return of UNEF, nor the visits of two special United States' envoys to Cairo, Robert Anderson and Ambassador Charles Yost, produced any result. Reports from Washington and other capitals indicated that the naval task-force initiative was encountering difficulties. The Pentagon, heavily engaged in Vietnam with half a million troops, was not keen to develop the international 'armada'. In the Foreign Ministry, we carefully sifted the incoming information. The top leadership of the ministry was divided. The assistant director-general for North American affairs, Moshe Bitan, and Joseph Tekoa, assistant director-general in charge of UN affairs, advocated war. The director-general, Aryeh Levavi, believed that we should continue to explore the diplomatic option. I reported to Eban in great detail the trends of thought in the ministry and suggested that, in view of the latest reports from Washington, he should consider withdrawing his opposition to war. He asked me to convene a meeting with the top officials on the morning of 1 June in Tel Aviv. In preparation for the meeting I wrote him the following memo:

> As you know, I am not among those who are pressing for military action, yet the considerations which led you to recommend to the government, on 27 May, to defer the military operation were as follows:
>
> The belief that the United States has committed itself to open the straits at an early date, if necessary alone, although she would try to ensure the participation of other maritime powers. The assumption that the opening of the straits by the US would be a blow to Nasser's prestige and snatch the initiative from him, and that after the lifting of the blockade a solution would be found to the troop concentrations. To these one must add the price of war, the casualties, the danger of a larger conflagration with possible involvement of the Soviet Union.
>
> After five days we can see that American attempts to enlist the support of other maritime powers have faltered. It is now clear that Canada and Norway would not join in the task-force. In the UK too there is hesitation. Holland and Portugal are prepared to take part in the force. Two influential Americans clearly indicated to us that the commitment by President Johnson (on the task-force) is not that categorical. Rusk is due to clarify this point officially.
>
> The situation in the area is deteriorating. The defence pact between Egypt and Jordan, the possibility that Iraqi troops will enter Jordan, the belligerent pronouncements in the Arab capitals, the news from Teheran that because of Arab pressure the government decided to announce that 'it was prepared to assist Islamic interests but only through the UN', all point to a downhill trend. Even if an international task-force were to open the straits, it is difficult to discern a solution to the military build-up. Even if Nasser agreed to disperse his troop concentrations peacefully, after having seen the effect it had on Israel (full mobilization) he could always revert to this option. Nasser may continue to stir the Arab states, and endanger the moderate regimes in Jordan, Lebanon and Saudi Arabia.
>
> During the 'waiting period' the credibility of Israel's deterrent capacity has already been adversely affected. I am obviously refraining from dealing with the domestic aspects of the situation.

Clearly, under the circumstances, I saw no point in continuing with the veto on war. Other Foreign Ministry officials who had opposed military action expressed similar opinions, prominent among them the deputy director-general, Arthur Lourie. Eban made up his mind and after the meeting ended we walked over to the office of the Chief of Staff, which was in the next building. With Rabin was General Yariv, and Levavi joined us. The Foreign Minister explained that he had come to the conclusion that there was no sense in postponing the operation further. After the meeting Levavi told me in a very stern voice that I was pushing for war, while ignoring the looming Soviet threat and the fact that the Russians had a long memory. I replied that I could see no alternative. After the Six Day War ended, Aryeh Levavi, who was a very conscientious diplomat, submitted his resignation.

Eban reached his decision in the morning of 1 June. During the course of that day the political roller-coaster gathered speed and with dramatic effects. The leaders of the religious party, Mizrachi, sensing that war was inevitable, pressed for a Government of National Unity. The country was fully mobilized and soldiers waiting in their trenches and tanks were not convinced that further procrastination was necessary. The newspapers clamoured for a government capable of taking decisions. Some members in the Labour Party were influenced by the anti-Eshkol rumours coming from Ben-Gurion's party, Rafi, and believed that a broader-based Cabinet, with Dayan as Minister of Defence, would improve morale and speed up a decision on the war. By late afternoon Eshkol concluded that he must respond to these pressures and invited Dayan to become Minister of Defence. He joined the Cabinet as the representative of the Rafi Party and Joseph Sapir and Menachem Begin joined as representatives of Gahal and became ministers without specific portfolios. Nineteen years after the state was established, Begin, the leader of the opposition, took up his first ministerial post. For him it was an important landmark on the way to power ten years later. The impact of Dayan's appointment as Minister of Defence was primarily on the morale of the country and of the army. The few changes that he introduced in the military planning did not decisively alter the course of the battle. The army was well prepared and ready for war and the operational plans were meticulously worked out by the Rabin General Staff.

One additional attempt was made to gauge, as precisely as possible, the American position. The Prime Minister dispatched to the US the head of Mossad, General Meir Amit, for talks with his CIA colleagues. He visited Washington on 31 May and 1 June, and met Richard Helms, the CIA director, and also the Secretary of Defence, Robert McNamara. Accompanied by ambassador Harman, Amit returned to Jerusalem and reported their assessments in a meeting at Eshkol's residence on the evening of 3 June, at which Dayan, Eban, Minister of Labour Yigal Allon, the army commanders, former Chief of Staff Yigal Yadin, the director-general of the Prime Minister's Office, Yacov Herzog, his bureau chief, Aviad Yaffe, and myself participated. Amit's conclusions were that the United States would not act alone to break the blockade of the Straits of Tiran. A huge question mark remained on the feasibility and practicability of the international naval task-force. Israel should not expect an explicit green light from the US; however the US well understood the dangers that Israel had faced, and that Nasser should not be allowed to triumph. If Israel decided to act, the US 'would not sit *shiva*', which meant that the US would not sit in mourning. Dayan reported on the Egyptian reinforcements; in the exchanges which ensued the consensus was that war was inevitable and should no longer be delayed. Now the only out-standing question was the timing.

In various writings on the June 1967 war it was suggested that in the course of his trip Amit received a 'green light' from the US for Israel to wage war on Egypt. In a conference held at Rosslyn, Virginia, on 3–6 June 1992, the twenty-fifth anniversary of the Six Day War, Amit gave a detailed account of his meetings in Washington. He said that in his talks with Richard Helms, director of central intelligence, he had received 'not a green, not a yellow, or any other light'. He explained that his trip to the US was intended to 'compare notes' and share with the CIA the Israeli assessment of the crisis; to find out if plans were under way to open the straits. He found none. He also intended to tell the Americans that he personally was going to recommend to the government that they should act against Egypt, and 'sense' their response. In the conversation with Secretary of Defence McNamara, Amit asked him to listen and not to react, and then told him what he personally was going to recommend to Eshkol. McNamara listened and then just asked two questions: 'How long will it take?' and 'How many casualties?' Amit replied, to the first question, seven days, and to the second he said that the casualties would be less than Israel had suffered during the War of Independence, which were about six thousand.[21] This meeting achieved two very important objectives: the US could not maintain that Israel surprised it by its preventive attack on Egypt and the Israeli government was indirectly informed that there was no American 'red light' and could therefore make its own decision with greater ease. Moreover, McNamara and Helms reported their conversation with Amit to Johnson, and he added to a letter to Eshkol, prepared by the State Department on 2 June, the following significant sentence: 'We have completely and fully exchanged views with General Amit.'[22] That was a clear indication that the President was fully aware of Israel's intentions, without being told explicitly of them and without sharing in any way the responsibility for the decision to wage war on Egypt. The agonizing 'waiting period' was coming to a close.

When I left Eshkol's residence in the late evening of 3 June, and walked out into a clear, somewhat chilly Jerusalem night it was apparent to me that, with this group of the most influential Cabinet Ministers actually having decided on the war, the next steps were mere formalities. On the following day, 4 June, the government adopted the formal decision on the Six Day War, which started on 5 June 1967.

A number of important principles guided Israeli thinking during the war: rapid attainment of full command of the skies; close and undisturbed air support for the infantry and armoured units; Israel's lack of strategic depth, which meant that the war must be fought on the enemy's territory and Jordan must be kept out of the battle unless she attacked first. Several channels were used to transmit this message to King Hussein on the morning of 5 June. A direct channel – an Israeli officer met the Jordanian Colonel Daud; another was through the United States; a similar communication from Eshkol was instantly passed on through the chief of the United Nations observers, General Odd Bull of Norway. It read: 'We are engaged in defensive fighting on the Egyptian sector, and we shall not engage ourselves in any action against Jordan unless Jordan attacks us. Should Jordan attack Israel, we shall go against her with all our might.'[23] The Americans had also cautioned the king against joining the war.

The king however, put his trust in the false information he had received from Nasser and his military chief, Field Marshal Amr, who had informed him that seventy-five per cent of the Israeli air force was destroyed. In his book, *My War with Israel*, King Hussein recounts the Eshkol message and adds: 'I answered Odd Bull, "They started the battle; well, they are receiving our reply by air." ' On the Amr stories Hussein writes: 'These reports, which were fantastic to say the least, contributed largely in sowing confusion and distorting our appreciation of the situation.'[24] From the Jordanian point of view, Hussein's decision to conclude a defence pact with Egypt, allow two regiments of Egyptian commandos to be stationed in Jordan, invite Iraqi troops into the Hashemite Kingdom, ignore Eshkol's warning and initiate hostilities against Israel, proved disastrous. In June 1997, King Hussein expressed publicly his regret for this decision. In a broadcast to the Jordanian people to mark the thirtieth anniversary of the Six Day War, the king said: 'In reality, it was probably our duty to try to prevent this country from being part of that battle.'[25]

At 7.45 a.m. on the morning of 5 June, Israeli aeroplanes, flying low over the Mediterranean to evade radar detection, attacked eleven Egyptian airfields. Surprise was total, and within three hours about 304 Egyptian aircraft, as well as runways and radar installation, had been destroyed. Most of the combat planes of the Israeli air force took part in the attack and only about half a dozen were left behind to protect the skies and the population centres in the case of a Syrian or Jordanian attack. By 11 a.m. an enormous sense of relief swept the army high command and senior Cabinet Ministers. Full air superiority had been achieved and augured well for a victory in ground battle. The infantry and armoured corps could advance into the Sinai free from fear of being attacked from the air and with close support from the Israeli air force. At 11.50 a.m. Syrian planes mounted an attack on kibbutz Deganya and a few other locations, causing minimal damage. At twelve noon Jordanian planes attacked Netanya and Kfar Sirkin and shortly afterwards three Iraqi planes bombed Nahallal. In retaliation, fifty-three Syrian planes, the whole Jordanian air force, consisting of twenty-eight planes, and ten Iraqi planes, were destroyed. By sundown on 5 June, about four hundred planes had been wiped out. Israel lost twenty-nine planes, eleven pilots were killed, four were captured and five injured.[26]

Jordan did not only mount air attacks. In the course of the morning of 5 June, the Jordanian army shelled Jerusalem and captured the UN headquarters on the southern outskirts of the city. Upon hearing the shelling, my wife Hana, like most parents, rushed to our son's nursery, to take the child home and into the shelter. The nursery teacher, who left the premises a few minutes later, was struck down by a shell which landed on the road close to the building. She was one of many killed and injured in Jerusalem on that day. It was the first land assault of the war on the civilian population and it demanded an immediate response. In late afternoon Eban and I drove to Jerusalem for a special Knesset meeting at which Dayan and Begin were to be sworn in as new Cabinet Ministers. The session was delayed time and time again because of Jordanian artillery shells falling close to the Israeli Parliament. If Israel had hoped to fight a single-front war with Egypt, it now had to redeploy for a two- and possibly three-front war. Syria, after absorbing the counter-attack of the Israeli air force and watching the developments with Jordan, was careful not to heed Nasser's calls to join the ground war in full force. Unlike Jordan, the Syrians had not put their army under Egyptian command.

From the very first hours of the war the thoughts and energies of Abba Eban, Yacov Herzog, my colleagues in the Foreign Ministry and myself were devoted to winning the diplomatic battle: to ensure that we would not be compelled to stop the war by Security Council resolutions before its major objectives had been realized; to prevent Soviet intervention; to secure American and Western support for the war; above all, to ward off any notion of withdrawal without peace. Urgent messages from the Prime Minister to President Johnson, Premier Kosygin and Prime Minister Wilson were drafted and dispatched. Eshkol's letter to Johnson was of particular importance. After outlining the 'catalogue of aggression' by Egypt, which had led to the war, Eshkol wrote: 'I hope that everything will be done by the US to prevent the Soviet Union from exploiting and enlarging the conflict. The hour of danger can also be an hour of opportunity. It is possible to create conditions favourable to the promotion of peace and the strengthening of forces of freedom in the area.'[27]

To prevent pressures for an immediate cease-fire, the government did not make detailed announcements of the impressive victories of the day. Eban, in consultation with the Prime Minister, decided to travel to New York to fend off attempts by the Security Council to impose a premature cease-fire and to prevent any calls for withdrawal without peace negotiations. After the Knesset session we went to see our families in the shelters, and left for Tel Aviv, travelling via side roads as the main highway was being shelled. It was a strange feeling to approach Tel Aviv, normally a city full of light, under a blanket of total darkness because of the tight blackout. At about 1 a.m. the Defence Committee of the Cabinet convened at Eshkol's Tel Aviv office to summarize the events of the day and set priorities for the future course of the war. I accompanied Eban to this memorable meeting and although it started very late the debate was lively. At that meeting it was decided to liberate Jerusalem and, in view of the Jordanian attacks, to capture the whole of the West Bank of the Jordan river. This was in addition to the targets on the Egyptian front: the destruction of the Egyptian armoured forces and the capture of Sharm el-Sheikh to open the straits to free shipping.

After the meeting we left for the airport and departed for Athens in a small chartered Arkia plane, en route for New York. We assumed that from Athens we would be able to catch the earliest scheduled flight to the US. At Athens we learned that the quickest route would be to fly to Amsterdam and board a KLM flight to New York, which we then did. About three hours before reaching Kennedy airport the pilot brought us a message from Gideon Rafael, the head of the UN Mission, that Eban would have no time to stop at the hotel but would have to drive from the airport directly to the Security Council, which was convening urgently. Eban, who for the past thirty-six hours had not even sat on a bed, let alone slept, asked whether I had the papers with me. I gave him a handful of telegrams and he set out to write his 7 June speech, a resounding defence of the war, which became a classic, and of which President Johnson said that it was 'worth several divisions' in the way it rallied public opinion in support of our cause.

The Security Council was bustling with diplomatic manoeuvring. At first Nasser did not have a clear picture of the extent of the defeat of his troops in the Sinai, and therefore Egypt and the Soviet Union delayed Security Council action. Later the Soviet ambassador, Nikolai Fedorenko, insisted on the inclusion of a strong condemnation of Israel in the resolution calling for a cease-fire. He encountered steadfast opposition to any condemnation of Israel or reference to withdrawal from the chief American delegate, Arthur Goldberg, who was supported by the Danish ambassador, Hans Tabor. Goldberg, an able and outspoken labour lawyer, was not impressed by Russian bullying and always made sure that President Johnson fully backed his policy line at the UN. Of the three Security Council resolutions on 6, 7 and 9 June, calling for a cease-fire on the Egyptian, Jordanian and Syrian fronts, not one of them called for withdrawal to the pre-war lines. How different from the combined American–Soviet pressures Israel had faced in 1956 and 1957.

While our minds concentrated on the diplomatic struggle in the Security Council, our hearts were with the troops fighting at home. Every tiny interval was used to receive updates from Jerusalem on the battles in the Sinai and on the West Bank. The third day of the war, 7 June was particularly significant. We were elated with the news that Jerusalem had been liberated and that, after a nineteen-year interval, Jews would again have access to the Wailing Wall, the long-cherished symbol of ancient Jewish sovereignty. On the same day the occupation of the entire West Bank was completed and Jordan accepted the cease-fire. Israel had never intended to wage war against Jordan, yet, when we were compelled to do so, the Israeli Defence Forces fought with great courage and sacrifice. In Jerusalem some of the Jordanian troops fought gallantly and inflicted heavy casualties on our paratroopers, who were under the command of General Mota Gur. Although the Jordanian war theatre was smaller than the Egyptian, the number of casualties we suffered on it was larger; 235 soldiers killed on the Jordanian front and 225 on the Egyptian. For Jordan the loss of the West Bank was definitive. Before the war there was a possibility that the West Bank would eventually become part of the Hashemite Kingdom. This was no longer possible. Instead Palestinian nationalism developed into a real force.

The reports on the battles in the Sinai were favourable beyond expectation. By 8 June the Egyptian divisions had been heavily defeated and Sharm el-Sheikh was found by the IDF paratroopers to have been abandoned. On that day Israeli troops approached the Suez Canal and completed their takeover of the Sinai peninsula. The Egyptian army lost thousands of soldiers, 590 tanks, hundreds of artillery pieces and other equipment. Tens of thousands of Egyptian soldiers made their way home. Over five thousand prisoners of war were taken by the IDF. President Nasser had belatedly realized the full extent of the defeat and eventually, on 8 June, agreed to a cease-fire. Both Israeli objectives vis-à-vis Egypt were achieved: the troop concentrations in the Sinai were smashed and the Straits of Tiran were opened for free shipping. Nasser cabled the Syrian President Atassi: 'We lost the battle; may God be with us in the future.'[28] Radio Cairo announced the resignation of Nasser and the commanders of the army, navy and air force; but within twenty-four hours Nasser cancelled his resignation, following demonstrations of sympathy and support.

With the war coming to a halt on the Egyptian and Jordanian fronts, the attention of the Israeli government turned to Syria. It was the continuous tensions and bloody confrontations with Syria which had led to Nasser's belligerency and caused the war. Moreover, Damascus had joined Egypt on the first day of the battle and its air force attacked Israeli targets. She also attempted some land assaults, which fortunately were swiftly repulsed. Could Syria be permitted to come out of the war practically unscathed? Should the settlements and towns in the Galilee continue to be exposed to the dangers of Syrian artillery shelling? These were the difficult questions that General David Elazar (Dadu), the commander of the northern front, and the representatives of the settlements were asking the government, as they pressed for action against Syria. Eshkol and Rabin, as well as the majority of the Cabinet, supported an operation and the Chief of Staff even ordered the Northern Command to engage in the planning and preparation for it. However, Dayan strongly opposed any decision to dislodge the Syrian troops from the Golan Heights. While recognizing the dangers of inaction, he argued that the army was already fighting on two fronts and should not open a third. He also felt that the Soviet commitment to Syria was very strong and he was apprehensive of direct Soviet involvement. The risk that the number of soldiers killed in action would increase also weighed heavily on his mind. However, in the early morning hours of 9 June Dayan suddenly changed his mind. Relying on a Cabinet decision that authorized the Prime Minister and Minister of Defence to decide whether to mount an operation against Syria, he notified Eshkol of his decision to order an offensive. Bypassing Rabin, he ordered General Elazar to attack the Golan Heights. The trigger to Dayan's sudden change of mind was a secret cable from Nasser to the Syrian President, Atassi, which Israeli intelligence intercepted on the night of 8 June. In it Nasser advised Atassi that the battle was lost. He therefore suggested that the Syrian President ask the UN for an immediate cease-fire in order to preserve the Syrian army. On reading the cable, the Israeli Defence Minister told his military aide that Israel should attack the Golan Heights.[29] In later years Dayan said that he regretted this decision, explaining that he knew that settlements would be built on the Heights and that they would be an obstacle to peacemaking.[30]

Eban and I returned from the Security Council debates in New York on 9 June. As the Syrian army was well entrenched on the hills and enjoyed a topographical advantage, the fighting on 9 and 10 June was, at times, tough. Nevertheless, within thirty hours the IDF reached the main town on the Heights, Kuneitra, and the whole of the Golan was then in our hands. Political pressures for a cease-fire with Syria were mounting by the hour. The Soviet Union mistakenly believed that Israel intended to march on Damascus, although there was not the slightest intention to do so. Nevertheless Moscow sent threatening messages to Washington. The 'hot line', a direct telephone emergency link between the White House and the Kremlin, was used by the Russians for the first time during the Six Day War. On 10 June, they kept it busy. Raymond Garthof of the State Department recounted the content and flavour of the Soviet threats: in a message which arrived at 9.48 a.m. Moscow warned 'that an attack on Damascus would create great danger and that the Soviet Union could not remain indifferent in that situation'. He further told of a conversation he had with a Soviet Embassy contact in Washington, a KGB man, who conveyed to him that 'this was a new war from Moscow's standpoint; that it now involved questions of the continuation of the Syrian government ... that they had changed their instructions to the Soviet military advisers with the Syrian forces, who previously had been told not to engage in any combat operations or put themselves in positions where they might be captured. They were now told that they could assist in the military defence of Damascus to the extent they were able.'[31] Not only was Israel in a fierce military confrontation with the Arab countries, but the Soviet Union was prepared to involve its military officers advising Syria in direct operations against the Jewish state in support of the Arabs.

In the afternoon of 10 June a Soviet Foreign Ministry official handed a stern note to the Israeli ambassador in Moscow announcing the severance of diplomatic relations with Israel. A similar message was delivered by the Soviet Ambassador in Israel, Mr Chuvakhin, to Eban. All East European countries, except for Romania, followed suit and cut off their ties with Israel. At 18.30 on 10 June the cease-fire with Syria became effective and the Six Day War, which started at 7.45 on 5 June, came to an end. Israel had lost 679 soldiers and 2,563 were injured. The Middle East landscape had changed dramatically and the Arab–Israeli conflict had assumed a new dimension.

This was a war that only four weeks before, on 10 May, no one in Israel had imagined or anticipated. There had always been tensions, terror and, at times, even military clashes, especially with Syria, but no one envisaged a full-scale military confrontation. One of the important lessons of the war was that in a volatile Middle East, unpredictability was ever present. Another was the ineffectiveness and unreliability of the UN machinery. The combination of a Secretary-General acting unwisely and the Soviet readiness to exercise a veto on behalf of the Arabs made any recourse to the UN hopeless. Israel's solitude during the three weeks of the 'waiting period' will remain engraved in its national memory as a painful experience in which it received plenty of advice to exercise restraint and no help in lifting the perils it faced. The General Staff concluded from this war that in the future, Israel must be prepared to fight on more than one front simultaneously. Israel repulsed Egyptian aggression by initiating an air and land battle, but Jordan and Syria joined the fighting on their own initiative. Also, when a ruthless Arab dictator decided to tighten the noose around Israel, the country had stood alone to confront the aggression. Therefore Israel's deterrent capacity must be strong and effective at all times, in war and in peace.

9

The Consequences of the Six Day War

The successful outcome of the Six Day War inaugurated a new era in the history of Israel. It both opened opportunities for peace and ushered in unfamiliar dilemmas. The immediate dangers facing Israel had been alleviated; its temporary borders extended from the Suez Canal in Egypt to Kuneitra, only forty kilometres away from Damascus. The border with Jordan was set on the western bank of the Jordan river. The concept of 'strategic depth' became meaningful. Israel could now be more relaxed about the danger of surprise attack and did not necessarily have to construct its defence doctrine on preventive strikes. It had enough depth to absorb a first strike.[1] It sharpened awareness in all Arab capitals and established in some the conclusion that Israel could not be defeated by war. The most Arab leaders could hope for now was to initiate hostilities, after which the big powers would quickly intervene and bring them political gains which they could not achieve as a result of war. In their frustration, Egypt, Syria and Iraq, the so-called 'front-line states', severed their diplomatic relations with the United States. A civilian population of about a million Palestinians was now under Israeli occupation. Arab pride was seriously wounded by the outcome of the war, as was Soviet prestige. Therefore revenge and further combat could be expected.

The debate on the necessity of the three-week waiting period before the war continued. Some suggested that had the war started in May, Eshkol would not have been forced to include Dayan and Begin in the Cabinet and the whole political map would have looked different. The most convincing answer to that question was given by the Chief of Staff. Speaking to high-ranking officers about a month after the war, Rabin asserted that the fact that the reserve troops were called to duty three weeks before the outbreak of the war, and used the time to train, 'greatly improved' the level of their fighting and brought them up to the standard of the regular army. From this point of view, Rabin said, the waiting period was very valuable. From the political standpoint it enhanced our ability to protect the achievements of the war. As Israel had allowed the United States time to try and prevent the war, which the US had been unable to accomplish, she could now oppose Security Council resolutions which tied the cease-fire to withdrawal and which were predicated upon a return to the fragile situation which had existed before 5 June. Rabin also stressed that the Israeli people fought differently when they felt that everything had been done to prevent war.[2]

The domestic impact of the war was far reaching and has influenced Israeli politics and thinking for the subsequent thirty years. Moreover, the results of the Six Day War continue to have a dominant effect on the peace negotiations and the shaping of Israel's coexistence with the Palestinians. As far back as 1931, Jabotinksy[3] and his followers had submitted a resolution to the seventeenth Zionist Congress stipulating that there should be a Jewish state on both sides of the Jordan River. The resolution was heavily defeated by the Zionist leadership, whose aim was to achieve the possible and not engage in setting unattainable goals for the movement.[4] A similar debate took place before the partition plan for Palestine was accepted, and this time again the pragmatic Zionists supporting partition, who were led by Ben-Gurion and Weizmann, won an overwhelming majority and the State of Israel was proclaimed. After Jordan joined Egypt in the Six Day War, Israel extended its control over the whole of the West Bank. This new situation revived the revisionists' drive, led by Menachem Begin's Herut party, for Greater Israel (Eretz Israel Hashlema). Many sites on the West Bank have profound biblical connotations, for instance Hebron or the tomb of the Patriarchs. Religious Jews therefore supported the nationalistic tendency of secular parties to hold on to all of the territories on the West Bank. Many of them settled in these areas and together with non-religious sympathizers form the core of the settlement population. Nevertheless Israeli governments, including those headed by Begin, Yitzhak Shamir and Netanyahu, refrained from annexing the West Bank in order not to block peace efforts. They recognized that the issue was not just the land, but the Palestinian people who live on the land and whose numbers have doubled in the past three decades. They must be part of any agreed solution. Consequently, the consensus on peace and security which existed between 1948 and 1967 was shaken and Israeli society became sharply divided. Concepts like strategic borders, defensible borders, strategic depth and the land of our ancestors became the subject of a passionate domestic debate.

Although it was easy to be carried away by euphoria in view of the crushing victory of the Israeli Defence Forces and the lifting of such a serious danger, this was not the mood of the first high-level inter-departmental brain-storming session after the war. The group was convened by Abba Eban two days after the cease-fire, on 12 June. In addition to the top leadership of the Foreign Office, which included the ambassadors Michael Comay, Mordechai Gazit and Shlomo Hillel, other participants were the director-general of the Prime Minister's Office, Dr Yacov Herzog, the chief of army intelligence, General Aharon Yariv, and the head of the Mossad, General Amit. Eban opened the meeting by asserting that Jerusalem would remain a united city and said that the two aspects which must be addressed were the holy places and the Arab population in East Jerusalem. On the West Bank we should consider two possible options: return of the territory to Jordanian control or the establishment of a Palestinian entity. What incentives could be offered to Jordan to bring it to the peace table, he asked, encouraging the participants to come up with options which could be suggested to the Cabinet. Amit stressed the importance of direct negotiations, called for public reiteration of the fact that we had not waged war in order to annex territory and suggested the formation of a working group that would consider the possibility of establishing a Palestinian state. Herzog warned that if we annexed territories we would alter the demography and the uniqueness of the Jewish state, but a return to the *status quo ante* was not possible because it would bring back the vulnerability which had existed before the war. He foresaw that the decisions we would have to make would cause deep rifts in the country. Yariv suggested that we convince Washington that Israel would need some time to formulate proposals for a settlement. The working assumption of all of us, in those early days, was that we would have partners to negotiate with. Unfortunately this was not a realistic expectation.

Having participated in many high-level meetings before and during the Six Day War, I am utterly convinced that the Cabinet Ministers, whether from secular or religious parties, who decided on the war, and also the Army General Staff, were not motivated by any desire to conquer land or dominate the Palestinian population. At every stage this war was forced upon us and its objectives were to lift the danger which emanated from Nasser's Egypt and to guarantee free passage to Eilat. The decisions of King Hussein and of the Syrian government to wage war against Israel led to the conquest of Jerusalem, the West Bank and the Golan Heights. This view is entirely borne out by an analysis of the war by Dayan only three days after it ended. Speaking before the Foreign Affairs and Defence Committee of the Knesset on 13 June, Dayan said: 'I heard and read that this was a pre-planned battle. The opposite is true. Of all the wars of Israel this was the least pre-planned. In the Sinai war we set the objectives and then followed them. This time we did not intend to conquer the West Bank, or Jerusalem, nor to wage war on Syria.'[5]

No sooner was the war over than the Eshkol Cabinet immersed itself in a heated discussion on how to promote peace and what Israel would be prepared to give up for the sake of it. The debate took place on 18–19 June, and the first issue was Jerusalem. Immediately after the city was liberated the Prime Minister met the heads of the Christian and Muslim communities and reassured them of free and full access to their holy places, and of the continuation of their activities.[6] In the Cabinet, Dayan stressed the importance of the continuation of Muslim prayer in the Omar Mosque, with free access to every Arab whether Israeli, from Gaza or from the West Bank. This line was approved by the ministers. Then the discussion examined each front.

On Egypt, it decided that in return for a peace treaty, Israel would be prepared to withdraw to the international border, subject to security considerations. The peace agreement should include freedom of passage through the Straits of Tiran and in the Gulf of Aqaba; freedom of passage through the Suez Canal; freedom to overfly the Straits of Tiran and the Gulf of Aqaba; demilitarization of the Sinai.

To Syria, Israel suggested the conclusion of a peace treaty on the basis of the international border and Israel's security requirements. The peace treaty would include demilitarization of the Golan Heights and assurances of non-interference with the flow of water from the headwaters of the Jordan River. Pending the conclusion of the peace treaty Israel would hold on to the Golan.

The Cabinet decided to postpone the discussion on questions related to Jordan.[7] On 19 June Eban conveyed this decision to the American Secretary of State, Dean Rusk, and Arthur Goldberg. The US transmitted its content to Egypt and Syria. It could have become the basis for negotiations of peace treaties between Israel and the Arab countries, but unfortunately they forfeited an important opportunity to break the circle of violence. The immediate Soviet re-supply of arms lost in the war, and their political support and military advice, gave Egypt and Syria the confidence to continue their belligerency.

With the unification of Jerusalem, the government and the Knesset, reflecting the views of the majority of Israelis, were determined that the city would not be divided again. On 27 June, Parliament gave official and formal expression to this policy in applying Israeli sovereignty over East Jerusalem.

Post-1967 Jordan was markedly different from the Hashemite Kingdom before the Six Day War. East Jerusalem and the West Bank, which Jordan had governed hitherto, would remain outside its control, as did the Palestinians living on the West Bank. A convergence of strategic interests characterized relations between Israel and King Hussein of Jordan for many years and made them unique. Israel had blocked Nasser's designs to control Jordan. It made it clear than an independent Jordan under King Hussein was a basic tenet of its policy. It appreciated that Jordan had made many efforts to control border incursions into Israel. It benefited from the commitment that Jordan had given the United States in 1965 that no tanks would be allowed to cross the Jordan River into the West Bank. (This commitment was broken when tanks raced into the West Bank in June 1967.) In later years, when Syrian troops moved towards the border with

Jordan and threatened its independence, Israel acted with determination, mobilized IDF units and was ready to intervene if it became necessary. With American mediation the two neighbouring countries reached an agreement on the distribution of water. Israel understood the constraints on the king – that he had to take into account the large Palestinian population living in Jordan. King Hussein in turn knew that without a meaningful, direct, high-level dialogue with the Israeli government, his strategic interests might be jeopardized. The first meeting between the king and a special envoy of Prime Minister Eshkol, Yacov Herzog, took place in London in September 1963 and, with brief interruptions, discussions continued for thirty-one years, until a peace treaty between Israel and Jordan was signed in 1994. Looking back over this long and, at times, troublesome period it is hard to overstate the importance to both countries of these private and secret talks with the king. They saved many lives and prevented numerous misunderstandings. In 1963, King Hussein explained his thinking to Dr Herzog: 'As it will take a long time to achieve a permanent settlement, it is our historic duty to develop, in a discreet manner, areas of cooperation that will aim at the permanent settlement.'[8] This unique relationship led Israeli leaders and military chiefs to believe that Jordan would stay out of the war. They underestimated the inter-Arab and domestic pressures to which the king succumbed. These emanated chiefly from Nasser and from his own military chiefs, who were apprehensive of unrest in the army should the kingdom not join the 'all-Arab effort'. The result of this decision was a crushing defeat of the Jordanian army and air force. About four weeks after Jordan decided to fight Israel, the direct dialogue resumed. In a meeting with Yacov Herzog in London on 2 July 1967, King Hussein explained his reasons for joining the war and expressed his regret.[9]

The Six Day War had its refugees, tens of thousands of Palestinians who crossed into Jordan, some from the refugee camps in the Jordan valley, others who wanted to join their families living there. They were allowed to return if they wished until August 1967. About fourteen thousand came back but the majority stayed away. The administration of hundreds of thousands of Palestinians living in the Gaza area and on the West Bank became one of the most urgent postwar tasks. As the status of these areas was undecided pending peace agreements, they remained under military government. Neither territory was an integral part of an Arab country before 1967. Since 1948 Gaza had been administered by Egypt and the West Bank was annexed by Jordan but only Great Britain and Pakistan recognized the annexation. This did not detract from the need to find immediate solutions to the many problems which had arisen. Dayon, who as Minister of Defence, was directly responsible for the fortunes of the Palestinians, set a liberal policy for their administration, which included free movement of people and goods between Israel and the territories; open bridges to Jordan; and the possibility of taking full advantage of the Israeli labour market wherever jobs were available. The first weeks after the war witnessed an intense traffic of Israelis visiting the West Bank and Palestinians visiting Israel. Many of them were surprised to find that there was no hate for Arabs among the Jews. They soon discovered that Israel is very different from the image they had formed from the anti-Israel propaganda. These visits were also their first encounter with a vibrant democracy, which many Palestinians wished to follow when their own administration evolved. However, the tranquillity was punctured before long by strikes, unrest and terror. The Palestinians refused to live under occupation, but at that important juncture in history when Dayan, Eshkol and other ministers would have, probably, gone a long way in order to work out an acceptable accommodation, they lacked the courage and leadership to start serious negotiations.

The role of the Soviet Union was disastrous before the Six Day War, horrendous during it and pathetic in the aftermath. From evidence that surfaced after the Soviet empire crumbled, it was clear that the Russians had conveyed to Egypt false intelligence about Israeli troop concentrations on the Syrian border. Their motivation had not been established. Did they wish to provoke a war? Did they fail to foresee Nasser's reaction of ordering a massive troop concentration in the Sinai? Was this manoeuvre part of a general Soviet trend to create instability? So far there are no unequivocal answers to those questions. During the war Premier Kosygin used the hot line to send threatening messages until the last phases of the war with Syria. He explicitly talked of the Soviet armed forces using appropriate means to end the 'Zionist adventure'. President Johnson, aware that Israel had already won the war with Egypt and Jordan and pleased that it had fought alone and successfully, ordered units of the Sixth Fleet to proceed towards the eastern Mediterranean.[10] The message was properly understood by Moscow.

Three days after the Six Day War ended, on 13 June, the Soviet Union took the lead in the United Nations. Fedorenko submitted to the Security Council a draft resolution condemning Israel and insisting on unconditional withdrawal to the 1949 armistice lines. The draft resolution was not passed. Frustrated by determined American opposition to their tactics, the Soviets decided to convene an emergency session of the General Assembly, where they enjoined the support of the Communist and non-aligned block of countries. To stress the importance of the initiative, their delegation was led by Premier Kosygin, who was followed by Prime Ministers of other Communist countries. The date was set for 19 June.

President Johnson was resolved to resist Soviet pressure to impose withdrawal without peace upon Israel. However, he also wished to avoid arguing with the Soviet Premier on the rostrum of the General Assembly. He therefore refrained from participating in the UN debate, but on the morning of the emergency meeting of the Assembly, he outlined the US position in an address to the National Foreign Policy Conference of Educators in Washington. Johnson's statement became the cornerstone of American policy in the Arab–Israeli conflict and included the following points:

> ... every nation in the area has a fundamental right to live and ... must accept the right of others to live.
>
> There must be justice for the refugees.
>
> Maritime rights must be respected. The right of innocent maritime passage must be preserved for all nations.
>
> That was 'a moment of choice' to limit the arms race.
>
> The nations of the region need recognized boundaries and other arrangements that will give them security against terror, destruction and war ... to move from 'uncertain armistice to durable peace'.

Johnson further suggested how these complicated objectives could be achieved by direct negotiation; 'the parties to the conflict must be the parties to the peace'.[11] This was a clear directive and a positive departure from the known US policy of strict adherence to the armistice lines. The President recognized the intrinsic fragility of the armistice regime, and pointed to the alternative: progress towards Arab recognition of Israel and to negotiations on peace. This policy did not only serve the Israeli interest; it was shaped in the belief that the Six Day War opened new opportunities which should not be missed and that it was contrary to the American interest to allow the Kremlin to bully a close ally, who had paid heavily in blood and material for this victory. To concede to Russian pressure and let them enhance their position in the Arab world at Israel's expense would certainly not have served the Western interest in the Middle East. Above all, it was in the interest of peace to break away from the circle of violence and promote negotiations. The origins of this change in the President's attitude could be traced to the Eshkol–Eban approach as expressed in the Prime Minister's letter to Johnson of 5 June 1967. Eshkol had asked for United States deterrence of Soviet involvement in the war and the President had acted with determination when this danger had arisen. Eshkol had also written of the 'hour of opportunity' which the war might create, and Johnson indeed grasped the chance. The new policy was born in the White House.

This was in sharp contrast to what Kosygin had to say when he addressed the General Assembly on the same day. He demanded condemnation of Israel, unconditional withdrawal of Israeli forces and compensation to be paid by Israel for damage in the war. Abba Eban, who arrived back in New York for this confrontation, gave Kosygin a forceful response, highlighting the Soviet role in the arms race, in encouraging the Arab countries to go to war, in paralysing the Security Council with their veto. Yet to the Arabs he again stretched out a hand of peace; 'The Arab States ... have come face-to-face with us in conflict. Let them now come face-to-face with us in peace,' he said. However, the speeches only set the stage for a fierce, nerve-racking diplomatic battle on the content of the resolutions which was to rage for weeks. Eban was assisted by Gideon Rafael, our chief delegate to the UN, and by his dedicated bureau chief, Emanuel Shimoni. This time it was not possible to fool the world, and the Soviet and Arab attempts to achieve a required two-thirds majority for resolutions reflecting their standpoint foundered. In the third week of July the emergency General Assembly adjourned and returned the issue to the Security Council. Deliberations resumed at the regular annual meeting of the UN in September.

The Soviet Union did not confine its activity to the UN. It moved swiftly to replenish the Egyptian and Syrian arsenals with modern aeroplanes, tanks and artillery. Russian advisers in their hundreds arrived in both countries to teach the armies how to make better use of their equipment in the future. The Soviet Chief of Staff, Marshal Zacharov, led a delegation of ninety-one officers, who arrived in Egypt in June and stayed for two months, studying the war and plotting for the next encounters. Within a short period the Russians instilled a new self-confidence in Nasser and in the Syrian President, Atassi, and his Minister of Defence, Assad, and removed any incentive for peace negotiations. When Arab leaders convened at the Khartoum summit, between 29 August and 1 September 1967, Nasser provided the lead, and the resolutions adopted reflected his thinking. In essence they stipulated: *No peace with Israel, no recognition of Israel, and no negotiation with Israel.* This was the most authoritative Arab reply yet to the statement of the Israeli government of 19 June, expressing its readiness to withdraw to the international border with Egypt and Syria in return for peace treaties. Many Israelis who had hoped that the Six Day War presented the region with a new opportunity to solve the Arab–Israeli conflict were deeply disappointed by this absolutely negative attitude.

Even after the three Khartoum noes, Dayan wanted to probe whether there was any opening for negotiations, using a private and informal channel to Nasser. He invited a well-known Palestinian writer, Fadwa Tukan, to see him. On 12 October 1967 she came to his home together with the mayor of Nablus, Hamdi Kenaan, and her uncle Dr Kadri Tukan. Dayan told his visitors about a conversation with Ben-Gurion in which the veteran leader had said to him that if the question 'peace or territories' were put to him, he would have preferred peace, except for Jerusalem, whose uniqueness Ben-Gurion fully appreciated. Dayan asked Dr Tukan to see Nasser and find out whether he was ready to make peace. Tukan's response was cool, but his niece picked up the idea. Fadwa Tukan met Nasser and in December reported back to Dayan. Nasser told her that Dean Rusk had suggested to him that he should settle with Israel on the basis of complete withdrawal from Sinai, but he had refused. The reason he gave was that the proposal did not include withdrawal from the West Bank.[12] This was not the case. Israel was prepared to talk to the Palestinians about autonomy and to King Hussein about the West Bank in the framework of a peace treaty and of territorial adjustments. However, the Palestinians in the territories felt compelled to follow the rejectionist attitude of the PLO and the king felt that he could not engage in a separate peace.

One thing the Soviet Union could not do was to restore Nasser's image in the Arab world. He was now seen as a loser. Irrevocably destroyed was his pan-Arabism, a dream which had appealed to many Arabs before the war. The moderate regimes in the Arab world now felt less threatened and their influence was in the ascendant. Yet the expectation, prevailing in many capitals, that Nasser would be ousted was not fulfilled. His policies continued to claim many victims, Israeli and Egyptian, and were devoid of vision or hope for the future.

As the General Assembly of the United Nations in September 1967 approached, unrest in the West Bank cities grew. A general strike was declared in Nablus, demonstrations took place in Ramalla and Gaza became a focus of terrorist activity. The Israeli euphoria in the wake of the victory and the shock of the Palestinians in defeat gave way to a new sense of realism. On the Palestinian side there was opposition to the occupation, accompanied by a readiness to cooperate on matters concerning day-to-day life. In Israel, a feeling arose that if after all that had happened the Arabs were not prepared to come to the negotiating table, then there was no alternative but to wait. Hence Dayan's cliché that we were waiting for 'the telephone call' from the Arabs. The first call came in October 1967, in the form of an Egyptian missile attack on the Israeli destroyer *Eilat*, which was outside Israeli's territorial waters. The destroyer was sunk and forty-seven sailors lost their lives. Israel retaliated by destroying oil refineries near the town of Suez. The civilian population along the bank of the Suez Canal fled inland and the canal zone became a focus of acute confrontation. The Security Council viewed the developments with increasing concern and accelerated the negotiations on an acceptable UN resolution.

From the third week of September I had been with Eban in New York, to attend the UN General Assembly and the continuation of the Security Council deliberations on the Middle East. In meetings with the heads of delegations, Eban found that more countries had become convinced that

Israel should not go back to the fragility of the armistice lines but should secure the boundaries established in peace agreements. The UK representative, Lord Caradon, also suggested the appointment of a special UN representative for the Middle East, who would assist the governments in their peace negotiations. Canada and Denmark supported the broad lines of this new approach. However, the Soviet Union, India, representing the non-aligned countries, and some South American delegations backed the Arab line demanding total Israeli withdrawal. The United States delegation started the complicated process of drafting a resolution which would be acceptable both to Israel and to the Arabs. The basic philosophy behind it was reiterated by Goldberg on 15 November. Speaking in the Security Council he said: 'To seek withdrawal without secure and recognized boundaries, for example, would be just as fruitless as to seek secure and recognized boundaries without withdrawal.' This is the essence of the 'land for peace' approach which became the cornerstone of UN Resolution 242.

The American draft encountered opposition and there was a need for wording that would balance the conflicting demands of Israel and the Arab countries. If it was impossible to write a resolution that would be acceptable to both parties, at least an attempt had to be made to compose a text that the parties could live with, and not reject instantaneously. Lord Caradon, a skilled and experienced diplomat, drafted what became Resolution 242. He struck a balance between the 'inadmissibility of the acquisition of territory by war' and 'the need to work for a just and lasting peace in which every state in the area can live in security'. The territorial aspect was particularly sensitive because there was no way in which Israel could acquiesce to any notion of withdrawal to the 1967 lines. Therefore he wrote that the just and lasting peace 'should include ... withdrawal of Israeli armed forces from territories [not from *all* territories or from *the* territories as some delegates demanded] occupied in the recent conflict'. The resolution also included 'acknowledgement of the sovereignty, territorial integrity and political independence of every state in the area', and the designation of a special representative of the Secretary General 'to promote agreement and assist efforts to achieve a peaceful and accepted settlement'. Gunar Jarring of Sweden was appointed as the special envoy for the Middle East.

In the drafting process, Caradon was in close touch with Gideon Rafael and with Eban, as he was with the US delegation and with other missions. When the final draft was ready, Eban felt that the Israeli government could live with the resolution, although there might be opposition from Begin and perhaps other ministers. To make sure that our delegation, which included members of the Knesset, was in concert with our thinking, he asked me to show the draft resolution to Mrs Golda Meir, the secretary-general of the Labour Party and the most senior member of the delegation. I went up to her suite at Essex House, told her about the latest negotiations with Caradon and showed her the text. She read it carefully and handed the paper back to me without the slightest word or even indication of criticism. In later years, when Golda Meir became Prime Minister, she did not always speak well of Security Council Resolution 242, but neither Abba Eban nor myself recalled publicly her attitude in 1967. On 22 November 1967 the resolution was unanimously adopted by the Security Council. To the present day it remains the basic document underlying all peace negotiations.

The Six Day War had a profound impact on the Palestinian issue. Resolution 242 referred only to the necessity of 'achieving a settlement of the refugee problem', and not to the broader aspects of self-determination, and was therefore rejected by the Palestinian leadership. Their opposition to the occupation of the territories was a powerful factor in forging a Palestinian national identity. Thousands of Palestinians were employed by the Israeli military government and helped in the administration of the territories. In later years many of them formed the core of the Palestinian administration. The human encounters after the Six Day War were completely different from previous meetings with Palestinians. Hundreds of thousands of Palestinians visited Israel, engaged in business activities and worked in industrial plants, tourism and construction. Goods, people and ideas moved easily across the 'green line', the former armistice demarcation line. However, there were painful aspects to these meetings as well; many refugees from the 1948 war came to visit their old homes, now occupied by Israelis, and then returned to the squalor of the refugee camps. Also, the gap in the standard of living of the two communities became evident. Above all, moderate Israelis and Palestinians, who welcomed this contact and believed that this was a opportune moment to reach a settlement, were deeply disappointed with the lack of political progress. Soon after the war, an informal, fairly discreet, political dialogue was launched. It took the shape of unpublicized conversations between Palestinian leaders in the territories and Dayan, as well as with other politicians and military people who had probed the possibility of an accommodation. In many minds, on both sides of the divide, the conviction grew that peaceful coexistence was inescapable, yet it was not possible to translate this conclusion into a viable negotiation. The option of autonomy for the Palestinians was first raised in these discussions and was utterly rejected by them. The concept of measured steps and of the need for a slowly evolving mutual confidence was alien to their thinking. They were afraid that autonomy would become their permanent status and would preclude statehood. Moderate attitudes by Palestinian notables were quashed by the militant leadership outside the West Bank and Gaza, led by Arafat and local extremists. Jordan too was not interested in the emergence of a Palestinian autonomous entity. The leaders of Al Fatah (the movement for the liberation of Palestine), who operated from the refugee camps in Jordan and of other factions were single-minded in their demands for a Palestinian state with East Jerusalem as its capital. They also insisted on the right of return and refused to recognize Israel. Nevertheless, Dayan wanted to learn first-hand of Arafat's point of view. A West Bank notable went to see Arafat in Jordan and suggested to him that Al Fatah cease terrorist activities, which were harmful to the Palestinians. He told Arafat that 70,000 Palestinians, peacefully working their land on the East Bank of the Jordan, had had to flee because they could not remain in the firing line between the Israeli army and Palestinian terrorists. If the Arab armies had failed to dislodge the Israelis, how could a handful of terrorists achieve that goal? The envoy suggested to Arafat a meeting with Dayan to try to reach an accommodation. Arafat reportedly replied that he did not care if thousands of peasants had to flee. He also said that, of all the Arab armies, the Palestinian was the only one to continue fighting. They were not fighting to push Israel back to the border of 4 June or for Kuneitra, but for Jaffa and Acre and what used to be the whole of Palestine. Arafat refused to meet Dayan.[13] This line was hard and uncompromising and suggested that little common ground existed. The Palestinians again became victims of their obduracy and reverted to violence and terror. Yet in spite of Arafat's negative attitude, Dayan left the door open for negotiations. He was asked whether, in view of Al Fatah terrorism, Israel would be prepared to negotiate with them. Dayan replied that if, in the future, they agreed to the cease-fire and renounced terrorism, if they came as part of an overall Palestinian delegation, with or without the concurrence of King Hussein, with the agreement by Nasser or without it, then we would accept them as interlocutors.[14]

The Palestinians did not agree to direct negotiations. Israel continued to fight terrorism and the view that the best 'Zionist answer' to continued Arab animosity was to establish possession on the ground, to build more settlements, gathered momentum. A few groups decided that they would pioneer the building of settlements and campaign for the annexation of the West Bank. The idea of Greater Israel received strong ideological and religious impetus. It was argued that the settlements, when built in strategic locations, would add a new dimension to Israel's defence capability. They would also help convince the Palestinians that the more they procrastinated in coming to the negotiating table, the more they would lose. Some of these views enjoyed considerable support around the Cabinet table, even from ministers of the Labour Party. The government had to decide where settlements could be built as part of a broader strategic outlook. Yigal Allon, the former commander of the Palmach, was Minister of Labour and headed the Cabinet committee on settlements. On 26 July 1967 he tabled a resolution outlining a long-term concept, which became known as the 'Allon Plan'. It was never approved by the Cabinet and in later years was modified by Allon himself. It did, however, serve as an unofficial guideline to the settlement policy in the late sixties and early seventies. According to the plan, on the east the border would be the Jordan River, so a strip of land of about ten or fifteen kilometres wide along the Jordan would be annexed to Israel. A similar strip, with minimal Palestinian population, stretching from the Dead Sea to Jerusalem, would be annexed. Territorial adjustments would be made in the area of Mount Hebron. In the areas designated for annexation, settlement building would be allowed. Allon also advocated in the plan autonomy for the Palestinians with close economic and defence links to Israel.[15] It was Allon who approved the first three settlements on the Golan Heights and the establishment of a theological seminary (yeshiva) in Hebron. Dayan also supported settlement activity, although he opposed the Allon Plan, fearing that it would be construed by the Palestinians as an attempt to cut off the West Bank of the Jordan from the East Bank. The idea that settlements would be confined to 'strategic locations' and would not be built near areas densely populated by Palestinians guided the policy of the government.[16]

In the months after the Six Day War Israel enjoyed the praise and admiration of Jews and non-Jews in every corner of the globe. Tourists flocked to the country to witness the new and exciting reality. The pre-war economic recession came to an end, books and albums detailing the sacrifice and heroism of the IDF appeared in abundance. A group of soldiers and officers, educated in kibbutzim recorded a different story: the agony of war, the pain of being compelled to kill, the anguish of seeing one's friends and colleagues fall in battle. Their thoughts were published in a sombre and reflective dialogue between warriors.[17] The twentieth Independence Day concluded Israel's second decade. It was celebrated in a united Jerusalem with prayers of thanksgiving and a military parade. The war had changed the entire Middle East landscape, inspired a new self-confidence in Israelis and developed war doctrines to be studied in military colleges in many countries. While it did not end Palestinian terror nor warfare with Egypt, it left Israel holding important cards for the day when serious peace negotiations would take place.

THE THIRD DECADE
1968–78

10

The Quest for Peace Continues

The third decade was eventful and dramatic. Three new leaders shaped the fortunes of Israel, Egypt and the United States – Golda Meir, Anwar Sadat and Richard Nixon. It started off with new diplomatic initiatives, continued with the most savage war Israel had endured, the Yom Kippur War, and came to a close with the historic visit of President Sadat to Jerusalem.

In diplomatic conversations during the seventies and eighties it was often said that, following the Six Day War, opportunities for making peace were missed. Even with the benefit of thirty years of hindsight it is difficult to see what additional steps Israel could have taken immediately after the war in order to encourage the Arab states and the Palestinians to come to the negotiating table. It had at the time a moderate, forward-looking, peace-oriented government led by Eshkol and Eban. At the beginning, Dayan also went along with the moderate line; only later, when he became convinced that no Arab country reciprocated Israel's wish to make peace, did he harden his attitude. Less than ten days after the end of the Six Day War Israel expressed its readiness to withdraw to the international borders with Egypt and Syria in return for peace treaties and the solution of security and water problems. By adopting this position, Israel was telling its neighbours that this had not been a war to conquer territories but to bring peace and security to a war-torn region. This was in line with the 'land for peace' concept; even before Security Council Resolution 242 was approved, it contained a fair basis for opening negotiations. From the Palestinians there was not the slightest disposition to negotiate. They continued their terrorism and adhered to the Palestinian National Covenant, which called for a Palestinian state in the whole of Palestine and the acceptance of the right of return.[1] In October 1968 the main Palestinian terrorist organization, Al Fatah, rejected 'all compromises aiming at halting armed strife'.[2] With Jordan, Israel was prepared to explore the possibility of a peace treaty in a direct dialogue with King Hussein. Messages were passed through the United States and other informal channels to Cairo and Damascus conveying Israel's readiness to make peace; however, they were met with zero response. Not a ray of light, not a shred of hope came back. The diplomatic front was paralysed by the negative positions adopted by the Arab heads of state at Khartoum, and the military front continued to be dominated by Palestinian terror and heavy artillery firing by Egyptian troops across the Suez Canal. Nevertheless attempts to bridge the wide gaps between the parties continued.

An intensive effort was made by the special UN representative, Dr Gunar Jarring, the Swedish ambassador to the Soviet Union, an experienced diplomat from a neutral country. Armed with a mandate from the Security Council enshrined in Resolution 242, he began to shuttle between Jerusalem, Cairo and Amman, Jordan. The Syrian government refused to receive him in Damascus because it did not accept Resolution 242. In our meetings with Jarring, Eban explained that we believed that peace could be achieved only in direct negotiations and that there could be no withdrawal of Israeli troops prior to a peace settlement. He further proposed to Jarring an 'agenda for peace' which would include discussions on political and juridical problems such as the replacement of the cease-fire arrangements by peace treaties; territorial and security problems, such as agreed boundaries and security arrangements; and navigation and economic problems. However, Egypt and Jordan insisted on withdrawal to the cease-fire lines as 'a basic preliminary step to a peaceful settlement'. As an indication of our strong desire to break the deadlock and start negotiations, Israel agreed to commence talks in a conference convened by Jarring in Nicosia, Cyprus. It was hoped that an 'indirect approach' would lead to direct negotiations at a later stage. Eban also expressed the view that 242 was 'a framework for agreement', a set of principles whose details must be negotiated. Egypt's stance was that the resolution was a plan for implementation. At the heart of the Arab position as presented to Jarring was a consistent refusal to negotiate with Israel. There was also a sharp divergence of views on the interpretation of the withdrawal clause of 242. The Arabs insisted on withdrawal from all the territories, while Israel's position was that the omission of the words *all* or *the* before the word territories was deliberate, and territorial adjustments should, therefore, not be excluded.[3] This interpretation was supported by the author of 242, Britain. On 17 November 1969, the British Foreign Secretary, Michael Stewart, was asked in Parliament: 'What is the British interpretation of the wording of the 1967 Resolution? Does the Right Honourable Gentleman understand it to mean that the Israelis should withdraw from all territories taken in the late war?' Mr Stewart replied: 'No, sir. That is not the phrase used in the Resolution. The Resolution speaks of secure and recognized boundaries. These words must be read concurrently with the statement on withdrawal.' A similar policy line was pursued by the United States. When the assistant secretary of state, Joseph Sisco, was asked, on an NBC 'Meet the Press' programme to address the same issue, he replied: 'That Resolution did not say "withdrawal to the pre-June 5th line" ... the question of the final

borders is a matter of negotiations between the parties.'[4] With such profound differences between the Israeli and Arab positions, the first phase
of the Jarring mission came to a halt.

In the summer of 1968, after two and a half rewarding years in the office
of Foreign Minister Eban, I left to take up my appointment as political
counsellor in our Embassy in Washington. Several months before, Yitzhak
Rabin had replaced Avraham Harman as ambassador to the United States.
In the first weekly staff meeting after my arrival, he asked me to analyse
the reasons for the failure of the Jarring mission. Having participated in
the Eban–Jarring talks in Jerusalem and in every possible attempt on our
part to turn the Jarring effort into a serious negotiating process, I could
report that Israel had displayed flexibility. The root cause for Jarring's lack
of success was, in my view, Nasser's reluctance to engage in any form of
negotiations with Israel and his hope that with the help of the Soviet
Union he could generate enough international pressure to achieve an
imposed settlement. He remembered that the Eisenhower–Dulles policies
in 1957 had compelled Israel to evacuate the Sinai peninsula and he had
hoped to see a repeat of that pressure. Notions of a peace agreement or a
peace treaty with Israel were simply non-existent in Nasser's discourse
with Jarring or with any other Western politician or diplomat. I stressed
that by his personality and nature Jarring was not able to come to grips
with the complexity of the Arab–Israeli conflict, whose intricacies were
new to him.

The collapse of the first phase of the Jarring mission and the absence of
any Arab willingness to negotiate peace hardened attitudes in Israel. The
movement for a Greater Israel gathered momentum and the Allon Plan,
which called for annexation of strategic areas on the West Bank, though
never officially adopted, influenced the thinking of many Israelis. Dayan
became quite pessimistic about the chances for peace and adopted a
hawkish line, supporting settlement activity. The persistent advocates of
peace had little to offer to the Israeli public except to point out the
long-term dangers of occupation. Nevertheless, on 8 October 1968, Eban
proposed a nine-point peace plan in the General Assembly of the United
Nations. It was well received by the United States and by public opinion
but unfortunately had no resonance in the Arab world. During the same
months the Israeli government stiffened its position of 19 June, that Israel
was not prepared to withdraw to the border of 5 June 1967 and would
expect border adjustments.[5]

While the War of Attrition – which began in September 1968 – was raging
and terrorist activity, emanating mainly from the Palestinian organizations
concentrated in Jordan, was continuing, important changes occurred in
Israel and in the United States. On 26 February 1969, Eshkol died and Mrs

Golda Meir was elected by the Labour Party to replace him as Prime Minister. Israel had lost a good and dedicated leader. Though underrated by some of his contemporary colleagues, Eshkol must receive credit for his part in the economic development of the country, for uniting the different factions of Labour into one party, for his contribution to building up the strength of the Israeli Defence Forces before the Six Day War and for his decisions prior to and during that war. Golda Meir was seventy, in poor health but with a wealth of experience and a good international reputation. The party pundits were afraid that there would be a struggle over the leadership between Moshe Dayan and Yigal Allon. Even more, they were terrified by the prospect that Dayan might emerge as the winner of that contest. They therefore turned to Golda Meir as the only person who could keep the party united. When the vote was taken in the Central Committee of the Labour Party, on 7 March, there was not a single dissenting vote. The Rafi faction led by Peres and Dayan abstained. Golda Meir described her feelings at that dramatic moment: 'I know that tears rolled down my cheeks and that I held my head in my hands when the voting was over, but all that I recall about my feelings is that I was dazed. I had never planned to be Prime Minister.'[6]

Mrs Meir did not introduce changes to the government or in Israel's foreign policy. However, her style was harder. This was most evident in our dialogue with the US. Her attitude towards the Arabs was less compromising. She gave her blessing to the adoption of the hawkish Galili Document, devised by Dayan and refined by Israel Galili. It called for a comprehensive effort to establish new settlements in the 'Rafiah salient, in the Jordan Valley and on the Golan Heights'. Her government approved the building of the town of Yamit.[7] Her relationship with her Foreign Minister, Abba Eban, was less cooperative than Eshkol's. She also had less direct experience of defence and relied heavily on Dayan in these matters.

In January 1969 President Nixon took over from Lyndon Johnson. The situation in the Middle East was quite explosive and dubbed a 'powder keg' by the new President. The Jarring mission was at a dead end and the Arab–Israeli conflict soon became a prominent issue both on Nixon's agenda and on that of his national security adviser, Henry Kissinger. The French government suggested four-power talks with the participation of the US, the Soviet Union, the British and the French, in order to work out a more detailed interpretation of Resolution 242. This new bluepirnt was to be proposed to Jarring as a basis for his negotiations with the parties. Just before Nixon assumed office, the Soviet Union had also proposed a new peace initiative, which did not differ in its essentials from the position Egypt had taken in its talks with Jarring, but indicated the Kremlin's recognition that the new administration in Washington had a key role to play, as well as expressing its own willingness to engage in a dialogue on the Middle East. Kissinger had serious reservations about both the French and Soviet initiatives, but on the recommendation of the US Secretary of State, William Rogers, they were both accepted by Nixon. Two-power talks were conducted between the assistant secretary of state, Joseph Sisco, and the Soviet ambassador to the United States, Anatoly Dobrynin, in Washington. The four-power talks were held in New York with the participation of the ambassadors of the US, USSR, France and Britain. Both were defined as 'exploratory'.

Both sets of negotiations were a source of concern to Israel. Two influential partners in the four-power talks, the Soviets and de Gaulle's France, wanted to push the country back to the lines of 5 June 1967 without a contractual peace. Similarly, there was apprehension that the Sisco–Dobrynin talks might allow Nasser to bypass direct negotiations and thus avoid mutual recognition. We felt that there was some distance between the Arab–Soviet demand for total withdrawal and the American position that border rectification should be 'minor'. We had every reason to believe that one of the Soviet objectives was to test the Nixon administration and find out whether, in comparison to Johnson, it would adopt a harder attitude towards Israel. Two weeks after the new President assumed office, I conveyed to Alfred Atherton, who was at the time director of Israel–Arab affairs at the State Department, a message containing Eshkol's concerns. The Prime Minister wondered how the US could believe that the Soviet Union, which had a very different view from America on freedom and peace, would agree with Washington on these issues in the Middle East.

Together with the Deputy Chief of Mission, Shlomo Argov, I accompanied Rabin to the Department of State to receive progress reports from Secretary of State Rogers and Joseph Sisco on these negotiations. After each session we spent long hours in the Embassy analysing every nuance and looking for signs of progress. The more we heard, the more apprehensive we became. We recognized that the United States had a much broader agenda with the Soviet Union, which, in addition to peace in the Middle East, included Vietnam and the need for East–West détente. We felt that in its eagerness to break the deadlock, the US might move away from the firm positions held since the end of the Six Day War while the Soviets stood fast, defending an uncompromising Arab line. In later years, Kissinger confirmed how justified our fears were. He wrote: 'Our position on frontiers had moved progressively in one direction – from the "weight of conquest" to "rectifications" to "insubstantial alterations". No corresponding shift had taken place on the radical Arab or Soviet side.'[8] It seemed to us that these fast-moving developments in a new administration, whose outlook and policies we had not yet fathomed, carried dangers for Israel. We obviously shared our anxieties with every branch of government, administration and Congress.

To overcome difficulties in the talks with Dobrynin, Sisco travelled to Moscow in July 1969, hoping to convince the Soviets to move closer to the American point of view. He returned to Washington disappointed, reporting that, as Nasser was the linchpin of Soviet influence in the Middle East, they were not prepared to press him to modify his position.[9] US efforts to work out with the Russians a joint paper on 'fundamental principles' for an agreement between Israel and Egypt faltered. Interestingly, they did not fail on the territorial question – because the Americans too agreed that the border between the two countries should not be different from the 5 June lines – but on Egyptian reluctance to make peace. Neither did the Soviets cooperate with attempts to limit arms supplies or revive the cease-fire. They fuelled the War of Attrition and succeeded in creating tensions between the United States and Israel. The failure of the two-power negotiations foreclosed any possibility of success of the four-power talks in New York.[10] It was additional proof that Soviet policy in the Middle East was shaped by Cold War interests, seeking predominance in the region, rather than reflecting an interest in peace and stability.

In view of the impasse in the negotiations with the Soviets, and the lack of progress in the four-power talks, William Rogers decided to publish the principles which guided American policy. They were included in a speech before the Adult Education Conference in Washington on 9 December 1969, and became known as the Rogers Plan. Underlining that peace 'must be defined in specific terms', Rogers spelled out the US view on the territorial issue by saying that 'any changes in the pre-existing lines should not reflect the weight of conquest and should be confined to insubstantial alterations required for mutual security'. Peace with Egypt would require withdrawal 'to the international border between Israel and Egypt'. The Israeli government was extremely upset by this. It believed that detailed delineation of the territorial issue would jeopardize negotiations with Egypt and would create difficulties in the negotiations with other Arab countries. If this was the US view, why should the Arabs accept less? Furthermore, on 18 December the American ambassador, Charles Yost, submitted a detailed proposal on Jordan to the four-power group in New York. Only two days earlier, Eban, in a conversation with Rogers, asked him specifically not to do so but to allow Israel to continue talking to Jordan via the private channel. Israel's opposition to the Rogers Plan was the first serious confrontation between Prime Minister Golda Meir and the Nixon administration. After a Cabinet meeting on 22 December the government rejected the plan. The lessons which the United States drew from this serious though unsuccessful attempt to advance peace were succinctly described by Alfred Atherton, who at the time was working with Sisco on the two-power and four-power talks: 'Washington was not again to put forth proposals on the specific elements of a comprehensive

Arab–Israeli peace settlement until asked to do so by both Israel and Egypt at Camp David nine years later. Nor ... was the United States again to use the Soviet Union as a principal channel to an Arab government on questions of Arab–Israel peace.'[11] The Cairo press also denounced the proposals. The kiss of death to both the two-power and four-power talks came when on 23 December the Soviet Union formally rejected the Rogers Plan. It relieved immediate US pressure on Israel. Elements of the plan were, in later years, incorporated into the peace agreement with Egypt.

Since September 1968, the exchange of fire across the Suez Canal had intensified. Nasser's intention to apply military pressure was, probably, at the root of the failed diplomatic efforts in Washington and New York. On 8 September 1968 Egyptian artillery opened fire on a wide front, killing ten Israeli soldiers and injuring eighteen. This was a notable escalation, the beginning of the War of Attrition. Less acclaimed yet very costly, this war raged for nearly two years, causing hundreds of Israeli casualties, killing thousands of Egyptians and displacing about a million Egyptians from the cities near the Suez Canal. In March 1969 Egypt announced that the cease-fire established after the Six Day War was no longer in force. Nasser's objectives were clear. With his army restructured and rearmed by the Soviets he had decided to harass the Israeli troops on the eastern side of the canal and destroy their fortifications. Soviet ground-to-air missiles provided cover for his troops and made it more difficult to attack them from the air. He also believed that shooting was the best means of keeping the conflict on the international agenda. He failed again to appreciate the full consequences of his policies. Israel reacted strongly to the artillery attacks. When the artillery barrages did not stop, it mounted a series of raids deep into Egypt, some not far from Cairo. The 'deep-penetration' raids would remain a subject of considerable controversy in the annals of Israeli military history. They had a harsh impact on Egypt but also resulted in an intensification of Soviet involvement. Highly placed American officials had believed that the stepping-up of military operations against Egypt might unsettle Nasser's regime and weaken the Soviet position in the Middle East. According to Kissinger, 'Nixon thought that Nasser would become more moderate if faced by overwhelming power.'[12] In his adroit style, Rabin reported the sentiment in Washington in sharp language, cabling home after a successful armoured raid across the Suez Canal in September 1969, that 'some sources have informed me that our military operations are the most encouraging breath of fresh air'. On 25 October 1969 Rabin advocated 'deep-penetration raids at military targets at the Egyptian heartland'.[13] The State Department approach to these raids was more cautious, yet I know from my own conversations in Washington at the time that Rabin reflected correctly the views of policy makers. This did not prevent the very same people from expressing reservations later on, when they learned of the considerable Soviet involvement which the raids had provoked. The suggestion of carrying out bombing raids deep inside Egypt was proposed to the Defence Committee of the Cabinet by Dayan and approved by it. The objective was to make the War of Attrition prohibitive for Nasser and compel him to stop it. Our impression in Washington was that the US government understood the decision and its motivation. The only negative signal was a refusal to sell Israel additional combat planes in order not to invoke criticism in the Arab world.

The deep-penetration raids were too much for Nasser to take; he felt that his army had no effective response to them. In January 1970 he went on a secret mission to Moscow to ask for help. The Kremlin did not hesitate to play brinkmanship, upgrading their arms supply to Egypt as well as their direct involvement. New surface-to-air missiles, of the Sam-3 type, were sent, with their Russian personnel, along with three squadrons of Soviet fighter planes, manned by Russian crews, to protect the missile bases and the skies of Cairo, Alexandria and Aswan. All in all about 15,000 Soviet advisors, officers and pilots were now stationed in Egypt.[14] The Soviet Union actually took on the responsibility for protecting the Egyptian airspace. The Soviet Premier, Alexei Kosygin, tried to pre-empt international criticism of increased Soviet involvement by writing to Nixon and the other leaders of the four-power group. The note delivered by Dobrynin to Kissinger on 31 January 1970 threatened that if Israel continued its attacks on Egypt, 'the Soviet Union would be forced to see to it that the Arab states have means at their disposal with the help of which a due rebuff to the arrogant aggressor could be made'.[15] Nixon refused to be impressed by the new Soviet threats and responded firmly that the US was watching the balance of arms and would not hesitate to provide arms to Israel 'as the need arises'. The President added a public warning to Moscow. In his report to Congress on 18 February Nixon wrote that the United States 'would view any effort by the Soviet Union to seek predominance in the Middle East as a matter of grave concern'.

Between January and March 1970, close to two dozen targets inside Egypt were bombed. The Soviets, seeing the dangers of a looming confrontation with the US in the Middle East, maintained a dialogue with Washington through discussions between Henry Kissinger and Dobrynin. In private as well as in public briefings, Kissinger added his own warnings against stepped-up Soviet involvement in Egypt. As the War of Attrition continued with even greater ferocity, it was only a question of time before the Israeli air force found itself in direct engagement with Soviet pilots. As Israeli fighter planes patrolled the Gulf of Suez coast on 30 June 1970, they were attacked by two formations (four planes each) of Russian combat planes. Five of the Soviet planes were downed, two of their pilots were killed and two were injured. The commander of the Soviet air force immediately rushed to Cairo to investigate the encounter. The Israeli government, conscious of its serious nature, was careful not to embarrass the Soviet Union.[16] Nothing was said publicly about the incident by Israel, the Soviets or the Egyptians.

The extended Soviet commitment *and* the upgrading of their arms supply to Egypt raised some serious questions in Washington. To what length was Moscow prepared to go in order to defend Nasser? Would they continue to further upgrade their arms supply with ground-to-ground missiles? If so, what sort of response would that require of the United States? Might not such an escalation compel Israel to undertake a pre-emptive strike against Egypt? The State Department felt that a new effort must be made to bring about a cease-fire, especially after Nasser signalled that he would be receptive to such a move. Despite past setbacks to American diplomacy, the US decided to launch a second Rogers initiative (as distinct from the 1969 Rogers Plan). It was communicated to Israel, Egypt and Jordan on 19 June, and announced publicly on 25 June 1970. On the Egyptian front it called for a ninety-day cease-fire. On the Jordanian front it aimed to get negotiations going. The parties were to agree to carry out Resolution 242 in all its parts and designate representatives for discussions under Jarring's auspices. The purpose of the discussions was to reach agreement between the parties based on mutual acknow-ledgement of each other's 'sovereignty, territorial integrity and political independence, and Israeli withdrawal from territories occupied in the 1967 conflict, both in accordance with Resolution 242'. Rogers was con-cerned that Israel might reject his new initiative even before Nasser or Hussein did so. When Rabin, Argov and myself met Rogers to receive his new initiative, he implored us not to reply negatively, at least until we learned what the Arab response would be. Rogers promised that the US would make sure that the arms balance was maintained, implying, however, that there would be a link between Israel's attitude towards his proposal and the supply of US arms, a notion which was emphatically rejected in all our contacts with the administration. He expressed himself strongly on deterring the Soviets, saying that further involvement on their part would risk 'more direct confrontation with the United States.

The Israeli government disliked the idea of limited cease-fires and of linking diplomatic efforts to vital arms supplies. Viewing a truce as a transition from a state of war to peace negotiations, it saw the time limit of ninety days as a licence to Nasser to start shooting anew at the end of that period. Golda Meir also knew that the acceptance of Rogers II would inevitably lead to a break-up of the National Unity Government, with Menachem Begin walking out of it. The initial reaction to the Rogers proposal was therefore negative and Golda Meir was prepared to convey it to Nixon in writing. In our Embassy in Washington we felt that it would be a grave mistake to enter into a head-on confrontation with the President on a proposal which might have some merit and which the Arabs had not rejected. Rabin asked permission to fly to Israel to explain our point of view to the government. It was granted, and in his conversations in Jerusalem, he succeeded in introducing a measure of moderation. Instead of outright rejection we now asked for clarification of this new diplomatic effort. Negotiations with the United States continued throughout July, leading to a series of important US commitments to Israel. Eventually the Meir government was pleased with a strong American hands-off warning to the Soviets, with a public statement by the President that withdrawal of Israeli troops must be to 'defensible' boundaries, and a detailed commitment on the supply of fighter jets in an agreed time frame. Above all it was the President's letter to Mrs Meir of 24 July 1970, which made the difference. These were its key undertakings:

> Our position on withdrawal is that the final borders must be agreed upon by the parties by means of negotiations under the auspices of Ambassador Jarring. Moreover, we will not press Israel to accept a solution to the refugee problem that will alter fundamentally the Jewish character of the State of Israel or jeopardize your security. We shall adhere strictly and firmly to the fundamental principle that there must be a peace agreement in which each of the parties undertakes reciprocal obligations to the other ... No Israeli soldier should be withdrawn from the present lines until a binding contractual peace agreement satisfactory to you has been achieved.[17]

The firm articulation of American policy on the key issues of withdrawal, the refugee problem and peace agreements, coupled with a commitment on arms supply to offset the losses in the War of Attrition, was one of the strongest in the history of US–Israel relations. Two days before this letter was dispatched Nasser replied affirmatively to the Rogers initiative and Washington was very keen that this new attempt at diplomacy take off and that Egypt and Israel 'stop shooting and start talking'. Nixon's assurances finally tilted the balance in favour of Israeli acceptance. Israel also saw it as an advantage that Rogers II was presented directly to the parties without the Soviet Union acting as a go-between for Cairo. A detailed agreement on the modalities of the cease-fire was now worked out with the United States. It stipulated that the truce would commence on 7 August and that Israel and Egypt would refrain from changing the military status quo in a zone stretching fifty kilometres east and west of the Suez Canal. In other words, there would be a 'standstill' cease-fire. Israel wanted to prevent a situation where, under the cover of the cease-fire, Egypt would position its anti-aircraft Sam-3 missiles close to the Suez.

On 4 August Golda Meir declared in the Knesset that the government had consented to the US proposal. The Gahal party ministers, led by Begin, resigned from the Cabinet. The reason was that the reply included the most explicit commitment 'to carry out Resolution 242 in all its parts', which was applicable not just to Egypt but to the West Bank as well. The cease-fire went into effect as agreed, only to be violated within hours by the Egyptians. Contrary to the 'standstill' agreement, they brought their missile batteries forward close to the canal. Israel appealed to the US to influence a pull-back of the Sam-3 missiles, but to no avail. The Soviets and Egypt refused to back down. Israel, reluctantly, took the position that it would not start the Jarring talks until the cease-fire violations were rectified. After independent verification, the US confirmed the forward deployment of the Sam missiles and agreed to supply Israel with sophisticated anti-missile warfare equipment. In September Mrs Meir came to Washington to meet President Nixon. He reiterated his strong commitment to Israel and to maintaining an arms balance but had no solution to the missile crisis. The only ray of light was that the cease-fire was holding and in December 1970 was extended for an additional three months. In the meantime attention focused on other developments – the death of President Nasser and the dangers to Jordan from a Syrian assault.

Between the end of the Six Day War and September 1970 there had been uninterrupted terrorist activity from the Palestinian camps in Jordan; 141 Israelis had been killed and hundreds injured during these three years. The Palestinians had built a terrorist infrastructure which threatened the stability of Jordan and the monarchy itself. When King Hussein accepted the Rogers initiative in July 1970, the Palestinians were dead set against it, and in early September they attempted to assassinate the king.

On 6 September the Palestinians stepped up terror in the air. A Pan-American Jumbo jet was kidnapped. After it landed in Cairo the passengers were released and the jet was blown up. Another two planes, one Swiss-Air and the other a TWA jet, were forced to land in Jordan. The passengers were held hostage in the steaming heat while the Popular Front for the Liberation of Palestine demanded of Israel, Switzerland, Germany, Britain and the United States the release of Palestinian prisoners. A few days later a British BOAC jet was kidnapped and its passengers endured a similar agonizing ordeal. Following strong international protests the terrorists blew up the three planes on their runways in Jordan and most of the passengers were released. The last group of forty were freed by the Jordanian army. In view of such a blatant infringement of Jordanian sovereignty, the Jordanian army attacked the terrorist bases, killing many, including the leaders. The Arab countries called on King Hussein to cancel the army operation but the monarch was determined to root out the terrorists in his kingdom. There were many Palestinian casualties during that month, which was dubbed 'Black September'. As the ferocity of the fighting grew, the Syrian army intervened and on 18 September, a Syrian garrison crossed the border into Jordan and occupied a police station. Additional Syrian armoured troops moved towards Amman and the Jordanian army engaged them, while King Hussein, knowing that the balance of forces was not in his favour, appealed to the United States, and to Israel, for help.

On the evening of 20 September, Golda Meir was attending the final engagement of her first trip to the US as Prime Minister, a gala dinner at the Hilton Hotel in New York. Together with a few of my colleagues in the Embassy, I flew to New York to attend the dinner. While we were sipping our cocktails, Rabin was called to the telephone. It was Kissinger calling from the White House to convey King Hussein's request for Israeli assistance, asking specifically that the Israeli air force attack the Syrian troop concentrations threatening Amman. A series of hectic consultations ensued between the acting Prime Minister, Yigal Allon, in Jerusalem, Golda Meir and Rabin in New York and Kissinger in Washington. Later in the evening Rabin flew back to the American capital to be on hand. After an independent assessment of the situation in Jordan, the Israeli government agreed to take action, provided the US guaranteed that should Egypt resume the fighting, a US 'umbrella' would be provided against Soviet intervention and Israel would receive arms to maintain the balance. Kissinger, on behalf of the President, gave a positive reply to the requests; the Israeli government mobilized units of the IDF and ordered a heightened state of alert. In the meantime the US demanded of the Soviet Union that it press Syria to pull back its troops from Jordan. To reinforce this message American naval forces were put on alert. The Jordanian army successfully repulsed the onslaught of three hundred Syrian tanks. The Syrian air force commander, General Assad (later President Assad), observing Israel's state of readiness, shied away from confrontation, and refused to provide air cover to the Syrian ground forces, who were forced to withdraw from Jordan. President Nixon was extremely gratified by Israel's positive response, which had helped protect a moderate Arab regime and at the same time prevented the need to obtain congressional approval for the dispatch of American troops.[18] Israel's swift action also had a lasting beneficial effect on its relations with Jordan. In November 1970 King Hussein met the Deputy Prime Minister, Yigal Allon, and expressed his thanks for the government's readiness to assist Jordan.[19]

By 1971 the Nixon administration had two years of experience of negotiating with the Soviet Union on the Middle East. It tested the Soviets time and again to find out whether they were prepared to change their pro-Arab position and apply pressure on Egypt to modify its radical anti-peace attitude. On both issues the answer was that they were not. The US nevertheless believed that despite the rivalry, the dialogue with Moscow was helpful in preventing a superpower confrontation in the Middle East. The new element in the regional equation was Nasser's successor, President Anwar Sadat. Not much was known about his qualities and policies, and the little that Western and Israeli intelligence had on file about him was not particularly complimentary. In the spring of 1971, Sadat paid his first visit as President to Moscow. His talks with the Soviet leaders were far from satisfactory to him, because his requests for more sophisticated weapons were not fulfilled and the Kremlin demanded greater control over the operational use of the arms supplied. The Soviets had no ready-made solution to assist Egypt to regain control of the Sinai.

In terms of the peace efforts, however, there was a slight degree of novelty in Sadat's approach. In December 1970 he renewed the cease-fire for another ninety days. Following the reassurances that Mrs Meir had received in her talks with President Nixon and his request to Congress to allocate $500 million for arms to Israel, she announced on 29 December the resumption of Israel's participation in the Jarring talks. In her speech before the Knesset she also expressed the hope that the 'new leadership' in Egypt would display the courage 'to set out on the road to peace'.[20] In February 1971 Jarring, believing that the only way to escape the impasse was to elicit 'parallel and simultaneous commitments', fired off a set of direct questions to Egypt and to Israel. Of Israel he asked for a commitment to withdraw to the international border in return for the establishment of demilitarized zones and arrangements that would guarantee freedom of passage in the Suez Canal and Sharm el-Sheikh. From Egypt he demanded a commitment to a peace agreement with Israel. Both countries replied within weeks, basically restating their position. However, in the Egyptian response the notion of *'achieving a peaceful settlement'* and readiness to *'enter into a peace agreement with Israel'* appeared for the first time. Egypt was prepared to terminate the state of belligerency provided Israel carried out Security Council Resolution 242 according to the Egyptian interpretation, meaning withdrawal from all the territories. A whole series of other conditions, including a 'just settlement of the refugee problem', was included in the Cairo response.[21] Though Jarring's intention was positive, the method which he had employed, of direct, clear-cut questions without prior consultations with the parties, was not conducive to solving such a complex conflict and inevitably led to the end of his mission.

At the same time, the possibility of an interim agreement with Egypt surfaced. In January 1971, Rabin was informed by Sisco that a high-ranking Egyptian military officer had suggested to an American representative in Cairo the possibility of a limited or interim settlement. It would lead to the reopening of the Suez Canal and include a withdrawal of Israeli troops to about forty kilometres east of the canal, a thinning out of the Egyptian forces stationed west of the canal and the resumption of navigation through Suez. The exact status of this proposal, presented in an informal Egyptian channel, was as yet unclear, but when we discussed it in the Embassy, some of us, including the ambassador, saw in it a different approach compared to Nasser's policies, and one which merited careful consideration. The general concept of an agreement on the reopening of the Suez Canal was not new. It had been raised by Dayan on various occasions. But this time it came from Egypt and could present a new opportunity. Moreover, on 4 February, Sadat addressed the National Assembly in Cairo, mentioning his readiness to reopen the Suez Canal in return for a partial withdrawal of Israeli troops 'as a first step' in a process that would lead to the implementation of the other provisions of Resolution 242. Sadat clearly indicated the interim nature of the first step on the way to an overall settlement. In an interview to *Newsweek* of 22 February 1971 he spoke of a much deeper withdrawal of Israeli troops than the 40 kilometres originally mentioned, to 'a line behind El-Arish'. The Jarring questions, which were submitted during the very same weeks as the interim agreement was considered, and independently of it, introduced a measure of delay. It was not clear which of the two efforts, Jarring or the partial agreement, had priority. It took about ten weeks for Mrs Meir to reply to this initiative (on 19 April), preceded by a lengthy Cabinet discussion on 22 March, at which Dayan proposed that Israel seek an interim agreement which would include the reopening of the canal in return for the end of belligerency. Some of the ministers, most notably Yigal Allon and Israel Galili had reservations about the new initiative.

In April, Rabin transmitted to Kissinger and Sisco the government's ideas for a partial settlement. They contained demands for an Egyptian commitment to a cease-fire of unlimited duration; a thinning out of Egyptian troops on the west side of the canal; a stipulation that Egyptian civilians engaged in clearing and operating the canal could cross to the east side, but no 'regular or irregular' forces would be allowed to cross. The distance of Israeli withdrawal was left open to negotiation. The proposal also stipulated that the interim agreement would not influence the negotiations on an overall settlement. In that context, Rabin was also instructed to stress Israel's insistence on Egypt's renunciation of the state of belligerency.

When a change of leadership occurs in a non-democratic society, some considerable time must pass before its full significance is understood. Years after Stalin's death the Soviet Union still had difficulties in shaking off its Stalinist image. In 1971, less than a year after Nasser's demise, Egypt was still seen to be ruled by a devious, untrustworthy regime. Sadat's intentions were unclear. In Jerusalem, his vision was neither understood nor appreciated and even less put to the test of negotiations. His approach to the

Soviet Union was ambiguous: in May, he purged a number of high-ranking pro-Soviet officials who threatened his regime, the Ali Sabri group, but to counteract this move he signed in the very same month a treaty of friendship and cooperation with the Soviet Union. Kissinger's reaction to this treaty is well documented by him: it 'reinforced my determination to slow down the process [of negotiations] even further to demonstrate that Soviet threats and treaties could not be decisive', he wrote.[22]

As the US had a representative in Cairo, Donald Bergus, their assessment of Sadat had more clarity. In March 1971 the US deputy assistant secretary of state, Alfred (Roy) Atherton, an astute and fair-minded diplomat, told me that the changes in Egypt were not just semantic but represented a shift in Egyptian thinking. At the beginning of May, Rogers, Sisco and Atherton visited Cairo and had talks with President Sadat and Foreign Minister Mahmoud Riad. Upon their return to Washington, Sisco told Rabin how impressed he was with Sadat's desire for peace. 'I found a great measure of flexibility in Sadat. He wants an agreement with Israel, but one that he can defend and justify *vis-à-vis* the other Arab countries.'[23] Moreover, Rogers and his assistants travelled on from Cairo to Jerusalem, and conveyed their impressions to the Prime Minister and to Dayan. The Minister of Defence met Sisco and Atherton on 6 May, and was prepared to be flexible on the interim agreement but felt bound by the official Cabinet position which Rabin had transmitted to the US. In his memoirs Dayan did not explain why he made no effort to persuade Mrs Meir and his Cabinet colleagues to modify the initial conditions for a partial agreement so that a breakthrough in the negotiations might have been achieved. Eban promised to support him if he were to raise the issue in Cabinet but Dayan refused to force a Cabinet decision against the Prime Minister's wishes.

A few weeks after the Rogers visit to Cairo and Jerusalem another complication arose. In the last week of May, the head of the US interest section in Cairo, Donald Bergus, helped the Egyptian Foreign Ministry to draft a reply to the Israeli proposals on the Suez agreement. This draft, which became known as the Bergus Memorandum, called for an Israeli withdrawal deep into the Sinai peninsula. Egyptian troops would be allowed to cross to the east side of the Suez Canal and between them and the Israeli forces there would be a United Nations presence. This memorandum in itself was quite unorthodox in diplomatic practice. Bergus raised expectations in Cairo because they believed that now a common position with the US had been forged. On 4 June, Egypt's answer was given to Bergus by the Foreign Minister, Riad, repeating the linkage of the partial withdrawal to the overall settlement but reacting positively to Bergus's unauthorized withdrawal proposal. The American envoy then travelled to Paris to brief Rogers on his accomplishment. When it was leaked to the press it raised hell in Jerusalem. America and Egypt were seen to have adopted positions which Israel had rejected. On 27 June 1971 the essence of the Bergus Memorandum appeared in the *Washington Post*.[24] We asked for a meeting with Rogers in order to protest at its content, a meeting which was fixed for the afternoon of 29 June. As my wife Hana was in her last stages of pregnancy, I dropped her off at George Washington Hospital and then joined Rabin at the State Department for the conversation with Rogers. The Secretary of State disowned the Bergus paper but the conversation was very tense. Suddenly Rogers's secretary walked in saying that a son was born to someone in the room. Rabin quipped, 'It's not mine.' I confessed that it was mine. Rogers stood up with a big smile and congratulated me, the icy atmosphere was broken and the conversation continued in an amicable and matter-of-fact manner. Instead of taking the usual route to the Embassy to write the report on the conversation, I went first to the hospital to see my wife and to meet Yuval, who twenty-six years later has been very helpful to me in the writing of this book. The Bergus Memorandum became a footnote to history.

During Mrs Meir's second visit to the US in December 1971, President Nixon made it clear that the supply of arms to Israel would be influenced by its flexibility in the negotiations. Golda Meir and Nixon agreed to give up temporarily the efforts to reach a comprehensive settlement with Egypt and concentrate on the interim agreement. In a subsequent meeting with Kissinger in New York on 10 December 1971, eleven months after the interim agreement was first proposed by Egypt, the Prime Minister modified the Israeli position. She agreed to the withdrawal of Israeli troops up to the western approaches of the Mitla Pass; that the duration of the cease-fire would be eighteen to twenty-four months; that Egyptian technical personnel and a 'certain uniformed force' would be permitted to cross to the eastern side of the canal. However, the Israeli and Egyptian positions were still quite far apart on a number of key issues: the extent of withdrawal, the link between the interim agreement and the overall settlement, Sadat's insistence on a timetable for complete withdrawal and the crossing of Egyptian uniformed personnel to the East Bank. A comparison of the Egyptian proposal with the Israeli approach to an interim agreement reveals not just a gap in the respective positions but a gulf in perception and expectations. Sadat intended to break the impasse in negotiations, reopen the Suez Canal, restore civilian life in the cities along the canal, demonstrate to his people that the first Egyptians were crossing back into the Sinai and negotiate further withdrawals.[25] Golda Meir saw it as an agreement which stood on its own and could have lasted for many years. She therefore attempted to uncouple it from the final settlement.

My father, David Herstig.

My mother, Elka Herstig-Biber.

With my mother, Elka Herstig-Biber, grandfather, Israel Biber, and my two brothers, Efraim and Yechiel.

With Foreign Minister Abba Eban, Chief of Staff Yitzhak Rabin and the Israeli Commander of the Northern Command, General David Elazar, 1967.

At Auschwitz Israeli Foreign Minister, Abba Eban, is joined on the ruins of the gas chambers by the Israeli ambassadors to the Eastern European countries, May 1966.

With Abba Eban at the UN Security Council in 1967,
during the debate on Resolution 242.

With Abba Eban, Ambassador Gunar Yarring, UN Special Envoy to the Middle East, and Teddy Koleck, Mayor of Jerusalem, 1967.

With Ambassador Yitzhak Rabin and Assistant Secretary of State Josef Sisko at the State Department, Washington, 1971.

With Deputy Prime Minister Yigael Allon and US Secretary of State William Rogers at the State Department, Washington, 1972. On my right, Alfred Leroy Atherton, Deputy Assistant Secretary of State. On my left, Yitzhak Rabin. Far right, Avner Idan, Deputy Chief of Mission, Embassy of Israel in Washington. Third from right, Josef Sisko.

With Bob Strauss, Chairman of the US Democratic Party, and later US Ambassador to Moscow, and Shimon Peres, Minister of Defence, 1975.

With Henry Kissinger, US Secretary of State, Defence Minister Moshe Dayan and Ambasssador Simcha Dinitz. On my right, Deputy Chief of Mission Mordechai Shalev, 1974.

With my children, from right to left Ilan, Orna and Yuval, on a trip to Paris after
completing my tour of duty as minister plenipotentiary in 1988.

Left At the Madrid Conference, October 1991. On the author's left, Eytan Bentsur, Deputy
Director General of the Foreign Ministry. On his left, Prime Minister Yitzhak Shamir.

With the Marshal of the British Diplomatic Corps, Admiral Sir James Weatherall, 1993.

With the Queen, 1997.

With my wife, after presenting my credentials to the Queen, 1993.

In the Israeli Embassy in London, after the terrorist bombing, 26 July 1994.
(Photograph courtesy of *The Times*)

With Margaret Thatcher, 1993.

With Douglas Hurd, British Foreign Secretary, 1995.

With John Major, welcoming him to Israel, 1995. On my right is my wife, on my left, Foreign Minister Shimon Peres. On his left, British Ambassador Andrew Burns.

With Tony Blair in Brighton for the Labour Party Conference, October 1995. On Blair's left, Norman Hogg MP, now Lord Hogg of Cumbernauld.

With Abba Eban in London, 1996.

With King Hussein of Jordan, after the signing of the Israel-Jordan peace treaty, 1996.

With Malcolm Rifkind, British Foreign Secretary, 1996.

Welcoming Foreign Minister Ehud Barak to London, 1996.

With my wife just prior to our return to Israel, 1997.

Substantial as these differences were, some or all of them could have been bridged in a serious, ongoing negotiation. Had they been reconciled and shaped into a partial agreement between Israel and Egypt, the Yom Kippur War would, in my view, have been avoided. Why then did this not happen?

Mordechai Gazit, Israel's former ambassador in Paris and director-general of the Prime Minister's Office, as well as a renowned scholar, wrote a thorough analysis of the interim agreement.[26] He ascribes its failure, *inter alia*, to mistakes in the American mediation effort and to the rivalry between Kissinger and Rogers. True, Kissinger's scepticism of the feasibility of such an agreement was so great that it led him to express his reservations to the President on Rogers's trip to Cairo, the first high-level contact between the US and Sadat. But Kissinger was also influenced by the Israeli stance. There was also Soviet opposition to the agreement, but this was not surprising as it was negotiated by the US. Moscow insisted on the condition of a commitment from Israel to total withdrawal. Given Sadat's determination to have a partial settlement, Soviet objections would not have blocked it, had there been progress in the negotiations.

I was then, and remain to the present day, concerned about the role that Israeli policy played in wasting an opportunity for peace. Important lessons for the future lie in a proper understanding of the Israeli approach, because a comprehensive peace in the Middle East is still far off and plenty of negotiations still lie ahead of us. Instead of recognizing the new opening and conveying to Sadat a clear and simple response, 'We are interested in a partial agreement, let's hammer out its terms together,' it took months of deliberations to reply. When Golda Meir's reply came it contained conditions which were totally unacceptable to the other side, like detaching the interim agreement from the final settlement with Egypt. Instead of seizing the initiative, every move had to be wrenched out of the Israeli government, as if we were doing the US a favour by displaying a modicum of flexibility. At the root of this approach was the mistaken belief that it was possible to achieve peace with Egypt without withdrawal to the international border. This is best illustrated by the Israeli Cabinet decision of 31 March 1971 which reads: 'A secure border for Israel requires changes in the former international frontier, including retention of the Gaza Strip, continued Israeli control at Sharm el-Sheikh, and a territorial link to the State of Israel. Continued control does not signify a presence but rather concrete military control, though the Israeli position regarding the legal form of such control has yet to be formulated.'[27]

From Sadat's point of view substantial border changes were incompatible with peace. By this decision the Israeli government tied its own hands and limited its freedom of action in the middle of a negotiating effort. It reflected the Meir–Dayan–Galili vision of a 'new map' for Israel. In

December 1969, barely a year after Nixon assumed the presidency I wrote to the Ministry of Foreign Affairs that the Nixon administration, like the Johnson administration before it, did not believe that it was possible to have both a 'new map' and a peace settlement. This reality had no influence on Dayan, who said that if he had to make a choice between Sharm el-Sheikh without peace or peace without Sharm el-Sheikh, he would choose the former. A whole generation of Israelis was raised on that slogan and when in later years Dayan was asked about it, he replied, 'So what,' and added that only fools believe in quotations as if they were the Bible.[28] He was also a driving force behind the construction of the town Yamit, near Rafah in the Sinai, at the cost of hundreds of millions of dollars, which was returned to Egyptian sovereignty with the signing of the peace agreement. Could these policies have been reconciled with a genuine attempt to reach a partial agreement with Sadat? Obviously not. No wonder that in her memoirs, Mrs Meir devoted less than eight lines to a major diplomatic effort in which she and her government were involved for over a year. In an interview with an Israeli journalist, Rami Tal, published only on 27 April 1997, Dayan actually confirmed that Golda Meir was against the interim agreement. He said that he had believed that a unilateral Israeli withdrawal from the Suez and the reopening of the canal would reduce the possibility of another war and might lead to negotiations. 'Golda did not believe in that ... Golda opposed it and I accepted her view.'[29] She was convinced that the Americans did not want the Suez reopened because it might have shortened the Soviet supply route to Vietnam. That was a poor argument. Rabin examined this question with Kissinger at the very beginning of the talks on a partial settlement. After checking with Nixon, Kissinger did not deny that such an interest existed but added that in view of the situation in the Middle East, the answer was that 'the United States favours discussions with Egypt about reopening the canal'.[30] On that issue there was a clear presidential answer and it could not serve as an excuse for not advancing the interim agreement.

In my attempts to form a comprehensive view on the failure of the efforts to reach an interim Suez agreement I wrote in June 1997 to Alfred Atherton, who was deputy assistant secretary of state at the time, asking him the following questions: (a) Why do you believe that the effort to achieve an (interim) agreement failed? (b) What were the outer limits of the concessions that Sadat was prepared to make? (c) Why did not Joseph Sisco, the assistant secretary of state in charge of the Middle East not come to Israel after his visit to Cairo in July 1971? Atherton, after discussing the issues with Joe Sisco, replied on 11 June 1997, and his answer further illuminates the US perception of that chapter in the relations between Israel and Egypt. I quote from his letter:

(*a*) The idea of an interim Suez Canal agreement, as you will recall, was initiated by Dayan. Sadat responded publicly indicating interest in the idea, but privately made clear any agreement would have to include stationing some Egyptian military personnel east of the Suez Canal. Our impression was that numbers and armament were negotiable, i.e., the force could be token – but some visible Egyptian military presence and flag across the canal was clearly Sadat's bottom line. (*b*) Given Golda's rejection of Sadat's bottom line, we never got to the point of probing what the outer limits might be of concessions Sadat would have been prepared to make. (*c*) Sisco and I did not return to Israel after the third visit to Cairo because there was nothing new to report. We gave Sadat the Israeli position on no military across the Canal, and Sadat made clear there was no use in pursuing the idea further.

There is one factor on the US side you should be aware of. While Joe [Sisco] had an OK from the White House and Secretary Rogers to give the interim Suez Canal agreement idea a try, his instructions were not to push it to the point of creating a crisis with Golda. Whether stronger White House backing would have made a decisive difference we will never know, but given Kissinger's lack of enthusiasm for the idea, the fact we were approaching an election year in the US and Golda's legendary toughness, I personally doubt it.

In recognizing and probing an opportunity for peace, flexibility and speed can be a greater virtue than 'legendary toughness'. Golda Meir was supported in her opposition to the Suez agreement by Chief of Staff Haim Barlev and General David Elazar.[31] I believe that had the Prime Minister told Kissinger that Israel was definitely interested in an interim agreement, his enthusiasm for it would have been considerably enhanced.

In our Embassy we had to navigate the conflicting currents flowing between Jerusalem and Washington. Rabin and the staff and our consulates around the country had to maintain a congenial dialogue with the United States, make sure that there was a robust posture against further direct Soviet involvement, secure a continued supply of fighter planes and economic assistance and ensure a supportive mood in Congress and public opinion. A hardworking counsellor for congressional affairs, Amos Eiran, spent most of his time on Capitol Hill, and the diplomatic personnel worked extremely hard to achieve these objectives. In the first three years after the Six Day War, 1968–70, Israel received $140 million in military credits. This figure was increased tenfold in the next three years. Between 1971 and 1973, we received $1,152.5 million.[32] Yet some of us could not but feel that because of a short-sighted policy we were missing an opportunity for peace – *a prime lesson for the future.*

By the end of 1971, the two-power talks had failed, the four-power talks had come to nought, the Jarring mediation had faltered, the Rogers Plan was inoperative, and now the Suez interim agreement had foundered. Sadat became increasingly disappointed with the lack of progress on the interim agreement and voiced publicly his criticism of American mediation. Nevertheless, he continued to signal his readiness for a partial Suez deal in the course of 1972. In July he expelled about 15,000 Soviet officers and advisers, a move which demonstrated his displeasure with Soviet advice and clearly implied a departure from Nasser's close relationship with Moscow. Egypt nevertheless remained exclusively dependent on Soviet arms. Sadat also initiated the opening of a secret channel to Kissinger which, unfortunately took eleven months to materialize. Kissinger received Sadat's national security adviser, Hafiz Ismail, only in February 1973. This was in line with Kissinger's belief that 'a measured pace fitted in with our strategy of creating in Egypt the maximum restlessness with the status quo'.[33] Kissinger, sceptical about the prospect of an interim agreement, discussed with Ismail a new concept in the framework of an overall settlement. Its shorthand definition was 'separating security from sovereignty', calling for the return of the Sinai to Egypt while maintaining an Israeli military presence in strategic locations. Sadat rejected this notion. Ismail further talked about the end of belligerency provided that Israel withdrew to the June 1967 line and a settlement of the Palestinian problem was achieved. The dialogue between Ismail and Kissinger led nowhere and only provided another impetus for Sadat to turn away from diplomacy. The diplomatic vacuum was starkly evident and Sadat turned to the other alternative – war. The countdown to the Yom Kippur War began.

11

The Yom Kippur War

The Yom Kippur War, which started on 6 October 1973, was a coordinated surprise attack by Egypt and Syria on Israel. Although
from all the evidence now available it is clear that there was a great
amount of information that war was imminent, the interpretation of the
information was completely incorrect. For the people of Israel, the two-
pronged onslaught came as a huge surprise. How was it possible that both
the Israeli and American governments, with two of the finest intelligence
services at their disposal, made such a colossal mistake in misreading a
series of warning signals?

Despite the tension between Egypt and the Soviet Union following the
expulsion of thousands of Soviet advisers, the arms supply to Egypt (and
to Syria) continued, the utter dependence of Egypt on Moscow was evident
and so was the strategic and tactical advice which Sadat and his government had received from the Kremlin. In September 1972, the Egyptian
Prime Minister, Aziz Zidky, visited Moscow and secured shipment of one
of the most sophisticated types of ground-to-air missile, the Sa-6. In the
ensuing months Egypt received ten batteries of Sa-6s and Syria fifteen.
These weapons, in addition to tanks, Sager anti-tank missiles and other
equipment, increased considerably the potential for aggression of both
countries and encouraged them to develop the strategy for the Yom Kippur
War. In March 1973, Sadat assumed the executive role of Prime Minister
in addition to his responsibility as President. He also formed a War Cabinet.
Later in the month he gave an interview to Arnaud De Borchgrave of
Newsweek, in which he explicitly said that war was imminent. The *Newsweek* correspondent, concerned about what he had heard, conveyed the
information to Kissinger before the magazine published it on 9 April
1973.[1]

In May an ominous deployment of Egyptian and Syrian troops was
observed. Israel responded by a high state of alert and by mobilizing
reserve units. Eventually the situation reverted to normal. The cost of the
call-up of reservists was $10 million, and became a cause for hesitation in
future decisions on mobilization. In the course of the same month Dayan
ordered the Israeli General Staff to be prepared for war against Egypt and
Syria by the end of the summer. Both fronts were reinforced and Israel's

rearmament programme was stepped up.[2] The US State Department held a similar view and believed that the likelihood of Sadat initiating a war in the autumn was 'better than even'.[3] On 5 May, the CIA director, James Schlesinger, informed Kissinger that a 'plan for crossing the canal' was being prepared by the Egyptian General Staff.[4]

Soviet warnings of impending war were not taken seriously by the United States. During the Summit Conference between Nixon and Breznev in San Clemente, California, in June 1973, at which Kissinger and the Soviet Foreign Minister, Gromyko, were present, Breznev warned 'that the Egyptians and Syrians were intent upon going to war and that the Soviet Union could not stop them'[5] unless a new initiative by the US were to be forthcoming and pressure on Israel exerted. Kissinger dismissed these warnings as 'psychological warfare' because he did not believe that Sadat had a serious military option. On 28 September Gromyko met Nixon at the White House. In their conversation he remarked: 'We could all wake up one day and find there is a real conflagration in the area' (the Middle East). Kissinger later maintained that Gromyko's remark had calmed US apprehensions because in the same conversation he had agreed that contacts with Israel and Egypt should resume in November.

In September 1973, Israeli intelligence observed increased military activity on both the Egyptian and Syrian fronts. In evaluating this information the chance of war was defined as of 'low probability'. However, the sudden rapprochement between Jordan and Syria and the movement of Syrian troops from the Jordanian border to the Israeli front puzzled Jerusalem and Washington. On 13 September a ferocious encounter between Israeli and Syrian fighter planes took place, in which thirteen Syrian planes were downed, while Israel lost one. Nine days later, on 24 September, the commander of Northern Command, General Hofi, predicted that a Syrian surprise attack on the Golan Heights was possible and as a result our troops in the north were 'reinforced' by a handful of tanks. In Washington Kissinger was told, on 26 September, that the Egyptian army was in a high state of alert and he promptly requested an intelligence estimate on the probability of war. One of the reports suggested a combined Egyptian–Syrian attack in 'the near future'.[6]

On 25 September, Prime Minister Meir met King Hussein in Israel. Having attended a meeting with Presidents Sadat and Assad in Cairo on 10 September, the king became very concerned with the possibility that Jordan would be sucked into another Arab–Israeli war against her best interests. The king conveyed his assessment of the situation, stressing his belief that the continued impasse must lead to war, given the heavy concentration of Syrian troops. Golda Meir was seriously alarmed at what she heard and interrupted the conversation to telephone the Minister of

Defence. Dayan replied that there was nothing new in the king's description of the situation. Our air reconnaissance had observed the Syrian troop deployment. Dayan and the military chiefs who were made aware of Hussein's views could have easily related the king's assessment to the mood of the Cairo meeting and seen that his apprehensions were well founded. But his realistic assessment contrasted with theirs. When, after the war, the Israeli chief of military intelligence, General Eliyahu Zeira was questioned about the '25 September warning' he displayed a fair measure of arrogance, regretting that Mrs Meir had not asked the king for more details. We now know that at the Cairo meeting the Egyptian and Syrian Presidents asked Hussein to secure the southern flank of the Syrian army and make sure that Israel did not attack Syria via Jordan.[7]

On 2 October Dayan was concerned enough to ask to brief the Cabinet of the dangerous situation. He told his colleague, Galili, that on the Syrian front we faced a build-up of 650 tanks and 500 artillery pieces, and asked to convene a meeting with Mrs Meir as soon as she returned from abroad. The first meeting on the impending war, chaired by her, was held on 3 October. The Minister of Defence and Chief of Staff, General Elazar, reported on the troop concentrations. The deputy chief of intelligence said that the troop deployments were such that they might become offensive at any time, but his estimate was that there would not be an attack and that the Egyptian army was engaged in their annual manoeuvres. The meeting ended without a decision to adopt special measures which could counter an emergency, such as the mobilization of reserve units.

In March 1973, Yitzhak Rabin had been replaced by Simcha Dinitz as ambassador to Washington. Dinitz was the director-general of the Prime Minister's Office and one of the closest confidants of Golda Meir. He continued the close and frequent dialogue with Kissinger and other top-level US officials. On 22 September, Henry Kissinger was sworn in as Secretary of State, replacing William Rogers. At the end of September, Kissinger too became concerned when information of heavy Syrian tank concentrations reached him. On 30 September he met Dinitz to discuss his plans to restart negotiations with Israel and Egypt in November. Dinitz raised another subject which was far removed from the evolving emergency, a terrorist attack in Austria on a train carrying Soviet immigrants and the subsequent decision by the Austrian Chancellor, Bruno Kreisky, to close Schonau Castle, near Vienna, as the main transit centre for immigrants arriving from the Soviet Union. Kissinger used the opportunity to question Dinitz on the tank concentrations on Israel's northern border. The ambassador replied that, according to the intelligence assessments available in the Embassy, these troop movements were 'manoeuvres or psychological warfare'. Kissinger could obtain no greater illumination from the American intelligence agencies. The Intelligence and Research Bureau of the State Department believed, on 30 September, that the 'political climate in the Arab world argues against a major Syrian military move'; they did not however exclude the possibility of a Syrian retaliatory attack for the shooting down of the thirteen aeroplanes in mid September. Three days later, on 3 October, the Defence Intelligence Agency (DIA) wrote that 'the movement of Syrian troops and Egyptian military readiness are considered to be coincidental and not designed to lead to major hostilities'. The evaluation of the Central Intelligence Agency (CIA) which Kissinger received twenty-four hours before war broke out, on 5 October, said that 'the military preparations that have occurred do not indicate that any party intends to initiate hostilities'.[8]

In the early morning of Friday, 5 October, information reached Jerusalem and Washington of the evacuation of families of Russian advisers from Egypt and Syria. Dayan ordered the Israeli army into the highest state of alert and the Prime Minister convened an urgent meeting with five of her Cabinet Ministers who were in Tel Aviv. As it was the eve of the most holy day in the Jewish calendar, Yom Kippur, she did not summon the ministers who were in Jerusalem. The troop concentrations were thoroughly discussed between Golda Meir, Dayan and the military before that meeting. The chief of intelligence estimated that no war would break out and the Chief of Staff did not dispute his assessment. Mrs Meir asked the defence chiefs whether the evacuation of Soviet families changed their assessment that war was not imminent, and they replied that it did not. She was reassured that Israel would receive ample warning time if the danger were serious and that more troops had been sent to the front lines. In the ministerial meeting that followed Dayan said that both Syria and Egypt were capable of starting a war in a matter of hours,[9] yet there was no suggestion of calling up reserves. Only two operative decisions emanated from that meeting, twenty-four hours before war broke out: to ask the US to contact Moscow and make sure that its clients were not going to cause trouble; to vest the Cabinet's authority to mobilize the reserves in the Prime Minister and Minister of Defence. Despite the confidence of the army chiefs, Mrs Meir was extremely uneasy about the situation. She may well have remembered her encounter with King Hussein. Yet present at the meeting were the Chief of Staff, Elazar, and two former chiefs of staff, Dayan and Haim Barlev, who was Minister of Trade and Industry in her government, and she felt that she should not overrule such a group of military experts. She regretted that decision very much, as she recounts in her memoirs: 'I should have overcome my hesitation. I knew as well as anyone else what full-scale mobilization meant ... That Friday morning I should have listened to the warnings of my heart and ordered a call-up.

[I] failed to make that one decision ... and I shall live with that terrible knowledge for the rest of my life.'[10]

At 4 a.m. on 6 October the Prime Minister and Dayan were awakened with intelligence information that Egypt and Syria would start the war at 6 p.m. on the same day. Dayan rushed to consult the military chiefs before meeting ministers. They weighed the options. The most obvious one was a pre-emptive strike by the air force. Elazar supported this course of action, Dayan opposed it, his main reason being that if Israel were to start a war, we might win some military advantages but risk the loss of US support during and after the war. An immediate mobilization of reserves and a strong warning to Cairo and Damascus via the US were other possibilities. Dayan believed that a limited call-up of reserves would suffice to stop the attacks; Elazar demanded a full-scale call-up. The definitive decision on these questions was left to Golda Meir. She decided against a pre-emptive strike, for the same reason as Dayan, and authorized a comprehensive call-up of over one hundred thousand troops. There was a dramatic contrast between the two Arab countries, which commanded large standing armies, and Israel, which was highly dependent on the reserves. This remains an inherent weakness of Israel's defence system.[11] The Prime Minister also told the US ambassador, Kenneth Keating, of the latest information we had of an imminent attack, stressing that Israel would not attack first, and asked the Americans to see whether war could still be prevented by US intervention, either in Moscow or directly with Egypt and Syria.[12] Then Mrs Meir convened her Cabinet. While the ministers discussed the situation, her military adviser, General Israel Lior, broke the news that shooting had started on both fronts at 14.05, four hours before the time predicted by the intelligence.

At the beginning of October the Israeli ambassador to America, Dinitz, had travelled to Israel because of the death of his father. The deputy chief of mission, Mordechai Shalev, a wise and experienced diplomat, acted as chargé d'affaires and carried the burden of the crucial exchanges with the American administration in the first week of October. In my meetings with State Department officials during these fateful months, I also leaned heavily on the assessments available to the Embassy, stressing the 'low probability' of war. A conversation on this subject which particularly stands out in my mind was with Michael Sterner, the head of Egyptian affairs in the State Department. He inquired what we thought of the possibility of a canal crossing by Egyptian troops. Without a shred of hesitation, I replied that we would sink them in the Suez Canal. Such was the confidence which repeated military assessments imbued in us. We sensed no special emergency and Embassy staff made their arrangements for the holiday. I decided to travel with my family to Boston to spend Yom Kippur with friends. On the way I stopped in New York on 4–5 October, to meet Foreign Minister Abba Eban, who had arrived for the General Assembly of the UN. I saw him and his skilful political adviser, Eytan Bentzur, after his meeting with Kissinger on 4 October, and we discussed some of the issues raised. Kissinger had asked Eban about the Syrian and Egyptian troop concentrations and Eban replied, according to the intelligence evaluations, that they were 'annual manoeuvres' and added the view, long held by our military analysts, that without attaining air superiority Egypt would not wage war. We wished each other well over the Yom Kippur holiday and I continued the trip to Boston so as to arrive before the fast set in. We stayed with Elva and Kuna Abroms. Our children and theirs were good friends. After the Yom Kippur eve prayers, 'Kol Nidrei', we chatted late into the night about everything except the possibility of war. As far as the American people were concerned it just was not on the cards. The next morning at 7 a.m. Boston time, the children rushed into our bedroom. They had seen a news flash on television, 'War in the Middle East'. I called the Embassy in Washington and Eban in New York. The shocking news was confirmed. Eban told me that he had been in touch with Kissinger since early morning and he too was surprised. I took the first available flight to Washington to join my colleagues at the Embassy for a non-stop, round-the-clock effort until the war was over.

On the same Friday, 5 October, Shalev received two messages which he transmitted to Kissinger's office in Washington. In the first, Israel asked the US to convey to the Soviet Union, Egypt and Syria that we had no intention of launching a pre-emptive strike. The rationale of that message was that if it was the fear of an Israeli strike which prompted Cairo and Damascus to order troop concentrations, then there was nothing to be alarmed about. This reassurance, which Kissinger conveyed to Dobrynin and to the Egyptian Foreign Minister, who was in New York, only about an hour before the war started, must have provided great relief to the planners of the Yom Kippur War. Its only advantage was that it helped dispel the notion in the US that Israel had attacked first. The message also stressed that, if attacked, Israel would retaliate with great force. The second message, which Shalev submitted in writing, included the up-to-date intelligence estimate and in essence, most surely reflected the views of the chief of military intelligence, General Eliyahu Zeira. It read: 'Our assessment is that the alert measures being taken by Egypt and Syria are in part connected with manoeuvres (as regards Egypt) and in part due to fears of offensive actions by Israel. We consider the opening of military operations against Israel by the two armies as of low probability.'[13] How could Israel and the United States misapprehend so badly a gathering storm of such immensity? First we must look at Israel because it was our security that was put in jeopardy and it is our responsibility to make sure that similar blunders never recur.

*

The security doctrine of Israel is conceived and nurtured by the Minister of Defence in careful deliberation and analysis with the General Staff of the IDF. Parts of it may be presented to the Cabinet and shared, in one way or another, with the top echelon of the bureaucracy engaged in defence and foreign affairs. It is based on military as well as political premises. Dayan's basic military concepts were shaped by his experiences as Chief of Staff in the Sinai Campaign in 1956 and Minister of Defence in the Six Day War in 1967. In both, the Arabs suffered resounding defeats and it was therefore inconceivable to him, as it was to the officers of the General Staff, that they would initiate a war which would most certainly end in their defeat (as indeed it did). According to this concept, an essential condition for an Egyptian decision to wage war was mastery of the air, so that a ground attack would have some chance of success. In 1973 Egypt and Syria had nothing like air superiority. The Soviet Union, which could have encouraged the Arabs to attack Israel and thereby demonstrate the superior quality of their weapon systems, had a cooler relationship with Sadat than in previous years. The Kremlin was currently giving priority to détente and rapprochement with the US rather than to the achievement of further gains in the Middle East. At the same time, Israel had improved its relations with the Nixon administration. All these developments were far from favourable to an Arab initiative. There was a strong belief, especially in the intelligence community, that if, contrary to all expectation, the Arabs decided to attack, there would be at least forty-eight hours' warning. On 6 October we hardly had ten hours of advance warning. If these, and other, assumptions were disproved and the Arabs nevertheless decided to attack, it was assumed that the fortified front lines (the Barlev line on the Suez) and the standing army and air force would be able to contain the onslaught and hold the line until reserves were mobilized and ready to counter-attack. As it turned out the front-line troops were inadequate, and had severe difficulty in holding the lines, being vastly outnumbered by Egyptian and Syrian forces. Moreover, the Arabs were shielded by an umbrella of fixed and mobile Sam missiles batteries, densely deployed, which limited the capability of the Israeli air force to block the offensive. True, they did not achieve air superiority, but the Russian missile defence system to some degree offset one of Israel's foremost advantages – air power. The new anti-tank Sager missile helped shield the Syrian and Egyptian tanks and inflicted heavy losses on our armoured corps. The assumption that the standing army and air force could contain a double-fronted attack proved erroneous. Furthermore, Israel paid a heavy price in casualties for its reluctance to deploy a precautionary number of reserve units. Hasty mobilization, the lack of time for units to rally and regroup properly, as they had done in 1967, and their swift dispatch into battle, caused initial setbacks in our counter-attack. The fact that the Egyptian and Syrian armies had mastered their new equipment, and were more determined to fight than in the past, compounded the difficulties of the Israel Defence Forces.

Part of the mistaken 'conception' was what Abba Eban called 'military euphoria' – like the statement of General Sharon in a newspaper interview that 'with our present boundaries we have no security problem'. Or the assertion of the Deputy Prime Minister, Yigal Allon, that 'Sadat has no military option', or Dayan proclaiming on Massada 'a new State of Israel with broad frontiers, strong and solid, with the authority of the Israel government extending from the Jordan to the Suez Canal'.[14] It was this concept, this confidence, that the Arabs had no option but to come to the negotiating table that was at the heart of the 1973 débâcle. It was a mixture of political and military euphoria which led to misjudgements, and the unfounded overconfidence which prevented vital precautionary measures such as mobilization. Dayan explained in later years that he shared the view that Egypt and Syria would not wage war until they were able to balance our military force.[15] He was not just a party to this conception, a bystander. His speeches and writings prove that, to a large extent, he was the author and one of the prime architects of the political and military thinking between 1967 and 1973, and few dared challenge his authority.

On the west side of the Suez Canal, on the other hand, Sadat assumed that unless there was a military move to shake negotiations out of their impasse, there was no chance of regaining the Sinai. Knowing that Egypt and Syria could not win an all-out war, he contented himself with a limited operation that would quickly establish a bridgehead on the peninsula and hold it until the big powers intervened. He succeeded in forging strategic and tactical cooperation with Syria, in maintaining a very high degree of secrecy and deceiving Israeli and Western intelligence by camouflaging his offensive preparations as military exercises. To achieve these limited purposes and thereby enhance Egypt's self-respect and self-esteem, he was ready to sacrifice the lives of thousands of his countrymen. The timing of the attack was carefully chosen by Sadat and Assad – Yom Kippur, the day of atonement, the most holy day in the Jewish calendar, when great numbers of Israelis were fasting and absorbed in prayer and meditation. It was the convergence of Sadat's deception and Dayan's self-deception, and the overconfidence of the Israeli High Command, which produced such a cataclysm in the history of our young state.

Still it is puzzling how the United States could be lulled into complacency and be surprised by the outbreak of the Yom Kippur War. The dialogue between Israel and Washington was close and wide-ranging. The Egyptian and Syrian theatres, which posed a direct threat to Israel, were kept under constant observation and surveillance by Israeli military and civil intelligence, and as far as the US was concerned there could hardly have been a more credible source of assessment than the Israeli briefings. There was no divergence of opinion on the facts which both intelligence services collected independently. This is why Kissinger could establish that 'our own reporting was a mirror image of Israel's'.[16] The problem was the evaluation of Sadat's intentions. No intelligence service can scrutinize the heart and mind of an opponent if he is determined to conceal his intentions. This was the case with Sadat; his deceptive intentions were kept a well-guarded secret. Like Golda Meir, Kissinger used strong words to lament the mistakes: 'We had become too complacent about our own assumptions. We knew everything but understood too little. And for that the highest officials – including me – must assume responsibility.'[17]

The combined attack by Egypt and Syria on 6 October commenced in the south with heavy artillery bombardment and air raids. After about ten minutes Egyptian forces started to cross the Suez along a very wide front. In the north the Syrians followed their initial artillery barrages with an assault of 500 tanks, attacking our troops and the 177 IDF tanks positioned on the Golan Heights. The forty-four artillery pieces, which our command believed could contain an offensive, were outnumbered fifteen to one by the 690 pieces of artillery which the Syrians deployed in this war zone. By midnight of the first day, thousands of Egyptian troops and 300 tanks managed to cross to the east bank of the Suez, and they were reinforced by another 600 tanks which traversed the canal on the second day. The 276 tanks and 48 artillery guns which our troops operated were no match for the 2,200 tanks and 2,000 artillery guns which Egypt threw into the battle. The discrepancy in the numbers of troops was even more staggering: Egypt started the war with about 100,000 soldiers compared to 8,500 on the Israeli side, while Syria deployed 45,000 troops against 5,000 Israeli soldiers.[18] It was the sacrifice and gallantry of our soldiers which blocked a deeper advance of the two attacking armies until the first reserve units arrived. When they did, fathers and sons often fought on the same front. Egypt and Syria (with Soviet advice) nevertheless accomplished a great deal: they surprised the IDF; they identified some of our weak points and built a strategy and battle tactics which required new answers; they inflicted heavy casualties on us and limited the ability of our air force to help the ground forces. All through the war they had an open supply line from the Soviet Union.

Eventually our newly mobilized reserve divisions arrived in the Sinai and on the Golan. The tank battles in both theatres were ferocious. After four days of fighting, by 10 October, the Syrian attack had been contained and during the next two days the IDF counter-attacked, recaptured the Golan and advanced some fifteen kilometres into Syrian territory. Other Arab countries rushed to assist them; an Iraqi armoured column attempted to reach the front lines and lost fifty tanks without a single loss to the Israeli forces, while a Jordanian armoured brigade also crossed the border into Syria. It was the bare minimum that King Hussein felt he must do in order to remain in step with Egypt and Syria. Basically he kept Jordan out of the war and thus saved many Jordanian lives. The Israeli air force braved the surface-to-air missile defences and suffered considerable losses. After six days of heroic fighting the tide on the Golan turned and IDF units stopped about forty-five kilometres from Damascus.

The Egyptian war theatre was very different from the Syrian. The desert expanses were vast and suitable for tank warfare. The largest tank battles since the end of the Second World War were fought in the Sinai. The first Israeli counter-attack, carried out only two days after the outbreak of the war, had been prepared hastily and underestimated the tenacity of the Egyptians. It could not but fail. It was one of the most difficult moments of the war. The army high command and the government then realized that this was not going to be a short war, like the Suez Campaign or the Six Day War, and that in view of the losses, there was an urgent need for more tanks and other equipment. After the IDF had consolidated their positions in the north, full weight was given to the battles with Egypt. Instead of a frontal counter-offensive it was decided to cross the Suez Canal, establish a bridgehead on its west side and clear out the surface-to-air missile batteries along the canal. Generals Ariel Sharon and Avraham Adan commanded this daring and costly operation. As the west side was not covered by the anti-aircraft missile umbrella, the Israeli air force had greater freedom of action and aided the advancing troops. The operation started on 16 October, the fighting was very heavy and the terrain completely new. Slowly our troops made their way north, destroying fortifications and missiles, and cutting off the two Egyptian armies – the Second and Third – on the east side from their main supply line on mainland Egypt. Hundreds of Israeli soldiers lost their lives and thousands were injured in this operation, but its success prompted Sadat to seek a cease-fire. When it came into force on 22 October, Israel held a line on the west bank of the Suez which stretched from the Gulf of Suez up to Ismailiah. The town of Suez and the Egyptian Third Army were completely encircled by Israeli troops. In sixteen days of severe fighting on two fronts Israel lost 2,564 soldiers and 6,923 were injured. These were the second highest losses since the War of Independence in 1948, and enormously painful. Egypt and Syria lost many thousands in dead and injured. Militarily, Israel won the war, but its deterrent capacity was adversely affected. The Arabs had proved that they could initiate a war and surprise Israel and the US. The extended lines, from the Suez to Kuneitra, were no guarantee against attack, though they made the defence of the country easier and the counter-offensive more promising.[19] It was a war in which modern technology, anti-aircraft and anti-tank missiles and sophisticated electronic equipment, played an important role. It was a battle of minds and of wills but also a testing ground of superpower high technology. It taught many lessons and required new thinking.

Parallel to the war, an ongoing diplomatic struggle was unfolding. Its centre was Washington, where President Nixon was immersed in the Watergate scandal and considerably weakened. In our Embassy, we struggled to maintain robust support from the administration, from Congress and from the American people, to ensure that everything would be done to deter direct Soviet involvement, to secure a constant flow of arms and ammunition to our embattled troops and to guard against hostile initiatives in the Security Council. Ambassador Dinitz, Shalev, the defence attaché, General Mordechai Gur (Chief of Staff after the Yom Kippur War), myself and a small group of highly dedicated foreign-service officers worked day and night towards these objectives. Our wives volunteered to help cope with a constant chain of inquiries from Israelis, and from the wider public, to enlist Israeli pilots and officers who were called up while studying or working in the US and insure that they had transport to Israel. Everything we did was under the shadow of success or failure on the battlefield; our hearts quickened with news of success and our spirits dipped when word of battlefield reverses and the names of fallen soldiers came in.

The most pressing issue from Israel's point of view was the rapid attrition of fighter planes, tanks and a wide range of other equipment, and the need for swift replacements. The fierce battles on the Golan Heights and in the Sinai were not only costly in human casualties, but also caused a very high rate of material losses. In anticipation of a rapid Israeli victory, the US adopted a low-profile policy, which, when translated into reality, meant great caution in supplying Israel with the weapons that, with every passing hour, became more vital. El-Al planes, stripped of their insignia, carried some equipment that was nowhere near satisfying the urgent requirements of the army and air force. On 9 October Dinitz and General Gur briefed Kissinger on the extent of the Israeli losses in the first three days of the war: forty-nine fighter planes (including fourteen Phantoms) and 500 tanks had been lost, (400 in the Sinai). Dinitz and Gur made every possible effort to impress upon Kissinger the urgency of new supplies.

The ambassador also told the Secretary of State that Golda Meir was prepared to travel to Washington for a special meeting with the President to convince him of the need for rapid shipments of armaments. Kissinger politely turned down this request, and rightly so. He knew that the visit would not remain a secret. It would be construed by the Arabs and Soviets as a sign of panic and exploited by their propaganda as evidence of collusion between America and Israel. Most importantly, he stressed that she was needed in Jerusalem, and this was true too. After the agony and qualms which the Prime Minister had experienced over the events leading up to the war, from the moment hostilities broke out she proved to be a tower of strength. While Dayan and army commanders were depressed at reverses on the battlefield and Dayan even offered his resignation, she remained cool and resolute, cutting through the complicated details of combat operations and leading the Cabinet to adopt tough decisions.

When the initial assumption of Kissinger and his colleagues on the Washington Special Action Group (WSAG) that it would be a short war and that Israel would win in a few days proved unrealistic, he became prepared to give up the low-profile policy and step up arms shipments. Some of his colleagues were apprehensive of the effect it would have on US–Arab relations and on the oil supply from Gulf countries. But Kissinger's view prevailed and he recommended to the President the acceleration of shipments of anti-tank weapons, air-to-air missiles and electronic equipment, assuring Israel that all her tank and aircraft losses would be replaced. This was a crucial decision, which instilled a measure of confidence in the army high command. However, the logistics had still to be worked out and they were not easy. European countries, including Britain, were reluctant to allow aeroplanes carrying weapons to Israel to refuel for fear of an oil embargo. Tanks could only be transported in giant American cargo planes. Officials in the Pentagon had referred Dinitz and General Gur to the State Department and vice versa. The mood in our Embassy turned very sombre in view of the delay. Israel was bleeding and in Washington we encountered first a low-profile policy and then, when a favourable presidential decision was eventually taken, logistical difficulties.

On 10 October, a massive Soviet airlift started to transport military equipment to Syria, and later to Egypt and even Iraq. After the Syrian battle reverses the Soviets became more bellicose, escalating their threats, and urging Jordan and Algeria to join the war. Kissinger and other top US officials realized that the arms balance might tilt against us, that the war might be prolonged and Israel exposed to increased danger. In spite of repeated attempts, Kissinger was unable to obtain Sadat's agreement to a cease-fire in the positions currently occupied.

A method had to be found to accelerate arms shipments to Israel. Kissinger informed Nixon that the Pentagon could provide three giant cargo planes for that purpose. President Nixon then made one of his boldest decisions, to mount an immediate airlift to Israel carried out by American planes. He told Kissinger: 'We are going to get blamed just as much for three planes as for three hundred.'[20] After a presidential decision of that magnitude the formidable capacity of the Military Airlift Command was ordered into operation. Giant C-141 and C-5a planes arrived the next day, 14 October, in Israel with tanks, anti-tank missiles and other essential equipment. The airlift could ship up to one thousand tons daily and for its duration 566 flights of the giant cargo planes landed in Israel, replacing lost equipment and providing the tools for the postwar reconstruction of the defence forces. To finance the arms Kissinger suggested to his colleague an aid package of $3 billion. Eventually President Nixon proposed to Congress, on 19 October, an aid bill of $2.2 billion, the highest Israel had ever received.[21] Israel would always remember this enormous US assistance in its hour of great peril. The Arab reaction was bitter and on 20 October King Faisal of Saudi Arabia announced an oil embargo on the United States.

As Secretary of State, Kissinger was the main anchor and architect of US policy during this crisis. The WSAG, under his chairmanship, convened daily.[22] He realized the dangers inherent in the coordinated attack on Israel and wanted to assure Israel's security, to deter any sudden involvement by the Soviets while at the same time maintaining détente. US relations with the Arab countries and the guarantee of a free flow of oil to the industrialized world were also of importance to him. From the very first days of the war he pondered how to promote peace negotiations. The first official message from Moscow to Nixon was phrased in a conciliatory tone, 'sharing' American concern at the developments and reminding Washington that they had warned in the past of the danger of a con-flagration. With this in mind Kissinger attempted to prompt the Soviets into joint action in the Security Council for a cease-fire. The Arabs, riding high on the battlefield, were reluctant to cooperate. Assuming that a cease-fire resolution calling for the return to the 6 October lines was unattainable, Kissinger aimed at a 'cease-fire in place', which would stop the fighting with the troops remaining in their positions when it went into force and move the conflict from the battlefield to the diplomatic arena. The Rus-sians came close to agreeing to such a resolution by the Security Council, with the US and Soviet Union abstaining. However, Sadat undermined the initiative and the Russians were reluctant to overrule him. Only after Israel's counter-offensive succeeded, with the IDF controlling an eleven-kilometre-deep salient on the Egyptian side of the Suez Canal, and Kos-ygin's visit to Cairo, did Moscow urge a 'cease-fire in place'. Israel had changed the course of the war and held important territorial cards in Syria and Egypt for future negotiations. On 19 October, Kissinger was invited by Breznev to Moscow to negotiate a cease-fire. The negotiations resulted in agreement on Security Council Resolution 338, which called on the parties to agree a cease-fire 'in the positions they now occupy', also to start 'the implementation of Security Council Resolution 242 in all of its parts'. The important achievement of this resolution was that it went beyond the cease-fire and, for the first time, specified that (direct) 'negotiations between the parties concerned under appropriate auspices' for a durable peace would take place. Together with Security Council Resolution 242, Resolution 338 remained an inseparable part of all the peace negotiations, from Camp David to Madrid and then Oslo.

During the war Kissinger kept in constant touch with the Soviet Union and maintained an open 'back-channel' to Sadat, exchanging messages with his national security adviser, Hafiz Ismail. The strongest signal to Moscow to refrain from direct intervention in the war was conveyed by moving the Sixth Fleet aircraft carriers to the eastern Mediterranean. But given Soviet behaviour in the war, their threats to Israel, the airlift to Arab countries and the fact that a number of Russian airborne divisions were put on alert, additional hands-off warnings were needed. This Kissinger achieved in his talks with Dobrynin. On 12 October, he told the Russian ambassador that 'any Soviet military intervention would be resisted and wreck the entire fabric of US–Soviet relations'. Similar words of warning were voiced by him on other occasions during the war, which was also a testing time for the détente, and had all the characteristics of Cold War confrontation.

During my years in Washington I participated in a number of meetings with Kissinger, including his conversation with Dayan after the Yom Kippur War. He had a profound understanding of Israel and of the Middle East, and an acute sense of our domestic scene. But he was first and foremost a strong defender of US interests and a champion of peace. The Arabs had also recognized this and they accepted him as a welcome negotiator in their courts and chanceries. During the first week of the war, when the US were following their low-profile policy and restrained arms supply to Israel, there was great anguish in Jerusalem and among our friends in the United States. But the policy was adopted by the admin- istration with the President and the Secretaries of State and Defence concurring in it, based on the belief that Israel could hold out even when she had been taken by surprise and was at a colossal disadvantage. For the US, the issue was its interests in the Arab world and its concern for Soviet reaction; for us it was the feeling that more and better equipment could have saved lives.

12

American–Soviet Confrontation and the Aftermath of the Yom Kippur War

The Yom Kippur War did not end on 22 October 1973 with the adoption of Security Council Resolution 338 on a cease-fire. Hostilities continued, and the Israeli army both tightened its noose around the Egyptian Third Army Corps and encircled the town of Suez. Tens of thousands of Egyptian soldiers were cut off from their supply line leading from Cairo to Suez and across the canal to the eastern bank.

The timing of the cease-fire was a subject of sharp exchanges between Kissinger and Prime Minister Meir, when the Secretary of State stopped in Israel for five hours (at Mrs Meir's request) on his way from Moscow. Israel, now on the offensive, could use any extra time to consolidate her military deployment in a way that might be helpful in future negotiations. It was felt in Israel that Egypt had started the war and now, after the military map had changed in Israel's favour and it was on the way to reaping the fruits of its sacrifices, it was to be robbed of them by an imposed, premature cease-fire. On 23–25 October there was acute tension between the US and Israel, to the point that President Nixon threatened 'to dissociate himself' from Israel if fighting continued. Once Resolution 338 was passed the US strongly urged Israel to hold its fire.[1] Having in mind future initiatives towards reaching an accommodation between Israel and Egypt and the need to salvage détente with the Soviet Union, Nixon and Kissinger decided to do all they could to save the Egyptian Third Army.

The Security Council reconvened on 23 October, and passed a second resolution, 339, calling for an immediate cessation of hostilities and for the dispatch of UN observers to supervise the cease-fire. The Soviets, aware that Egypt was in danger of having its Third Army destroyed, stepped up their threats and intimidation of Israel. On 24 October, Breznev wrote to Nixon that if the US could not 'act' together with the Soviet Union to stop the fighting, they would 'consider the question of taking appropriate steps unilaterally. Israel cannot be permitted to get away with the violations.'[2] American intelligence reported a series of ominous Soviet military moves which could have been a precursor to direct intervention: the alert order of seven airborne divisions was heightened; the cargo planes which had carried arms to Egypt and Syria returned to their bases in Russia and could serve as troop carriers, the Soviet fleet in the Mediterranean was reinforced.

In sharp contrast to Moscow's lethargic attitude towards a cease-fire during the first two weeks of the war, now, suddenly, every hour seemed to count. Breznev's message required a response in kind in order to prevent Soviet moves which might be irrevocable. When Kissinger conveyed its content to the President, Nixon authorized him to order the US forces to be on a state of alert. The Secretary of State convened the top security chiefs who decided the level of alert. At the same time, they resolved to increase pressure on Israel to stop the fighting. Nixon cautioned Breznev that any attempt to introduce Soviet troops into the area would contravene the American–Soviet agreement (of 22 June 1973) on the prevention of nuclear war. The confrontation continued and on 25 October American intelligence reported that a Soviet ship, which could be carrying nuclear arms, had arrived in Alexandria. The fear that the Soviet Union might misinterpret the Watergate crisis and view it as a weakening factor was very much on the minds of American policy makers. Nixon therefore ordered Kissinger to develop contingency plans for the dispatch of US forces to the Middle East, in case of direct Russian intervention. Soon afterwards, on 25 October, the Security Council reconvened and the two superpowers agreed on a resolution that excluded the participation of either Soviet or American forces in the supervision of the cease-fire. It was the third resolution to halt the Yom Kippur War, Resolution 340. This time it was respected by all parties and the war stopped. It also ended the Soviet–American nuclear confrontation which, although it had lasted only fifteen hours, on 24–25 October, had been fraught with danger.

Of the four wars Israel had fought in its first twenty-five years, the Yom Kippur War had the most potent global dimension, and the most dangerous one. In later years questions were asked whether the American forces should have been ordered to be on such a high state of alert. It is possible that now, after the crumbling of the Soviet empire, we shall learn more of Moscow's intentions at the time. Yet in October 1973 decisions had to be taken according to the available information and potential risks. Having followed this war hour by hour from Washington, I felt then, and am convinced now, that the decision was right. The clear and unequivocal assertion of US power probably prevented bolder Russian threats and strengthened the US position in the Middle East. The limitations of détente subsequently became apparent; as far as disarmament was concerned the Nixon–Breznev agreements were valuable. The Soviet decision to allow Russian Jews to emigrate to Israel must be credited to détente. However, the translation of détente into a meaningful superpower dialogue to prevent regional crises was still in its infant stages and less effective than had been hoped. Although it had a restraining effect during the crisis, the two superpowers still reached the brink of confrontation when they perceived a danger to their real interests in the Middle East.[3]

The oil embargo which the Arab states had imposed on the US, the cut in oil production and the increase in oil prices created a worldwide energy crisis which had adverse effects on the industrialized countries of Western Europe and Japan. As the US imported only 6 per cent of its oil from Arab sources, it was less severely affected. The fear of the oil crisis was one of the main causes for a reserved attitude on the part of Western Europe towards Israel in its hour of peril, a caution which permanently coloured Israel's perception of Europe.

In the wider Middle East context, US assistance to Israel was another demonstration that Washington would not stand idly by when needed by its friends and allies. In 1958 it had helped the government of Lebanon by landing marines on its shores. In 1970 it had enlisted Israel's help when King Hussein was in danger from Syria and in 1973 it had mounted a massive airlift to Israel. More recently, in 1991, together with Britain and others, it rescued Kuwait from annihilation by Iraq. In spite of the 1973 defeat, Sadat felt that Egyptian honour, indeed Arab honour, was restored by his, and President Assad's, coordinated attack on Israel, and that his limited objectives were achieved. He also recognized that American influence on Israel saved the Egyptian Third Army Corps and his country from a devastating defeat.

Postwar Agreements

The pivotal role that Kissinger played during the war placed the Nixon administration in a unique position to mediate peace. Taking the view that the Middle East conflict could not be left to simmer any longer, because the risks were too high, Kissinger moved swiftly to obtain the agreement of all parties to negotiate. At the end of October 1973 Golda Meir came to Washington to coordinate policy in light of the new situation. I vividly remember her visit. She was a changed person, her mood sombre, bordering on bitterness. The ordeal of the previous weeks had left deep wounds. The heavy casualties suffered by Israel during the war were a source of continuous pain, and she was disappointed that Israel had not been allowed to pursue its offensive. Her talks with Nixon and Kissinger were not all smooth sailing. The burning questions of the time were the need to supply the Third Army via Israeli lines, the disengagement of forces with Egypt, the early release of our prisoners of war and the reopening of free navigation to Elath by lifting the blockade at the entrance of the Gulf of Aqaba, at the Bab al-Mandam Straits. Following the talks with Prime Minister Meir, Kissinger paid his first visit to Cairo and on 7 November

met President Sadat, whose prime concern was the release of his beleagu-
ered Third Army and the encircled town of Suez from IDF siege. Once the
firing stopped, Israel had no intention of resuming it and the main thrust
of the postwar policy was to get the prisoners of war home and bring
Egypt to the recognition that direct contact was the best way to solve the
urgent military issues. The Cabinet therefore approved the supply of food
and medicines to the Third Army and to the town of Suez. Sadat was
relieved to learn of Israel's position and agreed to talks between Israeli and
Egyptian officers to work out the details of disengagement between the
two armies. They took place at kilometre 101 on the Cairo–Suez road and
were dubbed the 'Kilometre 101' negotiations. The Israeli team was headed
by General Aharon Yariv, and the Egyptian team by General Abdul Gani
al-Gamasi. It was an important step and a welcome change from the
Arabs' consistent refusal to talk directly to Israeli representatives. The talks
progressed well until slowed down by Kissinger, who wanted to preserve
his control over the negotiations and prepare the ground for the next
step – the Geneva Peace Conference. Moreover, in his talks with President
Sadat, Kissinger found the Egyptian leader amiable and secured his consent
to the re-establishment of diplomatic relations between Egypt and the
US.[4]

The convening of the Geneva Conference was beset by difficulties;
Kissinger laboured hard to ensure the participation of Syria, alas without
success. Assad's intrinsic obstinacy surfaced anew in his insistence that his
country's participation would depend on an agreement to disengage forces
with Israel, including the Golan Heights. Another stumbling-block related
to the Palestinian issue. In November 1973 an Arab summit conference in
Algiers recognized the Palestine Liberation Organization (PLO) as the 'sole
legitimate representative of the Palestinian people'. Israel objected to the
mention of Palestinian representation in the invitation to the Geneva
Conference. The Yom Kippur War had not directly affected the Palestinians, yet their participation at Geneva might have presented an opportunity for first contacts between Israel and the PLO. However, such a
notion sat ill with the Meir–Dayan perception of this organization as a
terrorist body. At the time, Israel's policy was still based on a mistaken
belief that accommodation with the Palestinians in the territories could
be reached without the PLO. The Geneva Conference convened on 21
December, with Foreign Minister Abba Eban representing Israel and his
colleagues from Egypt and Jordan taking part. Kissinger and the Soviet
Foreign Minister, Gromiko, were in the chair. Syria's absence only
reinforced the feeling that President Assad was a most difficult partner in
negotiations and Syria would therefore be the last to conclude an agreement with Israel. The participants agreed that the first step on the way to
peace must be agreement on the disengagement of forces. The conference

then adjourned indefinitely. Its achievements were modest but it had at least brought former combatants together around the same table.

The next phase was the agreement on the disengagement of military forces between Israel and Egypt. Soon after the Israeli elections on 31 December, at which the Meir government was returned to power, Dayan gave Kissinger a rough outline of a possible disengagement plan. He also encouraged him to return to the Middle East to help negotiate it. The American Secretary of State received similar signals from Sadat, who suggested that Kissinger stay in the area until agreement was accomplished. In this first attempt at shuttle diplomacy, travelling between Jerusalem and Cairo, Kissinger succeeded in narrowing the gaps and, on 18 January 1974 the disengagement agreement was signed at Kilometre 101.

The negotiations with President Assad of Syria were much more complicated and stretched over a longer period of time. They were described by William Quandt as 'murderously difficult'.[5] Between January and May 1974, Israeli and Syrian representatives came to Washington for talks on the agreement and Kissinger paid a number of visits to Jerusalem and Damascus. Assad wanted an agreement, but on terms that would show that he had done better than Sadat in the negotiations. He therefore insisted on an Israeli withdrawal beyond the salient it had occupied during the Yom Kippur War and also redeployment from the town of Kuneitra, which Israel had conquered in the 1967 war. Israel did not see any reason to reward the Syrian President for his aggression and refused to give in. After months of negotiations, sometimes on the verge of crisis and breakdown, Assad agreed that Kuneitra would become part of the United Nations buffer zone and on 31 May the Israeli–Syrian Disengagement of Forces Agreement was signed in Geneva by military officers. Prisoners of war were exchanged. The US committed itself to conduct reconnaissance flights and supply their results to both countries. It further promised Assad that the disengagement agreement was the first step towards peace according to Security Council Resolution 338. As Syria did not accept Resolution 242 this was her way of indirectly acknowledging that resolution, which remained an agreed framework for the solution of the Arab–Israeli conflict. Twenty-eight years later, in the absence of a peace agreement with Syria, the Disengagement Agreement is still the only legal document governing relations between the two countries. The Golan Heights area remains quiet and no Israeli soldiers have lost their lives in combat on this front since 1974. However, Damascus remains a centre for terrorist organizations and Syria is aiding the Hizbullah in Lebanon by allowing arms and money from Iran to flow freely to them. Following the agreement, Israel was assured of a continuous supply of aid and arms from the US to maintain the balance.

The seven months between November 1973 and May 1974 produced considerable success for Henry Kissinger's active diplomacy. The disengagement agreements with Egypt and Syria were the first Israeli–Arab accords since the armistice agreements of 1948–9. Both agreements were bilateral and contained reciprocal contractual undertakings. Both were accompanied by American political and economic commitments. Kissinger achieved a remarkable de-escalation in the conflict. He initiated direct contracts between Israel and Egypt; neutralized the Soviet Union, preventing it from participating, or rather interfering, in efforts to promote agreement; widened the rift between Sadat and the Soviet leadership; re-established relations between the US and Egypt in February 1974; and negotiated the lifting of the oil embargo on the US. Kissinger's step-by-step diplomacy proved to be the correct approach, possibly the only one, to the long road leading to the solution of this complex conflict. These achievements demonstrated to the Arabs that only the US had the power, influence and resources to promote peace. In the case of Egypt the first bricks were laid for the future peace agreement with Israel. The rapport between Kissinger and President Sadat served American interests well and Egypt, in turn, received an aid package of $250 million from the US. Kissinger's envoys constantly updated King Faisal of Saudi Arabia, King Hussein of Jordan and other Arab leaders. They, in turn, broadened Arab support for his diplomacy and helped in creating an atmosphere conducive to President Nixon's visit to the Middle East in June 1974.

The Yom Kippur War was first and foremost a supreme test of Israel's ability to cope with a two-pronged surprise attack by Egypt and Syria. Although it ended in victory, the war tempered the boundless self-confidence resulting from the Six Day War and led to a more energetic effort to work for peace. The US commitment to Israel had also been tested in an unprecedented manner, and the stalwart alliance between the two countries proved to be resilient and valuable to both. For its part, Israel was true to its policy of not asking for US troops to defend the country; all we wanted were the 'tools', and the rest was left to the Israeli Defence Forces to accomplish. The other side of the coin was that Israel's dependence on the US was more evident than ever before. It henceforth became an inseparable element of our policy-making and provided Washington with an added leverage to promote peace on the basis of a reasonable compromise.

The war had a traumatic effect on the Israeli domestic scene. Golda Meir described the postwar feeling in the country very succinctly: 'Much of the outcry was genuine. Most of it, in fact, was a natural expression of outrage over a fatal series of mishaps that had taken place.'[6] A commission of inquiry headed by the president of the Supreme Court, Justice Shimon Agranat, was nominated; the term 'political earthquake' was frequently used to describe the consequences of the war. The preliminary findings of the commission were published in April 1974. They absolved the politicians of 'direct responsibility' for their erroneous assessments before the war and for the unpreparedness of the IDF, and put the burden of responsibility on the army high command. The Chiefs of Staff and of Intelligence were forced to resign. The findings remained controversial, because they evaded the question of ministerial responsibility; people could not accept that Dayan, as Minister of Defence, carried no responsibility for the surprise attack and would emerge unscathed. Dayan sensed that he no longer enjoyed the confidence of the nation and twice submitted his resignation to the Prime Minister, the first time while the war was still raging and then again after it was over. On both occasions Golda asked him to stay on. Her notion of collective responsibility meant that she shared the blame for the Defence Minister's mistakes. However, the criticism and soul-searching went beyond this to the basic assumptions of the Meir–Dayan–Galili approach that Israel must cling to the territories, establish an unassailable position on the ground and wait for a telephone call from the Arabs expressing their readiness to make peace. Dayan nevertheless repeated his hard-line convictions on the eve of the December 1973 elections. On 5 December he said that if the Labour Party were to decide to allow Palestinian self-determination, he would leave the party. He also reiterated his belief in the building of the town of Yamit and of the settlements.[7] The military victory of the war gave him some sense of vindication and he would have greatly preferred the public to concentrate on the end results of the war rather than on its origin. In spite of the criticism, the Labour Party led by Golda Meir won the December 1973 elections, but with a reduced majority. Shortly after the preliminary report of the Agranat Commission was published, Dayan resigned from the Cabinet, and on 11 April 1974 Mrs Meir resigned as Prime Minister, after holding the post for five years. Both stayed on until a new government was sworn in in June 1974. Golda Meir was the last Labour Prime Minister to belong to the generation of the founding fathers. The leadership now passed to a new generation. The first Israeli-born Prime Minister, Yitzhak Rabin, formed the new government.

The First Rabin Government

The elections for the leadership of the Labour Party were held in April 1974. The two contesting candidates were Yitzhak Rabin and Shimon Peres; 552 Central Committee members participated in the vote and Rabin won by a margin of seventy-four. However, the rivalry between Rabin and Peres plagued the Labour Party for the next twenty years, contributing to the later loss of power by Labour to Likud and making it harder for the party to regain the confidence of the electorate. Only the cooperation of the two leaders during and after the Oslo negotiations in 1993 eased their antagonism. On 3 June 1974 Rabin presented his government to the Knesset. He declared peace with the Arab countries to be 'the central goal of our policy' and offered his view of why peace had eluded Israel for the preceding twenty-six years: it was, he said, because of the Arab demand for a commitment to withdrawal to the 1967 borders as a precondition for negotiations and their refusal to accept direct negotiations with Israel. Shimon Peres became Minister of Defence and the new Foreign Minister was Yigal Allon. Thus the ministerial career of the brilliant Abba Eban came to an end after nine years as Foreign Minister.

On the eve of Nixon's visit to Israel I cabled from Washington a detailed analysis of his presidency as it related to Israel. Without ignoring the periods of tension and the divergence of views at times, I stressed his unequivocal commitment to the security of Israel; the fulfilment of his promises to ensure that the arms balance would not tilt against us; his strong opposition to an imposed settlement, while constantly seeking ways to promote negotiation and peace and maintain American interests in the Arab world; the unprecedented level of economic assistance which we received under his presidency and his deterrence of the Soviet Union.

On 16 June two weeks after Yitzhak Rabin replaced Golda Meir as Prime Minister, Nixon arrived in Israel. His itinerary in the Middle East started with the first official visit of an American President to Cairo. He received a tumultuous welcome from the Egyptian people. Considering that Egypt had been under strong Soviet influence for twenty years and had received enormous military assistance from Moscow, the warm reception accorded to the American President must have caused reflection in the Kremlin. In Damascus, Nixon obtained Assad's agreement for the re-establishment of diplomatic relations between the US and Syria. In Israel, he received the gratitude of the government and of the Israeli people for his assistance during the Yom Kippur War. As he was being cheered by the welcoming crowds, Nixon remarked to Rabin: 'They know what I have done for Israel.'[8] In talks, the Prime Minister stressed that the next step towards peace with Egypt must include political issues, aiming to attain an agreement to end the tension. The President conveyed his impressions from Cairo, saying that although Sadat had not changed his basic conditions for peace and was insisting on withdrawal to the 1967 border, he did want a political solution and was aiming to move towards economic development.

Only six weeks later Nixon was forced to give up his presidency. On 8 August, Mordechai Shalev hosted a farewell dinner in our honour as we were due to leave Washington shortly. At 9 p.m. we broke with etiquette and assembled around the television screen to watch the President's dramatic announcement of his decision to step down. It was a move designed to forestall his impeachment by Congress because of the Watergate scandal. Although neither I nor my colleagues in the Washington Embassy could find any justification for the Watergate transgressions, we felt that as far as Israel was concerned Nixon had played an important role during a crucial period. Between 1969 and 1974 he had supported our basic policy that there could be no withdrawal without a real contractual peace. Under his leadership the US had provided Israel with unprecedented economic and military assistance. He and Kissinger had taken a firm line against the Soviet Union, deterring direct involvement in the Yom Kippur War. Above all, in our greatest hour of peril, he had ordered a massive airlift of arms and equipment. After the war he gave his full backing to Kissinger's efforts to promote peace. It was a remarkable record. On 9 August President Gerald Ford was sworn in as the first non-elected US President and promptly asked Kissinger to remain as Secretary of State.

One of my last assignments in Washington was to accompany the Israeli Foreign Minister, Yigal Allon, to his meeting with Kissinger on 30 July 1974. Allon came as the representative of the new Rabin government, and brought a clear message to the US: the disengagement agreements were only the first step and we must decide together how to make further progress toward peace. He represented a government whose striving to achieve peace reflected the will of the people. The government was keen to negotiate peace agreements with both Egypt and Jordan. Allon explained that in the Jordanian context Rabin was committed to having an agreement ratified by a general election (a commitment that Golda Meir had made and Rabin adopted). There could, however, be no return to the 1967 lines, and Allon reiterated the essence of the 'Allon Plan' which, practically, would divide the West Bank between Israel and Jordan, but stressing that it had not been approved by the Cabinet. The government was also prepared to return to the Geneva Conference. Kissinger was very receptive to the first part, but thought that an unprepared Geneva Conference, with Russian participation, would be the worst possible course for Israel. He encouraged Allon to formulate proposals for a second, limited agreement with Egypt.

A few days later Hana, our three children and I left Washington after six rewarding years of diplomatic service. During our stay in the US I had had the opportunity to observe closely three Secretaries of State, Dean Rusk, William Rogers and Henry Kissinger. In talent, vision, negotiating skill and drive, Kissinger was outstanding. True, his excessive use of 'constructive ambiguity' made it, at times, difficult to gauge his intentions. Yet his historic role in identifying opportunities for progress toward peace in the Middle East, his step-by-step approach, his untiring efforts to negotiate the agreements with Egypt and Syria and his unfailing commitment to a strong Israel, were enduring landmarks of his statesmanship.

The tasks before Rabin were daunting: to instil a new self-confidence in the country, to oversee the rebuilding of the army under the new Chief of Staff, Lieutenant General Motta Gur, to balance the economic losses of the war and continue with the peace negotiations with Egypt. In September 1974 Rabin travelled to Washington for his first meeting with Gerald Ford. Both men knew each other from earlier meetings and the dialogue between them was easy. Ford wanted to pursue the Kissinger drive for a negotiated settlement; Rabin supported the step-by-step approach, although he was aware that this obliged Israel to return land, which would be irreversible, in exchange for vague commitments. During one of Kissinger's shuttles to Cairo, Rabin asked him to find out from Sadat privately whether he would be willing 'to conclude a separate and full peace agreement with Israel in return for most – or possibly all – of Sinai'. Kissinger's reply was that Sadat could not conclude a separate agreement, 'so the question of what Israel is prepared to pay in return is not relevant now'. Furthermore, at Kissinger's suggestion Rabin wrote a personal letter to Sadat which Kissinger took to the Egyptian President, but he received no reply.[9] In 1974 Sadat still lacked the courage and conviction which he so stirringly displayed in later years. Rabin agreed with Ford that Kissinger should continue with his mediation efforts; the President approved a remarkable list of arms to be sold to Israel, its value amounting to about $750 million.

Soon afterwards, Kissinger embarked on the second stage of negotiations with Egypt, the 'interim agreement'. The Israeli government had hoped that this would include the end of belligerency, but this was not Sadat's idea. He knew exactly what he wanted to achieve; the return of the oil fields at Abu Rodeis and Egyptian control of the strategic Mitla and Giddi passes in the Sinai. He offered very little in return and basically viewed this step as another military disengagement, refusing to move on to broader political issues and terminate the state of war. He knew that his ally, President Assad, was vehemently opposed to an interim agreement and so was the Soviet Union. The Russians did not like the increased American influence in the Middle East brought about by Kissinger's successful diplomacy. From Israel's standpoint Sadat's demands represented major concessions. Abu Rodeis supplied about fifty per cent of Israel's oil requirements and the passes were important militarily if the possibility of war was not to be ruled out. Another important issue was Israel's insistence on keeping the intelligence early-warning station at Umm Khisheiba. Rabin conducted the negotiations together with Peres and Allon, and the three of them felt that Israel could neither grant such far-reaching concessions nor give up such important negotiating cards without a more substantial quid pro quo. Sadat was adamant in his refusal to commit

Egypt to non-belligerency but agreed to the 'non-use of force', which again was vague. To salvage the talks, President Ford decided to pressure Israel, he wrote to the Israeli Prime Minister on 21 March 1975 telling him that he had ordered 'a reassessment of United States policy in the region', which in reality meant a suspension of new military and economic aid to Israel. Rabin read to the Cabinet the full text of Ford's message, which was tough and threatening. Concerned at the implications of an American policy reassessment, the Cabinet was nevertheless convinced that Rabin's opposition to the content of the agreement was justified and that the President's threat did not produce a change of mind. This led to one of the more dramatic confrontations between two statesmen, who were on the most cordial terms, who had known each other for years and held similar views on many strategic issues. Yet in March 1975, Rabin and Kissinger defended different interests. Kissinger was momentarily convinced that the risks of an interim agreement were acceptable to Israel and that failure to reach it spelled the end of his step-by-step policy. As a result Sadat might move closer to Assad's demand to reconvene the Geneva Conference, with Soviet co-chairmanship, and the US would lose control of the process. He was obviously very reluctant to see a major Ford–Kissinger initiative founder. Rabin was conscious that barely eighteen months had passed since the Yom Kippur War, in which the lines in the Sinai had been defended at immense sacrifice. With the resumption of war still possible, he could not concede major negotiating cards in return for vague promises. He did his utmost to explain his views to Kissinger, who construed them, mistakenly, as political weakness. The two statesmen, friends, parted dramatically at Lydda airport on 22 March, with Kissinger's voice choked with tears and many of the journalists who were present also having difficulty in controlling their emotions.[10]

As often happens, time and the imperatives of life have a great healing effect. Kissinger's assertions that Israel had no foreign policy, only a domestic policy, although not totally far-fetched, were superseded by widely held views in the US that the administration should not punish Israel for guarding its security interests. On 21 May seventy-six Senators wrote to the President that every withdrawal by Israel must be conditional on practical steps toward peace by its Arab neighbours, and asking him to be 'responsive to Israel's economic and military needs'.[11] A hard look at other options, like the overall settlement approach, convinced the administration that step-by-step was still the most promising route to progress. At the beginning of June Presidents Ford and Sadat met in Salzburg. Sadat indicated his willingness to pursue the interim agreement, and although he still insisted on receiving the oil fields and the passes in the Sinai, he was now prepared to accept an American presence at the warning station at Umm Khisheiba. Israel also made a unilateral gesture.

On 5 June 1975 the Suez Canal was reopened for international maritime traffic. On 2 June, while President Ford was meeting Sadat in Austria, Rabin notified the President that Israel would thin out its forces in the canal area. On 4 June Allon announced the decision in the Knesset, adding that it was designed to reduce tensions, increase confidence and engender peace. This unilateral decision was appreciated by Sadat.[12] The US and Egypt concluded that the time was ripe to renew the effort for an interim agreement. By mid-June Rabin was back in Washington and the negotiations resumed. In August Kissinger returned to the area and after lengthy negotiations completed the details of the agreement. Sadat agreed that the conflict between the two countries 'shall not be resolved by military force but by peaceful means' and that US personnel would man the Israeli and Egyptian early-warning stations in the newly established buffer zone. Both countries pledged to reach a final and just peace settlement. Egypt obtained control of the passes and of the Abu Rodeis oil fields.

Rabin also negotiated with Kissinger the text of the accompanying Memorandum of Agreement between Israel and the US, guaranteeing the supply of oil if it became unavailable to Israel, and the assurance of consultations in the event of Soviet intervention, as well as arms supply and the granting of a generous aid package ($2.25 billion for 1976). The US also agreed to vote against any attempt in the Security Council to change Resolutions 242 and 338. Israel agreed that the next step with Egypt as well as with Jordan would be a final peace agreement.

Since the Rabat Arab Summit Conference in October 1974, in which the heads of state had recognized that the PLO was 'the sole legitimate representative of the Palestinian people',[13] the PLO and the Palestinian issue had achieved greater prominence. In that context, the US commitment in the memorandum that it would not recognize or negotiate with the PLO until that organization recognized Israel's right to exist and accepted UN Resolutions 242 and 338 was very important. The interim agreement with Egypt was signed on 4 September in Geneva and represented another important step forward in the search for peace.

The first Rabin government, like its predecessors, was compelled to fight terrorism. On 27 June 1976 an Air France plane flying from Tel Aviv to Paris was hijacked and diverted to Entebbe, Uganda; its passengers, among them many Israelis, were held hostage. For days the government negotiated with the hijackers via France; however, when the Chief of Staff told the Prime Minister that a proper military option was available, that was his preferred course of action. After the operational plan was presented to Rabin, to Defence Minister Peres and other top ministers, the decision was made to use force. On 4 July one of the most daring raids ever to be embarked upon was successfully carried out. The Entebbe airport, thousands of miles from Israel, was stormed and the hostages freed. In the afternoon Hana and I went to the American Embassy for the traditional 4 July celebration, which turned into a party to applaud the success of the Entebbe raid. When Rabin arrived he was engulfed in well-deserved congratulations.

In November 1977 the American elections took place and Jimmy Carter, the Democratic candidate, was elected by a narrow margin. Shortly after his inauguration President Carter invited the Israeli Prime Minister to visit the US. In March, Rabin travelled to Washington. He had known Presidents Nixon and Ford personally and, in spite of occasional differences, had had good working relationships with them, while Carter, the man and his policies, were unknown to him. By then, the Secretary of State, Cyrus Vance, had made an exploratory visit to Israel and Arab capitals, and the Carter administration had conducted its own review on the Middle East. The policy which had emerged was based on an unequivocal commitment to the security of Israel and an 'active' peace role for the US. They felt that the step-by-step approach had come to an end and the administration must pursue a comprehensive peace. The Palestinian question, which Kissinger had avoided, must become part of their mediation effort. 'The President and I were convinced that no lasting solution in the Middle East would be possible until, consistent with Israel's right to live in peace and security, a just answer to the Palestinian question could be found, one almost certainly leading to a Palestinian homeland and some form of self-determination,' wrote Vance in later years.[14] In policy towards the Arab world, Carter adhered to the traditional US interests of strengthening moderate Arab regimes, ensuring the flow of oil and preventing superpower confrontation.

Rabin had no difficulty in agreeing with Carter on the main objective; that the US and Israel should aim at achieving an overall settlement during 1977. However, being aware of the restrictive view of peace that prevailed in Arab capitals, Rabin explained that peace was not just the absence of belligerency, but must include concrete steps that would demonstrate the existence of a peaceful relationship. Cyrus Vance conveyed his impression, based on talks he had had with Arab leaders, that the Arabs considered peace to consist in the termination of belligerency and claimed that all the other issues like trade, free movement of people and diplomatic relations, were subject to their own sovereign decisions.

Rabin clearly detected the shift in US policy – a greater emphasis on the Palestinian issue. Carter told him that he saw 'no evidence of Palestinian leaders other than the PLO leadership'.[15] The President also supported the reconvening of the Geneva Conference, another indication that he veered away from the step-by-step approach. Before long, Carter's public statements spelled out the change in policy. He spoke of Israeli withdrawal to the 1967 borders with 'minor modifications', of PLO participation in the negotiations and of a 'Palestinian homeland'. Above all, Carter involved himself in the details of the negotiations to a degree unknown in former administrations. Rabin was unprepared for such a radical shift of policy. His last experience of negotiations was in the excruciating talks on the interim agreement. It was an election year in Israel and the domestic imperatives were hardly taken into account in the American policy review and the timing of the statements indicating change. Party leaders could be expected to bring before the Knesset and the country negotiated agreements for approval, but to embark on an election campaign with untested policy changes was risky. Consequently Rabin reacted somewhat brusquely and the encounter with Carter was less than successful. The tensions with the US found their way into the press and did not add to the popularity of the Rabin government, already in serious difficulty.

Since the beginning of 1976 I had headed the North American Division of the Foreign Ministry. Among my responsibilities was the preparation of the weekly briefings for the Foreign Minister, Allon, to deliver to the Cabinet and I would often discuss the contents with him. Two related issues to which he devoted considerable thought were Jordan and the Palestinians. We detected a slow but constant shift in the US attitude towards the PLO, a change sharper in American public opinion than in the administration. Arafat's appearance at the UN in November 1974 drew attention to the problem and, perhaps in spite of his showmanship, the main issue received prominence. On 12 November 1975, the Deputy assistant secretary of state for Near Eastern affairs, Harold Sanders, stated before a congressional subcommittee that the Palestinian issue was the 'heart of the conflict' and that 'the legitimate interests of the Palestinian Arabs must be taken into account in negotiating an Arab–Israel peace'. A report by a study group of the Brookings Institute published in the same year recommended that 'credible Palestinian representatives who are prepared to accept the existence of Israel should participate in the peace settlement negotiations',[16] so the change of policy on the Palestinian question which Carter articulated was no surprise to us. Yet the prevailing belief in the Israeli government was that despite the Rabat resolutions, King Hussein would be our partner in negotiation on the West Bank. It was wishful thinking, because the Palestinians would not accept it and, after numerous meetings with the king, Allon knew his terms for a peace agreement with Israel. They were total return of the West Bank, including East Jerusalem, and therefore could not constitute a basis for negotiations. Kissinger at some point explored the possibility of a disengagement agreement with Jordan conditional on Israeli withdrawal from the main security line to the east, the bank of the River Jordan, which again was unacceptable to us.

The Rabin government was in any case running out of time. Coalition squabbles caused early elections in May 1977. The agony of the Yom Kippur War was still plaguing the country and a new party, the Democratic Movement for Change, was formed. It split the centre of the political spectrum and reduced support for the sharply divided Labour Party. The result was that for the first time in twenty-nine years the Likud, led by Menachem Begin, won the elections.

13

Begin Elected Prime Minister

The ramifications of the Yom Kippur War were deep and lasting, and the splits and rivalries in the Labour Party distanced it from the electorate. Shortly before the elections, Rabin resigned for personal reasons and Shimon Peres was elected leader of the party. According to the opinion polls he led the election campaign. However, when voting took place on 17 May 1977 the results were devastating for Labour. The Likud Party, headed by the veteran opposition leader, Menachem Begin, won the elections. It emerged with forty-three seats in the Knesset, four more than it had enjoyed in the former Parliament, while Labour lost nineteen seats, leaving it with thirty-two members compared to fifty-one in the eighth Knesset. The Democratic Movement for Change (DMC), composed, to a large degree, of former Labour sympathizers, won fifteen seats. Its leaders, Yigal Yadin, Meir Amit and others, bore a good measure of responsibility for Labour's loss of power after it had headed every government for twenty-nine years. Joining Begin's coalition, the DMC accorded it a more balanced image, being a left-of-centre party, but had limited influence on shaping policy. On 20 June Begin presented his government to the Knesset, after nominating a former Labour leader, Moshe Dayan, as Minister for Foreign Affairs. Ezer Weizman, the former general who had become a Likud politician and was one of the main architects of the Begin victory, became Minister of Defence. In his speech, Begin, like other Prime Ministers before him, called on Arab leaders to meet him to discuss the 'establishment of true peace'.

Dealing with North American affairs in the Foreign Ministry I was the recipient of a large number of inquiries from Americans, individuals as well as organizations, who were extremely concerned by the election of Begin. The US press gave him a less than friendly welcome and fuelled the apprehensions. His reputation as a right-wing hard-liner was at the root of the concern, which was shared by many Israelis. I had known Begin personally since 1967, when he was a member of the Eshkol National Unity Cabinet. I had accompanied distinguished American visitors, people like Senators Yacov Yavetz, Richard Stone and others, who had visited him as the leader of the opposition. In reply to the expressions of concern, I made the point that Begin was now the democratically elected leader and had often displayed statesmanship and responsibility. For the rest, of course, we had to wait for his policies to unfold. From my remarks in various conversations Begin understood that I was not a Likud sympathizer. In 1983 when I was nominated as deputy chief of mission in London he asked my ambassador, Yehuda Avner, whether he was sure that I was 'one of them'. Avner could not reassure him on that point, but said that I followed the practice of the civil service and was a-political in representing the government of the day. Begin left it at that, and to his credit I must add that in his approach to the civil service he followed the British practice of viewing it as non-political, more than other Israeli Prime Ministers before him or after him. I had no doubt that Begin was an ardent believer in his ideology and in his oratory. Now he had to reconcile both with an unsettled reality.

The nomination of Moshe Dayan as Foreign Minister and his acceptance of the post was as meaningful as it was controversial. Begin had a high respect for Dayan's talent and his international reputation. His own party offered few personalities of such high standing and Begin thought that, in spite of his mistakes, Dayan could make a valuable contribution to his government. He knew that on some issues Dayan held hard-line views close to his own, although their approach to the Palestinian question differed. Dayan's presence would also give the government a more moderate appearance. Four days after the elections Begin offered Dayan the Foreign Ministry. It was a difficult decision for a Labour member of Knesset and he asked for some time for reflection. As an ardent follower of Ben-Gurion, who loathed Begin, Dayan basically shared the Labour view of the new Prime Minister, which was less than complimentary. Why then did he accept the job? After the disengagement agreement and the interim agreement with Egypt he was convinced that Sadat wanted peace and saw a historic challenge in helping to forge it. Personally, he was well aware that his public image had been seriously tarnished by the Yom Kippur War and he wanted to be remembered not as the Defence Minister blamed for the outbreak of the war, but rather as a peacemaker. After a few days of soul-searching, Dayan asked Begin for clarification on a number of key points. Aware that the Likud election platform stipulated that Israel's sovereignty should apply to the whole territory between the Mediterranean Sea and the Jordan River, Dayan inquired whether Begin's government would refrain from annexing the territories. Begin agreed that 'while negotiations were in progress' he would not annex the territories. He later added that in any case he would seek Knesset approval by a special majority of sixty-one votes for such a decision. Would Begin agree that the Geneva Conference could reconvene without prior conditions and that the basis for negotiations with the Arabs would be Resolution 242? Begin agreed and added that his government would honour all the agreements entered into by former governments. Would he maintain the status quo on the Temple Mount, prohibiting Jewish prayer near the Mosque, and the existing arrangements at the Tomb of the Patriarchs in Hebron? Begin agreed and said that Dayan could quote him publicly on these issues. Reassured that there was a good measure of pragmatism in Begin's policies, Dayan gave his consent.[1]

Even before the DMC joined the coalition, Begin's alliance with the religious parties enabled him to form a government. For nearly three decades these parties had been partners with Labour in the achievements of modern Israel. After the Six Day War a slow but constant shift to the right became evident in the National Religious Party. The support for 'Greater Israel' became the guiding principle in its platform and the more realistic, moderate elements in the party lost influence. Begin built on that affinity and hammered out a lasting alliance between Likud and the religious parties that kept his party in power for the next fifteen years, long after the Democratic Movement for Change had dissipated. Begin appreciated that he was propelled into power by great numbers of Jews of Sepharadic and oriental origin. He demonstrated respect and affection for this section of the community by bringing some of their prominent leaders, like David Levy, into his government.

After Begin had presented his government to the Knesset, he and Dayan set out to explore possibilities for peace. Both agreed that the attainment of a peace treaty with Egypt should be their main priority. In July 1977 the Prime Minister went to Washington for his first encounter with President Carter. Dayan went with him, which was novel, as Israeli Prime Ministers and their Foreign Ministers seldom travelled together to Washington. The reasons for these solo trips were rooted more in personality clashes than in principle. The meetings with Carter and his team were held on 19–20 July. By then the new US policy principles on the Middle East had been shaped and Carter outlined them to Begin. The main objective was a comprehensive settlement. There would be no imposition of a settlement by the US or any other outside country. The basis of negotiations was peace in exchange for territories according to Resolutions 242 and 338. Final boundaries would be negotiated by the parties and should be defensible. Full peace must include 'full normalization' of relations, open borders and diplomatic relations. The Palestinian issue must be part of the settlement. Carter did not support a Palestinian state but a 'homeland linked to Jordan'.[2]

Begin came with proposals that had been meticulously crafted. He agreed to the convening of the Geneva Conference under the auspices of the US and Soviet Union in accordance with Resolution 338. That implied acceptance by him of Resolution 242, which was part of 338 and was the reason for his walking out of the National Unity Government in 1971.

The Arab sovereign states would participate but a Palestinian delegation or PLO participation in the conference was ruled out. The conference should convene without any prior conditions and with no combined Arab delegation – just national delegations. After the plenary session it should split into bilateral commissions or committees with rotating chairmanships of the two parties, which meant that direct negotiations would be conducted without American or Soviet presence. Should the Arabs reject this procedure, the fall-back position could be bilateral committees convened by the US or 'proximity talks', where both delegations would be in the same building and the US would circulate between them to bridge the gaps. From Begin's position it was clear that he was prepared to embark on a serious negotiating effort. His proposals dealt mainly with procedure, consistent with the view shared by Israeli politicians of both Likud and Labour that the hard-core issues had to be negotiated with the Arabs and not with the US.

Carter made it clear that the West Bank must be part of the negotiations and that the administration strongly objected to settlement building. Begin stated that Israel could not agree to a Palestinian homeland or entity and, on settlements, he said 'we would just have to disagree'.[3] Hence his statement after returning to Israel that Carter and he agreed to disagree. It is hard to establish whether Carter's encounter with a second Israeli Prime Minister left him more favourably impressed than he had been with Rabin. The clash of personalities and conflicting outlooks on how to proceed towards peace undoubtedly created dissonance. Carter was more impressed by Sadat than by Begin, but the President and Vance refrained from confrontations with Israel.

The tense negotiations between Israel and the US on an agreed approach to the Geneva Conference continued during the visit of Dayan to Washington in September. In talks with Vance and Carter, Dayan reiterated the position of the Begin government, offering a slight modification on immediate settlement building. Carter ferociously attacked Israel's settlement policy and maintained that Israel was less flexible than the Arabs. He complained bitterly about statements in Jerusalem that Israel was going to settle hundreds of thousands of Jews in the territories and that there would be no other foreign sovereignty on the West Bank, and said that these statements made it difficult for Sadat and King Hussein to progress towards peace. They actually made him sceptical about whether Israel really wanted peace. Vance explored with Dayan the question of whether Israel would be willing to accept US guarantees against attack. Dayan said that the only guarantee we were looking for was against Soviet intervention. We would deal with the Arabs ourselves. He appreciated the importance of US guarantees but they could not be a substitute for holding on to territories. To Israel's consternation, Dayan finally worked out an agreed Israeli–American document on Geneva, but a joint American–Soviet declaration was published on 1 October, and the gaps remained wide.

Despite the state of war with the Arabs, the Labour governments under Eshkol, Golda Meir and Rabin, had carefully fostered relations with the three Muslim monarchs whose interests converged with Israel's in many fields: the Shah of Iran, King Hussein of Jordan and King Hassan of Morocco. All of them supported moves towards peace. After the first talks with the Carter administration, Dayan met King Hussein on 22 August 1977, in London. Dayan found the king still upset by the Rabat Arab summit decision that the PLO was the sole legitimate representative of the Palestinians and reluctant to take any initiatives relating to the Palestinian question. In two conversations with Dayan, King Hussein opposed any settlement that would be based on the division of the West Bank between Israel and Jordan. He explained that dividing the West Bank would mean ceding Arab territory, which he could not do. He insisted that a settlement must be based on withdrawal to the 1967 lines, including East Jerusalem. The king also refused to meet Begin. Given Begin's unequivocal stance on Yehuda and Shomron, the biblical names for the West Bank areas, a meeting of minds between the two leaders was unlikely. Dayan felt that under the circumstances a peace process could not start with Jordan and efforts must therefore be concentrated on Egypt.

Dayan's next stop was Morocco, where he met King Hassan on 4 September 1977 and asked him whether he could arrange a meeting with a high-level Egyptian politician, maybe President Sadat or his deputy, Hosni Mubarak. The king promised to reply shortly and cautioned Dayan against the idea of establishing a Palestinian entity within the framework of a federation with Jordan. He was convinced that such an arrangement would spell the deposition of King Hussein. Within days King Hassan had arranged a meeting between Dayan and the Egyptian Vice-President, Dr Hassan el-Tuhami, at which Tuhami said that Sadat was serious about peace, that he believed in Begin and in his government, and agreed to open a dialogue. However, he would meet him only after Begin had accepted the principle of total withdrawal, which was the key to peace. He would not shake Begin's hand before being assured that Israel would withdraw from all the territories. After such a commitment by Israel, it would be possible to discuss security arrangements. The negotiations should be completed before the Geneva Conference convened. The parties should arrive at Geneva with an agreed accord and in the negotiations there should be no Soviet participation.[4] At the beginning President Assad would oppose the agreement but after King Hussein had accepted it, he too, would come round. A full peace would take between three and five years to establish. Dayan answered that he was Begin's emissary and he would report to him.

From the meeting it was clear that for the first time the leader of the most important Arab country, Egypt, had decided to embark on direct negotiations with Israel on all political issues and, perhaps even move ahead on a separate agreement. Although the gulf between the positions of the parties was wide, it was a significant step. From Tuhami's tactical approach on the Geneva Conference, Israel learned of Sadat's distaste for any Russian involvement, his aversion to negotiations in a multilateral forum with all the other Arab delegations present and his correct reading of the situation in the Arab world, especially in Syria.

Dayan reported the conversation to Begin, who asked that the US be notified of the contact with Egypt and agreed that in the next meeting with Tuhami there should be an exchange of draft peace treaties.[5] In a second meeting, which was also held in Morocco, on 2 December, Dayan outlined elements of a peace treaty with Egypt, based on the assumption that Israeli presence in Sharm el-Sheikh and the settlements in the Rafah salient would remain intact.

But there was a surprise move before that date, on 9 November, when Sadat addressed the Egyptian Parliament. After agreeing to attend the Geneva Conference he made the most stunning announcement: 'I state in all seriousness that I am prepared to go to the end of the world – and Israel will be surprised to hear me tell you that I am ready to go to their home, to the Knesset itself, to argue with them, in order to prevent one Egyptian soldier from being wounded. Members of the People's Assembly, we have no time to waste.'[6]

A *Jerusalem Post* reporter called the director-general of the Prime Minister's Office, Eliahu Ben-Elissar, with the news and he instantly replied that Sadat 'would be more than welcome'. Only the next morning did he notify the Prime Minister of Sadat's statement and his comments. Begin and Dayan were puzzled, at first hesitant. But Sadat had notified President Carter of his intention to go to Jerusalem the day before his astounding statement. Cyrus Vance described the American reaction: 'We were momentarily stunned by the decision, although we knew that he [Sadat] was intensely frustrated at the prolonged and tedious negotiations.'[7]

Begin's reaction to this dramatic announcement came two days later, in an English broadcast to the Egyptian people, carried by Kol Israel on 11 November. Begin said that 'it would be a pleasure to welcome and receive your President' and reiterated his call for 'no more wars'. On 13 November, he invited the Egyptian President publicly and officially to Jerusalem 'to conduct talks on permanent peace between Israel and Egypt'.[8] On the same day I went with a congressional delegation, led by the house majority leader, to see Begin. After their visit to Israel the Congressmen were travelling to Cairo and were due to meet Sadat the next day. Before Begin joined us in the conference room I asked his bureau chief, Yehiel Kadishai, to tell the Prime Minister that I suggested he open his remarks by conveying a direct message to Sadat, saying that he would be a welcome guest in Israel. Kadishai faithfully conveyed my proposal and Begin indeed started his exposé by asking the delegation to communicate to Sadat a personal message from him to that effect. The US ambassador, Samuel Lewis, who was present duly reported the conversation to Washington and Cairo. Additional moves in that drama were the joint Sadat–Begin interviews with Walter Cronkite of CBS on 14 November, in which the Egyptian President asked for a written invitation. Begin promptly sent a formal letter via the American Embassy. In it he stressed that Sadat's announcement to the People's Assembly 'has been noted here with deep and positive interest' and invited him to address the Knesset and meet the leaders of the other parties.

Saturday evening, 19 November 1977, and Sadat's arrival in Jerusalem will remain engraved in the national memory of the State of Israel as one of the most dramatic and exciting moments in our history. In Jerusalem people were either in the street waving to Sadat or glued to the television watching his every move. I waited, with a small group of officials, at the King David Hotel in Jerusalem for his arrival. When he entered the lobby he was surrounded by outstretched hands welcoming him. His broad smile and cordial response evoked instant sympathy. We were not naïve enough to think that all the difficult problems would be solved in one visit. But I recall two constant and overpowering impressions: admiration for his personal courage in the face of the animosity towards Israel in the Arab world, and hope. Everything that Sadat brought to Israel on that visit could be condensed into this single word, hope. A sense was born that the conflict was not intractable, that the slogan of 'no more war' might become reality, that on the other side of the fence there was a humane leader who wanted peace.

Dayan described his hesitations and restraint, and what he called the 'shadows' which accompanied Sadat's announcement of his visit. He was thinking of the price that Sadat would ask in return for such a dramatic gesture. He must have sensed that on 19 November his dream of retaining Sharm el-Sheikh and the salient of Yamit had come to an abrupt end. The problem was that it had been an unrealistic dream from the beginning, but one which he had unfortunately instilled in many hearts and minds. I must confess that I had visited both places and never felt that they were essential to Israel's security in peacetime. I therefore felt no sense of impending loss. On the contrary I was elated by the prospect of real peace with Egypt, although knowing full well that difficult negotiations lay ahead.

What made Sadat decide to come to Jerusalem? In the preceding four years he had fought a terrible war against Israel. It had restored Arab honour but done nothing to change the realities in the region. Since the war he had negotiated two limited agreements with Israel, but most of the Sinai remained in Israeli hands. Now he wanted to do something dramatic, something that would break the psychological barriers of fear and distrust in Israel and demonstrate that he was sincere in his desire for peace. Only then might Israel be willing to give back the Sinai. Moreover, he was frustrated by the lengthy negotiations over the convening of the Geneva Conference, disappointed by the American–Soviet communiqué of 1 October and by the tendency of the US Secretary of State to drag the Russians back into the negotiations; he decided that he must do something bold. In June 1979, after the peace treaty with Egypt was signed, Dayan asked Sadat what had made him decide to come to Jerusalem. He said that before making the decision he had wanted to convince himself of two things: that Begin was a strong man and had the courage to make far-reaching concessions, and that he was sincere. He put both questions to the Romanian President, Nicolae Ceausescu, who had spent hours talking to Begin, and who reassured him on both counts. The idea to come to Jerusalem occurred to him while flying to Teheran. He had been looking for something that would shock Israel in a positive way. He admitted to Dayan that his talks with Dr Tuhami in Morocco had had some influence but the reason he sent Tuhami was that he wanted an Israeli–Egyptian agreement worked out before the Geneva Conference was convened.[9]

The Egyptian writer and journalist, Mohamed Heikal, described how Sadat explained his decision, the day after his announcement in the Assembly, to the six members of the National Security Council: 'The US effort had virtually come to a halt, the Soviet Union was unacceptable to both Israel and the Arabs as peacemakers, the Europeans were in no position to help, leaving only direct Arab–Israeli negotiations as a way forward ... the difficulties are psychological and the Israelis are the ones who need assurances. They are right when they ask how can we live in peace if we are not prepared to talk peace.'[10]

After Sadat's visit to Jerusalem, some politicians asked why he had not decided to travel to Israel during Golda Meir's or Rabin's premiership. I believe the reason was that in the early seventies his thinking was not ripe enough for such a decision, nor his position in the first years of his leadership strong enough to absorb its shocks. Moreover, Golda Meir was the Prime Minister of the Yom Kippur War and the one who had refused to have a Suez interim agreement with Egypt before the war. Rabin had probed the possibility of a full peace with Sadat through Kissinger and had even sent him a personal letter, to which Sadat did not respond.[11] Now he had been President of Egypt for seven years, he was confident that he could carry the Egyptian public with him, single-minded in his determination to regain the Sinai and less concerned about the reactions in other Arab capitals. Although his decision appeared sudden, it had evolved over time in Sadat's thinking. Four months before he arrived, in July 1977, he had said that he would consider a peace treaty with Israel five years after the last Israeli soldier had left the territories.[12] During his visit he voiced the opinion that a just peace according to UN resolutions did not require the signature of a peace treaty and the establishment of diplomatic relations. In the talks that he, and his ministers, had in Jerusalem they insisted that Egypt would not sign a separate peace. All these positions he later abandoned. The intense diplomatic activity led by the Carter administration, and his conversations with Begin, Dayan and Minister of Defence Ezer Weizman, convinced him that unless he was prepared to sign a contractual peace treaty, he would not get the Sinai back. This bold decision to break the ice paved the way to full peace between Israel and Egypt, and the later breakthrough with the Palestinians in Oslo, as well as the peace treaty with Jordan. It was a brave move.

The highlight of Sadat's visit to Jerusalem was his speech to the Knesset. On 21 November I took my seat in the gallery well before 4 p.m., the time scheduled for his speech. The house was packed. President Efraim Kazir, the army chiefs and dignitaries from all fields of endeavour came to this extraordinary session. I was sitting between the American ambassador, Samuel Lewis, and the house majority leader, Congressman Jim Wright, who had returned with his delegation from Cairo to be present at this historic moment. As Sadat spoke Arabic and the only interpretation was into Hebrew, I translated the speech from Hebrew into English for Lewis and Wright as Sadat was speaking. The speech, flowery in style, was a clear reiteration of the Egyptian position: an end to the Israeli occupation of the Arab territories seized in 1967; self-determination for the Palestinians, including their right to establish their own state; the right of all the states in the area to live in peace within their boundaries; an end to force and the solution of differences by peaceful means; a conclusion to the state of belligerency.[13] The last two points were duly noted. The resolution of differences by peaceful means and the end of belligerency, reiterated in the Knesset, were important steps down a long road of negotiations. The speech made no mention of the PLO, but it contained an emotional appeal to the people of Israel which was not lost. Sadat said: 'I have chosen to come to you with an open heart and an open mind. I have chosen to give this great impetus to all international efforts exerted for peace. I have chosen to present to you, and in your own home, the realities devoid of any schemes or whims ... for us to win together, the most dangerous of rounds and battles in modern history – the battle of permanent peace based on justice.'[14] Little did Sadat know that his prophecy of 'the most dangerous battle' would cost his own life.

In his reply Begin outlined our relentless quest for peace since 1948, and the repeated Arab rejection of our outstretched hand. Then he focused on the future, repeating our readiness to negotiate on all issues without preconditions, in direct talks or at the Geneva Conference. He also made the point that the end of belligerency should be in the context of a peace treaty with normal relations. Which meant that we were aiming at a much broader peace than just the termination of the state of war. He invited President Assad and King Hussein to follow Sadat to Jerusalem, speaking only of Arab countries without mentioning the Palestinians. However, touching on Sadat's reference to the Balfour Declaration, he said: 'No, sir, we took no foreign land, we returned to our homeland. The bond between our people and our land is eternal. It was created at the dawn of human history. It was never severed. In this land we established our civilization ... here we became a nation ... Even when we were far away, we did not forget this land.'[15]

The special Knesset session ended with a speech by Shimon Peres, the leader of the opposition, in which he cited, chapter and verse, the passionate calls from Ben-Gurion, Moshe Sharett, Levi Eshkol, Golda Meir and Yitzhak Rabin for peace with our neighbours. It was inevitable that such a climactic atmosphere, filled with expectation, would end with a measure of disappointment. The audience and millions of television viewers could see the gulf in our positions and the absence of bridging opportunities. Just as it is impossible to govern by rhetoric alone, without the accompanying decision on detail and implementation, it is not feasible to negotiate from a rostrum, well placed though it might be. Sadat abhorred details, formulations and drafts. He had made the daring decision to come to Jerusalem and expected in return a bold move by Begin, one that would refer to the withdrawal from the Sinai and self-determination for the Palestinians. The Prime Minister, however, took the view that the gesture of the visit was reciprocated by the warmth of the welcome and the rest should be left to detailed negotiations. The talks with Begin and his ministers before and after the speech revolved around the same issues and the same differences. The only conversation that the two leaders had alone, during Sadat's visit, was not documented. But Dayan was told of its content and wrote that it included three principles on which both leaders agreed: no more war between Israel and Egypt; sovereignty over the Sinai would return to Egypt; most of the Sinai peninsula would be demilitarized and limited Egyptian forces would be stationed in areas close to the Suez Canal.[16] So Sadat did not leave Jerusalem empty-handed. On the contrary, as far as Egypt was concerned, he had a basic commitment for withdrawal. True, it had to be embodied in a proper peace treaty. But the visitor had

had an opportunity to become acquainted with the Israeli leadership and develop a good rapport with Ezer Weizman, whose style Sadat had come to like. He had prayed at the holiest Muslim shrine in Jerusalem, the Al Aqsa mosque, met the Security and Defence Committee of the Knesset and before returning to Cairo agreed on a joint communiqué with Begin. It stated that the negotiations between the two countries, leading to peace treaties, would continue.

On his return to Cairo, Sadat was welcomed by millions of people lining the streets. He saw this as a resounding endorsement of his initiative. Yet the bureaucracy was more sceptical and attentive to negative reactions in the Arab world, and his Foreign Minister, Ismael Fahmi, resigned. The follow-up to the visit was also slow and difficult. In mid-December Sadat convened the Cairo Conference, at ambassadorial level, to which the other Arab states and Israel were invited. When the talks started, only Egypt, Israel, US and UN representatives were present. The outcome was disappointing. At the same time, Arab countries, including Iraq, Syria, South Yemen, Algeria, Libya and the PLO, convened in Tripoli, rejected Sadat's initiative and decided to isolate Egypt and impose an economic boycott on it. Jordan and Saudi Arabia did not join in. These reactions hardened the Egyptian stance in the negotiations and they insisted on a declaration of principles in which Israel would state its commitment to withdrawal to the 1967 lines on all fronts, and on self-determination for the Palestinians.

Begin realized that Israel must address the Palestinian question and prepared a plan proposing the autonomy of the Palestinians in Judea and Samaria and the Gaza District (the West Bank and Gaza). On 16 December he met President Carter in Washington to present him with the Israeli response to Sadat, which was: withdrawal, in two stages, to the international border with Egypt in return for a peace treaty and self-rule for the Palestinians after a transition period of five years. Carter and Vance did not endorse the plan but reacted favourably because they saw in it an important opening for further negotiations on the future of the West Bank and Gaza. The Prime Minister also stopped in London to discuss the plan for Palestinian autonomy with the British Prime Minister, James Callaghan, who, without sanctioning Begin's scheme, also reacted positively. Now came the most crucial part, its presentation to Sadat. For this purpose the two leaders met, this time in Ismailia, Egypt.

The meeting took place on 25 December. Although it was the first summit on Egyptian soil, there were no ceremonies, no warm welcome, just business talks. Sadat continued to press for a declaration that would include a commitment to withdrawal and self-determination for the Palestinians. The proposal on withdrawal to the international border with Egypt was very important to Sadat. It also represented a fulfilment of a promise that Begin had given him during his visit to Jerusalem. In Ismailia

Sadat made it clear that he would not accept an Israeli military or civilian presence in the Sinai after withdrawal. The two leaders agreed to continue negotiations in two committees, one political, one military.

The first – and last – meeting of the political committee, at Foreign Minister level, convened in Jerusalem on 17 January 1978. The negotiations stalled. At a dinner tendered by the Prime Minister in honour of the delegations, Begin delivered a speech which the Egyptian Foreign Minister, Kamel, saw as an affront, and in spite of Vance's and Dayan's pleas, the Egyptian delegation aborted the talks and left abruptly for Cairo.

Sadat's battle now concentrated on winning self-determination for the Palestinians. He knew that the Egyptian–Israeli peace treaty could be negotiated successfully. For Begin's government the West Bank was the heart of the matter. Begin's ideology and his policy was based on the premise that it would remain under Israeli control, although for the time being it would not be annexed. He had hoped that by compromising with Egypt on the Sinai, there would be less pressure on him for flexibility on the West Bank. His solution for the Palestinian population was self-rule, which he hoped would become permanent. Neither Sadat nor the US accepted his vision and there was a convergence of interest between the US and Egypt, aiming to achieve something more substantial for the Palestinians. If Begin suggested a five-year transition period, they wanted to know there and then what would happen after the five years. The spring of 1978 was fraught with disagreement and tensions between Israel and America and Begin and Sadat. Begin went to Washington in March and again in April. Dayan held extensive talks with Carter and Vance, but with scant results. However, the American administration did not give up, because the stakes were too high. Sadat could not be let down after such a revolutionary and courageous move. The momentum had to be kept up. Vance was assisted by a highly experienced team of Middle East experts. They included Alfred Atherton, who became ambassador at large for Middle East negotiations, Harold Saunders, assistant secretary of state for the Middle East, and William Quandt, who was the area expert on the National Security Council. They worked tirelessly to keep the negotiations going. If proposals were rejected, new ones had to be devised until common ground was identified and the gaps between the parties could be bridged.

Then, as often happens in the Middle East, terrorists intervened. On 11 March two rubber boats with eleven terrorists landed between Haifa and Tel Aviv. They made their way to the main highway and commandeered a bus full of men, women and children on holiday. About eight miles from Tel Aviv the security forces stopped the bus and in the ensuing battle nine of the terrorists were killed and thirty-five Israelis lost their lives. From the interrogation of the two surviving terrorists we learned that they had come from Tyre in the Lebanon. Palestinian terrorists had done their best to thwart the negotiations.

Israel retaliated by launching a major attack against terrorist concentrations south of the Litani River (Operation Litani). After five days the IDF withdrew but the security zone in southern Lebanon remained under the control of the Christian militiamen led by Major Saad Haddad. Hundreds of terrorists were killed and sixteen Israeli soldiers lost their lives.

With Israel nearing its thirtieth Independence celebrations, two conflicting trends of thought dominated the political discussion: the dream of Greater Israel versus the logic of territorial compromise and acceptance of the 'land-for-peace' concept. Sadat's visit had introduced a new and promising element in the Arab–Israeli conflict. Would Begin have the courage and vision to agree on an acceptable compromise? Only time would tell.

THE FOURTH DECADE
1978–88

14

From Camp David to Intifada

B y the summer of 1978 it was clear that another effort must be launched to get Israeli and Egyptian officials talking to each other. After endless discussions with Begin and Dayan the Americans concluded that there was no way to persuade the Begin government to make commitments on the final status of the West Bank and Gaza. Begin's position had been that after a transition period of five years, Israel would be entitled to propose the annexation of the West Bank. Should the Palestinians reject the prospect of living under Israeli sovereignty, autonomy would continue indefinitely. Unrealistic as that position was, the Americans believed that, to circumvent it, negotiations must take place on the shape of the five years of autonomy, which in itself would represent progress. Talks would continue on the permanent status during the period of autonomy. In a meeting with Sadat in April, Alfred Atherton conveyed this assessment to him and urged him to put forward an Egyptian proposal. In a conversation with Carter in May, Begin agreed not to press Israel's demand for annexation of the West Bank for the next five years and with this small measure of flexibility achieved, the Americans set out to work more energetically towards an accommodation. Vance invited Foreign Ministers Dayan and Kamel, accompanied by small delegations, to meet him in Britain. The chosen venue was Leeds Castle and the two-day conference started on 17 July. The main issue was again the Palestinian question and, specifically, what would happen to the West Bank and Gaza after the five-year transition period. Usama al-Baz, the special adviser to Vice-President Mubarak, stressed the centrality of the Palestinian issue. If it were ignored, it would come back and 'erupt as a volcano', he said. Dayan, although uncertain of Begin's position, probed whether the Allon Plan, the division of the West Bank, would be acceptable. Kamel responded categorically that it would not. Dayan now had unequivocal rejections of the Allon Plan from King Hussein as well as Egypt.

In an attempt to lessen Israel's security concerns, Vance had asked Dayan whether membership of Nato would satisfy Israel. Although suggestions of a Nato-type guarantee had been voiced before, it was the first time that such a far-reaching proposal, from an authoritative source, had reached Israel. It demonstrated how far the US was prepared to go to advance peace. In the grim reality of a Middle East under the shadow of the Cold War, Nato membership could be a powerful deterrent to direct Soviet involvement. Dayan replied that he would welcome such a move but not as a substitute for an Israeli military presence on the West Bank and Gaza.

The free and open exchanges at Leeds Castle impressed the Israeli Foreign Minister, who was constantly searching for new ideas acceptable both to Begin and Egypt. He decided to submit a 'personal' three-point proposal which had not been cleared with Begin. First, Israel would not accept an agreement that called for a return to the 1967 lines with only minor modifications and the establishment of Arab sovereignty over the territories, even if it received security guarantees. Secondly, if a plan based on territorial compromise were to be tabled, Israel would consider it. Thirdly, the main point: should the autonomy plan be accepted, Israel would be prepared, after five years, to discuss the question of sovereignty or permanent status of the West Bank and Gaza. The ambiguous phrasing would allow Israel to demand annexation and the Palestinians to claim a state.

Upon his return Dayan reported the outcome of the conference to Begin and the Cabinet. At first Begin had not been pleased at Dayan's submission of a personal paper, which had not been cleared with him. But he had Dayan's suggestions approved by the Cabinet and even sanctioned by the Knesset. Sadat's demand for a declaration of principles did not figure highly in the Leeds Castle discussions, which reinforced the American view that negotiations must now concentrate on a peace treaty with Egypt and on autonomy arrangements for the territories. Vance and his advisers had also decided that the time had come for an American proposal to be tabled. The US and Israeli delegations were pleased with the outcome of the conference; not so Sadat. He was still apprehensive of being accused of engaging in a separate agreement with Israel and abandoning the Palestinian cause. The Leeds Castle Conference was the last stop before the summit meeting with Carter, Begin and Sadat was convened at Camp David, Maryland.[1]

The talks which had taken place since Sadat's visit to Jerusalem, in Cairo, Ismailia, Washington and Leeds Castle, convinced him that without the full participation of the US, the negotiations might reach a total impasse. Hence his continued pressure on Carter to join them and put forward bridging proposals. In the first week of August, Vance travelled to Jerusalem and Cairo to hand Begin and Sadat President Carter's invitation to attend a conference at Camp David. Begin accepted it immediately, though he was anxious that the US should not table proposals. Sadat was pleased that, at last, the Carter administration was joining the talks as a 'full partner', and agreed to attend. In the autumn of 1978, Begin's political standing in Israel was resilient enough to withstand, if necessary, failure at Camp David. However, for Sadat success was essential. Nine months had passed since his historic visit to Jerusalem and he had little to show his critics to justify such an unusual move. For Carter, too, failure had a political price.

The Camp David summit was held on 5–17 September at the presidential retreat in the Maryland mountains. These were thirteen days of difficult negotiations and high drama, and produced a Framework for Peace in the Middle East consisting of two parts; a framework agreement for the West Bank and Gaza, and principles for a peace treaty with Egypt. The US team, led by Vance, invested a tremendous amount of work in the preparations for the summit. They had chosen a secluded venue away from media and other pressures, had decided that only one spokesman would issue statements on behalf of all three delegations and, above all, had drafted an American bridging proposal, to be tabled if an impasse were reached.

Like the pioneering visit of Sadat to Jerusalem, this American–Israeli–Egyptian summit was unprecedented. During the first meeting of the three leaders, which took place on 6 September, Sadat explained that he would be prepared to conclude a settlement for the West Bank and Gaza before signing a peace treaty between Egypt and Israel, but would be reluctant to do it the other way round. In this there was no change in Sadat's position since his visit to Jerusalem; it is to be hoped that the Palestinian people realize how hard and long President Sadat fought for their cause. Reluctantly, Begin agreed to give priority to the Palestinian question. Then Sadat tabled a draft framework for a comprehensive peace in the Middle East, but this was rejected outright by Begin, who explained that it would lead to a Palestinian state, to which both Carter and Sadat had objected in the past. Sadat replied that the Palestinian state he was proposing would be demilitarized, not independent and linked to Jordan. Still insisting on a referendum among the Palestinians on whether they should join Jordan, his belief was that the majority of Palestinians on the West Bank and Gaza would opt to become part of the Hashemite Kingdom. Furthermore, if King Hussein refused to sign for the Palestinians, he would act on their behalf. Begin further rejected Sadat's demand for Arab sovereignty over East Jerusalem, explaining that it would lead once more to the division of the city.

The Egyptian Foreign Minister, Kamel, maintained in later years that Sadat had decided to submit a detailed proposal in order to provoke a confrontation with Begin in which Carter would side with him and Begin would be isolated.[2] This view is sustained by the tactics Sadat adopted. He handed Carter a three-page confidential paper containing fall-back positions which Carter could use at the appropriate moment. In it, he agreed to accept reservations on the return of refugees and on other sensitive issues, and to meet Israeli demands for normalization, including the establishment of diplomatic relations. On Jerusalem, Sadat had agreed that the city should not be divided again.[3] These were important points, helpful to Carter in the delicate negotiations, and the President used them at appropriate moments. They also eased the drafting of the American compromise proposal and reflected Sadat's sense that Carter was close to his point of view and that they could collaborate for the greater success of the summit.

At the second meeting of the three leaders, the next day, Begin refuted, point by point, the Egyptian draft and Sadat accused him of wanting territories more than peace. The atmosphere was charged with tension and Carter soon concluded that it was better to meet each leader separately, and distil the issues on which a compromise was possible, rather than have direct confrontations. The session on 7 September was therefore the last at which all three met together, until the agreement was ready for signature. The US team worked informally and diligently with each delegation and had many conversations with their key participants, to understand the issues, identify the outer limits of compromise and negotiate the terms. Vance had special praise for the contribution of three members in the Israeli delegation: Dayan, 'very helpful in the darkest moments', Minister of Defence Ezer Weizman (later President of Israel), who was 'most helpful' and the Attorney-General, Aharon Barak (now President of the Supreme Court), who 'was indispensable in finding imaginative ways to overcome ... insurmountable stumbling blocks'.[4] Israel's ambassador to Washington, Simcha Dinitz, the legal adviser of the Foreign Ministry, Meir Rosen, and Dayan's political adviser, Elyakim Rubinstein, were also on the very strong and balanced team led by Begin.

On 10 September, after completing the twenty-third version, Carter handed the US draft proposal to Begin. After receiving the Israeli response some changes were introduced and the next day Carter gave the document to Sadat, who did not react negatively. However, the negotiations with the Egyptian delegation were complicated because, contrary to the moderating influence which Dayan, Weizman and Barak had on Begin, Sadat's advisers, headed by Foreign Minister Kamel, took a harder line than their leader, to the point that Kamel, at the end, resigned. The submission of the American document made an Israeli counter-proposal to Sadat's superfluous, and the negotiations took a more promising turn. Dayan urged the Americans to present a draft treaty with Egypt so that it could be discussed simultaneously with the draft on the Palestinian issues. Carter also felt that the unique opportunity at Camp David should be used to construct a framework for a peace treaty between Israel and Egypt and wrote the first draft himself, based on his conversations with the two leaders. The two agreements were now negotiated in parallel, although most of the time was spent on the Palestinian issue.

The summit was not without tension and crisis. Two days before it ended Sadat threatened to leave, and at other times Dayan cautioned the Americans of Begin's disposition to give up. The two issues on which Sadat was adamant were the evacuation of the fourteen Israeli settlements in the Sinai and the dismantling, over a period of time, of the three air-force bases there, so that Egypt would regain full sovereignty over the peninsula. After many attempts to convince Sadat otherwise, the Israeli delegation concluded that the two were make-or-break issues for the Egyptian President. Begin then agreed to bring the removal of settlements to the Knesset, making it clear that the peace treaty with Egypt hinged on the decision. Defence Minister Weizman explored the possibility of receiving US aid for the construction of new airfields in the Negev as a substitute for the Sinai ones. Carter and Secretary of Defence, Harold Brown, agreed to this, and the way to a peace agreement with Egypt was now open.

The critical issues on the Palestinian question were Sadat's demands for a settlement freeze on the West Bank and phrasing on Jerusalem. On the former, Begin refused to sign an agreement that stipulated a freeze on settlement activity. The final evening of the conference saw a decisive conversation between the President and Begin. In it, according to Vance, Begin told Carter that he would be prepared to write to the President 'that Israel would establish no new settlements until the autonomy negotiations were completed'. When Begin's letter arrived it referred to a moratorium on settlements only during the negotiation of a peace treaty with Egypt which was to last three months.[5] Carter sent the letter back to Begin but he refused to change it. Vance was the only American present at that nocturnal Carter–Begin encounter on 16 September, at which Begin was accompanied by Dayan and Barak. Dayan maintained that Begin's letter truly reflected his commitment, which Carter and Vance may have misunderstood.[6] William Quandt, who kept a daily journal at Camp David, did not participate in this important meeting but recorded the report that Vance conveyed to the American delegation on it. According to him, Begin and Dayan made it clear that they could not agree to a moratorium on settlements to last until after the completion of the autonomy talks. He noted: 'Begin will write a letter to Carter that will be made public. There will be no new settlements during the negotiations except by agreement. It means that there will be a freeze on settlements. (Begin sees the freeze lasting only three months, but it may be extended ...)'[7] What later transpired was that Begin had stressed that it was a period of three months that he had in mind. Carter seemed to be right that Begin's commitment was originally given in the context of the agreement with the Palestinians, and not with Egypt. Carter then agreed to remove from the framework agreement on the Palestinian question the paragraph on settlements, on the assumption that Begin's promise would be spelled out in the promised letter. He was therefore surprised when Begin linked the moratorium to the negotiations with Egypt. Some Americans had suspected that Begin changed his mind because he knew that the duration of the autonomy talks would be long and also that he had become increasingly concerned about adverse reactions in Israel to such a commitment. It was a serious misunderstanding which clouded relations between Carter and Begin to the end of his presidency.

Begin also refused to include in the autonomy agreement any clause on Jerusalem. The Americans then decided to exclude all reference to the city from the accord and suggested that each participant state his country's position in a letter to the President. However, Begin did not want the US to reiterate its detailed policy challenging the annexation of East Jerusalem. The limitation on American statements did not go down well with Carter, but the success of the conference was of paramount consideration. Carter wrote that the US position on Jerusalem remained as stated by the ambassadors Goldberg and Yost in the UN.

On Palestinian rights, Begin agreed that the Framework for Peace include the following: 'The solution from the negotiations must also recognize the legitimate rights of the Palestinian people and their just requirements; in this way, the Palestinians will participate in the determination of their own future...'[8]

Begin was the first Israeli Prime Minister to recognize 'Palestinian rights'. In this phrasing he went beyond declarations of other Prime Ministers before him. He surely had his own interpretation as to how these rights should be exercised. He believed that the Palestinians had the right to autonomy but not to self-determination, but this did not change his undertaking and the fact that after Camp David it became an inseparable part of Israel's commitments, which rhetorical acrobatics could not alter.[9] Furthermore, Begin had agreed that the negotiations would be on the basis of Resolution 242 'in all its parts', a resolution which he had fiercely repudiated in 1970. This is not to detract from Begin's strong defence of Israel's interests, especially on Yehuda and Shomron, as he perceived them. As the future would show, his vision consisted of a mixture of realism and dream at Camp David. Fortunately for Israel and peace, the balance tilted toward the former.

The principles which would form the peace treaty with Egypt constituted the second part of the agreement, and both Israel and Egypt committed themselves to complete the detailed negotiations within three months. On 17 September the Camp David Framework for Peace in the Middle East was signed by Prime Minister Begin and President Sadat in the East Room of the White House, with President Carter signing as a witness. Dayan wrote: 'Tonight was one of the greatest hours of my life. I was delighted to have had the privilege to be one of the architects of the Camp David agreement.'[10] Secretary of State Cyrus Vance, whose tenacity and perseverance made the agreement possible, wrote that Camp David reflected 'the outer limits of the possible at the time'.[11] Sadat was subdued, his Foreign Minister Kamel submitted his resignation and some members of the Egyptian delegation, including Usama al-Baz, did not attend the signing ceremony. They reflected the criticism in the Arab world of what was perceived as a separate peace with Egypt. In November an Arab summit gathered in Baghdad and decided to sever political and economic relations with Cairo. Especially disappointing to Sadat were the decisions of the pro-Western rulers in Saudi Arabia and Kuwait to withdraw their economic assistance to Egypt. But as the leader of Egypt, Sadat knew the truth; he had achieved for his people what had been unattainable for eleven years, the full restoration of the Sinai to Egyptian sovereignty. He had also given them the chance of a better and safer future, with 'no more wars'. Begin and Sadat later received the Nobel Peace Prize for their efforts to conclude the Camp David Accords.

American political and public opinion were jubilant at Carter's achievement. In Israel, the returning delegation met criticism, mainly from the right-wing, who objected to the loss of the settlements in the Sinai, a decision which caused considerable controversy. It was difficult for settlers who had devoted years of sweat and toil to building their farms – and also for the country – to accept that it was these settlements which prevented peace with Egypt. But this was Sadat's unalterable condition for peace. On 24 September, the government approved the agreement by eleven votes to two, with one abstention and four religious ministers not participating in the vote. A few days later, the Knesset ratified it, again by a considerable majority. Of the 120 Knesset members, eighty-four voted for the Camp David Accords, nineteen were against and seventeen abstained. In the debate, Dayan took the floor and, after a resounding defence of the achievements at Camp David, explained the reasons for his own reversal of position: 'What has changed since the period when I said Sharm el-Sheikh without peace was preferable to peace without Sharm el-Sheikh,' he explained, was that when he made that statement, during the Nasser period, he genuinely thought that it was so. Since then eight years had passed, and there was a new administration in Egypt. Looking towards the future he now preferred 'peace without Sharm el-Sheikh to Sharm el-Sheikh without peace'.[12] The change in rhetoric was easier than the uprooting of fourteen settlements including the town of Yamit, however.

Twenty years later, the Framework for Peace in the Middle East can be seen as a major building block on the way to the solution of the Arab–Israeli conflict. Another seven months were required, and painstaking negotiations led by Carter and Vance, before the peace treaty between Israel and Egypt was signed on 26 March 1979, at the White House.

When Begin returned from Washington, he was welcomed by a special reception at the Knesset Plaza. President Yitzhak Navon, who had replaced President Kazir, thanked him warmly on behalf of the nation for his 'persistence', and stressed that 'you wrestled with yourself before our eyes'. This was a correct description of Begin's difficulties both at Camp David and during the negotiations over the peace treaty. A few weeks later, on 2 April, Begin departed for his first official visit to Cairo and talks with President Sadat. The implementation of the agreement was now very much in the minds of the two leaders and Begin announced that we would withdraw from El-Arish ahead of schedule. On the Palestinian issue, Sadat relied on the joint letter which he and Begin had dispatched to Carter before signing the peace treaty, on 26 March 1979. In it both leaders had agreed that the two governments would 'negotiate continuously' on the self-governing authority on the West Bank with the goal of 'completing the negotiations within one year'.[13] (It took more than fourteen years until the modalities of self-government were eventually agreed in Oslo). Begin was welcomed in Cairo by sizeable crowds, which was a demonstration of popular support for Sadat's peace policy.

The temperature of the peace between the two countries was not perhaps as warm as we would have liked it to be, and the relationship would, most probably, continue to be subdued until a comprehensive settlement was achieved. Nevertheless, the agreement has withstood many a turmoil in the past nineteen years and has proved to be robust. The tragic assassination of President Sadat did not disrupt it. President Mubarak continued Sadat's policy and, like his predecessor, is very vigorous in attempting to help the Palestinians. There have been other tremors, like the war in Lebanon in 1982, the intifada of the Palestinians in the territories, the continuous campaign of terror and the Gulf War. However, the inherent self-interest of Israel and Egypt in maintaining peace has remained an overriding consideration in both countries and the peace has endured. Also, during the past twenty years, and as a result of Camp David, relations between Egypt and the US have taken on a new and more friendly dimension. American aid to Egypt has topped the $50 billion figure. For a while Egypt was isolated in the Arab world, but in 1991 Syria, Jordan and the Palestinians at last accepted the principle of direct negotiations, which had made Camp David possible.

The experience of Camp David and the subsequent negotiations on the peace treaty showed that direct negotiations did not mean that the US would be debarred from its crucial mediation role. Face-to-face meetings between leaders is a key to mutual acceptance and mutual recognition, but it does not always lead to successful negotiations. Begin and Sadat slid easily into confrontation, and their dialogue on peace had to be supplemented by active US involvement. Without President Carter's drive, his readiness to put the weight and prestige of the United States of America behind the negotiations, his personal commitment and mastery of detail, the visit of President Sadat to Jerusalem would have remained a courageous episode and a wasted opportunity.[14]

In Israel even the tiny minority of Camp David sceptics, which included Yitzhak Shamir and Moshe Arens, came to realize the strategic advantages of peace with Cairo. With Egypt out of the circle of war, the likelihood of Arab countries attacking Israel diminished and Israel could gradually reduce its defence budget. The peace treaty with Egypt made it possible, in later years, for Jordan to be the second Arab country to conclude peace. For the Palestinians and their vehement rejection of Camp David, the autonomy scheme with certain modifications became the foundation of the Oslo Agreement.

In the summer of 1978, I was nominated as ambassador to the Philippines. Shortly after I took up my appointment, I presented my credentials to President Ferdinand Marcos. During our conversation he was most interested to learn more about the negotiations with Egypt and the deteriorating situation in Iran. The intricacies of Palestinian autonomy were of little interest to him, but a change in relations with Egypt held out the promise of a different Middle East. He was well disposed towards Israel but also had more than a million citizens working in Arab countries, as well as other interests in the Arab world, and therefore welcomed an easing of the Israel–Arab conflict. His anxiety about Iran was based on his fear of upheaval in the Persian Gulf area and the danger to oil supplies. I shared his concern about Iran and echoed the historic achievements of the Camp David Accords, with which I associated myself with all my heart.

The implementation of the peace treaty with Egypt took time but was faithfully carried out. Jordan did not accept the Camp David Accords and the Palestinians totally rejected them because they did not include self-determination. Their terror campaign continued in the course of 1978, with over two hundred terrorist attacks recorded. Sadat, true to his commitment, decided to negotiate self-rule for them, an effort which had little chance of success.

Changes in the Israeli domestic scene also hindered a successful outcome for the autonomy talks. Begin, who was convinced that the sacred mission of his government was to preserve Judea and Samaria as part of Greater Israel, aimed at a most limited scheme for self-rule. The government had resumed settlement building after a three months' interval, and he did not believe that the pragmatist Dayan would go along with his restricted view of administrative self-rule. He therefore nominated the Interior Minister, Dr Yosef Burg, whose National Religious Party was close to his own ideological outlook, to lead the Israeli team in the negotiations with Egypt on Palestinian autonomy. Dayan saw this as a clear expression of no confidence in him, and after observing a few sessions of the negotiations, resigned from the government in October 1979. Weizman, too, could not see that the very limited autonomy which Begin suggested would lead to an agreement and, a few months later, resigned as Minister of Defence. The Egyptian and Israeli delegations met infrequently between 1978 and 1980. Carter appointed as special envoy to the negotiations first Robert Strauss and later Sol Linowitz. Neither could find a formula for self-rule that would both satisfy Sadat and be acceptable to Begin.

In mid-1980, the right-wing Techia Party initiated a 'fundamental law' declaring Jerusalem as the united and indivisible capital of Israel. Begin did not oppose the law and made it impossible for the Labour Party to reject it. Israeli law had been applied to Jerusalem in June 1967, under the Eshkol government, and from any legal or political standpoint there was no need of further legislation. However, the Knesset voted on 30 July, passing the law and repeating the guarantee of free access to the holy places. The result was uproar in the Arab world. Sadat suspended the autonomy talks, and eleven countries which had their Embassies in Jerusalem took them out of the capital and transferred them to Tel Aviv. Following Carter's strong encouragement to resume autonomy negotiations, Sadat agreed, provided another Camp David conference were convened. Carter would have followed up on Sadat's request had he won the elections. But as so often happens in the Middle East, unpredictable developments entered the scene. Carter became bogged down in the Iran hostage crisis, which led to his defeat. In November 1980, Ronald Reagan was elected President of the US.[15]

For Sadat this was a personal loss. He had developed a unique amity with Carter. In their discourse there was also a shared belief in the centrality of the Palestinian problem to the solution of the Arab–Israeli conflict. This was one of the reasons why Begin did not regret Carter's defeat. Begin was in no hurry, and did not want to accelerate the negotiations on autonomy but preferred instead to continue settlement activity, which Carter had vehemently opposed. No wonder that when President Reagan was inaugurated in January 1981, Begin congratulated him profusely. Reagan's hard-line attitude toward the 'evil empire', as he called the Soviet Union, and his abhorrence of the PLO was more to Begin's liking. The new President had great sympathy for Israel's struggle and a number of his pre-election statements reflected that sentiment. The peace process was not a major priority of his administration and the Israeli government was looking forward to a more relaxed dialogue with the US. In March, however, the first strains appeared when Israel and the US clashed over Washington's decision to supply sophisticated parts for F-15 fighter planes and advanced

AWACS aeroplanes (Airborne Warning And Control System) to Saudi Arabia.

The situation on the border with Lebanon deteriorated throughout 1981. The Palestinians had decided to step up terror on a large scale in order to undermine peace with Egypt. Katyusha rockets were fired into townships and villages in the Galilee. From Naharyah to Kyriat Shmona people were killed and injured, and Israel retaliated by repeated bombings of terrorist concentrations. As the danger of escalation was ever present, the US decided to intervene and dispatched the special ambassador Philip Habib to negotiate a cease-fire. In July he succeeded in brokering a truce on the northern border, which more or less held for eleven months, yet it did not stop horrendous terrorist attacks on Israeli targets in Europe. In April an Israeli diplomat was assassinated in Paris and in June the Israeli ambassador in London was gravely injured.

At the beginning of the eighties, information persistently reached Israel that Iraq was on the verge of developing a nuclear bomb. This was seen by the military, as well as by politicians, as a grave danger, and the army was ordered to prepare contingency plans for the destruction of the Iraqi nuclear reactor near Baghdad. There was some discussion about how long it would take until the reactor, built by French companies, became operative, but the basic consensus in the government was that Israel must not allow this to happen. Begin set the date of 7 June 1981 for an attack, three weeks before the elections. Sixteen Israeli F-15s and F-16s flew low over Arab territory to Osiraq, the nuclear installation near Baghdad, a distance of about six hundred miles, destroyed the nuclear reactor and returned safely to their base. In Israeli terms this was a brilliant military accomplishment and a courageous and far-sighted decision, although the Security Council condemned Israel's attack and the United States suspended arms shipments. Condemnations from the Arab world were harsh in tone, but Sadat did not waver on his peace commitments and many Arab leaders felt that they could breathe more easily. From Israel's security standpoint the action was essential, but its full significance for the region and the world was realized nine years later, when Saddam Hussein attacked Kuwait in 1990. Had Saddam possessed a nuclear bomb, the decision of the US, the United Kingdom and the other allies to attack Iraq would have been much harder, Kuwait would not be on today's world map as an independent state, Saudi Arabia and the whole Gulf area would be under Iraqi domination and the supply of oil to the industrial world would be at Saddam's mercy.

In June 1981, my family and I were due to leave Manila and return to Jerusalem after close to three years of service in the Philippines. Following the attack on the reactor I was asked to stay on for another few weeks to defend the action. In fact, the destruction of the nuclear plant received prominence in the media there but met with very little criticism. On the contrary, there was considerable understanding for the government's decision and my colleagues in the five Asian capitals in which we were represented experienced similar reactions. The attitude towards Israel in the Philippines was very friendly. As a Catholic country, reared on the Bible, they regarded our nation as important. Their close relations with the US also led to a greater awareness of Middle East realities.

When we reached Jerusalem, election fever in Israel was soaring. The Labour leader, Shimon Peres, mounted an outstanding campaign and was close to defeating Begin. However, the result of the vote on 30 June, was the smallest margin; forty-eight Knesset members for Likud led by Begin and forty-seven for Peres' Labour Party. Begin's majority was a mere 10,000 votes, but with the support of the religious parties he formed his second coalition. Yitzhak Shamir continued as Foreign Minister and Ariel Sharon was appointed Minister of Defence. Little pragmatism and plenty of ideology characterized the second Begin administration.

The process of normalization with Egypt continued via ministerial visits and the meetings of joint working groups on trade, tourism, energy and other subjects of mutual interest. Israeli and Egyptian airlines scheduled daily flights to the two capitals and a two-way traffic developed. Soon after our arrival in Jerusalem I was nominated director of the Economic Department of the Foreign Ministry and within weeks left for Cairo to attend the joint committee on trade. My first call was at the Israeli Embassy to receive a briefing from our ambassador, Moshe Sasson, one of the foremost Middle East experts in the ministry. Our delegation was very excited by the visit to the first Israeli Embassy in an Arab capital. Sasson's work was fraught with difficulties, stringent security precautions, resentment by intellectual groups like the lawyers' association and others, but sympathy from the average Egyptian who supported peace. It was obvious that in spite of the peace treaty we were still a long way from true reconciliation. The negotiations were professional and businesslike; however, while our delegation had authority to make decisions, our Egyptian colleagues had to refer to their superiors on nearly every issue. The main problem was that there was little Israel could import from Egypt to balance exports except oil, which was handled in a different context. As Egypt develops its industrial and technological base, this structural difference will diminish. Walking in the streets in Cairo, visiting the Pyramids and the Cairo Museum were experiences which one could hardly have dreamed of before Sadat's visit to Jerusalem. We left Cairo determined to make every effort to enhance trade between our countries.

A few months later, on 6 October, tragedy struck. While President Sadat was taking the salute during a military parade to commemorate the October 1973 war, a young army officer stopped his truck in front of the reviewing stand and, together with three other military conspirators, opened fire and killed the President. The assassin belonged to an extreme fundamentalist group which aimed to turn Egypt into an Ayatollah-type Islamic republic and was utterly opposed to peace with Israel. The assassination shocked Egypt, Israel and the world. President Navon eulogized Sadat and described him as an 'extraordinary human being and an outstanding statesman'. Prime Minister Begin, accompanied by Shamir, Sharon and the Minister of Interior, Joseph Burg, represented Israel at the funeral. However, Radio Damascus announced that 'the traitor is dead'.[16]

By a miracle Vice-President Hosni Mubarak escaped unhurt, and he took power with remarkable speed and efficiency. He legitimized his rule by a quick referendum which gave him over ninety-eight per cent of the vote and provided continuity in fighting fundamentalism, maintaining the peace process and following a clear pro-American administration. On the day of the funeral Begin and the delegation had a meeting with Mubarak in which the Prime Minister pledged to adhere to the timetable of withdrawal from the Sinai and Mubarak promised to continue Sadat's peace policy. It was a powerful affirmation of how resilient the peace treaty was.

In the late autumn of 1981, Israeli and American teams completed their work on a framework for strategic cooperation between the two countries, mainly designed to counter Soviet threats. On 30 November, Sharon and the US Secretary of Defence, Caspar Weinberger, signed the Memorandum of Understanding on Strategic Cooperation in Washington. Its main features were: joint naval and air military exercises, joint readiness activities, cooperation in research and development and a number of other subjects. In some of the fields cooperation existed before the memorandum was signed and others were a declaration of intent, but the government attached importance to their incorporation in a joint document. The agreement received considerable publicity and naturally a wave of Soviet and Arab criticism followed. Before long it was overtaken by events.

On 14 December, the Prime Minister was due to leave hospital following a hip operation. In the early morning hours he invited Foreign Minister Shamir and Defence Minister Sharon to his bedside and disclosed to them his plan to table a law annexing the Golan Heights on that very day. The ministers concurred. The Cabinet was called to Begin's home, for a special session, approved his initiative and the same afternoon the Prime Minister appeared before Parliament, in a wheelchair, and proposed 'extending Israeli law, jurisdiction and administration to the Golan Heights'. The law was hurried through the committee stage and the three required readings on the same day. Protestations from the opposition were of little avail. The basic situation on the Golan had not changed; the thirty-one settlements and four townships were already there. Begin must have understood that without territorial compromise on the Golan there could be no peace with Syria. True, Assad did not respond favourably to peace feelers, whether direct or through the Americans, but this could not be a reason for Israel to add difficulties on the road to peace. Begin's motives and the sudden and dramatic manner of carrying out the decision were puzzling. Was he driven by domestic considerations or did he really believe that he was making history and creating an irrevocable reality? Its immediate effect was to enrage the Arabs and attract scathing criticism from the United States, leading to the suspension of the Memorandum of Understanding, which had been signed only two weeks before.[17]

'Peace for Galilee' – the War in Lebanon

Terror on the northern border plagued the Begin government as it had others. In 1981–2 the incidence of Katyusha rockets and artillery attacks on populated areas in the Galilee intensified. The PLO had built up a considerable network of terrorist bases and underground arms depots – it was receiving an ongoing supply of weapons from Syria and the Soviet Union, including heavy artillery guns with a range of up to forty kilometres – and was harassing our villages and towns. The problem was compounded by the PLO in western Beirut becoming a command centre for terrorist activities against Israeli and Jewish targets in Europe.

Armed to the teeth and with about fourteen thousand fighters at their disposal, the PLO became involved in Lebanon's domestic affairs and upset the precarious balance between Muslims and Christians. The Christian community lived in clusters of villages in south Lebanon and between east Beirut and Jounieh in the north of the country. They viewed with trepidation and a sense of foreboding the growing influence of the Palestinians. In 1975, a representative of the Phalangists, the more militant of the Christian groupings, approached a representative of Mossad in Europe and suggested cooperation with Israel. He explained that Israel and the Christian Maronites had a common enemy in the PLO, and a common interest in fighting it. David Kimche, who was a top Mossad representative in Europe, passed on the request, supporting it. The Rabin government saw the advantages of such a relationship but imposed constraints on it: Israel was not to get involved in the continuous strife between the various Christian clans nor be dragged into confrontation with the Syrians. Kimche, back at Mossad headquarters, assumed responsibility for forging the relationship. Soon a programme of military training, for the members of the Phalangists and the faction led by Camille Chamoun, started. Israel also sold them weapons, mainly from the arsenal of captured arms from Egypt and Syria. The common objectives were clear: to rid Lebanon of the PLO and terminate their attacks on Israel from bases in the Lebanon.

Israel also hoped that when the Christians assumed power, Lebanon would be the second Arab country to conclude peace.

After Begin became Prime Minister and learned more about this extraordinary relationship, he encouraged it and saw a moral justification in extending a helping hand to Christians in distress. His major concern was to pacify the Galilee; the information that came from the Phalangists as well as their attitude towards the terrorist build-up also served Israel's interest. In July 1981 six Israelis died and sixty-five were injured in shelling attacks. Israel retaliated by bombing PLO targets in western Beirut. The US condemned the attack, in which innocent civilians were also hurt, and dispatched ambassador Philip Habib to arrange a cease-fire. In August, Foreign Minister Yitzhak Shamir outlined the government's objectives in Lebanon: '... Israel has only one desire. We want to see a free Lebanon. We want to see the last Syrian soldier removed from Lebanese soil. We want to see the terrorists disarmed and forced to respect Lebanese laws and sovereignty. We want peace with our Lebanese neighbours.'[18]

In August 1981, Ariel Sharon became Minister of Defence. From his very first days in office he concluded that a major operation against the terrorist bases in Lebanon was inevitable and set out to plan it with the General Staff of the Army. Chief of Staff Rafael Eitan held a similar view and a number of contingencies were already on the drawing-board. Sharon had additional political objectives in mind; the weakening of the PLO leadership in Beirut would lift their pressure on the Palestinians in the territories and make the Palestinians more amenable to a settlement with Israel. Also, a flood of Palestinians fleeing Lebanon might arrive in Jordan and increase the chances of Jordan becoming the Palestinian state. Begin did not necessarily share these broad designs and they were not presented to the government for approval. But the Prime Minister did believe that a serious offensive, cleaning out the terrorist strongholds, must be mounted. At his invitation Sharon outlined plans for the 'big operation' to the Cabinet in December 1981, as a precaution in case the Syrians reacted to the annexation of the Golan with violence.[19] Sharon's broad concept was discussed in many meetings with the army and it basically envisaged the following aims: to destroy the terrorist bases in south Lebanon and Beirut, to compel the Syrians to withdraw from Beirut and station their troops closer to the Syrian border, to link up with the Phalangists forces on the Beirut–Damascus road and have them install a new government in Lebanon that would make peace with Israel. His ambitious plan evoked the resentment of ministers and was shelved for a while.

Encountering the lack of enthusiasm in Cabinet for a sweeping operation, Sharon and the Chief of Staff worked on a more modest scheme, that would start 'small' but could be steamrollered into a broader operation with the wider objectives. On 9 May the Israeli air force attacked terrorist bases in Lebanon; heavy shelling of the Galilee followed. The next day Begin convened the Cabinet and maps of Lebanon were rolled out; plans for an offensive were again discussed. The army looked at 17 May as a possible date for it; however, ministers had their reservations and Begin sensed little eagerness to support the operation. A week later, Sharon travelled to Washington and, in a lengthy conversation with Secretary of State Alexander Haig on 19 May, explained the inevitability of dealing with the PLO terrorist infrastructure. He further outlined his main concept of the operation and told Haig that 'our aim is not to bring about an independent Lebanon, or to expel the Syrians; these, however, could be by-products of our operation'.[20] The US recognized the Israeli government's dilemma, with the Galilee exposed to continuous terrorist harassment, buttressed by Syria and the Soviet Union, but Haig expressed the opinion that unless there was provocation that justified the proposed operation, it would be severely criticized. Begin concluded that Israel had the under-standing of the Reagan administration for the 'Peace for Galilee' operation. A letter from Haig to Begin following his talk with Sharon, in which he stressed the need for absolute restraint, contained mixed signals but did not change Begin's view that there was no American 'red light' and he was right. However, 'by May 1982 those Americans most in the know seemed to accept the inevitability, if not desirability, of such a move,' wrote Quandt.[21]

On 3 June, Israel's ambassador to London, Shlomo Argov, one of the foremost diplomats in our foreign service, was shot and severely injured as he left the Dorchester Hotel. His assailants, two terrorists of the Abu Nidal group, were chased and apprehended by Special Branch detectives. The next day Begin told his Cabinet that the assault on the ambassador was tantamount to an attack on the state. It was the Prime Minister's declaration of the war in Lebanon. Argov, who was paralysed in the attack, resented very much the fact that the assault on him was used as a *casus belli* when the operation had in fact been planned long before. At the suggestion of the Chief of Staff, a number of bombing raids were approved, including targets in Beirut. The PLO response was as expected, hundreds of shells and Katyusha rockets on the Galilee. On 5 June the Cabinet convened again, this time to approve Sharon's proposal for a land offensive on Lebanon. A considerable debate ensued, at the end of which the plan was approved, with several provisos: that Beirut was not included in the attack; that the forces would advance up to forty kilometres from Israel's northern border; the operation would last twenty-four to forty-eight hours; and that there was no intention of a confrontation with the Syrians.[22] Leaders of the opposition Labour Party were briefed and did not object to these limited goals.

Sharon and the Chief of Staff had much wider objectives in mind. To them it was clear that unless the terrorist concentrations in Beirut were tackled, the offensive would not solve the basic problem of PLO terrorism. They also believed that some sort of encounter with the Syrian troops stationed in Lebanon was inevitable in order to destroy their ground-to-air missile batteries. The IDF advance began, and Sharon obtained Begin's approval and Cabinet sanction as the army advanced. Begin himself described the strange procedure by saying that sometimes he knew about military moves before they had happened, and at other times he became aware of them only after they had occurred. By 11 June Israeli troops were at the outskirts of Beirut and two days later, the Chief of Staff, General Eitan, drove into Christian sections of Beirut to the cheers of the inhabitants. The siege of Beirut was complete. The expectations that the Phalangist units would link up with the IDF and take responsibility for fighting the terrorists in west Beirut faded away. Their elders cautioned them against such a confrontation, as they would have to continue living in a Lebanon with a Muslim majority. Syrian missiles in the Lebanon were attacked and fourteen batteries destroyed. Attempting to protect them, the Syrian air force lost twenty-four MiG fighter planes. People recalled Begin's pledge in the Knesset only days earlier, when he said on 8 June: 'We do not want war with Syria. From this rostrum, I call on President Assad to instruct the Syrian army not to harm Israeli soldiers, and then nothing will happen to them ... We do not want any clash with the Syrian army.' On the IDF advancing up to the forty-kilometre limit, Begin said, in the same speech: 'If we achieve the forty-kilometre line from our northern border, the job is done; all fighting will cease.'[23] But there was no correlation between the initial offensive which the government had authorized and the reality on the battlefield; between the Prime Minister's statement to Parliament and the actual situation on the ground; between Sharon's designs and objectives and the more restricted views of Cabinet Ministers.

Begin was pushed by Sharon into taking military decisions whose implications he did not perceive, and his government and the country were sucked deeper and deeper into a prolonged war claiming 650 casualties with many hundreds injured. On 17 May 1991, Uzi Benziman published an article contending that Begin knew Sharon had deceived him. Sharon sued the journalist for libel. After a six-year trial, and sifting through heaps of evidence, the district court judge, Moshe Talgam, ruled on 4 November 1997 that the evidence presented was enough 'to prove that what was published was the truth'. The judge added: 'The green light given by the Prime Minister and the government to commence with Peace for Galilee cannot, therefore, be interpreted as a conscious consent for the Lebanon war.'[24]

During these weeks the American special envoy, Philip Habib, shuttled between Jerusalem, Beirut and Damascus arranging cease-fires which repeatedly broke down. The US felt let down by Begin, having believed his undertaking that Israeli troops would not advance beyond the forty-kilometres line and passed assurances to Damascus that Israel had no intention of attacking Syrian troops. The Prime Minister wrote to President Reagan on 6 June that the army had been instructed 'to push back the terrorists to a distance of forty kilometres', and the administration believed that to be the objective of the war. Habib's reports and the continuous fighting conveyed a very different picture. The Americans looked at a number of options. In a conversation with the Israeli ambassador in Washington, Moshe Arens, Haig talked about the possibility of using the shock of the war to achieve the evacuation of all foreign forces from Lebanon–Israeli, Palestinian and Syrian. It was a very attractive thought. If only it had been achievable! The possibility of the PLO leaving Beirut was nevertheless raised and subsequently followed up.[25]

In the third week of June Begin travelled to New York for the UN Special Assembly on Disarmament and was invited to Washington for talks with Reagan. In their meeting on 21 June the President, though angry with Begin, focused on the future rather than dwelling on the past, and attempted to chart a course out of the war. He identified three points which served the Israeli as well as the US interest; the evacuation of all foreign forces from Lebanon, the establishment of a stable government and the creation of a security zone up to forty kilometres from Israel's northern border. Haig tried to impress upon Begin the need for an immediate cease-fire. However, Sharon tightened the noose around west Beirut and eventually Haig was compelled to resign as Secretary of State. His support for the war in Lebanon was too obvious and had been increasingly criticized by Defence Secretary Weinberger and by other members of the administration. He was replaced by George Shultz.

Israeli bombing raids of west Beirut aroused worldwide censure. Public opinion in Israel became extremely weary of the war, which caused more and more casualties and the intemperate behaviour of Sharon infuriated ministers like the Minister of Trade and Industry, Gideon Patt, the Minister of Energy, Berman, who resigned from the government, and others. In a Cabinet meeting on 12 August, Begin decreed that Sharon could not order any more air-force, naval or artillery operations without prior approval by the Prime Minister. The Defence Minister protested, saying that he could not operate within such constraints, and asked for a vote. Begin agreed and all the ministers, except Sharon and one other colleague, approved Begin's decision. It was an important move for getting the war under control, or so Begin hoped. Yitzhak Shamir, who was Foreign Minister at the time, later wrote that 'mistakes and miscalculations of a most serious nature were made and cost precious lives'. He described Sharon as possessing an 'inborn extremism and recklessness' and of having 'disregard of accuracy'.[26]

On the same day Yasser Arafat agreed to Habib's plan to evacuate the PLO fighters with their personal weapons from Beirut, under the protection of American marines. It was a major achievement, although it was clear that some terrorists would remain behind, even in areas under IDF control like Tyre and Sidon.

On 23 August Bashir Gumayel was elected President of Lebanon, to be sworn in a month later. It seemed that some of the objectives of Peace for Galilee were slowly taking shape. Begin and Sharon met the President-elect to discuss a peace treaty with Israel; he was cautious and hesitated to commit himself. But he agreed that the Lebanese army and the Phalangists would deal with the Palestinians in west Beirut and in the refugee camps. However, on 14 September, while the newly elected President was visiting a Phalangist branch, a powerful bomb devastated the building and killed him, with dozens of his supporters. The general assumption was that the plot had originated in Damascus. The Christian community lost a charismatic leader and Israel was stripped of an authoritative ally in the Lebanese quagmire. Without Begin's permission, Sharon authorized the advance of the IDF into west Beirut, as well as the entry of the Phalange into two refugee camps, Sabra and Shatila. The Maronites, anguished and grieving, expressed their wrath over the killing of their leader by committing a horrendous massacre of Palestinian civilians. About eight hundred were killed in areas under the control of the IDF. A huge outcry resulted and massive demonstrations took place in Tel Aviv. After heavy public pressure, Begin reluctantly established a commission of inquiry to investigate the atrocities.

The commission was chaired by the president of the Supreme Court, Justice Yitzhak Kahan, with Justice Aharon Barak and General Yona Efrat as the other members. Its report was published on 8 February 1983; it asserted that 'the massacre at Sabra and Shatila was carried out by a Phalangist unit, acting on its own but its entry was known to Israel'. Since this was an area under the responsibility of the IDF, the commission determined that Israel had 'indirect responsibility for the massacre'. The Prime Minister was responsible 'for not exercising greater involvement', Sharon was accused of 'not taking appropriate measures to prevent blood-shed' and his removal from the Defence Ministry was recommended. General Eitan, according to the findings, 'did not give the appropriate orders to prevent the massacre'. As his term of office was to end a few weeks later the commission did not demand his resignation. Three other high-ranking officers lost their command. The government accepted the report and Sharon resigned but stayed on in the Cabinet as minister without responsibility for a specific department.

In Lebanon, Amin Gumayel was elected President after the death of his brother and his government entered negotiations with Israel on a peace agreement. After thirty-five sessions, under American chairmanship, an agreement was signed on 17 May 1983, by the Director-General of the Ministry of Foreign Affairs, David Kimche, and Mr Fattal on behalf of Lebanon, ending the state of war between the two countries. Israel was to withdraw its forces within eight to twelve weeks, as part of 'all external forces' being removed from Lebanon. It was a short-lived accord. Syria had no intention of withdrawing its army from Lebanon and its relentless pressure forced the Lebanese government to abrogate the agreement.

The summer of 1983 marked the first anniversary of a war that was intended to last between twenty-four and forty-eight hours. In the country there was a profound sense of dissatisfaction. Hundreds of Israeli soldiers had lost their lives; the troops in Lebanon were exposed to continuous terror, from Palestinians as well as from the Shia Muslims. Demonstrations with daily updates of the number killed were staged in front of Begin's home; thousands of Palestinians and Lebanese, including civilians, were killed; acute tension with the US and erosion of public support for Israel from the world followed. The consensus which had existed in the country at the beginning of the war was long dissipated and the continuous strain took its toll on Begin. By August 1983, he was a very sick man. During his premiership he had suffered a number of heart attacks and a slight stroke. A year earlier, in July 1982, the American ambassador reported to the State Department that 'Menachem Begin was sinking into a mood of deep depression.'[27] His Cabinet, his close entourage and his doctors covered up for him and did not disclose to the nation his real state of health. Thus, the country, in the midst of war, was being led by a Prime Minister at less than his full capacity and a Minister of Defence who was less than candid. This should never have happened in a vibrant and open democracy like Israel. At the end of August Begin told his Cabinet, 'I cannot go on,' and left the room. This was his resignation; it was the truth and said everything. No more explanations were given or needed. He left a disastrous legacy in Lebanon, an economy at four hundred per cent inflation, a country that was polarized by his vitriolic rhetoric. Yet his historic achievement in signing the peace treaty with Egypt will stand as an important turning-point in our struggle for peace and security.

The Reagan Plan

A year before Begin left office the Reagan administration made a serious attempt to contribute to the solution of the Palestinian problem and encourage Jordan to join the peace process. After Shultz became Secretary of State he asked a group of top officials, which included Lawrence Eagelburger, Nicholas Veliotis and others, to prepare an outline for a presidential initiative on the Middle East. By August 1982, the plan was finalized and Shultz discussed it with the President on a number of occasions. The issue which 'weighed most heavily' on Reagan's mind was the security of Israel.[28] Shultz reassured the President on that point and prepared the launch of the plan, which was announced by the President in a televised speech, on 1 September 1982, later called the Reagan Plan. The timing of the speech coincided with the successful evacuation of the PLO from Beirut. The US ambassador to Israel, Samuel Lewis, had given Begin notice of the plan the day before. Its essence was: the war in Lebanon and the evacuation of the PLO from Beirut opened a new opportunity for peace. 'The question now is how to reconcile Israel's legitimate security concerns with the legitimate rights of the Palestinians,' Reagan said. After calling for direct negotiations he proposed that the Palestinians and the Arab states recognize and accept the 'reality of Israel', and advocated the participation of Jordan and the Palestinians in the process; peace would not be achieved either by a Palestinian state or by Israel's annexation of the West Bank and Gaza, and therefore the US would not support these alternatives; the best option was self-government in the territories in association with Jordan; Resolution 242 applied to 'all fronts, including the West Bank and Gaza'. The President also said that Jerusalem must remain undivided, but that its final status should be decided through negotiations. Palestinian inhabitants of East Jerusalem could participate in the elections to the Palestinian authority. He suggested a settlement freeze but stressed that 'Jews must have the right to live on the West Bank, historically Judea and Samaria.' No President had ever previously gone that far in accepting the right of Jews to live in the territories. Reagan also made it clear that in the negotiations to follow 'the US will ... oppose any proposal from any party and at any point in the negotiating process that threatens the security of Israel. America's commitment to the security of Israel is iron-clad.' This was strong and friendly language, written and spoken by two staunch friends of Israel, Shultz and Reagan.

Lewis met Begin at his holiday retreat in Naharyah on 31 August, and conveyed the Reagan Plan to him. The Prime Minister's reaction was totally negative, for the plan envisaged a territorial compromise on the West Bank and called for a freeze on settlements. Upon hearing the details, he told Lewis that it was the 'saddest day' of his life. It certainly was one of the tougher and more unpleasant talks that the experienced and friendly American envoy had with the Prime Minister. The next day, 2 September, the Cabinet supported Begin's position and rejected the plan point by point as a deviation from the Camp David agreements. Nevertheless, the Reagan Plan had a number of very positive elements, and had it been accepted by Israel and the Arabs as a basis for negotiations, it might have accelerated the peace process and prevented anguish and bloodshed. The Arab reaction was evasive but after Begin's criticism of the plan they did not need to say much. It was another missed opportunity, because at that point the PLO was weakened after their eviction from Beirut. The Syrians also had domestic problems after their troops had massacred thousands of its citizens in Hama in an attempt to put down the Muslim Brotherhood rebellion. Thus the atmosphere was ripe for restarting negotiations.

On 1 September 1983 the Likud Party elected Yitzhak Shamir as their new leader to replace Begin. On 10 October he presented his government to the Knesset, retaining the post of Foreign Minister as well as taking on that of Prime Minister. A few weeks later Shamir departed for Washington for talks with the President and in their first conversation told him that the proposals in the Reagan Plan were unacceptable. If the Americans entertained any hope that the change of leadership would lead to more flexibility in negotiations with the Palestinians, Shamir dispelled it.

After my return from the Philippines, until I was appointed minister plenipotentiary (deputy chief of mission) in our Embassy in London, I worked under Shamir, heading the Economic Department of the Foreign Ministry. I appreciated his businesslike, forthright manner, and on any subject that was not related to the West Bank or to settlements, it was easy to get his opinion or decision. As Prime Minister, Shamir managed domestic affairs with a surer hand than Begin. However, his vision on Judea and Samaria was as ideologically oriented and as hard-line as Begin's. Yet the articulation of his beliefs was sometimes more carefully worded and designed to maintain Israel's relations with the US and the world. He believed that 'Israel should not pay for peace with parts of its land.'[29] In other words his policy, like Begin's, was based on the negation of the land-for-peace formula or any notion of territorial compromise on the West Bank. It was clear that under these conditions there could be no Palestinian partner for negotiations. The policy denied that 242 was applicable to the West Bank. When the New York Times correspondent Thomas Friedman asked him whether Israel still adhered to 242 and the implicit land-for-peace formula, Shamir replied: 'We don't accept that formula any more.' Israel must keep building West Bank settlements 'without any pause'.[30] In reality that meant continuing occupation, continuing resistance by the Palestinians, continuing repression and continuing casualties. In this policy there was no solution to the ultimate fate of two million Palestinians, or to the impact of prolonged occupation on Israeli society; nothing was said about how to reduce tension and hostility with the neighbouring Arab countries, who believed that the Palestinian issue was the heart of the conflict, or how to advance the peace process. The final aim of this line of thought was the annexation of the West Bank; little attention was given to the vexing question of how Israel could remain a Jewish state if it incorporated another 2.2 million Palestinians and how it would maintain its democratic system if the Jewish population and the Arab population were nearly at par. The priorities were set according to the single-minded goal of building more settlements as quickly as possible and therefore urgent needs – more roads, assistance to less-developed towns, more funds for education – were put on the back burner. Shamir explained his sense of mission to the Knesset on 12 March 1984: 'Please listen to what the Arabs are saying ... Let the Likud government work for another two years, and there won't be anything left on which to negotiate. This is what they say when they point to the map, which is gradually filling up with Jewish settlements. This is our pride, and for its sake we are ready to absorb a great many things, and to suffer, since these are the things that determine history.'[31] In this scheme, peace was to be sacrificed for the sake of more settlements.

On 23 July 1984 the country went to the polls to elect the eleventh Knesset. Likud lost seven seats and had forty-one members; Labour lost three seats and became the largest party in the Knesset with forty-four representatives. However, neither party was able to achieve an absolute majority, the sixty-one members necessary to form a government. Shamir supported a national-unity Cabinet composed of the two large blocks; Labour had no better option. A bizarre arrangement called 'rotation' resulted. As the government would hold office for fifty months, twenty-five months would pass with Peres as Prime Minister and twenty-five months with Shamir. Each party had ten ministers and they did not change with rotation. Peres became Prime Minister from 1984 to 1986 and then Shamir replaced him, between 1986 and 1988. Each of them became Foreign Minister when his colleague was Prime Minister. On 13 September the National Unity Government was voted in by the Knesset.

On domestic issues and on top security policy the two parties reached agreement easily. Yitzhak Rabin was Minister of Defence in both administrations and shortly after the inauguration of the new government he set up an army team to prepare a proposal for the withdrawal of the IDF from Lebanon. After a massive army presence in Lebanon for two years and seven months, and hundreds of casualties, Peres suggested to the Cabinet on 14 January 1985 that the IDF withdraw in phases. The last phase included withdrawal to the international border and the establishment of a security zone in south Lebanon which would be operated by the South Lebanese Army with the backing of the IDF. There was a fierce debate in Cabinet with Shamir and Likud ministers opposing the resolution. David Levy, a prominent Likud minister, supported the need to disengage and voted with Labour, and so the resolution was passed. Thus the Peres government extricated Israel from the difficult situation in which Begin and Sharon landed the country in 1982. It did not entirely solve the problem with Lebanon, which continued to fester and is still claiming its toll in human lives and suffering, but it reduced it very considerably and made it more manageable.

The second issue which plagued the country was rampant inflation. By the end of June Peres was ready with the Economic Stabilization Plan, which radically reformed the economy. It was approved by the Cabinet and had lasting beneficial effects.[32]

The guidelines of the National Unity Government contained the pledge that it would 'spare no effort to promote peace' and it was on this issue that the big divisions between Peres and Shamir surfaced. Peres was farsighted, and dedicated himself to exploring every opening in order to launch a negotiating process. Shamir was in no hurry. He was content with the status quo as long as it allowed for more settlement activity; he insisted on direct negotiations, for which the Arabs were not yet ready, and ignored the long-term dangers. He was against what he called 'illusory short-range and temporary gains'.[33] Both supported Rabin's initiatives to maintain a modern and highly sophisticated army. But the two leaders held particularly divergent views on the possibility of convening an international conference on the Middle East, which was supported by the US. Shamir opposed such a conference in the most vehement terms. He believed that it was a deviation from the Camp David Accords and that its purpose was to circumvent the need for direct negotiations. He was also wary of a possible Soviet role in the conference. This last point was well taken care of by Shultz, who obtained the agreement of the Soviet Foreign Minister, Edward Shevardnadze, that the negotiations would be done 'by the parties directly and bilaterally'.[34] Peres obviously preferred direct negotiations or any other more plausible alternative to an international conference. The problem was that no better alternative existed at the time. Jordan seemed to be the second Arab country willing to engage in peace negotiations and, in conversations with American statesmen, King Hussein promised publicly to declare non-belligerency. Peres met the king in July and October 1985 in London[35] and Hussein insisted on an international conference. In conversations with Israelis and Americans the king had stressed the need for such a conference in order to overcome the problem of Palestinian representation and to have an international umbrella against Syrian criticism. Peres therefore saw it as the only alternative which could pave the way to direct negotiations and break the impasse. This was also the opinion of George Shultz, who was attempting to build a Jordanian–Palestinian delegation that would be acceptable to the US and Israel. As a terrorist organization, the PLO was barred from participation by Israel and by President Reagan, who refused to sanction any meetings of US representatives with Palestinians who were 'even remotely associated with the PLO'.[36] The political clock was ticking fast and the Americans knew that in 1986, when Shamir was to replace Peres according to the rotation agreement, it would be harder to launch a dialogue. The assistant secretary of state, Richard Murphy, and others worked very hard for many months to overcome the obstacles to an international conference which would allow for direct negotiations under its wings, but with no success.

Before Peres could attempt to muster Israeli support for an international conference Hussein needed the support of the Palestinians or of Syria for such a move. He failed to obtain either and in February 1986 he castigated the PLO for their blunders. 'I and the government of the Kingdom of Jordan announce that we are unable to continue to coordinate politically with the PLO leadership until such time as their word becomes their bond,' the king said.[37]

Peres and King Hussein made another attempt to start peace negotiations in the spring of 1987. On 11 April 1987 they met again in London in Lord Mishcon's apartment. Lord Mishcon, a perceptive and highly discreet attorney, had a long-standing friendship with the king and his family. Peres was accompanied by Yossi Beilin, political director-general of the Foreign Ministry, and the king had with him Zaid Rifai. After a long discussion the two statesmen agreed on the modalities of an international conference. Moreover, the king had no objection to embodying the main points of the agreement in a joint document, which became known as the Peres–Hussein London Agreement. Its main features were that the Secretary-General of the UN would convene an international conference whose objective would be to reach a comprehensive peace in the Middle East and achieve a peaceful solution to the Palestinian problem 'in all its aspects'. Then came a series of restrictive procedures: the conference would not impose solutions, the negotiations would take place in bilateral committees, the Palestinian issue would be dealt in the framework of the Jordanian–Palestinian delegation, all the parties would have to accept Resolutions 242 and 338. The agreement was subject to the approval of the two governments.[38]

The Jordanian monarch had no problems with getting approval, but Peres encountered a huge obstacle – Shamir's opposition. To achieve a smoother acceptance of the accord, the king and Peres had agreed that the Americans should present the plan as a US initiative. After Peres briefed the Prime Minister on the outcome of the London talks, Shamir decided to undermine the initiative without rejecting it formally. Following a telephone call from Shultz indicating that he intended to travel to the area with the Peres–Hussein agreement, Shamir instructed the secretary to the Cabinet to call Shultz and express reservations about the international conference. According to the Secretary of State, Rubinstein said that Shamir 'would not welcome' a visit by him.[39] Moreover, without notifying his Foreign Minister, he dispatched the former Israeli ambassador to Washington, Moshe Arens, to meet Shultz and convince him not to present the agreement on the international conference. Shultz, now aware of the polarized views, became reluctant to get involved in a domestic argument between the Israeli Prime Minister and Foreign Minister, and dropped the initiative. Hussein expected Peres to have a parliamentary showdown with Shamir, and if necessary resign on the issue. However, with Labour's narrow margin in Parliament, the result of such a clash, on a subject not terribly popular, could have lead to a loss of influence and prestige. To the king's chagrin, Peres stopped short of such a confrontation. Instead, many of the procedures of the London Agreement were adopted four years later, when another Secretary of State, James Baker, negotiated the Madrid Conference, to which Shamir agreed. In 1987, the picture was gloomy: the autonomy talks had stopped, there was no prospect of any political negotiations and the Palestinians, in their despair, took to the streets and to violence. The intifada was born. Had Hussein agreed to the same London document a year earlier, when Peres was Prime Minister, many lives and much suffering could have been spared. In the sad catalogue of missed opportunities, the failure to follow up on the London Agreement figures prominently.

As deputy chief of mission in our Embassy in London I followed very closely, together with the ambassador, Yehuda Avner, the unceasing efforts to achieve a breakthrough in the peace process. The British Prime Minister, Margaret Thatcher, was kept in the picture by King Hussein and Shimon Peres, and was very supportive of these endeavours. She also encouraged the Reagan administration to be involved and to soften its line on the PLO, although her opposition to terror was as strong and unyielding as possible. I conducted a continuous and fruitful dialogue with her private secretary, Sir Charles Powell, who had a fine understanding of the Middle East and an appreciation of our difficulties. My American colleague, minister plenipotentiary Raymond Seitz, was close to George Shultz and together with the Middle East expert in the US Embassy, Ms Robin Raphel, gave us a comprehensive picture of the Reagan administration's thinking and its desire to promote peace. (When I returned to London as ambassador, I was delighted to find Ray Seitz as the ambassador of the United States. Despite all the uncertainties involved, I felt that we should have given the London Agreement a chance.

In October 1987 Shultz attempted to arrange a different version of an international gathering on the Middle East. Presidents Reagan and Gorbachev would invite Prime Minister Shamir and King Hussein together with the UN Secretary-General and representatives from Syria, Egypt and Lebanon to meet in Washington as part of the American–Soviet summit.

This time Shamir agreed but King Hussein rejected the idea. According to Shultz, the king explained that he did not believe that 'Shamir would ever give up an inch of territory or work for "final status" agreement for the territories'.[40] Despite the setbacks Shultz did not tire; he made two additional attempts to start a negotiating process, in February–March and June 1988, without success.

Shultz outlined his new plan in a speech before the Council of Foreign Relations on 9 February 1988 and proposed it officially in March. It was carefully prepared and took into account a more favourable Soviet approach as well as the influence of the intifada. It centred again on a formal opening of negotiations in an international conference, or an international 'event' that would continue in direct negotiations. It also advocated the shortening of the transition period of autonomy to three years and that direct talks on permanent status be completed within a year. Foreign Minister Peres reacted by saying that he was pleased 'by the move', while Shamir on the next day, 12 February, said that Peres' statements were 'irresponsible' and later rejected the initiative.[41] Shultz later wrote: 'I was frustrated by Shamir's inflexibility and by the fact that divided government, as had existed in Israel since late 1984, meant that no one could be held responsible and accountable.'[42]

During 1987 there was a marked increase in violent incidents in the territories. In late December, the Minister of Defence, Yitzhak Rabin, made an unscheduled stopover in London on his way back from the States. As we had not arranged any meetings for him, it afforded us time for a comprehensive chat. Rabin asked me about our relations with Britain and the prospect of the Thatcher government's lifting the embargo on the sale of arms to Israel. I told him that in view of the interest in London in a very substantial arms deal with Saudi Arabia I doubted whether a favourable decision on the embargo was forthcoming. Also, the British knew that even if the embargo were lifted, the US would remain our major arms supplier. Rabin then recounted his successful talks with the American Secretary of Defence. As we were talking, his military assistant brought in updates on the latest violence in Gaza and the West Bank. Rabin was concerned that this time it seemed to be a more prolonged campaign. But he could not have imagined that it would be a popular uprising, sustained for so long and claiming 409 Palestinian and fifteen Israeli lives between December 1987 and June 1989. During the same period 1,869 Israelis and 6,594 Palestinians were injured.[43]

The outbreak of the intifada, the Palestinian uprising in the territories, is technically tied to an occurrence on 8 December 1987, a road accident involving an Israeli lorry and a car carrying Palestinians from the Gaza Strip, in which four Palestinians were killed. Soon rumours spread that the driver smashed into the Palestinian car on purpose and thousands of people took to the streets in the Gaza area, throwing stones, burning tyres and igniting bottles filled with petrol. The small Israeli army contingent, caught completely unprepared, defended themselves with live ammunition and before long another Palestinian was dead. Fire fuelled fire, pent-up hatred turned into fury and twenty years of frustration and despair under Israeli occupation turned into a tidal wave of violence which swept the towns, villages and refugee camps in the territories. Neither the Israeli government nor the PLO were ready for such an outbreak. It was not planned or premeditated and neither were the counter-measures which had to be adopted while the uprising went on. The road accident was only the trigger, but the mood was ripe for rebellion. Abject poverty, a desire for some national expression, despondency under occupation, disillusionment with the lack of support from Arab governments, all these combined to cause an eruption of violence on an unprecedented scale. Once it had begun, the PLO made every attempt to direct it and use it politically. Israelis, anguished that their children had to confront and fight civilians, men, women and children, reflected more than ever on how to solve the Palestinian problem. In 1986 Prime Minister Peres had paid the first Israeli public visit to Morocco. Peres promised King Hassan that he would report their talks, the 'Ifrane summit', to the Knesset. On 26 July 1986 Peres told Parliament how King Hassan spoke of the hundreds of thousands of young Palestinians; 'they have no flag, they have no identity, they have no state. But they do have national feelings ... Their frustration is liable to lead them to rebellion and violence.' These were prophetic words, spoken seventeen months before the intifada started.[44]

The uprising had many lessons for all parties in the Israeli–Arab conflict. To Israel it proved that the status quo was untenable and that force alone could not solve the Palestinian problem. Supporters of annexation of the West Bank, proponents of Greater Israel, had to ponder anew the feasibility of that option. The persistence of the Palestinians was remarkable and their suffering and sacrifice compelled the PLO leadership to take a more realistic attitude towards negotiations and accept the imperative of compromise. The intifada proved to Jordan that a Palestinian national political force had been forged and that it was preferable for the kingdom to concentrate on the East Bank rather than seek to restore Jordanian control over the West Bank. To all involved it became apparent that without the PLO there could be no serious negotiation on the Palestinian issue, though Shamir still refused to admit that.[45] Before long the US opened a dialogue with the PLO.[46]

In London, as in other capitals, the ambassador, Yehuda Avner, and the whole Embassy staff made every effort to explain to the British government, to Parliament and to the public that violence would not solve the Palestinian problem and that the real answers lay around the negotiating table. Public opinion had hardly forgotten the telecasts of the bombings of civilians in Beirut when this new and ugly confrontation began to appear day after day on their television screens. Keeping the media and the wider public friendly towards Israel during the intifada was a formidable challenge. Three weeks after the outbreak of the uprising, on 31 December, I analysed the events at an Embassy staff meeting by saying that a fortnight of violence coupled with civil strife had achieved more for the Palestinians than the combined efforts of Arab countries on their behalf and more than their futile campaigns of international terrorism. It placed the Palestinian issue at the centre of Israeli and international attention. Being seen to respond to violence with an 'iron-fist' policy tarnished our image around the world. The Palestinians in the territories had outmanoeuvred the PLO and the Palestinian issue could not be ignored any more.

The daily confrontations with stone-throwing children in the streets of Gaza and West Bank towns overshadowed preparations for the fortieth anniversary of Independence, which included a grand celebration at the Grosvenor House Hotel.

As the fourth decade drew to a close, Israel was making little progress on peace; however, our foreign relations were enhanced when several African countries recognized the futility of refusing diplomatic ties with Israel. The Ivory Coast, Cameroon and Togo resumed relations. Israel also established diplomatic relations with Spain and solved the Taba dispute with Egypt. A remarkable policy shift towards South Africa, in line with US and European policy, was adopted by the government. It was the result of a persistent initiative by Yossi Beilin, then political director-general of the Foreign Ministry. The overall friendly dialogue with the US continued, but the main issue, peace with our neighbours, would still have to wait.[47]

THE FIFTH DECADE

1988–98

15

The Peace Process Continues

The fifth decade found Israel more confident of its future. The struggle for sheer survival was past. The battle for international recognition and legitimacy had become part of history. Peace with Egypt, though not completely satisfactory, had its dividends. The defence burden had eased and the army could concentrate on modernization and quality enhancement rather than on guarding our southern frontier. The Israeli flag flew continuously in the most influential Arab capital, Cairo, and the Egyptian ambassador in Israel became a prominent member of the diplomatic corps and a welcome guest in many Israeli homes. The advent of Gorbachev and the Soviet Union's new policy of openness towards the West had a favourable impact on its relations with Israel. More Jews were allowed to emigrate. The dialogue between Gorbachev and President Reagan, and Gorbachev's meeting with Margaret Thatcher, clarified the new trends in Soviet thinking. They included reduced hostility towards Israel and a diminishing commitment to aggressive Arab designs. Yosef Govrin, the deputy director-general of the ministry and our top Soviet expert, concluded that the two major irritants in the relations between Israel and the Soviet Union, Soviet support of the Arabs and the immigration of Soviet Jews, had lost their thrust in the Gorbachev era.[1] In June 1988 Shamir met Shevardnadze in Rome and the Soviet Foreign Minister agreed to the first step in the resumption of relations, the establishment of an Israeli consular mission in Moscow. By October Aryeh Levin, a high-ranking diplomat, was appointed to head the Mission. For about two years it operated as part of the Royal Netherland Embassy[2] but in December 1990, as a result of a meeting between Foreign Minister David Levy and Shevardnadze in New York, our mission was elevated in status and Levin became consul-general. After an absence of twenty-three years the Israeli flag was raised again in Moscow. The most important feature of this new relationship was the increasing exodus of Soviet Jews to Israel.

The beginning of the fifth decade also saw increasing international recognition of Israel's achievements in science and technology. During talks between Rabin, President Reagan and the Secretary of Defence at the end of June, the Americans agreed to joint development of the Arrow anti-missile missile. It was a unique project, part of the sophisticated Star Wars scheme. At the time of writing, considerable progress has been achieved in developing the Arrow. Later in 1988, the first experimental Israeli satellite, Ofeq 1, was successfully launched into space.

There was also progress in broadening Israeli diplomatic representation around the world. In October we resumed low-level relations with Poland by opening an information office in Warsaw, which later became a full-fledged Embassy. However, the biggest advance was in Asia. In the autumn of 1988 we established a 'scientific exchange' office in Beijing. For quite some time we had had trade and other contacts with China and the new office normalized these contacts until full diplomatic relations were set up. Shortly thereafter a representative of the Chinese Tourist Corporation established himself in Tel Aviv. Science and tourism provided an elegant facade for the forging of a meaningful relationship between two ancient peoples.

Closer to our shores, the intifada and its impact continued to influence the Middle East lack-of-peace agenda. Islamic fundamentalist organizations, especially Hamas, used the misery of the Palestinians in Gaza refugee camps to further their particular designs. They were inspired and financed by Iran and by 'Muslim Brotherhood' movements whose aim was to engulf the Arab world in Islamic republics that would stretch from Morocco to Pakistan, with Palestine being part of this sinister map. At the beginning, the PLO did not take this movement seriously but as they increased their influence during the intifada, used Friday sermons in mosques to fuel violence and established a web of social welfare and educational institutions to spread their ideology, the PLO and Arab governments recognized the long-term dangers. Tension between the PLO-led Palestinian authority and Hamas continues.

The London Agreement between Peres and King Hussein had been the last attempt by the Jordanian monarch to play a dominant role in the fortunes of the West Bank and Gaza. The tide has now turned, on 31 July 1988 King Hussein delivered a televised speech to the Jordanian people recognizing the right of the PLO to secede from Jordan and have self-determination, emphasizing that Jordan was not Palestine and announcing the severance of legal and administrative ties between Jordan and the West Bank. There were many reasons for this far-reaching move; the king was upset by the impasse in the peace process and by years of unsatisfactory dealings with Arafat and the PLO. The underlying cause was their continuing antagonism over influence on the West Bank Palestinians. Now there was a danger that the intifada would spill over into Jordan and the king felt compelled to act. His step was also a recognition of the growing force of Palestinian national aspirations, which were led not only from the PLO headquarters in Tunis, but also by a new leadership emerging from within the territories. It was an admission of a new reality, radically different from the situation which had existed before June 1967, when Jordan ruled the West Bank.

Although there had been earlier indications that Hussein might contemplate such a move, his announcement, clear and unequivocal, created a new situation. For the Labour Party, it was the end of the 'Jordanian option', which supported a solution to the Palestinian problem in concert with Jordan. Israel would now have to negotiate with the Palestinians directly, though a Jordanian–Palestinian delegation was later put together for the Madrid Conference. But to all intents and purposes it was like talking to two separate delegations. Rabin pondered the immediate influence of the speech on the inhabitants of Judea and Samaria; Shamir maintained that the king was in any case cut off from developments on the West Bank and wondered how he could support self-determination for the West Bank Palestinians while ignoring 'the right of self-determination of the Palestinians living in his kingdom'. Shamir further stressed that 'if he [the King] quits the process, we have no reason for regret'.[3]

Arafat and the PLO, encouraged by the intifada and attempting to translate it into more lasting political gains, convened the Palestine National Council (PNC) in Algiers. On 14 November 1988 it issued a long declaration enumerating a catalogue of demands and calling for an international conference to be convened on the basis of Resolutions 242 and 338. It was the first time that they had accepted these Security Council Resolutions and agreed to negotiate with Israel within the framework of an international conference. The PNC also declared the independence of Palestine, with Jerusalem as its capital, without delineating borders. Israel reacted to this declaration by a Cabinet statement on 20 November, which said that the 'PLO has not changed its covenant, its policy, its path of terrorism or its character', and called on other countries not to recognize their declaration of independence. The PNC declaration came nowhere near Israeli requirements for accepting the PLO as a partner, but it paved the way to fulfilling American conditions for opening a dialogue.

At this time I was deputy director-general of the ministry in charge of information. I found it an interesting assignment, with responsibilities that were not tied to a specific geographical area but were of a global nature. In addition to ensuring that our missions abroad were well informed of political developments, I dealt with policy towards the media and with the need to adapt quickly to the media revolution, which was racing ahead. Our major challenge was to maintain the understanding and goodwill of world public opinion towards Israel, a task in which I was assisted by two able division directors, Yacov Levy and Yossy Gal. In early November it had become clear to us that the PNC meeting in Algiers would be different from previous gatherings of that body and that this time they might proclaim a Palestinian state. In line with government policy, supported by Labour and Likud, I had instructed our Embassies that should the Palestinians declare a state at Algiers, it would be fictitious. The accepted basis for negotiations was Resolutions 242 and 338, and they did not include any reference to a Palestinian state. Such a state might be able to conclude alliances with radical Muslim countries and so threaten Israel and Jordan; in any case progress could only be achieved in negotiations and not by unilateral acts.

The US insisted on a clear and unequivocal commitment from the PLO to meet American conditions for dialogue and until then Shultz refused to grant Arafat an entry visa to the US to participate in the forty-third session of the UN General Assembly, on the grounds that he headed a terrorist organization. The Assembly, however, defied US opposition by voting to reconvene at the UN European headquarters in Geneva, to discuss the Palestinian problem and listen to Arafat. At the same time, Shultz gave his discreet consent to the Swedish Foreign Minister, Stan Anderson, to work for a clear-cut PLO declaration that would meet the American requirements. On 7 December Anderson transmitted to Arafat the following points to be included in this commitment: readiness to negotiate with Israel a comprehensive peace on the basis of Resolutions 242 and 338; that the PLO was prepared to live in peace with Israel and 'respect their right to live in peace within secure and internationally recognized borders'; that it condemned terrorism 'in all its forms' and was prepared for 'a moratorium on all forms of violence, on a mutual basis once negotiations begin'.[4] Shultz refused to endorse any US support for Palestinian self-determination. However, he agreed that the Palestinians could table their demand in negotiations.

In his speech before the General Assembly in Geneva on 13 December, Arafat made some of these points. When he was told that his lack of clarity was unsatisfactory to Washington, he supplemented his UN statement in a press conference declaration on 14 December, saying: 'Yesterday ... I also made a reference to our acceptance of Resolutions 242 and 338 as a basis for negotiations with Israel within the framework of the international conference ... In my speech also yesterday, it was clear that we mean ... the right of all parties concerned in the Middle East conflict to exist in peace and security and, as I have mentioned, including the State of Palestine, Israel and other neighbours according to the Resolutions 242 and 338.' The language this time was more explicit and on the renunciation of terrorism he was even more specific: 'As for terrorism, I renounced it yesterday in no uncertain terms, and yet I repeat for the record that we totally and absolutely renounce all forms of terrorism, including individual, group, and state terrorism.'[5]

On the same day, 14 December, Shultz obtained Reagan's approval for authorizing a dialogue with the PLO, which in the first instance was conducted by the American ambassador in Tunis. Shultz's decision to change American policy *vis-à-vis* the PLO just weeks before he stepped down as Secretary of State reflected a recognition that without the PLO there could be no peace process. In his own reaction, President Reagan described the new developments as an 'evolution in Palestinian thinking' and reassured Israel of the 'unshakeable' US commitment to its security and well-being.[6]

For the PLO it was a major landmark, as one of their leaders described it in later years: 'It meant that we, the PLO, had definitely become an official and integral part of any dialogue on the Middle East conflict.'[7] It is a matter of great regret that it had taken full forty years after Israel's independence before the representative organization of the Palestinians, our next-door neighbours, recognized the state's existence, accepted 242 as a basis for negotiations, and most importantly, understood that the future lay in a negotiated compromise and not with the gun. The conditions for a dialogue with the US were part of the Rabin–Kissinger understanding of 1975, which compelled the PLO to be clear and explicit in their undertakings. As for the renunciation of terror, the PLO leadership was either unable or unwilling to impose discipline on all factions. (In May 1990, when two boats with terrorists belonging to the 'Palestine Liberation Front' were intercepted by the Israeli navy on their way to mount an attack on crowded beaches, Arafat refused to condemn the attack, compelling Baker to suspend the talks.

Once the UN had decided to have a Special General Assembly in Geneva in December, I was asked by Foreign Minister Peres to join our delegation there and ambassador Yochanan Bein travelled from New York to head our team. The expectations of Arafat's speech were considerable, as a result of Swedish and American accounts that this time the PLO leader would announce a radical change of policy. The encounter was also a battle for public opinion. In a press conference following Arafat's speech, I said that Israel's security could not depend on vague formulations, recalled the twenty-five years of terror by the PLO and stressed that what was important for us was not just what Arafat said but what he did.

We reported back to Jerusalem all the nuances of the speech and Arafat's press conference, together with the reactions of American and European diplomats. The consensus was that, in spite of ambiguous formulations, they represented recognition of Israel, acceptance of 242 and at least verbal renunciation of terror, though the PLO leader did not fail to encourage the violence of the intifada. The reactions from Israel to the speech reflected the conflicting opinions in the country. Prime Minister Shamir released a statement saying that the speech was 'an act of deception ... a mirage ... an illusion of moderation'. Foreign Minister Peres offered his views in a statement to the Knesset on 14 December in which he said that

Israel could not simply criticize what Arafat was saying but must offer its own programme. He also declared that we were ready for a dialogue with the Palestinians 'without Jordanians' if they stopped shooting. Rabin expanded his views on the changes of PLO policy in a television interview, saying that Israeli readiness to talk with the PLO was tantamount to agreeing in advance to a 'PLO-Palestinian state'. He added that Arafat's statements were not important because they were not 'intended primarily for Israel, but ... at reaching a political dialogue with the US'.[8]

The Israeli Prime Minister and Foreign Minister at this period were members of a transition government. Elections for the twelfth Knesset had been held on 1 November 1988, and the result was again a cliff-hanger: Likud won forty seats and Labour thirty-nine. The religious parties had eighteen seats, and right-wing small parties ended up with seven members. The election gave Shamir the option of forming a government without Labour. Yet the ultra-orthodox Knesset members, sensing their ability to decide which block would head the coalition, conditioned their participation in it on amending the 'law-of-return' to exclude automatic citizenship to Jewish immigrants converted by Conservative or Reform rabbis. At first Shamir tended to comply, but a wave of protest by American Jewry convinced him that the danger of splitting the Jewish people was more serious than the problems of a coalition with Labour. It was the right decision, because no issue carries more peril of driving a deep wedge into the great partnership between Israel and Diaspora Jewry than that amendment. He was also aware that, with the Reagan–Shultz period ending, there was a likelihood that the Bush administration would increase US pressure on Israel. Thus he negotiated with Peres a second National Unity Government, which was sworn in on 22 December 1988.

In the new Cabinet Moshe Arens became Foreign Minister, Peres was Vice-Premier and Minister of Finance and Rabin continued as Minister of Defence. Peace negotiations were now under the control of a Likud team led by Shamir and Arens. Rabin, the Chief of Staff of the Six Day War, had to carry on with the daunting task of containing the intifada within the rule of law and the moral ethos of the State of Israel. Rabin understood that there was no military answer to the wave of Palestinian popular resistance and that political steps were imperative. By January 1989 he proposed that the inhabitants of the territories should be offered elections and meaningful autonomy if they stopped the intifada. In February Arens reached a similar conclusion. The suffering caused by the intifada, and the views of European Foreign Ministers, persuaded him that an Israeli initiative was essential. He presented Shamir with a five-point plan which also included elections on the West Bank and Gaza. At the beginning Shamir was reluctant to embark on any initiative, but when US pressure mounted and he was invited to visit Washington, he realized that it was preferable to come up with an Israeli proposal rather than face an American blueprint. He then incorporated some of the Rabin and Arens suggestions into what became known as the 'Shamir Plan'.[9]

The plan called for direct negotiations based on the Camp David Accords: no negotiations with the PLO; elections to produce a representative delegation of Palestinians; the end of violence and no PLO intimidation of voters; after the elections Israel would negotiate autonomy as an 'interim arrangement'; following a 'testing period' of five years, negotiations on the permanent status of the territories would take place, with the participation of Egypt and Jordan. An ending to the state of belligerency, of economic boycott and 'collective action' to solve the refugee problem was also called for.[10] The initiative was further refined with input from Rabin and Cabinet Secretary Elyakim Rubinstein and approved by the government on 14 May 1989. In supporting the logic of the plan, Rabin explained that the National Unity Government could not exist either on the basis of the land-for-peace formula or on a Greater Israel platform. Therefore the efforts should concentrate on the interim settlement (autonomy) on which Labour and Likud could agree.

The Bush administration, with James Baker as Secretary of State, was conversant with Middle East problems. Bush had been Reagan's Vice-President and Baker his Chief of Staff. Both had followed closely the Shultz efforts to launch a negotiating process. In the first part of 1988 Shultz paid no less than four visits to the area and returned frustrated, being unable to secure Shamir's cooperation on an international conference as an opening forum for direct negotiations. Upon assuming office Baker, who was less reluctant than Shultz to pressure Shamir, was helped by the direct US dialogue with the PLO, which in most capitals was considered the leading political organization of the Palestinians. Our ambassador in Washington, Moshe Arad, an experienced and able diplomat, believed that the new administration would adopt a more vigorous attitude towards the peace negotiations and differences with Israel would sharpen. In March 1989 Foreign Minister Arens visited Washington for talks with Bush and Baker and he was the first Cabinet Minister to sense a more assertive line. After talking to Arens, Baker reaffirmed publicly the US commitment to Israel's security and economic well-being and focused on the 'need for progress' in the peace process as the 'highest priority'; comprehensive peace must be based on 242; a way must be found to meet 'Israel's legitimate security needs' and at the same time address 'the legitimate political rights of the Palestinian people'.[11] The widening gap between the new administration and the Shamir government was evident and was the essential message that the Foreign Minister conveyed upon his return.

On 6 April Shamir met Bush and Baker. One of his main concerns was the US–PLO dialogue because, according to his thinking, the only peace the PLO could produce was 'the peace of the cemetery'.[12] When Baker asked him about his views on permanent status, he replied that 'there will be Israel's demand for sovereignty'. When Shamir presented his plan for negotiations, Bush supported elections but the overall impression of the talks was that if peace were to be advanced the Israeli government must move away from some of Shamir's positions. This prompted an outspoken and blunt statement by Baker delivered to the American Israel Public Affairs Committee (AIPAC) conference on 22 May 1989, in which he said, *inter alia*: 'For Israel, now is the time to lay aside, once and for all, the unrealistic vision of Greater Israel ... Forswear annexation; stop settlement activity, reach out to Palestinians as neighbours who deserve political rights.'[13] Baker's speech stunned the government in its articulation of the depth of divergence in perception between the US and Shamir. Ambassador Arad was not surprised by the content of Baker's statement, but the tone was harsher than expected. The next day the Prime Minister reacted by saying that it was 'ironic' to speak of Greater Israel, when Israel was a very small country, adding that he did not see a connection between the settlements and the peace process.

A lasting misunderstanding between the President and the Prime Minister developed over the settlement issue. When Bush raised the subject, Shamir said, 'Don't worry, they won't be a problem.'[14] Bush's impression was that settlement activity would be halted. As building continued, 'the President's sense that Shamir betrayed him worsened' according to Baker, and he condemned the settlement policy on many occasions. Shamir wrote to the President in 1990 regretting that his words 'may have given the wrong impression,' but the anger remained with Bush until he left office.

Between May 1989 and March 1990 there were continuous efforts by Baker, President Mubarak, Rabin, Peres and Arens to breathe life into the Shamir Plan and translate it into a negotiating process, but to no avail. Shamir always found a reason to stall and delay. Endless discussions took place on how the Palestinian representatives would be chosen. On 23 February 1990, in a conversation in Washington, Baker asked Arens whether the government would 'be ready to consider on a name-by-name basis any Palestinian who was a resident of the territories'. Arens reported to Shamir the conversation with the Secretary of State and his recommendation to reply affirmatively to Baker's question. It is interesting to read Arens' description of that conversation. He told Shamir that 'we should have no problem' with the question once it was established that no resident of Jerusalem would participate in the Palestinian delegation. 'Shamir was sitting there ... sipping tea ... Except for some cynical comments I received no real reaction. My impression was that the whole process, about which he was sceptical from the beginning, was not to his liking and that he preferred to dig in rather than go along with the process.'[15] Arens later wondered how Shamir envisaged a solution of the Israeli–Arab conflict without meaningful contact with the Palestinians.[16] The Labour leaders insisted on a positive reply to the Baker question. Reacting angrily to this pressure, Shamir fired Peres from the government. The other Labour ministers resigned instantly and on 15 March the National Unity Government was voted down by the Knesset. The peace initiative had had no chance to take off. Baker, who had invested a remarkable effort in launching negotiations, felt 'battered, beaten and betrayed' by Shamir's ambivalence. 'Shamir was not even willing to embrace his own plan,' he wrote.[17]

After three months of negotiations on forming a coalition, two religious members of Knesset gave Shamir the necessary majority and he again formed a narrowly based right-wing government, which lasted until 1992. Arens became Minister of Defence and David Levy was nominated Minister of Foreign Affairs. In the meantime, major international developments deflected attention from the peace negotiations; the fall of the Berlin Wall in November 1989 brought freedom to Soviet Jews and an unprecedented wave of immigrants arrived in Israel. They generated excitement and new hope, uniting the country in an all-embracing absorption effort. The Gulf War focused attention on Iraq's aggression against Kuwait and exposed Israel to a new danger, Iraqi missile attacks.

Four months before Iraq invaded Kuwait, its ruler, Saddam Hussein, voiced one of his more dire threats against Israel. Speaking to his General Command on 2 April he said that if Iraq were attacked, 'by God, we will make fire eat up half of Israel'.[18] It was a declaration that sent shock waves not only to Jerusalem but to Washington and other capitals as well, and was taken as an indication that Iraq was prepared to use chemical weapons. For many months now Israeli intelligence had focused on Iraqi capabilities of producing unconventional weapons and it was a leading subject in exchanges with Washington and other friendly governments. We knew that in addition to other sinister designs, Saddam wanted revenge for the destruction of the Iraqi nuclear reactor, Osiraq, by the Israeli air force in June 1981.

On 2 August 1990 Iraq invaded Kuwait, threatening the national existence of Saudi Arabia. Only the power of the US could save these two countries from becoming Iraqi protectorates and safeguard the oil supply to the industrial world. President Bush, prepared to stand up to the brutal aggression of Saddam, was encouraged by Mrs Thatcher and Arab leaders to take a firm stand. For that he needed the support of Congress and the American people; he also needed to ensure that the US acted in concert with other nations. In November the United Nations had authorized the use of force against Iraq to reverse its aggression. Baker succeeded in forging an international coalition, while countless diplomatic efforts to achieve a retreat of Iraqi forces without war continued, but to no avail. The anti-Saddam front included Arab countries led by Saudi Arabia, the Gulf states, Egypt and even Syria. However, Jordan had a very complex relationship with Iraq, having served as its main gateway and supply route during the war with Iran, and an open anti-Iraqi stand would have endangered King Hussein's regime. The PLO supported Saddam and couldn't wait to see his threats against Israel realized.

With the constant escalation of Saddam's threats, Shamir and the government decided not to fall into the trap of deflecting world opinion from the Iraqi aggression against Kuwait on to the Arab–Israeli conflict. Saddam's repeated attempts to draw a parallel between the occupation of Kuwait and the occupation of the West Bank and Gaza had little resonance. The Israeli government adopted a low-profile policy, while intensifying intelligence exchanges with the US, closely monitoring events, raising the state of alert of the Israeli Defence Forces and, by October, when war seemed inevitable, distributing gas masks to the population. As Saddam had used chemical weapons before against Iran and the Kurds, every precaution had to be taken. To prevent Iraqi troops from moving closer to our borders, Defence Minister Arens had announced that if Iraqi forces were to enter Jordan, Israel would act. Within the confines of the 'low profile', I guided our Embassies to stress that Saddam's aggression proved anew how difficult it was to predict events in the Middle East; in many capitals the Iraqi despot was considered a source of instability but few had predicted that he would consume another Arab country in the belief that he could get away with it. Israel was sceptical that this crisis could be solved by negotiations; our view on the PLO was well known, and their support of Saddam's assault on Kuwait was very telling; even more disappointing was the sympathy expressed by the Palestinians in Judea and Samaria for the Iraqi action. I concluded by emphasizing that Iraq was the only country which manufactured and used chemical weapons, and that a solution to the crisis must ensure that this threat would end. From the beginning of this conflict deputy foreign minister Benjamin Netanyahu was the main spokesman for Israel on the unfolding events.

The key to Israeli decision-making was close coordination with the US. In September Arens travelled to Washington and met the Secretary of Defence, Dick Cheney, and a group of friendly Senators to explain the implications of the new developments, military and economic, on Israel. Our ambassador in Washington at the time was Zalman Shoval. Arens assured a package of military supply, but encountered a great reluctance to share strategy with Israel or coordinate tactics. The main message was 'stay out and let us do the job'.

In December the Prime Minister met President Bush. The relations between Shamir and the Bush administration were strained as a result of the differences on the peace process and on settlements, but now a new and dangerous situation had arisen and the communality of interests in confronting the Gulf crisis dictated that other subjects be shelved. Shamir was praised for the low-profile policy and for the restraint Israel had displayed. The President outlined the coalition objectives: to re-establish Kuwait's sovereignty, to smash the Iraqi military machine, to lift the threat to other Gulf states. The President assured Shamir that there would be no trade-off with Iraq on any Israeli interest. He also stressed that the US did not want Israel as part of the coalition for it would inject the Arab–Israeli conflict into the Gulf crisis. Shamir told Bush that Israel had no intention of making a pre-emptive strike and that if the country were directly attacked by Iraqi forces he would consult the US.[19] With firmness and resolve he stood by his commitment.

The coalition attack on Kuwait started on the night of 17 January 1991. On 18 January the first Scud missiles exploded in Tel Aviv. Israel was faced with a new danger, missiles launched from a distance of five hundred kilometres with the potential to kill and destroy property. Although I had lived through many of Israel's wars, I had never experienced such a sense of utter helplessness as during our exposure to those attacks. We prepared a sealed room in our flat, and did not go anywhere without gas masks. As our daughter Orna and her family lived in Tel Aviv, we invited them to join us in Jerusalem, which we assumed would not be directly targeted by Scud missiles. This was how most of the country handled the new dangers, but Palestinians in the territories cheered from rooftops as the exploding missiles hit central Israel. Between 18 January and 28 February, life was completely disrupted. The question before the government was how to react. In the past when Israel was attacked we retaliated swiftly. The army quickly established that the Scud missiles were launched from fixed and mobile launchers in western Iraq and prepared plans for an independent Israeli operation to dislodge them. Arens and the army chiefs presented the plans to the Cabinet for approval and a number of hawkish ministers, headed by Ariel Sharon, pressed for action. Shamir averted a decision by insisting on prior coordination with the US.

The Americans were determined to prevent any Israeli move that might split the international coalition, since an Israeli attack on Iraq might have evoked hostile opinion in Egypt, Syria and Saudi Arabia, and complicated their participation in the coalition. The Bush administration was, however, aware of the anguish and of the damage the Scuds had caused, and noted the domestic pressures on Shamir, which intensified with every explosion. Before the crisis they had installed a direct, safe telephone line between Arens and Defence Secretary Cheney. Now it served not only for the exchange of information and assessments but also as a channel for urging restraint on the Minister of Defence. The Americans used their satellite communication system to increase the warning time of missiles launched against Israel; it took only seven minutes for a missile to reach Israel. An instant signal of the launch would be sent to Washington from an orbiting satellite, and that would then be directed to Tel Aviv within three minutes. This left a four-minute warning time to alert the population. The Americans also supplied Patriot ground-to-air missile batteries, which boosted morale but proved ineffective in intercepting Scuds. Two top officials from the State and Defence Departments, Larry Eagelburger and Paul Wolfowitz, arrived in Israel shortly after the missiles started to fall, to keep in close touch with Shamir, Foreign Minister David Levy, who supported restraint, and Arens. A group of high-ranking American military officers accompanied them to exchange views with the army command. As the missiles continued to explode Arens intensified his demands for action. In early February he went to Washington to persuade the administration either to assign an air corridor for an Israeli operation or to give us the identification codes so that our air force would not clash with coalition planes. When, however, he was asked how Israel could do better than the coalition with its immense fire-power and sophistication, he had difficulty in explaining how we could do more. The US intensified its attacks on western Iraq and the missile assaults became less regular and frequently overshot their targets. They nevertheless caused havoc and injuries. Thirty-nine missiles exploded in about six weeks of war and by sheer good fortune only a few Israelis were killed, although hundreds were injured, and thousands of flats were destroyed. Above all, Israel's strategic planning had, from now on, to take into account a new and dangerous dimension – missile warfare. The Israeli public supported Shamir's policy of restraint, appreciating the considerable risks that were involved in an independent operation. They sensed that pride and questionable arguments on the need to demonstrate our deterrent capacity were hardly worth the life of a single Israeli pilot.

On 28 February, President Bush announced a cease-fire. Kuwait had been liberated, the Iraqi war machine had been seriously damaged and Iraq would be compelled to destroy its arsenals of weapons of mass destruction. A stringent, UN-led regime of intrusive supervision was to ensure that Saddam would comply with these decisions. Only after the war did the UN team discover how close Iraq had been to acquiring nuclear capability. Saddam Hussein remained in power and six years later the need to contain him created a new crisis. In November 1997 there was evidence that Iraq was continuing to develop and store biological weapons. In 1991, Bush was criticized for failing to carry on with the war until the brutal dictator had been deposed. The American, indeed coalition, rationale for ending the war was that the UN mandate had been to liberate Kuwait and not to topple the Iraqi despot. More importantly, to search for and destroy Saddam, who was surrounded by loyal troops, would have called for a sustained operation on Baghdad, exposing American soldiers to prolonged urban terror. There was also a strategic danger: no visible alternative to Saddam existed, to govern the country and ensure that a united Iraq would survive the shock. Iraq's fragmentation would have left Iran as the dominant power in the Gulf area and boosted the spread of extreme Islamic fundamentalism.[20]

A week after the end of operation Desert Storm, Baker embarked on a new Middle East peace initiative. It partly represented the fulfilment of a promise to Arab coalition partners that after the Gulf War ended, the US would make a renewed effort to bring about a solution to the Arab–Israeli conflict. But essentially it was an attempt to build swiftly on the outstanding accomplishments of the war and construct what was dubbed 'a new world order'. This ambitious term raised expectations, but it was no more than a desire to strengthen traditional Western objectives: providing stability, working for peace, de-escalating regional conflicts and spreading democracy and market-economy principles.

The peace initiative rested on two pillars: an aspiration to break the Arab taboo of resisting direct negotiations with Israel; and the agreement of the Shamir government to an international peace conference that would launch negotiations. US standing in the Arab world was at an all-time high point. America, sacrificing its soldiers, had returned an Arab country, Kuwait, to the map of independent nations and guaranteed the freedom and independence of Saudi Arabia and the other Gulf states. It had demonstrated the strength of its commitment to its friends. Although in its fifty years of independence Israel had never asked for foreign troops to fight for its security, there was a stark message in Desert Storm that even after the trauma of Vietnam the US would never allow its friends, including Israel, to be overwhelmed by force. Our security was also enhanced by the fact that an eastern front, with the participation of Iraq, was now less likely, while the standing of the PLO had weakened as a result of their support for Saddam. The Soviet Union, the great protector and arms supplier of the Arabs for the past thirty-five years, had crumbled. Gorbachev's regime was prepared to show pragmatism and cooperate with the US on negotiations, this time not only to further their interests but to find a way of de-escalating the conflict. This radically new situation, what Washington called 'a window of opportunity' or a 'strategic moment' to promote peace and stability, Bush and Baker seized.

A week after the war ended, on 6 March, President Bush outlined before both houses of Congress the American policy on a solution to the Arab–Israeli conflict:

> ... we must work to create new opportunities for peace and stability in the Middle East ... We've learned in the modern age, geography cannot guarantee security and security does not come from military power alone ... A comprehensive peace must be grounded in United Nations Security Council Resolutions 242 and 338 and the principle of territory for peace. This principle must be elaborated to provide for Israel's security and recognition, and at the same time for legitimate Palestinian political rights.[21]

The principles were not new. The challenge was their translation into a viable process in the new realities of the Middle East. To achieve this, Baker set out on 8 March on his first shuttle to the area to prepare a conference in Madrid. His objectives were to launch direct talks, on which Israel insisted, starting at a regional peace conference, which the Arabs favoured. The negotiations were to take place on 'two tracks' – with the Arab states on peace treaties and with the Palestinians on self-government. This concept was suggested by the able and experienced deputy director-general for North American affairs (later director-general), Eytan Bentsur, to a prominent member of the Baker team, Denis Ross.[22] The Secretary of State adopted it and made it part of the new initiative. In order to facilitate the conference Baker was seeking agreement on 'parallel reciprocal steps' which would bolster confidence. He was greatly encouraged by the reaction of King Fahd of Saudi Arabia, whom he met first. Saudi Arabia had also suffered sinister Scud missile attacks and appreciated Israel's restraint, which allowed the anti-Saddam coalition to hold together. Supporting the two-track approach, Fahd told Baker that 'if a homeland could be found for the Palestinians he was prepared to approve full economic and diplomatic relations with Israel'.[23]

The difficult part was to obtain Shamir's consent to the modalities of the conference and to the composition of the Palestinian delegation, and to get the Palestinians to accept non-PLO participation. After eight shuttle trips in as many months, Baker finally secured the agreement of all concerned to convene the Madrid Conference in October 1991. Shamir had agreed to a joint Jordanian–Palestinian delegation and promised Baker not to boycott the talks if the Palestinians declared openly that they represented the PLO. All Palestinian delegates had to be residents of the territories; those living in East Jerusalem or outside the territories were excluded. Endless discussions were held on procedural matters, which prolonged the arduous process of pre-negotiations and gained time for Shamir, who saw that as an objective. The parties received letters of assurances from the US which protected their positions on condition that all assurances were made available to all the parties to avoid mis-understandings. In his letter to the Palestinians of 18 October 1991, Baker reiterated the US adherence to the principle of 'territory for peace', stated the objective – a comprehensive settlement of the Arab–Israeli conflict – and outlined the agreed modalities: the co-sponsors were the US and the Soviet Union; the European Union would be represented by its presidency; the UN would be represented by an observer of the Secretary-General and the US would not support attempts to have a 'parallel process' in the Security Council. The US also reiterated its position on Jerusalem: 'It remains the firm position of the US that Jerusalem must never again be a divided city and that its final status should be decided by negotiations. Thus we do not recognize Israel's annexation of East Jerusalem or the extension of its municipal boundaries.' The letter also stated that a Pale-stinian who resided in Jordan and was a member of a Jerusalem family could be part of the Jordanian delegation.[24] There was little doubt that the members of the Palestinian delegation were approved by the PLO.

The eight months of negotiations with Baker were accompanied by tensions within the Cabinet and with the US. Foreign Minister David Levy supported a more flexible stand and pushed Shamir to respond favourably to some of Baker's questions. Without his contribution, the Madrid Con-ference might have been delayed. Minister of Defence Arens described Shamir's 'general strategy' of delay: 'There was no way I could introduce sense into his head,' he wrote, following a conversation with the Prime Minister on the Baker suggestions. Arens advocated a halt to the building of new settlements, while strengthening existing ones, but Shamir was adamant in refusing to stop settlement building. According to Arens, Shamir also did not like the idea of elections in the territories.[25] Sharon and two other ministers objected to the whole Baker process. Shamir insisted that the UN repeal the notorious resolution equating Zionism with racism. Baker promised to work to that end and the resolution was indeed repealed. He also gave a commitment that the US would not allow a 'competing process' in the Security Council. For its part, the Soviet Union renewed full diplomatic relations with Israel before the conference started.

On 18 October 1991 the US and Soviet Union issued the invitation to Madrid: 'The President of the US and the President of the USSR invite you to a peace conference, which their countries will co-sponsor, followed immediately by direct negotiations. The conference will be convened in Madrid on 30 October 1991.' The invitation stipulated that direct bilateral negotiations would commence four days after its opening and multilateral negotiations after two weeks. The latter would deal with 'arms control and regional security, water, refugee issues, environment, economic develop-ment, and other subjects of mutual interest'. The countries invited were

Israel, Syria, Lebanon and Jordan, Egypt as a participant and Palestinians 'as part of a joint Jordanian-Palestinian delegation'. The representatives were to be at ministerial level.

As all other participants were represented by their Foreign Ministers, David Levy asked a small group of officials to start preparing for this historic event. During one of the sessions that Director-General Yosef Hadas, my colleague, Eytan Bentsur, deputy director-general for North American affairs and myself had with Levy on Madrid, a phone call from the Prime Minister came through. We offered to leave the room but Levy signalled us to stay. Shamir told Levy that he had decided to travel to Madrid himself and asked the Foreign Minister to join him. Levy was taken aback; he reminded Shamir that the Arab countries would be represented by their Foreign Ministers and angrily stated that if Shamir went he would not be at Madrid. Knowing Shamir's hesitations, Levy was very puzzled by the decision. Shamir did not in fact expect much to happen at Madrid except a reiteration of known positions, but he realized the importance of sharing a platform with Bush and Gorbachev and taking part in a huge media event covered by two thousand journalists. Together with a group of Foreign Ministry officials I too travelled to Madrid as deputy director-general for information, to deal with the media. Netanyahu was in charge of the communication effort. I appreciated the unique gathering, the beginning of direct negotiation, and saw Madrid as an important achievement in the long struggle for direct negotiations. Bentsur and most of my colleagues took a similar view. However, when we gathered every evening in Shamir's room to report on the events of the day, we were struck by his dismissive demeanour and his desire to see this first direct encounter between Israeli and Arab officials outside the UN over and done with as soon as possible. To a suggestion that the Israeli delegation might extend its stay in Madrid for another day to explore possibilities of private contacts with Arab participants, the answer was that Shamir wished to be back in Jerusalem before the onset of the Shabat, a less than convincing argument.

The Madrid Conference was a landmark in the long quest for peace. The principle of direct negotiations was accepted by all the Arab countries; it started a process of bilateral and multilateral negotiations and for the first time in the history of the conflict Israelis and Palestinians negotiated officially face to face. The joint Jordanian–Palestinian delegation was a face-saving charade to please Shamir – the Palestinians spoke for themselves and the fact that they were part of the joint delegation was no more than a technicality. They declared their allegiance to the PLO and fulfilled their instructions. The PLO in fact appointed a special coordinator for the bilateral talks, Nabil Shaath, and Arafat's financial adviser, Abu Ala, later became the coordinator for the multilateral negotiations. Saudi Arabia was again, for the first time, represented at a peace conference by Prince Bandar Ibn Sultan, their ambassador in Washington. After three decades of hostility towards Israel, the Soviet Union displayed a more balanced attitude as co-sponsor of the conference and demonstrated to the Arabs that the Cold War was over. The bilateral talks started five weeks later in Washington and the multilateral negotiations were launched in Moscow in January 1992.

Towards the end of January I left for Moscow with a small Foreign Ministry team as an advance party to prepare for the international conference that would inaugurate the multilateral talks. The conference opened on 28 January, and our delegation was headed by David Levy. As we circled over Moscow I reflected with trepidation on the hardships and suffering of three million Jews under Stalin and his successors. I recalled the war years my family and I spent in the Romanian-occupied Ukraine. Of my four grandparents, three did not survive the ordeal and were buried in Moghilov Podolsk. I remembered my army service in Israel in the fifties when the first news about the supply of Soviet weapons to Egypt arrived, and the uninterrupted chain of Soviet hostility towards Israel since. All in all, the Jewish people and Israel suffered greatly from the animosity of successive Soviet regimes. Before long the aeroplane touched down and we drove through the streets of Moscow. My first impressions were of utter disbelief. Poverty and dilapidation were visible at every corner. Empty shops were common, with people queuing for bread and other basic food supplies. Was this the capital of the dreaded Soviet Empire? How had everything crumbled with such speed?

Only four weeks before, on 24 December 1992, Gorbachev had resigned after the Soviet Empire disintegrated and split into the Commonwealth of Independent States. From the international point of view, Russia became the 'successor' state, assuming the Soviet seat in the Security Council and retaining responsibility for all international commitments and treaties. Boris Yeltsin, the President of Russia, replaced Gorbachev as the leader of the most powerful country in the former Soviet Union.

Our first meetings with Russian officials to discuss the modalities of the conference were somewhat vague. They were all grappling for instruction, but our ambassador Ayre Levin, found his way through the bureaucratic labyrinth. As much as I was interested in the conference, I was fascinated by the events that had led to the break-up of this vast and cruel empire. I knew the American ambassador, Bob Strauss, and asked Levin to set up a meeting with him. In a wide-ranging discussion Strauss expressed confidence that Yeltsin was in control and could handle the transition to a democratic system provided economic assistance would be forthcoming.

David Levy arrived on 27 January from China, having agreed on the establishment of full diplomatic relations between our two countries.

During the conference we were informed that India had also decided to establish diplomatic ties with Israel. The Madrid momentum was kept up, breaking barriers that had lasted for over four decades. Two visits with David Levy remained engraved in my memory. One was a prayer service at the Moscow Synagogue, filled with emotion. Beside me stood the governor of the Bank of Israel, Yacov Frenkel, who was also a member of the delegation, and both of us thanked God Almighty for the redemption and liberation of this wonderful tribe of Soviet Jews. Had the repressive communist regime continued for another twenty-five years, very few of the three million would have remained Jewish. The visit to the Kremlin, built by the Tsars of Russia and the hub of decision-making during the seventy-two years of a bygone system, was fascinating. A relic of a forlorn ideology, which had fired the imagination of so many people, started off with good intentions and developed into one of the most despotic tyrannies, also evoked sombre reflection. Although Gorbachev was out of power and out of favour, Levy called on him. It was he who had taken the momentous decision not to use force when the Soviet empire started to unravel and it was he who had opened the gates for the exodus of Soviet Jews to Israel.

Our conference was the first major international event of the new Russia, and the Foreign Ministry made a supreme effort to run it smoothly. Syria boycotted the multilateral negotiations, but the other Arab countries participated. This track, which was complimentary to the political, bilateral talks, was to lay the groundwork for regional cooperation. The working groups on economic development, water problems and the environment had useful meetings. I was involved in them as co-chairman of the group on the environment. Although there were always political overtones, the experts in this field got to know their counterparts, identified problems of common interest and initiated more than a dozen surveys on subjects concerning our area. I believe the fields for regional collaboration were well chosen and that the multilateral process, which came to a complete halt after Netanyahu became Prime Minister, should be reinvigorated.

The bilateral talks started in Washington on 4 December 1991. The 'peace for peace' policy which guided the head of our negotiating team with Syria precluded any serious movement. In the absence of progress with Syria there was no possibility of reaching agreement with Lebanon. Jordan was prepared to negotiate seriously but did not want to conclude a peace treaty before there was agreement either with the Palestinians or with Syria. The key to progress was in the negotiations with the Palestinians. Within the constraints of Shamir's policy – restricted autonomy, no linkage with the permanent status agreement and no contact with the PLO – the head of the Israeli delegation, Elyakim Rubinstein, and his deputy, Eytan Bentsur, tried hard to persuade the Palestinian delegation to inch forward. Between December 1991 and September 1993, there were eleven rounds of talks. Endless time was spent on procedural matters, while on substance the gaps became more evident. The Palestinians had a clearly defined aim, a Palestinian state, and therefore reiterated their demand for self-determination. They also insisted on the right of return of 1948 and 1967 refugees and the cessation of settlement building. Despite the lack of progress, there was nevertheless some merit in these meetings, as they lowered tension in the area, allowed Israeli and Arab officials to get acquainted, and entrenched the principle of direct negotiations. But no agreements emerged.

In the first part of 1992 the small right-wing parties deserted Shamir's coalition, because the Madrid process was not to their liking. The Prime Minister decided to call early elections and they were set for 23 June. The result was a substantial defeat for Shamir's Likud. It dropped in size from forty Knesset seats to thirty-two, while the Labour Party, led by Yitzhak Rabin, went up from thirty-nine to forty-four members. The balance between the right-wing plus religious block against Labour plus smaller left-wing parties, was still very precarious: fifty-nine to sixty-one.

The Shamir era drew to a close in bitter controversy with President Bush over an Israeli request for a \$10 billion loan guarantee from the US government, to help absorb the large number of immigrants from the former Soviet Union. Bush made its availability contingent on a halt in settlement activity but Shamir would not relent. The mounting tension with the Bush administration had its influence on the electorate but it was not the only reason for Shamir's defeat. The Israeli public started to realize that Shamir's policies were leading to a dead end. Arens attributed the cause of defeat to 'Shamir's inflexibility' and to the divisions within the Likud (the Shamir–Levy rift).[26] History will make a more definitive judgement of his leadership, but the question must be asked: why did Shamir reject so many attempts to engage in serious negotiations, against the best advice of his Foreign Minister, Arens, Labour leaders and the Bush administration? Shamir was a dedicated patriot but held a totally unrealistic vision of the future. His policy was inspired by deep conviction and best defined in his own words: 'We will not give the Arabs one inch of our land, even if we have to negotiate for ten years,' he told the Likud Central Committee in May 1989.[27] He was Prime Minister for seven years and, during that long period Israel did indeed hardly inch towards peace, despite the Madrid Conference. These years were characterized by terror, a popular Palestinian uprising – the intifada – and continuous bloodshed. He fought against the notion of 'land for peace' saying that it was 'no longer relevant' and that peace could be arrived at 'without the help of such formulas'.[28] In a speech before a rabbinical conference in July 1989, he expressed fierce opposition to any territorial compromise and branded the supporters of such compromise as 'traitors'.

I say, and I believe, that it is absolutely possible and necessary to arrive at peace without conceding, Heaven forbid, one bit of the land of our forefathers, the holy land. On the contrary it is incumbent on us to convince and to show that people who believe with all their hearts and with all their might in Eretz Israel are also capable of a breakthrough on the road to peace, and that peace is not the monopoly of traitors, of those who surrender and give in.[29]

It was the 'peace for peace' supposition which no Palestinian would ever accept and no Arab country would ever support. There was simply no matter for negotiation on that basis. However, it allowed its supporters to claim that Israel wanted peace and was always for peace, albeit on terms which were delusive and completely unacceptable to the Arabs. Shamir, like Begin, was prepared to grant the Palestinians limited autonomy, considering it the end of the road. He never explained how he would force two million Palestinians to live permanently under Israeli dominance. His biggest achievement, in his view, was the increase of the settlement population, which numbered about ten thousand settlers when the Camp David Accords were signed and was more than ten times as large when he was voted out of office in 1992. This, he believed, would render the creation of a Palestinian state impossible.

For the Palestinians these years were a time of deepening frustration and bitterness; they saw the violence of the intifada and the ascendancy of Islamic extremist movements like Hamas and Islamic Jihad. Shamir demonized the PLO and paid little attention to the rise of Islamic extremism in the territories. In his memoirs he attacks the PLO in the fiercest terms and mentions Hamas only once. I wonder whether he ever asked himself what were the real causes for the ascendancy of Hamas and Islamic Jihad extremism, apart from the inspiration and support such groups received from Teheran.

Shamir's vision for the solution of the Israeli–Palestinian conflict was as unrealistic as the claim of the Revisionists before the Second World War to have a Jewish state on both banks of the River Jordan. Had Ben-Gurion followed that line there would never have been a Jewish state. And it was as impractical as Shamir's own opposition to the Camp David Accords. Had Begin insisted on more than was absolutely attainable in the negotiations with Sadat, there would not have been a peace treaty with Egypt. How then was the Israeli public persuaded to follow Shamir and accord him his slim majority in elections? In Israel, voters decide on life and death matters, on whether they condemn their children and grandchildren to an endless chain of killing and bloodshed or whether they support real efforts for peace. Yet for years support flowed to parties with extreme ideological convictions which perpetuated animosity, refused to explore options for peace and engendered bloody confrontations. The absence of credible Arab bargaining partners and the bitterness that Palestinian terror had produced in the Israeli public encouraged uncompromising positions, especially when the West Bank was at issue. The Palestinians never failed to supply an alibi for those who wanted to stall and delay peace. Nevertheless, credit must go to Shamir for his firm stand against independent Israeli action during the Gulf War, for the mobilization of an all-out effort to absorb the Soviet immigration, for the in-gathering of the Jews from Ethiopia and for the good economic growth rate during his premiership.

Within three weeks of the elections Rabin formed a government, which he presented to the Knesset on 13 July, pledging to continue the peace process based on the Madrid formula. Retaining the Ministry of Defence in his own hands, he set out to change the national priorities; instead of diverting considerable resources to settlement building, the new government allocated larger budgets to education, unemployment and infrastructure. As Minister of Defence he renewed his efforts to strengthen the army and ensure that it had the most sophisticated equipment while, at the same time, he fought terrorism in every possible way. At the same time, his main thoughts centred on the need to advance peace. He defined the relationship between peace and security in a realistic manner, explaining that peace constituted 'a very important component' for guaranteeing the security of the state. He also signalled to Syria that peace would contain territorial concessions on the Golan Heights and reiterated to Lebanon that Israel had no territorial problems and recognized its international border.[30]

Shimon Peres was appointed Foreign Minister. Upon assuming office he made it very clear to us in the ministry that he was determined to instil new life into the peace negotiations. While Rabin was considering options for progress with Syria or with the Palestinians, Peres concentrated on the Palestinian issue. Eytan Bentsur, deputy head of delegation to the bilateral talks with the Palestinians and Jordan, summed up the situation: the Palestinian delegation was receiving its instructions from the PLO in Tunis; in view of the election result the PLO was holding back, testing the new government; to increase confidence it was necessary to build a link between the interim – and permanent-status agreements. Bentsur also suggested establishing contact with the PLO.[31]

On 2 August the top officials in the ministry joined Peres for the first briefing to foreign ambassadors serving in Israel. He told them that in the negotiations with the Palestinians he wanted to move away from trivialities and go to the 'heart of the matter', elections in the territories. A week later, Rabin travelled to the US and met the President in Maine. Bush received him very cordially and agreed to put at Israel's disposal the $10 billion loan guarantees which he had denied Shamir, saying that Rabin had convinced him that he was committed to 'making the talks succeed'. He called on the Arabs to 'respond in kind'. On 4 November, in spite of his overwhelming popularity of only eighteen months earlier, Bush lost the elections. Bill Clinton was elected President and Israel had to establish relations with the new administration.

By March, Rabin was back in Washington for his first encounter with President Clinton. It was the beginning of a relationship marked by openness and friendship, and which propelled the relations between Israel and the US to new heights. Clinton took a keen interest in the peace process and Rabin outlined his thoughts on every track of the negotiations. Clinton fully shared the Israeli concept on normalization of relations with the various Arab partners, spoke about zero tolerance of terror and pledged to maintain Israel's 'qualitative military edge'. However, as terror continued to plague the country, Rabin was compelled to take harsh measures, including the deportation of Hamas operatives. These acts caused tensions with the US and with more pragmatic Palestinians, who had had high expectations of the Rabin government.

Our delegations to the bilateral talks with Jordan, the Palestinians, Syria and Lebanon were instructed to concentrate less on procedural differences, more on substance. However, progress in the talks with the Palestinians was minuscule, if there was any at all. Rabin had promised to reach an autonomy agreement with the Palestinians within nine months of taking office, yet with every passing month it became clear that there was little chance of implementing that timetable. To both Rabin and Peres it was clear that the Palestinian problem was the core of the conflict. Without a solution to that, there could be no progress on resolving the Arab–Israeli conflict. In the Palestinian camp, too, there was frustration at the lack of movement in the bilateral talks. Abu Mazen, Arafat's top aide in charge of the negotiations with Israel, wrote after studying the exchanges between the two delegations in Washington: 'I set them aside since they were dominated by political literalism and dealt more with formalities than with substance.'[32] No wonder, because the leader of the Palestinian delegation, Dr Haidar Abdel-Shafi, was a militant hard-liner and much less pragmatic than Abu Mazen or their chief negotiator at Oslo, Abu Ala. Peres tirelessly looked for direct channels that could speed up negotiations. So did deputy foreign minister Yossi Beilin, a man with a creative mind who had for years championed a more realistic approach to the Palestinian question. Both wanted to find a back-channel in which negotiations could take place directly with the PLO leadership in Tunis, who made the decisions for the Palestinians. They believed that the Washington talks were slow because they were conducted under the glare of the media and because the Palestinian negotiators referred every issue back to Tunis.

Beilin was in touch with a Norwegian official, Terje Larsen, who headed a research institute that worked closely with Palestinians and was therefore acquainted with Abu Ala, Arafat's finance adviser. Larsen's wife Mona was the assistant to Norway's deputy foreign minister, Jan Egeland. It was Egeland, who, on a visit to Israel in September 1992, suggested to Beilin that Norway should host secret negotiations, promising that the Norwegian government would fund this effort. Beilin and Egeland were convinced a back-channel was crucial if the negotiations were to be successful. Beilin also worked on a project that looked at future economic cooperation between Israel and the Palestinians. His chief collaborator here was Dr Yair Hirshfeld of Haifa University.

However, contact with the PLO, a terrorist organization, was still a criminal offence in Israel. Only in early December 1992 was the law forbidding such contacts repealed. On 3 December 1992 Hirshfeld had a meeting in London with Abu Ala and the London representative of the PLO, Afif Safieh. Abu Ala stressed that the moderates in the Palestinian camp were losing ground to Hamas and that it was essential to reach agreement soon on a declaration of principles for an interim agreement. He also gave Hirshfeld a draft of points to be included in such a declaration. Hirshfeld reported the content of his talk to Beilin, who was in London for the same reason as Abu Ala, the meeting of the steering committee of the multilateral talks. Beilin, Larsen and Hirshfeld decided to continue the talks with Abu Ala in Norway. It was a bold decision by Beilin because he did not consult Peres or Rabin on this major policy step – direct talks with the PLO. But as long as the contacts were informal, conducted by a university don, the risk was acceptable. Hirshfeld was joined by Ron Pundak, also of Haifa University, and Abu Ala's team included Hassan Asfour and Maher al-Kurd. On 20 January 1993 one of the most successful ventures in diplomatic practice commenced in Norway.[33]

At first these unorthodox negotiations were completely unofficial, conducted on the Israeli side by two dons, Yair Hirshfeld and Ron Pundak. Their reports to Beilin impressed him with the seriousness of the PLO approach. At the beginning the idea was that a declaration of principles would be negotiated and placed by the Americans before the official delegations in Washington to work out the details of implementation. It soon became clear that Abu Ala and his two assistants were speaking with the full authority of Arafat; also, that they were prepared to accept the 'Gaza first' principle which Peres had proposed some two years earlier and which called for Israeli withdrawal from Gaza as a first step. After a few weeks Beilin apprised Peres of the negotiations and although the Foreign Minister had reservations on some of the details he recognized their potential and before long became completely immersed in directing them. His experience was vast and his imaginative drive for peace was invaluable in the process. Peres reported the Oslo contacts to the Prime Minister and although Rabin was cautious and sceptical at the beginning, he authorized their continuation. In a series of tête-à-tête talks, Peres convinced Rabin of the seriousness of the Oslo channel and received his backing for the line that the Israeli negotiators were to take. It had become clear that the talks were not an academic exercise but a focal negotiating arena where the future coexistence of Israel and the Palestinians could be shaped. There was now a need for a more official representation and for legal expertise. Peres nominated the director-general of the Foreign Ministry, Uri Savir, and the legal adviser, Yoel Singer, to head the team. Savir, courageous and articulate, impressed the PLO interlocutors. On Arafat's insistence the 'Gaza first' idea was broadened to include Jericho as well, so that the first Israeli withdrawal would also include some of the West Bank territory. (Like the 'Gaza first' concept, the idea to add Jericho was originally proposed by Peres to Mubarak.) Singer contributed substantially to formulating the Declaration of Principles and suggesting that the agreement with the PLO should go beyond the declaration and include mutual recognition.

On 19 August 1993, after seven months of intensive negotiations, the Declaration of Principles on Interim Self-government Arrangements was initialled at Oslo by the director-general of the Foreign Ministry, Uri Savir, and by Abu Ala. Both delegations agreed 'it was time to put an end to decades of confrontation and conflict, to recognize their mutual legitimate and political rights, and strive to live in peaceful coexistence ...' The declaration set out details on the framework for the interim self-government for a period of five years, elections on the West Bank and Gaza, security and economic issues, withdrawals of Israeli troops and the nature of the transitional period. More negotiations were needed to hammer out the agreement on mutual recognition and here the Norwegian Foreign Minister, Johan Joergen Holst, was instrumental in achieving the exchange of letters between Rabin and Arafat of 9 September 1993. In his letter to Rabin, Arafat recognized the right of the State of Israel to exist in peace and accepted Security Council Resolutions 242 and 338. He committed the PLO to a 'peaceful resolution of the conflict'; renounced 'the use of terrorism and other acts of violence' and pledged to assume responsibility 'over all PLO elements and personnel to ensure their compliance'. Rabin was worried that the commitment to cease violence did not include all the Palestinians and was limited to the 'elements of the PLO'. Arafat then supplemented his letter to Rabin with a letter to Holst calling upon the people in West Bank and Gaza to reject violence and terror. He also wrote to Rabin that 'those articles of the Palestinian Covenant which deny Israel's right to exist ... are now inoperative and no longer valid' and undertook to submit to the Palestinian National Council the necessary changes for their approval.[34]

Rabin confirmed in his reply to Arafat that in view of the commitments in his letter, the government of Israel 'had decided to recognize the PLO as the representative of the Palestinian people' and negotiate peace with it. The way was now open to the full signature of the declaration by Peres and Abu Mazen in Washington in the memorable ceremony of 13 September 1993. It was followed by the historic handshake between Rabin and Arafat on the White House lawn which shook Israel and the world. The US government, which was not part of the negotiations, but was periodically kept in the picture through talks between Beilin and deputy assistant secretary of state Dan Kurzer, and by Holst, was pleased with the outcome, and ready to involve the personal prestige of President Clinton in this key agreement. The White House ceremony accorded this historic breakthrough the prominence it deserved.

In 1992 and 1993 the PLO had been in great financial difficulties because their funding by Saudi Arabia and the Gulf states was cut off due to their support of Saddam Hussein. For the same reason, their international standing was adversely affected and due to terrorist activity the US had suspended its dialogue with them. In the territories Hamas was in the ascendancy, while the influence of the PLO had declined. Also, a local Palestinian leadership had begun to emerge which could eventually pose a threat to them. On the Israeli side settlement building continued, though at a much more controlled pace. Arafat and his lieutenants realized that the Rabin–Peres government presented them with their best opportunity for many years to forge an agreement, offering them the prospect of returning to the territories and forming a self-governing authority. The PLO had abandoned their claim for a democratic Palestinian state in 1988 and agreed to the two-state solution which was originally envisaged in the partition of Palestine scheme. In Oslo they progressed further towards realism in agreeing to mutual recognition and to work for the abolition of those clauses in the Palestinian Covenant which negated Israel. They had never abandoned their core-objective, a Palestinian state, but now aimed for a state that would exist alongside Israel and in close cooperation with it.

In order to achieve a real breakthrough, Israel wanted recognition as a Jewish state, a firm commitment to ending terror and an undertaking to abolish the Palestinian Covenant. Rabin also insisted on assurances on two crucial points; that both Jerusalem and settlements be excluded from the interim agreement. He used an alternative channel to Arafat to probe these questions. The Minister of Health, Haim Ramon, put them to Dr Ahmed Tibi, an Israeli Arab with close links to the PLO leader. On 26 July 1993 Ramon received from Tunis the answer that the issues of 'Jerusalem, refugees, settlements, security arrangements, borders and other issues' would be specified in the declaration of principles as belonging to the permanent-status negotiations. A similar assurance was given by Arafat that external security would remain Israel's responsibility in the interim stage.[35] Rabin and Peres knew that self-government for the Palestinians would free Israel from the burden of occupation and of the responsibility of running the lives of two million Palestinians, and would open the way for peace with Jordan and, later, Syria and Lebanon. They were also aware that it was possible to reach agreement with the PLO without the participation of Palestinians in the territories while it was impossible to agree on anything with Palestinians from Gaza and the West Bank without the PLO. The conclusion was that the key to progress rested with the leadership in Tunis; hence the necessity to communicate with them directly. On timing and urgency, the interests of the Israeli government and Arafat converged. The political clock was ticking in Jerusalem too. The coalition's majority in the Knesset was scant and continuous terror strengthened the right wing. The concept and the determination were there but a credible framework for their realization was missing.

The setting was provided by Beilin, Hirshfeld, Larsen and Egeland, and by the support of two Norwegian Foreign Ministers, Stoltenberg and Holst, who set the stage for a private dialogue between Israel and the PLO, and provided the rural setting in Norway, which was conducive to secrecy and to amicable talks. The results of the Oslo talks were a triumph of face-to-face negotiations, for the Norwegians let the parties work out the difficult questions and only occasionally offered their help. Secrecy was essential for both parties. For decades the PLO had been synonymous with the devil in the perception of most Israelis. To alter such an emotionally coloured view required the proof that the PLO had changed from a terrorist organization to a political movement. Otherwise public opinion would have been enraged. With the agreement in hand Rabin and Peres could face the public and the Jewish world and convince them of the important shift among the Palestinians. This is why Rabin did not reveal, either to Ehud Barak, the Chief of Staff, or his personal staff, the secrets of Oslo. He worked with Peres and the small group set up originally by Beilin, and reinforced by the two negotiators, Savir and Singer.

Critics have maintained that if the Israeli government had made the same concessions in the bilateral talks in Washington, agreement could have been reached there. This is doubtful, because a delegation composed of the PLO and local leaders would have been more militant, more demanding. Every Palestinian concession would have been debated publicly in the territories and used to fuel opposition in Israel. There was also the argument that the Oslo declaration had many 'holes' in it and could have been tighter. This criticism could apply to nearly any agreement. More often than not if negotiators attempt to achieve everything, they are likely to attain nothing. Oslo was a first step, a framework to be supplemented by more detailed agreements later, like the Cairo agreement of May 1994, detailing the self-rule arrangements for Gaza and Jericho, and the Oslo II accord signed in Washington on 28 September 1995, expanding autonomy to the West Bank.

Critics may ask, why, if the Oslo Agreement was so historic, did it not live up to expectations. Five years after Oslo we can say that an opportunity to change the direction of the Israeli–Palestinian conflict, from bloody confrontation to negotiation, was seized upon with drive, talent and foresight. The difficulties that have arisen were caused by inflated expectations and slow implementation of the interim agreement. The Palestinians anticipated rapid economic development and Israel expected an instant cessation of terror. Huge amounts of international money flowed to the Palestinian Authority. Some of those funds were mishandled and others spent on running costs which did nothing to create jobs or improve the infrastructure. However, the crux of the problem was and is terror. In the first three years after the agreement horrendous acts of terrorism, including many suicide bombings, were committed by Palestinians.[36] The perpetrators belonged mostly to extreme Islamic organizations such as Hamas and Islamic Jihad and not to the PLO, which, under the Palestinian Authority consolidated a strong armed police and a number of other security arms. (Though in September 1996 members of the Palestinian police fired on Israeli soldiers.) Thus the most important security commitment by Arafat, to end violence, was not fulfilled. Israelis believed that Arafat, with the armed law-enforcement forces, could and should have stopped the terror. Yet he, and the Palestinian Authority, were reluctant or unable, or both, to put an end to the most serious and damaging block to peaceful coexistence. The result was that to protect its citizens and allow the daily flow of life to continue, Israeli governments had to undertake stringent measures against terror, which included closure of the territories and barring Palestinians from working in Israel. Tens of thousands of Palestinians lost their incomes and the already poor standard of living in Gaza and the West Bank dropped further. Abject poverty strengthened extremism. Negotiations on subsequent steps towards autonomy were slowed down as Israeli confidence in the Oslo Agreement eroded. This in turn increased Palestinian frustration. Later, the advent of the Netanyahu government made progress still more difficult.

Nevertheless substantial advance was achieved in other areas: orderly elections of the Palestinian Council and its chairman, Arafat; Israeli forces redeployed from the populated cities and other areas; two million Palestinians emerged from occupation and the Palestinian Authority became responsible for their lives and well-being; the road to peace with Jordan was opened; Israel established ties with Morocco, Tunis, Bahrain, Oman, Qatar; and the Arab boycott began fading away. Given the history of the conflict in the preceding forty-five years these were historic developments and although the road to peace is still fraught with difficulties, few Israelis or Palestinians would advocate a return to belligerency and more blood-shed. Rabin, Peres and Arafat received the Nobel Prize for achieving the Oslo Agreement and it was well deserved. The political risks that the three leaders had undertaken were very considerable. Indeed, Rabin paid the ultimate price, when he was assassinated by a Jewish zealot who opposed the agreement.

Hana and I arrived in London in October 1993, and shortly afterwards I presented my credentials to Her Majesty the Queen. In nearly every conversation I had at the time, people praised the courage and foresight of Rabin and Peres in forging the Oslo Agreement. In early December I received an invitation from the Foreign Secretary, Douglas Hurd, to attend a lunch in honour of Yasser Arafat. I accepted the invitation, viewing his visit as a direct consequence of Oslo. The Jewish organizations, however, hesitated over whether they should meet the PLO leader. They had diffi-culties in accepting Arafat as Israel's legitimate partner in negotiations and there was also right-wing pressure against such a meeting. In a lengthy conversation with the president of the Board of Deputies, Judge Israel Feinstein, I described the radical change of policy in Israel, and how, as a result of mutual recognition and Arafat's commitment to stop violence, we were negotiating with the PLO, and this new reality had to be recog-nized and accepted. Rabin and Peres, who had shaken Arafat's hand in Washington, were strong defenders of Israel's interest and no Jew could claim to be more upright than they. Rabin's words on the White House lawn reverberated in my ears: 'We who have fought against you, the Palestinians, we say to you today in a loud and clear voice: enough of blood and tears. Enough.' Judge Feinstein, a distinguished historian and jurist, and a life-long Zionist, took the point and resisted pressures to the contrary. Lord Rothschild, a staunch supporter of Israel and of peace joined the delegation that went to see Arafat. They outlined the concerns of the community on fighting terror and exchanged views on a wide range of subjects. It was an important turning-point, because the negotiations at Oslo had been secret and their outcome a surprise. Time and effort would be required to bring Jewish opinion round.

The signing of the Oslo Accords opened the way for negotiations on a peace treaty with Jordan. King Hussein, who for years had maintained a secret dialogue with Israeli leaders, felt that the peace momentum must be maintained. On 26 September 1993, just two weeks after the Washington ceremony, he invited Rabin to his royal yacht in the Gulf of Aqaba. He had not been told about the Oslo negotiations until they were finalized and obviously wanted to know whether and how the new agreement would affect Israel's relations with Jordan. The agreement had many practical implications for Jordan. Rabin reassured the king and tested his readiness for a peace treaty with Israel. When convinced that King Hussein had no more reservations and was ready to move swiftly, negotiations were set in hand.[37] The need for secrecy was again paramount, and Rabin nominated a team who would report to him directly. It was composed of Elyakim Rubinstein, who had headed the delegation to the Washington talks with the Jordanian–Palestinian delegation, Efraim Halevy, deputy head of Mossad and General Danny Yatom, Rabin's military aid. On 25 July 1994 a second White House ceremony took place. Rabin and King Hussein with President Clinton at their side signed the Israeli–Jordanian Declaration of Non-belligerency, ending the state of war and 'generations of hostility'. The two leaders agreed to take immediate action to normalize relations and resolve problems of border delineation, water allocation and an air corridor for Jordan. It was the first public meeting between King Hussein and an Israeli leader since the private contacts had begun in London thirty-one years earlier, in September 1963. It was also the last step before the signing of a full-fledged peace treaty with Jordan. The next day, the US Congress, in a unique gesture, held a joint session of the Senate and House of Representatives to honour Prime Minister Rabin and King Hussein.

The enemies of peace reacted swiftly, this time in London. A day after the signing of the declaration, on 26 July, I was in Jerusalem for a conference of Israeli ambassadors accredited to countries of the European Union. This conference saved my life. At about five minutes before 2 p.m., while visiting the Foreign Ministry, I was contacted by my personal assistant in London, Zipora Allon, who passed on a number of messages. While we were talking there was a bomb blast and the telephone went dead. She and my able English executive secretary, Mandy Bendel, were closest to the explosion, and both suffered injuries. Within minutes a number of top officials and myself gathered in the 'situation room'. I established contact with the Embassy on an emergency telephone link, and was told by the chargé d'affaires, Yacov Hadas, that there were no fatalities, although a number of Embassy staff had suffered injuries and the damage was considerable. A car bomb had exploded behind a wall of my office, and the steel plate which was attached to the wall for added protection had been ripped off by the blast and had fallen on my chair. Thanking the Almighty that I was in Israel, I called the Foreign Office in London, asking them to step up protection, and after consulting my colleagues, left for the airport to return to London. Before landing at Heathrow, I asked the El-Al pilot to convey to the Embassy that all uninjured diplomatic staff should convene at 10 p.m. It was very difficult to be cut off from events during the five-hour flight and I was greatly relieved when we landed. I called *The Times* to issue a forceful condemnation of the atrocity, and then drove to the Embassy.

On the way, I received a preliminary report of the events from my Special Branch team. After the assassination attempt on the life of one of my predecessors, Shlomo Argov, the British government had decided to accord Israeli ambassadors Special Branch protection. I was privileged to have exceptional people on my team, devoted, resourceful and hard-working, and during these difficult hours I particularly valued their opinion. The Embassy staff gathered in a sombre mood. After inquiring about the injured I inspected the considerable damage. The staff told me that the same morning Hadas had asked the Foreign Office to step up security. I remarked that when terrorists are determined to inflict damage they always find loopholes. Unfortunately there was a slack point in the perimeter security, which fell within the responsibility of the Diplomatic Protection Group of Scotland Yard. This was the third terrorist attack involving the London Embassy. Our agricultural attaché, Ami Shechory, was killed by a letter-bomb in 1972; and ambassador Shlomo Argov was severely injured and paralysed from the neck down in 1982.

I asked the staff who felt able and unaffected by the shock to report for work the next morning, stressing that we must continue business as usual. I arrived home at midnight, shared my impressions with Hana and fell asleep. After about an hour I was awakened with the news of a second blast at Balfour House, the headquarters of a number of Jewish organizations.

I received many warm messages of sympathy, including one from Her Majesty the Queen, and a telephone call from John Major. The Prime Minister expressed his sense of outrage and wished a speedy recovery to the injured. Douglas Hurd invited me to his office and promised that Her Majesty's Government would bear the costs of repairing the Embassy, which indeed it did. Scotland Yard conducted a most thorough investigation and after six months it apprehended the Palestinian terrorist cell which had committed the atrocity. Two years after the blast, on 16 December 1996, Jawad Botmeh, twenty-eight, and Samar Alami, thirty, were convicted and sentenced at the Old Bailey to twenty years' imprisonment. Mr Justice Garland explained that these two were not the only ones responsible for the terrorist attack. The others had not been caught, and in their sentencing, his duty was to judge the offence and not the politics. I reacted to the sentence in a statement to the press, saying 'Terrorists must know that nothing can or will be achieved by terrorism and that in the end they will be brought to justice.'

Far more devastating acts of terror took place in Israel. They included the kidnapping of soldiers and suicide bombings, the latter performed by fanatical young Palestinians blowing themselves up in populated areas, killing many women and children indiscriminately. On 18 October 1994 Lea and Yitzhak Rabin arrived in London for a working visit. From Heathrow we drove straight to the Embassy in Kensington, so that the Prime

Minister could observe the damage caused by its bombing. After inspecting the devastation, Rabin told me that until he saw the Embassy, he had not imagined that the destruction was so extensive. Later in the afternoon we drove to Downing Street for a comprehensive discussion with John Major. Rabin expressed the view that without the progress with the Palestinians, the signing of the peace treaty with Jordan would have been impossible. But peace had no meaning without security. He said that the real test of Arafat's leadership would be the way he dealt with the fundamentalist Islamic extremists of Hamas and Jihad. Drawing an analogy with Northern Ireland, he said that Britain had achieved a cease-fire without a political settlement while Israel had concluded a political settlement without the cessation of terror. It was a very friendly and wide-ranging conversation, which included an overview of the Middle East situation, covering Iran and Iraq, as well as the bilateral relations. On the latter point Rabin told Major that under his leadership 'dramatic changes in our relations occurred'. The day was full of engagements and concluded with Rabin's address to the International Leadership Reunion of the United Jewish Appeal. Rabin recounted to his listeners the agony of having had to order a risky military operation on the house where a kidnapped soldier, Nachshon Waxman, was being held; Waxman had been killed and Rabin had visited his bereaved parents just before departing for London.

We started the second day of the visit with an interview on BBC Radio Four's 'Today' programme. I was alone with Rabin in the special hotel suite which we used for press interviews, when the presenter told us, at about 8.10, of reports coming in of a bus explosion on Disengoff Street in Tel Aviv. It was news to us, but by the time we returned to Rabin's suite all the telephones were ringing with reports of the suicide bombing and the terrible carnage in which twenty-two people had been killed. It was a devastating tragedy. Rabin decided to cut short his visit to London and return home. Three major engagements were pending: a meeting with Tony Blair, a lunch for sixty distinguished guests in Rabin's honour at our residence, and a lecture to nine hundred students in Oxford. We decided not to cancel the meeting with Blair, which was very warm and friendly, and was in fact the last time that the two statesmen met. Rabin asked me not to accompany him to Heathrow airport, but to attend the lunch and address the Oxford Union on his behalf, which I did. About nine hundred students and faculty members gathered in the Oxford Union lecture hall. In my opening remarks I said that in many years of diplomatic practice I had replaced speakers but never before had I taken the place of a Prime Minister who was leading Israel during such a trying period. It was Rabin's last visit to Britain.

Terror did not deflect the Rabin government from the business of peace-making. On 26 October 1994, a week after his return from London, Rabin and the Jordanian Prime Minister, Abdul-Salam Majali, signed the Treaty of Peace between Israel and Jordan. The ceremony was held at the Arava border crossing and was witnessed by King Hussein and President Clinton. It was the culmination of very intensive secret negotiations conducted in Israel and Jordan. The final obstacles were ironed out in a marathon seven-hour meeting between Rabin and the king on 16 October. One of the most difficult issues was the allocation of water. The Prime Minister agreed that Israel would supply Jordan with fifty million cubic metres above the agreed distribution and Jordan gave up any claims of access to the Kinneret, the Sea of Galilee.[38]

When I arrived in Tel Aviv, on the morning of 26 October – to help prepare for a private visit by the Duke of Edinburgh to receive the Yad Veshem medal on behalf of his mother, who had saved a Jewish family during the war – the whole country was electrified by the signing ceremony in the Arava, which was televised live. I was only sorry that Dr Yacov Herzog, who started the contacts with King Hussein, did not live to see this modest but impressive ceremony. A few days later I met Rabin and his satisfaction at the Jordanian Treaty of Peace was manifest.

Several weeks later, at a dinner at the home of our friends, Lord and Lady Weidenfeld, I was chatting with Lord Howe, whom I had known when he was Foreign Secretary. I asked him whether, upon leaving the Foreign Office, he would have predicted that at the end of 1994 Israel would sign a peace treaty with Jordan. Howe replied that he had not predicted the crumbling of Communism, the election of Mandela as President of South Africa or the peace process in the Middle East. So sudden and unexpected was the pace of change.

Ever since the end of the Six Day War in 1967, whenever decisions about an agreement with the Palestinians were being made, the domestic debate was fierce and passionate. However, we were confident that no matter how tough the decisions, they would be taken within the framework of the democratic system and respected by the people. Tragically, this hope was not borne out by events. The fringes of Israeli society harboured a dangerous and fanatical brand of extremism. Begin and Shamir had had to address it when twenty-seven Jews were tried, in June 1984, for committing atrocities against Arabs. After the Oslo Accords these zealots stepped up their violence. On 25 February 1994 Dr Baruch Goldstein, an orthodox Jew, deluding himself that he could single-handedly stop the tide of history and jeopardize the Oslo Agreement, entered the Tomb of the Patriarch and gunned down twenty-nine innocent Muslims praying in this holy shrine. Another 125 people were injured before he was over-powered and killed. The next chapter in this atrocious fanaticism was to see Jew turning against Jew.

On 28 September 1995 the Oslo II Agreement was signed, stipulating the withdrawal of the IDF from the populated West Bank cities. The right-wing opposition stepped up its protest demonstrations, viciously attacking the Rabin government. On 4 November 1995, Hana and I went to the theatre to see *Three Tall Women*. About twenty-five minutes into the play, one of my Special Branch guards whispered in my ear: 'Sir, your Prime Minister has been shot.' Within minutes we were speeding in our car on the way to the Embassy. On the car radio we picked up reports on the Tel Aviv demonstration and the assassination attempt. We had known of the big peace rally taking place and had expected to hear of its success, not this shocking news. We prayed and hoped that Rabin was only injured, but shortly after our arrival in the Embassy the bitter report of his death reached us. As my colleagues gathered around, grief-stricken, our pain was intensified by the intolerable thought that a Jew, Yigal Amir, had murdered our leader. It was so abhorrent, so unbelievable, so much against our ethos, our tradition and our values that we were confounded into painful silence. In addition to the national catastrophe, it was for Hana and me a personal loss. I had known Rabin well since 1966. As Abba Eban recounts in his memoirs,[39] I suggested to him in 1968 that he nominate the then Chief of Staff of the Six Day War as ambassador to the US. We later worked with Lea and Yitzhak Rabin for five years in Washington and felt close to them. I observed his transition from army commander to diplomat, and then watched the combined qualities of his two former careers blend into Rabin the politician. On 7 November, Lea had been due to arrive in London to address a charity dinner. In view of prevailing terrorist threats at the time, I had mentioned my concern to one of the Special Branch officers, who later notified me that Mrs Rabin would be accorded police protection. That same evening Rabin was assassinated. Recollections of my last talks with him rolled through the mind like a reel of film, especially our last meeting in London, the talks with John Major in Jerusalem in March 1995 and a memorable helicopter trip with Rabin and Major to the Galilee in which the Prime Minister was our guide and explained, using a map, the security problems with Syria and Lebanon. I could not indulge in reflection for long, as telephone calls expressing condolences soon started to come in. One of the first to call was Tony Blair, expressing shock and disbelief. Soon Downing Street and the Foreign Office informed us that the Prince of Wales and John Major would fly to Israel for the funeral. Major invited the leaders of the other major parties, Tony Blair and Paddy Ashdown, and they were joined by the Chief Rabbi of Great Britain, Dr Jonathan Sacks, on their special flight to Jerusalem.

My next concern was to arrange a proper memorial service at the end of the seven-day mourning period. I consulted Sir Trevor Chinn, the president of the United Jewish Appeal, and the president of the Board of Deputies, Eldred Tabachnick, and both were of the opinion that the Albert

Hall would be the most suitable venue for the service. On 12 November a packed Albert Hall, with many people crowding the square outside, paid tribute to our assassinated leader. Addressing the audience, I said that the question of whether man made history or whether history created its heroes was irrelevant in the case of Yitzhak Rabin, whose whole adult life had been closely intertwined with the history of our young state.

The profound sense of loss was compounded by concern for the future of the peace process, for the fate of his legacy, for the impact of the murder on the relations between Orthodox and secular Jews in Israel and on the political system. In every speech I cautioned against any notion of collective guilt, pointing out, however, that the educational system which helped create such extreme tendencies must examine its conscience.

Despite the pain and anguish, Israeli democracy had proved to be strong and resilient, and within a short while Shimon Peres was nominated acting Prime Minister to succeed Rabin. Ehud Barak, a brilliant army general and former Chief of Staff who had joined the Labour Party, became Minister of Foreign Affairs. In the whole political spectrum in Israel there was no politician more experienced, more charismatic and more courageous than Peres. Yet his second term as Prime Minister lasted only seven months and ended in his defeat in the general elections. It was a period marked by an upsurge in Hamas terror and increased violence on the Lebanese border. In January 1996 a top Hamas terrorist responsible for engineering the suicide bombings was assassinated. Hamas retaliated with the utmost fury and during February and March fifty-eight Israelis lost their lives in a series of suicide bombings in Jerusalem and Tel Aviv. The public became despondent and support for the peace process dropped steeply. In April, Hizbullah rocket attacks on the Galilee injured scores of people in Kiryat Shemona. Peres ordered a massive air and artillery retaliation on targets in Lebanon, operation 'Grapes of Wrath'. The killing of civilians in Lebanon by artillery fire had serious ramifications on world public opinion and on the support of Israeli Arabs for Peres.

In his short span as Prime Minister, Peres speeded up the implementation of the Oslo accords and attempted to achieve a breakthrough in negotiations with Syria. In January 1996 I travelled to Jerusalem and met Barak. The Foreign Minister said that we were expecting to hear the Syrian position on normalization of relations and on the structure of security arrangements. Peres nominated Uri Savir, the director-general of the Ministry of Foreign Affairs and chief negotiator in the Oslo talks, to head our delegation in the negotiations with Syria. He worked jointly with our ambassador in Washington, Itamar Rabinovich, who had led the contacts with Damascus during the Rabin period. Both attempted to accelerate the talks; instead of concentrating primarily on security, Savir widened the scope to include other subjects of mutual interest. The Americans encouraged this new effort to achieve a breakthrough by offering the Wye Plantation in Delaware, a country house removed from media attention, as the site for the talks. However progress was painfully slow.

The approach of President Assad to the negotiations with Israel was baffling. As far back as June 1967, the government led by Levi Eshkol had decided that, in the context of a peace treaty, Israel would be ready to withdraw to the international border with Syria, subject to security arrangements. At that time there had not been a single Israeli settlement on the Golan, and a solution to security concerns and to problems connected with water could have ushered in a peaceful relationship between the two countries. However, for twenty-seven years there had been no opening whatsoever for negotiating peace with Assad. In July 1994 Rabin authorized Secretary of State Warren Christopher to convey to the Syrian President 'his own impression' that should Syria agree to full normalization of relations with Israel and to proper security arrangements on the Golan Heights, Israel would be ready to withdraw from the Golan as part of a peace treaty. Rabin added that 'the Israelis will not spell it [this position] out before all our needs are met'.[40] When Peres became Prime Minister, he followed a similar line on the question of withdrawal. However, Assad continued to move very slowly, seeking a commitment to total withdrawal, declining to meet Peres, as he had been reluctant to meet Rabin before him, and refusing to agree on a peace package. A question mark was thus left in the minds of Americans and Israelis on whether he was at all interested in peace. The very same question continues to puzzle the wits of politicians and diplomats to this day. Some observers believe that the present situation, in which Assad can rally support against the enemy, Israel, may seem preferable from his point of view. Ambassador Itamar Rabinovich, who was our chief negotiator with Syria, also maintained that in August 1993 when Rabin probed the option of a peace treaty with Damascus, and also shortly after Peres became Prime Minister in November 1995, Assad could have concluded a peace agreement with Israel. However he missed these opportunities. During the four years of contacts, Syria had nevertheless agreed to a peace treaty which included a restricted normalization of relations in return for total withdrawal.[41] This was an unacceptable formula to Israeli governments.

On 31 January 1996, Shimon Peres arrived in London for a working visit. I recalled that when I last welcomed Peres as Prime Minister in 1986, Mrs Thatcher and Geoffrey Howe were his British counterparts. Now both had left the political scene and Peres had become Prime Minister again. In the Heathrow lounge I told him that while he had been in the air, there was a report on the radio that he wanted to advance the elections. He said that he had not yet decided to do so. While in London, he expected to receive a more forthcoming reply from Assad on his suggestion that the two leaders meet and set the stage for stepped-up negotiations. Had the Syrian President replied favourably to Peres' approach, he would have delayed the elections to November 1996. In the absence of such a commitment, Peres felt that no progress with Syria and continuous Palestinian terror risked further erosion of his political standing, and decided to advance the elections to May 1996. In the event, the results took many by surprise. Binyamin Netanyahu was victorious with 50.49 per cent of the vote while Peres had 49.51 per cent. He had lost by 29,500 votes, a margin of less than one per cent. After four years of a Labour government Likud was back in power.

Netanyahu Elected Prime Minister

Overnight, a completely new situation had emerged. Israel was in a quandary. In the Arab world, a feeling of deep apprehension and dejection was evident, and among the Palestinians a sense of foreboding. Arafat was reported to be in shock.

Most prominent among the factors that were responsible for Netanyahu's victory was the impact of the murderous terrorist suicide bombings in Jerusalem and Tel Aviv in February and March 1996. Fears for personal safety outweighed the trauma of the Rabin assassination and the ground swell of support for the Rabin–Peres approach to peace. With Likud putting the sharpest emphasis on these fears, the politics of delusion and fear had triumphed over those of hope and promise inherent in the Peres approach. Likud's electoral rhetoric had encouraged the belief that Netanyahu would fight terror more effectively, and this was combined with support for him from all shades of the religious spectrum. Religious voters doubted Peres' firmness on the Jerusalem issue. Encouraged by the rabbis, they flocked to the polls and voted for Netanyahu, although he was as secular and as agnostic as Peres.

The founding fathers of the State of Israel, especially David Ben-Gurion, understood the importance of having a religious component in Israel's coalition governments. Unfortunately, the main partner in early coalitions, the National Religious Party, had drifted to the right. The Labour Party under Rabin and Peres was influenced by its junior partner, the strictly secular Meretz Party, and in the last few years had not included a single religious faction in its governments. Thus Labour was perceived by the rabbis as anti-religious. Demographic growth worked in favour of the religious groups, and was evident in the composition of the newly elected Knesset. It contained twenty-three religious members, compared to sixteen in the former Knesset – 19.5 per cent of Parliament. Netanyahu had no difficulty in obtaining their support for the government he was forming.

Netanyahu, the eighth Prime Minister of the State of Israel, had also fully mastered the media. With his telegenic personality, well-versed in the craft of sound-bites and trained by American media experts, he had grasped the potential of media politics. It was the short and simple message, well articulated, rather than profound reflection, that carried the masses. Character, experience, morality and personality are less easily conveyed by the small screen.

Many people I met in London pondered on the question that thousands of Israelis were now asking themselves; how could half of the electorate in Israel ignore the remarkable accomplishments, indeed historical break-throughs, of the Rabin–Peres government in the preceding four years? There had been advancing negotiations with the Palestinians; the peace treaty with Jordan; diplomatic ties with Morocco, Tunis, Qatar and Oman, and a number of less formal contacts with other Muslim countries; erosion of the Arab boycott; an influx of foreign investment and a wave of international goodwill unparalleled since 1948. The achievements in the domestic field were no less striking: extensive road construction; expansion of education; sustained economic growth of five to six per cent in the years before the elections; advances in science and technology. The answer appeared to be that these achievements were eclipsed by fear of boarding a bus, or going to the market-place, by a unfounded apprehension that Peres would concede too much too fast in the negotiations with the Palestinians. The public mood was fickle.

Both Rabin and Peres knew that their drive for peace was fraught with danger and political risk. Yet they also understood that to strengthen the pragmatic Palestinians led by Arafat, and to reduce the influence of the extremists such as the Hamas, it was imperative to move swiftly and shorten the dangerous transition period. This, they had hoped, would also lead to a reduction, if not elimination, of terror. Little did they imagine that their strategy would result in the assassination of Rabin by a Jewish terrorist and the downfall of Peres by the narrowest of margins in an election. For three difficult years the Israeli government had pledged that it would not allow terror to undermine the peace process. It had negotiated while constantly fighting terrorism. Now, the two courageous architects of that process were gone. Yet the movement towards peace did not die, and their legacy had become part of a new reality.

On Friday, 30 May, I made my way to 10 Downing Street, to give the first assessment of the election results to John Major's private secretary, John Holmes. I told him that the results clearly indicated that the country was divided right down the middle on the peace process. From my personal acquaintance with Netanyahu, I believed that he was a pragmatist rather than an ideologue and from his service in our Washington Embassy and later as head of our Mission to the UN in New York, he appreciated the importance of our relations with the United States as well as the role of Europe. He understood that in an interdependent world Israel could not remain isolated. He would therefore have to find a way to reconcile the pressures in his party and his campaign commitments with the real world. Holmes asked me about his statements that Israel would not withdraw from the Golan Heights. I replied that these were pre-election speeches and that if and when Netanyahu negotiated with Syria he would soon find that it would be impossible to attain peace while holding on to the whole of the Golan. I asked that HMG make no judgements on Netanyahu's policies based on his election rhetoric, but rather to wait for the formulation of the guidelines of his new government.

Holmes replied that the British government would cooperate with the newly elected government of Israel without prejudice. He added that he found my analysis useful, for Arafat would be arriving in London the following week and would meet the Prime Minister. The same afternoon, the first British reaction was published in a statement from the Foreign Secretary. Congratulating Netanyahu, Malcolm Rifkind stated that the British government was looking forward to working with him in the future, and hoping that he would keep up 'the momentum in the peace process'.

In the coming days, my staff and I spent a considerable amount of time allaying the fears of the business community, which was greatly concerned that any notion of stalling negotiations with the Palestinians might produce an environment hostile to doing business with Israel. Two conversations were remarkable in this context: Lord Weinstock, the chairman of the General Electric Company, called me expressing the view that only a Likud–Labour coalition government would generate confidence in the Israeli economy. A conversation I had with the chairman of Marks & Spencer, Sir Richard Greenbury, started off by him saying that the election results were very disappointing. Sir Richard, a creative leader in business and a staunch friend of Israel, was also the chairman of the Israeli–British Business Council, and M&S was the largest importer of Israeli goods into Britain, amounting to over £100 million a year. I reassured Sir Richard that trade with Israel would not be adversely affected. Sir Trevor Chinn, who participated in the meeting, and had been instrumental in establishing the Business Council, explained that Netanyahu was committed to privatization and to a market economy, and that business would continue as usual.

The inseparable connection between business and progress in the peace process was emphasized in the letter of congratulation which John Major sent to Netanyahu on 3 June 1996. 'Many of the individual business decisions will have been taken because of the new confidence in peace between Israel and her neighbours, including the Palestinians, which has held out the prospect that a base in Israel will serve not only customers in Israel but also a wider regional market. It is obviously important that British business retain that confidence,' wrote the Prime Minister. He also invited Netanyahu to visit London. On 4 June, Major replied in Parliament to a question by John Butterfill, MP, saying, 'This country has perhaps, a better relationship with the State of Israel today than it has had in any stage in the history of the State of Israel and I know that the new Prime Minister is determined that that should continue and so am I.'

However, the overriding theme in conversations remained concern for the peace process and fear that one of the most encouraging advances in the Middle East might be halted. This anxiety was not confined to the United Kingdom, it was quite universal. Letters and statements addressed to the Prime Minister-elect echoed it. In his very first phone call, congratulating Netanyahu, President Clinton discussed the peace process and expressed the US commitment to working with him and with all those in the region 'to realize the goal of a comprehensive peace between Arabs and Israelis'. The American administration, in messages to Arab leaders, asked them not to rush to conclusions and to wait for Netanyahu's policies.

None the less, the sense of gloom and pessimism in Arab capitals and among the Palestinians grew, and a flurry of meetings of heads of state ensued. The President of Egypt, attempting to forestall a militant line led by Syria, convened an Arab summit in Cairo. It supported a just and comprehensive peace while warning against any retraction by Israel of its commitments under agreements already reached. The heads of state also reiterated their demand for a Palestinian state with East Jerusalem as its capital.

Outlines of the Israeli government's guidelines, published in the press on 7 June, heightened Arab concern. Although they contained a pledge to widen the circle of peace with all our neighbours, they also spelled out the negatives: the government would insist on Israel's sovereignty on the Golan Heights and would strengthen the settlements there; the government would allocate the necessary resources to ensure 'the existence and the development of the "new settlements"' (in the West Bank); it would oppose the establishment of an independent Palestinian state; united Jerusalem, the eternal capital of Israel, was one city under Israel's sovereignty, indivisible, though every religion would enjoy freedom of worship and access to its holy places. The policy on Jerusalem enjoyed a wide consensus in Israel and was understood, though not accepted, by the Palestinian and Arab world. But the impact on the Arabs of these cumulative negatives was stark, decreasing incentives to negotiate. From the Arab point of view they represented retrogression. If Rabin and Peres had succeeded in strengthening the pragmatist majority in the Arab world, the new messages fuelled radical fires.

Nevertheless, King Hussein of Jordan, who was the first Arab leader to be invited to Washington after the election of Binyamin Netanyahu, sounded cautiously optimistic. Following a meeting with Secretary of State Warren Christopher, on 11 June 1996, the king talked to the press. Recognizing the need to consolidate past achievements, he added, 'I have every reason to be, I believe, optimistic, hopeful, determined to see us move ahead towards that goal.' A journalist present wondered how, of all the Arab leaders, the Jordanian monarch was the only one to sound positive about the future after the election of Mr Netanyahu, and asked what his optimism was based on. The king replied: 'There are many reasons if you look back into the history of the region', a reference to the fact that the peace treaty with Egypt, and the very substantial concessions required in order to achieve it, were made by a leader of the right-wing Likud party, Menachem Begin. Then, referring directly to the elections, King Hussein added, 'the issue was not one of peace and the opponents of peace. I believe the overwhelming majority of Israelis have opted for peace and realize that it is our only way. I believe that the issue of the elections was for a person, a leader, the Prime Minister and in that regard the Israelis made their choice.'[42] It was clear from the remarks that King Hussein was unruffled by the election results.

Only a few weeks before, on 20 May, I had met the king at a dinner hosted by the Friends of the Haifa Technion, at which he received the Churchill Award. Before dinner I discussed with him the impending visit of Foreign Minister Ehud Barak, who was due to arrive in London the next day to meet him. The king had opted not to have a meeting with Barak in Amman, which was only an hour away from Jerusalem, since such a high-profile meeting might have been construed as interference in a domestic elections campaign. Hussein, who always valued a low-profile attitude, was concerned about press coverage. In the course of his speech he said that he was accused of supporting this or that party ahead of the elections; he recalled that Prime Minister Rabin had told him that peace with Jordan is peace between the Israeli and Jordanian peoples. But King Hussein's attitude had more to it than just political caution. The assassination of Rabin had robbed him of a friend and collaborator whom he trusted and with whom he had signed the peace treaty. The history of Hussein's relations with Peres was more complicated. He had been disappointed that Peres had not resigned after Prime Minister Shamir rejected the London Agreement, concluded by both of them in 1987. He also believed that he should have been apprised of the Oslo Accords earlier than he was and, above all, he was afraid that in the negotiations on permanent status with the Palestinians, the interests of Jordan would not be fully protected by a Labour government. Hence, subjectively, he viewed the change of prime ministers in Israel as not totally unsatisfactory.

During the first eighteen months of the Netanyahu government there was no movement on the negotiations with Syria. If President Assad was serious about his contention that he had made a strategic decision to negotiate peace with Israel, he had forfeited an opportunity to do so while Rabin and Peres led Israel. Both were prepared to offer a far-reaching withdrawal on the Golan Heights in return for a peace treaty based on full normalization of relations, satisfactory security arrangements and an agreed time-frame for implementation. Assad persisted in his demand for an unequivocal commitment to total withdrawal from the Golan Heights ahead of negotiations. Whether he realized that in the Middle East a 'window of opportunity' to make peace is very limited in time it is difficult to know.

The focal endeavour remained negotiations with the Palestinians. After discrediting Arafat at the beginning of his term, Netanyahu realized that there was no point in weakening the main negotiating partner and the only leader who could make the crucial decisions to reach agreement. He eventually met Arafat and established negotiating channels. In January 1997 the government concluded and swiftly implemented the Hebron Accord, turning over most of the city to the Palestinian Authority and agreeing to a timetable for further redeployments of Israeli troops from the West Bank. In March 1997, the government decided to initiate a housing project in a new Jerusalem suburb, Har-Homa, to which the Palestinians objected fiercely. For the next nine months negotiations were stalled, and Hamas terror continued unabated. In July, Netanyahu talked about the lessening of terror and two days later, on 28 July, suicide bombers blew themselves up in the Machne-Yehuda market in Jerusalem, killing twelve Israelis and injuring 170. Inevitable countermeasures ensued and trust between the parties dropped steeply; the tense relationship and lack of progress adversely affected Israel's international position.

In June 1997, Ehud Barak was elected leader of the Labour Party, replacing Shimon Peres. Barak, briefly Foreign Minister, former Chief of Staff, and chief of military intelligence, was well acquainted with our defence and foreign-policy dilemmas. As the top commander of the Israeli Defence Forces he possessed the necessary skills to set the right priorities and oversee an immense budget while shouldering the responsibility of sending soldiers into battle. A few months before his election, in January 1997, he set out his vision for peace with the Palestinians and with Syria. He followed the Rabin concept, advocating separation between Israel and the Palestinian entity which must be 'beyond the borders of Israel'.[43] He admitted that a Palestinian state, with constraints on exercise of sovereignty, might be 'the outcome of the process', and outlined the Labour

Party positions on the permanent-status talks: a united Jerusalem; no return to the 1967 borders; settlements to remain under Israeli sovereignty; no Arab army to cross to the west of the River Jordan; coordination with the Palestinians on water resources.

Barak's position on negotiations with Syria was based on the principle of 'land for peace', noting the content of the talks with Syria that had transpired in contacts during the Rabin and Peres periods. These were reasonable positions reflecting the views of Israelis at the centre of the political map.

In June, the Prime Minister moved away from the right towards the centre, suggesting to his Defence Committee an outline for an Israeli proposal to the permanent-status negotiations. It called for the return of areas on the West Bank to the Palestinians while retaining the Jordan Valley and a narrower strip on the western edges of the West Bank. Jerusalem, including the Etzion Block and Ma'ale Adumim, would also be retained. This represented a considerable shift in Likud policy, with Netanyahu stating that Israel would achieve a permanent-status agreement that 'would surprise the world'.[44]

The impasse nevertheless continued. The Palestinians demanded a freeze on settlement activity, a request which was endorsed by the US and by European countries. Netanyahu suggested that Israel and the Palestinians change course and instead of tortuous negotiations on interim steps, move to permanent-status talks and work out a definitive settlement. The Palestinians insisted on parallel progress on the implementation of the Oslo accords. They were apprehensive that in case of a crisis in the permanent-status talks, which would include Jerusalem, settlements and refugee issues, they would lose both the internationally recognized commitments under Oslo and the chance to move swiftly to a final settlement. The gaps, therefore, remained wide and the difficulties were heightened by a considerable lack of mutual trust.

In November 1997 Netanyahu arrived in London for his second visit since becoming Prime Minister. In his friendly and business-like talks with the British Prime Minister, Tony Blair, and Foreign Secretary, Robin Cook, he expressed a preference for negotiations on the permanent status. However, the British view was that there must be parallel movement on the interim agreement. During his visit to Britain he also had, on 17 November, a crucial encounter with the American Secretary of State, Madeleine Albright, in which she impressed upon him the need to carry out a further redeployment of Israeli troops from the West Bank before it was possible to start final-status talks. Albright was on her way to the Gulf States and in the middle of a serious effort to revive the anti-Saddam-Hussein coalition in view of Iraq's violation of the inspection of arms of mass destruction and the possibility of military action against Baghdad.

The Arab countries did not fail to voice their disappointment with the lack of progress on peace with the Palestinians, and were reluctant to grant the US the same support as during the Gulf War in 1990.

In all my meetings with Israeli leaders I have never encountered a Prime Minister as embattled as Binyamin Netanyahu was on his visit to London in November 1997. A few days before his arrival the Likud central committee voted on a change to the party electoral system designed to strengthen his authority and weaken the influence of ministers and members of Knesset. Top Likud leaders like the mayors of Jerusalem and Tel Aviv, Ehud Olmert and Roni Milo, were furious, and indirectly challenged Netanyahu's leadership. Relations with the United States were under serious strain, to the point that President Clinton had refused to meet the Prime Minister unless there was movement in the negotiations with the Palestinians. Similarly, the European Union and other countries were extremely sceptical about his intentions. Diaspora Jewry was concerned about his commitments to the religious parties to enact legislation that would alter the recognition of conversions to Judaism. Egypt, Jordan and the Palestinians had lost faith in his willingness to make progress in the negotiations. His national and international standing and credibility was at very low ebb. Shortly after returning to Israel the Prime Minister initiated Cabinet discussions on a 'further redeployment' of Israeli troops from the West Bank.

The irony was that Netanyahu had become the first Likud leader to accept the principal of 'land for peace' and the need for territorial compromise on the West Bank, giving up the unrealistic dream of Greater Israel. In time, this policy switch will ease the way to a permanent settlement. However, scepticism about his ability to carry through this policy and doubts whether his right-wing coalition partners would support this approach plagued the country. The disbelief rests on the fact that in the first twenty-two months of his premiership, negotiations with the Palestinians have been stalled; talks with Syria stopped; the multilateral peace process ground to a halt, and the process of normalization of relations between Israel and Muslim countries slowed. Had he turned to Labour and invited Barak to join a national unity government, he would have had a broad base for a permanent settlement with the Palestinians. Together, the two large parties could also have forged agreements on other crucial issues like relations between the religious and secular, and introduced constitutional changes essential to stability. Netanyahu's constraints, personal and political, remain a source of great uncertainty. Despite transient difficulties, the long-term imperatives dictate that Israelis and Palestinians must re-engage because there is no alternative. Five million Israelis and two million Palestinians must reason together and work out their peaceful existence.

Epilogue

On 4 December 1997, Hana and I paid a farewell call on the Queen. In a very friendly and informal conversation, Her Majesty remarked on our long periods of service in the United Kingdom. It was the remarkable culmination of fourteen years of diplomatic service in Britain, in three different positions, spanning a period of over three decades.

In 1959, I worked for a short while under Ambassador Eliyahu Elath, Israel's second envoy to Great Britain and a well-respected diplomat. His successor, Arthur Lourie, was my first teacher of classical diplomatic practice. As one of the founders of the diplomatic service he was a model of integrity, impeccable in style and behaviour and seasoned in the art of understatement. Returning to London as minister in 1983, I served under ambassador Yehuda Avner, a hard-working diplomat and good friend, who had the right perception of the dual role of an Israeli envoy, as representative to both the UK government and the Jewish community.

The three British prime ministers with whose governments I worked during my tenures in London were Baroness Thatcher, John Major and Tony Blair. Lady Thatcher pursued a friendly policy towards Israel, took a strong stand against Palestinian terrorism and was extremely supportive of the efforts of Shimon Peres and King Hussein of Jordan to start direct negotiations between Israel and the Arabs with an international conference, which eventually took place, at Madrid. However, she failed to lift the embargo on the sale of arms to Israel, which adversely influenced our relationship in the field of defence. Her government had negotiated a £20 billion arms deal with Saudi Arabia and she was concerned to avoid anything that would upset the Saudi king. Before I left London, in the winter of 1997, I accompanied Peres to a meeting with her. She was full of vigour, outlining in considerable detail the dangers Britain would face if it became part of the single currency mechanism. When we had touched on developments in the Middle East, Lady Thatcher remarked that she did not like the expression 'peace process' because it implied that we were dealing with a lengthy course of action. I thought that the description 'process' was fitting because the resolution of such a complex issue as the Arab–Israeli conflict was a 'process'. Neither Peres nor I felt that it was worth arguing with the Iron Lady on semantics. I thanked her for the understanding she had displayed towards Israel during her premiership and thought to myself that here were two extremely able although very different leaders, both of whom the democratic process, in their respective countries, had decided to sideline in this period of change.

My acquaintance with John Major was much closer than that with Lady Thatcher. He occupied Downing Street for over three years of my term as ambassador, and I had the privilege of meeting him on many occasions. From our first encounter I felt that, while he was a strong defender of British interests in our region, both he and his wife Norma were true friends of Israel and staunch supporters of peace. Accompanying him during his visit to Jerusalem in March 1995 was a high point in our discourse. Major said that it was extraordinary that his visit to Israel was only the second visit of a serving British prime minister in the forty-seven years of the state. 'Your leaders should be over there and our leaders should be over here,' he remarked. He had a thorough understanding of our security imperatives and he saw clearly the dangers posed by Syria as well as the complicated situation on the border with Lebanon. Rabin, who explained to him the strategic and tactical problems with our neighbours in the north, also reiterated that Israel had no territorial claims on Lebanon and that in the context of peace we were ready to withdraw to the international border. During that visit Rabin and Major established the Business Council, which has taken an important role in enhancing the economic relationship between our two countries. By inviting a group of top businessmen to accompany him to Jerusalem, Major sent a powerful signal to the City that as far as the British government was concerned, the Arab boycott had come to an end. He and his Foreign Secretary Malcolm Rifkind also ended the embargo on the sale of arms to Israel, and gave their blessing to the first royal visit when His Royal Highness the Duke of Edinburgh came to Jerusalem on a private visit. His government invited President Weizman for the first state visit of an Israeli President to Britain. In 1994 we established the UK–Israel Science and Technology Research Fund, supported by the Israeli and UK governments and private funding, which included a contribution from the Rothschild Foundation. It promoted collaboration in science and technology between the two countries, especially in the fields of biotechnology, electro-optics, lasers and high-performance materials. Two conversations with John Major will always remain in my memory: his telephone call to my residence following the bombing of the Embassy, a warm and compassionate call at a time of distress, and a conversation at Northolt airport on 5 November 1995, when I saw him off on his flight to Israel for Rabin's funeral. The assassination of Rabin touched him deeply on a personal level, as a colleague and as a great supporter of peace, for he was concerned that the process of negotiation would be slowed down as a result of the murder.

Major extended a very warm welcome to the Israeli Prime Minister, Shimon Peres, in January 1996. After a wide-ranging discussion between the two leaders on negotiations with Syria, the successful elections to the Palestinian Council and the future prospects for peace, they faced the press. Major stated that he could not 'remember a time when the bilateral relationship was as close over a whole range of issues as it is at the present time and I think a great deal of the credit for that goes to Prime Minister Rabin and Prime Minister Peres'. The Labour Party, on the suggestion of Gordon Brown, invited Peres to address the Shadow Cabinet. It was an exceptional gesture of friendship and appreciation.

I also followed closely Major's domestic policies; the way he pulled Britain out of an acute economic recession, reduced unemployment and kept inflation low. However, with a very narrow majority in Parliament he was unable to discipline members who opposed his policies on Europe and the single currency and thus left an impression of weakness. His greatest difficulty was that after eighteen years of Tory government the mood in Britain favoured change and on 1 May 1997, Tony Blair won the election by a landslide.

Our work in the Embassy was based on the premise that the British approach to the Middle East conflict rested on a broad multi-party consensus and close relations with the opposition as well as with government had to be an essential part of our effort. When I left London as Minister Plenipotentiary in 1988, I recommended to my successor that two young Labour Members of Parliament, Tony Blair and Gordon Brown, be invited to visit Israel at an early date. Upon returning as ambassador I developed a good rapport with the Labour leaders, John Smith and his successor Tony Blair. In the three years prior to the British elections in May 1997, the Labour leaders visited Israel and got acquainted at first hand with our leaders and with the problems in the peace process. These visits included Tony Blair, Lord Irvine of Lairg, Gordon Brown and Robin Cook.

An important component of Blair's 'New Labour' policy was to change the unfriendly attitude of the left wing of his party towards Israel and win the support of the Jewish community in Britain. In the course of 1996 and 1997 he succeeded in both. Yet the Labour government, like its predecessor, was extremely concerned that a lengthy impasse in negotiations with the Palestinians would endanger the peace process and set back the important achievements of the Oslo Accords. This serious anxiety was at the heart of the discussions that Prime Minister Netanyahu had with Tony Blair and Robin Cook in November 1997. A week before we left London, on 9 December, Blair spoke at the Labour Friends of Israel annual luncheon and delivered the most authoritative policy statement of his government on the peace process.[1] He stressed that he had considered himself a friend of Israel all his adult life and understood the need for 'peace with security'.

The Oslo Accords made it possible 'to imagine' a 'lasting and comprehensive peace' and therefore the process would have 'to be taken forward'. He also reiterated the British view of the foundations for peace. It was only on the basis 'of a just exchange of land for peace that the future of the region can be secured'. The Prime Minister expressed his support for the American call to freeze settlement activity and for a substantial redeployment from the West Bank. The Blair statement did not represent a change of British policy since the Six Day War, but it reflected friendship for Israel and understanding of its vulnerability. In thanking the Prime Minister for his support and his personal tribute to me, I remarked that his concern for peace was fully consistent with his friendship for Israel. This, in my view, was the case even if we differed on some of the details.

I also followed closely Tony Blair's attempts to introduce revolutionary change in the life of Britain. He inspired a hopeful public mood and possessed a singular combination of youth, courage, public trust, a huge parliamentary majority and an imaginative programme. These were valuable assets, which he used to win over the City by continuing Tory economic policy and holding referendums in Scotland and Wales for a Parliament and an Assembly respectively. Britain must now hope that Scottish nationalism will not go too far and move from devolution – which in essence is meant to be decentralization of government – to secession. Three major issues seem likely to dominate the Blair administration for the foreseeable future; Northern Ireland, Britain's role in Europe, including the single currency, and the restructuring of the welfare state.

Relations between Israel and Britain have undoubtedly weathered stormy periods. The most difficult was of course the post-mandate Attlee–Bevin term. British interests in the Middle East were perceived as excluding a friendly rapport with the Jewish state. For many years there was an abundance of experts in the Foreign Office who would argue the Arab cause and few who would defend Israel's security imperatives. This situation began to change during the Wilson years and continued with the advent of Margaret Thatcher. The Oslo Accords and the serious attempt to solve the Palestinian problem opened up new opportunities and released a wave of latent sympathy towards Israel. It was our task in the Embassy to translate this empathy and understanding into lasting cooperation. By the time I left London I felt that although there still were serious differences between us on the shape of the final settlement, on Jerusalem and on the solution to the refugee problem, the relations between Israel and Britain rested on a solid base of shared values. These include adherence to the ethical code of the Judeo-Christian heritage, a relentless quest for peace and respect for democracy and the rule of law. These relations also benefit from a wide knowledge in Israel of the English language and literature, love of theatre and the arts, cooperation in a considerable number of academic fields and a lively volume of trade. Further progress in the peace process will certainly open new vistas for cooperation. However, a continuing impasse would create friction.

Maintaining relations with the Jewish community in Britain was an essential part of our work. The affinity between Israel and Diaspora Jewry is unique and it places a special responsibility on Israeli diplomats, who must devote time and effort to strengthening this important bond. Simultaneously loyal to their countries of residence, Jews living abroad have made considerable contributions to the phenomenal growth of the State of Israel. Israel adds status to their existence and remains a source of inspiration to generation after generation. They, in turn, are proud of our achievements and concern themselves with the trials and tribulations of the young state. A report by the Institute for Jewish Policy Research on the attachment of British Jews to Israel found that eighty-one per cent are moderately to strongly attached to Israel.[2]

The Jewish population in Israel is constantly growing while the number of Diaspora Jews is declining, partly as a result of the natural process of ageing and death, but mainly because of assimilation, which has become the greatest danger to Jewish survival outside Israel. The pressures of a rapidly changing environment are immense. True, Judaism has successfully faced the challenges of many cultures, Roman, Greek, German and others, but the age of liberalism, in which Jews are accepted as equals more than at any time before, and the changes in the second half of the twentieth century require different approaches. It is not just another clash of cultures. It is the scope and intensity of change and its hurricane force that the traditional Jewish society must learn to cope with. The simple answer is to say 'let them come to Israel'; however, the majority of American, British and French Jews, and Jews of other Western communities, will not immigrate to Israel. Therefore, as Israel celebrates its fiftieth anniversary, it must face the task of assisting Diaspora Jews to remain Jewish; it must intensify the dialogue with these communities, devote more thought and effort to educational programmes, and think and act creatively in order to help counter assimilation.

In the course of our diplomatic service I was in close touch with Jewish leaders in the US while we were serving in Washington and devoted much attention to the Jewish community in the UK during our stay in London. The Embassy staff and I supported the communal efforts initiated by the Chief Rabbi, Jonathan Sacks, to launch an educational programme under the banner of 'continuity' and worked closely with the United Joint Israel Appeal, the Board of Deputies and other organizations. From the very beginning I made it clear that I am Israel's envoy to all shades of the community – Orthodox, Reform, Liberal, Masorty, Sepharadi and Ashkenazi – and we enjoyed the unfailing support of all of them. We were extremely fortunate that the spiritual leaders of the community were strong supporters of the peace process. The former Chief Rabbi, Lord Jacobovitch, spoke out gallantly in support of the negotiations for peace · and for the need to separate religion from politics in Israel. Sacks was always supportive of the Oslo Accords and maintained that 'even a difficult peace is better than an easy war'. I kept a friendly, ongoing dialogue with both, and with the late leader of the Reform movement, Rabbi Hugo Gryn, a great Zionist and peace-lover. As a result the Jewish community in Britain was spared the sharp controversy on peace and territories that split Jewish communities in America and France.

The political issues dividing Israel undoubtedly have an impact on Diaspora Jews. Foremost among them is the need for a territorial compromise on the West Bank, which contradicts the dream of 'Greater Israel'. Although a noble cause, 'Greater Israel' is not an absolute value, and does not stand on its own. It must be balanced against a whole set of other considerations and long-term objectives. For instance, there can be no comprehensive peace without a solution to the Palestinian problem, as there can be no solution to the Palestinian problem without territorial compromise. Attempts to undercut the peace process for ideological reasons would renew the spiral of terror and bloodshed and could lead to total war, contradicting the adherence to the sanctity of human life which is a supreme value in our ethos. Israel must also remain a Jewish state; it is the only state the Jews have. Any notion of annexation of the West Bank would mean sliding into a binational, Jewish–Palestinian state. Israel must maintain its robust democratic character, and the majority of Israelis would accept territorial compromise if it led to peace with security. Peace and the unity of the Jewish people are two fundamental pillars of our existence and neither can be undermined by extremism. Peace cannot be held hostage by the craving for territorial advantage, for it is an inseparable component of long-term security.

Shortly before his assassination, Rabin wrote to Chief Rabbi Sacks thanking him for his 'unfailing support' for the peace process. In his letter, dated 18 October 1995, Rabin also included some prophetic words:

> Thank God, we are a democratic nation and all voices are heard. But even within the democratic framework, obstructions, the call for violence, the use of undemocratic means to destabilize our system and our way of life, cannot and should not be permitted. Compromise and tolerance are essential if peace is to be achieved.

Two weeks later he was assassinated.

Speaking to Jewish audiences at a number of farewell functions, I focused on the need for greater tolerance for bridging gaps between the religious and the secular, inside and outside Israel, and on the prohibitive price we had paid for extremism. Diversity remains a distinctive characteristic of the Jewish experience. Looking towards the future and our common destiny, we must forge greater unity while respecting diversity.

We live by the calendar and it is only natural that the fiftieth anniversary of the state provides a landmark date both for justified celebration and for intense introspection. As a guide to the future the latter is the more important, because we are still in the midst of the struggle for peace and many lessons can be drawn from past experience. Personally, I am very pleased to have returned home on the threshold of 1998 because to be in Israel in this important year is for us the biggest celebration of all. Going back to my birthplace in Dorna (Bukovina) in the Carpathian mountains, an unfriendly environment, typical of Eastern Europe, and remembering what it meant to live without a Jewish state, enables me to appreciate the difference fully. I vividly recall the orthodox background of my father, David Herstig and his family, the ardent Zionism of my mother Elka Biber and my grandfather Israel Biber, and their stories about Palestine, which were more like a fairy tale than real. If someone had told them, at the end of the Second World War, that soon we would have a strong, viable independent state, they would probably have replied 'not in our lifetime'. They had instilled in me and in my two brothers, Yechiel and Efraim, a love for Zion that only increased with the years. The proclamation of the state in 1948 was the realization of our dreams. To be part of the diplomatic corps of the newly independent Israel, to work to establish its place among the nations, gain legitimacy and help forge peace with our neighbours was a singular privilege which I shall always cherish.

The two principal peace treaties, with Egypt and Jordan, have moved us away from confrontation to a new and promising relationship. We hope to be able to resolve our differences with the Palestinians by peaceful means and to build lasting coexistence. The Palestinians will have to accept that Jerusalem will remain the united capital of Israel, with guaranteed safeguards of free access to Muslims and Christians of all denominations, and that there can be no return to the 1967 borders. Israelis will have to accept that a Palestinian state is a historic inevitability. The sooner it is established, by mutual consent and with certain agreed limitations arising from security considerations, the shorter the road to peace will be. The definitive configuration of the triangular relations between Israel, Jordan and Palestinians must be worked out. One possibility is to have a confederation. To make peace comprehensive we must conclude peace agreements with Syria and Lebanon as well. However, progress on these tracks is largely dependent not only on the Israeli leadership but also on President Assad and the leaders of Lebanon.

On the domestic scene Israel must choose its own pace in moving towards a full market economy. Of all the industrialized countries it is the only one to absorb large numbers of immigrants and therefore cannot afford prohibitive unemployment levels. The adjustment of the welfare state to a market economy will be slower than in Europe. In the coming years Israeli leaders will need to improve the flawed constitutional system which allows for a large number of small parties, each exercising excessive political influence. Checks and balances on the executive branch are insufficient; one possible way of improving them might be the introduction of a second chamber in the Knesset. Cooperation between the religious and the secular populations requires a constant dialogue and tolerance on both sides, which should eventually lead to greater harmony and a new code of conduct, reducing friction. It will be difficult but should be achievable once constitutional changes have corrected the present imbalances. More attention, and more money, will have to be devoted to the Arab minority, which numbers about 800,000. Israel has adjusted well to the computer age and the revolution in telecommunications and information technology. It is already a prominent member of the 'global village'. Inching further towards peace, it should be able to place education before defence in budget allocation.

The media revolution has a considerable impact on democracies, not least on diplomacy. Information can now pass instantly from capitals to embassies and vice versa. Ambassadors have opportunities to reach large audiences and acquaint them with their countries' policies and they must, therefore, be conversant with the media. CNN has drastically changed the global news flow and can set the agenda for governments. When I started my career in the Foreign Office, ninety per cent of diplomatic transactions were secret. Today only ten per cent, at most, are secret and that usually for no more than twenty-four to forty-eight hours. Nevertheless the human factor remains paramount in diplomacy, for computers, fax machines and mobile telephones cannot think, analyse, negotiate or decide. The technical aspects of diplomatic practice have changed but the nature of diplomacy – representation, negotiations, proper access to decision-makers and perceptive analysis – has not. It is to be hoped that the diffusion of information will, in time, encourage our neighbours to adopt democracy. Until that happens, Israel will have to live in a non-democratic environment.

Israel's map of diplomatic representation tells the full story. At the time of writing we have diplomatic relations with 161 countries, with the Vatican and Ireland being the last in Western Europe to exchange ambassadors. The three pillars of Israel's foreign relations remain the region in which we live, the United States and Europe. Relations with our neighbours will be dominated by progress in the peace process. Relations with America were pivotal in the first fifty years of our statehood. Most of the agreements reached between Israel and Arab partners have a distinct American input. The Oslo Declaration of principles was achieved without US participation, but the US has played a crucial role in its implementation. Moreover, results of negotiations have depended a great deal on the personal commitment of American presidents. President Nixon accorded his full support to Kissinger's shuttle diplomacy, which resulted in the 'separation of forces' agreements with Egypt and Syria. Carter's tireless negotiations with Begin and Sadat produced the Camp David Accords and the peace treaty between Israel and Egypt. Since it was signed in 1979, Israel and Egypt have received about $110 billion in American aid. This is an enormous amount of assistance, and it has contributed to peace and stability. President Bush took a personal interest in Baker's diplomacy, which led to the Madrid Conference, and President Clinton and Secretary of State Madeleine Albright are deeply involved in the negotiations with the Palestinians. America is Israel's only strategic ally, in an unwritten alliance, and its contribution to Israel's defence and economic prosperity is immeasurable. Stability in the Middle East and the Persian Gulf area will, for the foreseeable future, depend on the US presence and a close understanding with the US must continue to have priority with Israeli governments.

Israel's relations with the European Union are not uniform because of the nature of the bilateral ties with each member state; these are influenced by historical memories and by the way they have been shaped in the past fifty years. The Holocaust remains an ever-present factor. The way European countries behaved when Israel was at peril during the Yom Kippur War and the British mandate over Palestine also had their impact. The Jewish contribution to European culture is enshrined in universal works of art, philosophy, music and literature. There is a cultural, emotional and geographical affinity with Europe which has no parallel, and many Israelis are keen Europhiles. However, the close friendship and mutual respect between Israel and Western Europe is nowhere near an alliance. Security remains a major consideration in Israeli policy-making and it can hardly rely on European assistance in times of danger. The common foreign policy of the European Union would require a broad consensus and the practical agreement of fifteen governments for any major policy decision. Europe, after the end of the Cold War, does not face major threats to its existence and expects Israel, as a liberal democracy, to conduct its policy in a European style, something that is not always possible given the dangers Israel still faces. Forty per cent of Israel's exports flow to countries of the EU and our imports from the union are considerable; there is therefore an important economic component to the relationship. The preferential agreement between Israel and the EU, which was first signed in 1975, was updated and broadened to include scientific cooperation. Europe obviously takes a keen interest in the peace process. It has contributed to multilateral discussions on specific subjects, like regional economic cooperation. It allocated large sums of money to Palestinian development after the Oslo Accords. Stability and peace in the Middle East is of prime interest in EU capitals. However, the role of Europe in the peace negotiations is limited because it cannot replace the US as the dominant power in the area and the major mediator in the Arab–Israeli conflict.

When my family and I arrived in Israel in 1948 there were about 700,000 Jews living there. On reaching the first million, the country celebrated passionately and fiery speeches were delivered in the Knesset. This feeling of elation continued with every additional million. No less exciting was the forging of people from such diverse backgrounds and cultures into one nation, the creation of an educational system that compares with the most advanced in the world, the building of a strong and sophisticated army, of a caring social structure, of a vibrant economy and a scientific and technological base that allows us to compete with advanced industrialized countries. The absorption of millions of people while fighting five bitter wars and coping with continuous terror was a major challenge. Heroic as these achievements were, we cannot dwell too much on the past and must look to the future and the formidable challenges which lie ahead.

I often think about the kind of Israel I would like my children and grandchildren to live in. All three are married. Our daughter Orna is a successful journalist and our two sons, Ilan and Yuval, are bankers. The four of us devoted twelve years of our lives to regular army service, not including periods of reserve duty. They and our five grandchildren give Hana and me immense pleasure. It would be simplistic to say that I would like our children to live in peace and tranquillity, for Israel is not the sole master of its destiny. Just as we cannot forge peace without the cooperation of our Arab partners, so we shall not be able to ignore developments which might affect us adversely and over which we have no control. Given the large Arab populations, the vast expanses of land they possess and their oil resources, there will always be a lack of equilibrium between Israel and its neighbours. The wider area includes Saddam's Iraq and fundamentalist Iran, adding to the measure of unpredictability with which Israel must live. It is therefore imperative that at all times Israel should have a strong, credible, sophisticated defence force as a deterrent. Arab leaders must be convinced that Israel has no aggressive designs or extensive territorial claims, no desire for hegemony of any sort and no interest in setting the regional agenda. Israel–Arab relations must be based on non-interference in internal affairs and on a readiness to cooperate in a true partnership for the stability and economic prosperity of the region as a whole.

For peace to be lasting and coexistence to be meaningful there is a need to work for true reconciliation between Jews and Arabs. As the conflict is basically political and not religious, and the root cause of friction is the Palestinian problem, agreement with the Palestinians should be accompanied by active efforts on both sides towards such reconciliation.

As Israel commences its journey into the second fifty years and the millennium dawns, I am confident that we have the will, the capacity and the innovative spirit to cope with the challenges of the twenty-first century. From a broad historical perspective we can see that the two hostile, anti-Semitic doctrines which dominated the twentieth century – fascism and Stalinist communism – have perished. They claimed the lives of millions of people. Zionism has triumphed and produced an independent and sovereign Israel, which is, however, far from being a perfect state in an imperfect world. But its first fifty years are a remarkable success story. Historians will make their detailed judgements on individual events and their consequences. This retrospective is merely a diplomat's narrative with the focus on the struggle for legitimacy and peace.

Notes

From the British Mandate to Jewish Sovereignty
1 HMSO, p.106
2 Noah Lucas, *The Modern History of Israel*
3 Crossman to Attlee, 7 and 9 May 1946, Crossman papers; PREM 8/302
4 PREM 8/627/5, Foreign Relations State Department archives
5 Roy Jenkins, *Nine Men of Power*, essay on Bevin

The Partition of Palestine
1 Jonathan Daniels, *Man of Independence*

THE FIRST DECADE, 1948–58
Independence and War
1 Howard M. Sacher, *A History of Israel*, Vol.I, p.332
2 Moshe Maoz, *Syria and Israel*
3 David Ben-Gurion, *Israel*, p.351
4 *Minutes of the Middle East Conference*, 21 July 1949, FO 371/75012
5 *Israel's Foreign Relations, Selected Documents*, ed. Meron Medzini, p.296
6 Elyahu Elath, *Through the Mist of the Days*
7 Holmes to Lovett, USSD 501 bb Palestine, 12-2248 box
8 WM Roger Louis, *The British Empire in the Middle East 1945–1951*, pp.566–7
9 FO Documents 371/75337
10 *Hansard, House of Commons*, debate on 26 Jan. 1949
11 Gideon Rafael, *Destination Peace*, pp.38–9
12 Abba Eban, *Personal Witness*, and Rafael, op. cit.
13 Sir Anthony Eden, *Full Circle*, p.330

The Suez War and the Sinai Operation
1 Egypt received 530 armoured vehicles (230 tanks, 200 armoured troop carriers and self-propelled guns), some 500 artillery pieces and nearly 200 combat aircraft. Chaim Herzog, *The Suez Sinai Campaign: Background*; and Cole C. Kingseed, *Eisenhower and the Suez Crisis*
2 *Eisenhower Diaries*, ed. Ferrell, pp.318–19
3 Eden, op. cit., p.331
4 Ibid., p.426
5 Moshe Dayan, *Story of My Life*, p.218
6 Department of State Press Release 413, 1956
7 Kingseed, op. cit., pp.51–3

8 Ibid.
9 Eden, op. cit., p.470
10 Ibid., p.480
11 Radio Cairo, 27.9.55, as quoted in Ben-Gurion, op. cit.
12 It was agreed that France would sell Israel seventy-two Mystere planes and two hundred tanks
13 Shimon Peres, *David's Sling*, pp.154–6
14 The details on the cooperation between France and Israel are based on *David's Sling* and *Battling for Peace* by Shimon Peres and Dayan, op. cit.; both were the architects of that unique relationship
15 David Ben-Gurion, *Selected Documents (1947–1963)*
16 Keith Kyle, *Suez*, p.324
17 Ben-Gurion's diary entry for 26 October 1957
18 Kyle, op. cit., p.334
19 As quoted in Kyle, op. cit., p.359
20 Kyle, op. cit., p.364
21 Abba Eban, *Autobiography*, p.216
22 *Selected Documents*, op. cit., p.557, 569
23 Abba Eban, *Autobiography*, p.232
24 Letter from Eisenhower to Ben-Gurion, 2 March 1957, in *Selected Documents*
25 Kyle, op. cit., p.497
26 *Hansard, House of Commons*, Vol. 562, 20 December 1956

Israel Celebrates its Tenth Anniversary

1 Ben-Gurion, *Selected Documents (1947–1963)*, p.436
   See also Bibliography on page 288 for further sources on the First Decade

THE SECOND DECADE, 1958–68

1 Golda Meir, *My Life*, p.259
2 Conversation with Israeli Foreign Minister Meir, 27 Dec. 1962, DOS, DD 193A (1979) as quoted in Moshe Ma'oz, *Syria and Israel*, p.86
3 Ibid.
4 Terrence Prittie, *Eshkol of Israel*
5 Ibid.
6 Sachar, op. cit.
7 Ben-Gurion, *Israel*
8 The ambassadors from Bucharest, Budapest, Prague, Belgrade, Moscow and Warsaw were present, see also Eban, *Autobiography*, p.307
9 As quoted in the State Department letter to Senator Keating of 17 June 1964, in *Selected Documents*, op. cit., Vol.I, p.496
10 Eric Johnston, 'A Key to the Future of the Mideast', *New York Times Magazine*, 19 Oct. 1958. *Selected Documents*, Vol.I, p.489
11 Ma'oz, op. cit., p.74
12 Eban, *Autobiography*, p.320

The Six Day War

1 Letter for U Thant to Foreign Minister Mahmoud Riad, 18 May 1967, *Selected Documents*, op. cit., vol.2, 713

2 *Selected Documents*, op. cit., vol.2
3 As told by ambassador Salah Bassiouni Richard Parker, *The Six Day War*, p.42
4 Cable from Eshkol to General de Gaulle, 19 May 1967, as quoted in Eban, *Autobiography*, p.327
5 *Selected Documents*, op. cit., vol.2, p.740
6 Moscow: Institute of International Relations, 1994, pp.129–33, as quoted by Parker, op. cit.
7 Parker, op. cit., pp.42, 71
8 Dr Vitaly Naumkin, Director of the Russian Centre for Strategic Research and International Relations, in Parker, op. cit., pp.38–9
9 Parker, op. cit., p.18
10 Shmuel Segev, *Sadin Adom*, pp.88–9
11 *Selected Documents*, op. cit., vol.2, 'The Six Day War'
12 From captured Egyptian documents, reprinted in *Basic Documents on the Arab–Israel Dispute*, E6, MF
13 See Eban, *Autobiography*, chapter 13 for accounts on the Paris, London and Washington talks
14 Yitzhak Rabin, *The Rabin Memoirs* (Steimatzky edn.), p.69
15 William B Quandt, *Decade of Decisions*, p.52
16 Efraim Evron, quoted in Parker, op. cit., p.133
17 *Selected Documents*, op. cit., vol.2, p.743
18 Eban, *Autobiography*, p.356
19 All quotes on the conversation with Johnson are from Eban, *Autobiography*, chapter 13
20 *Selected Documents*, op. cit., vol.2, p.747
21 Amit, as quoted in Parker, op. cit., p.140
22 William B Quandt, 'The View from the White House', Parker, op. cit., p.204
23 *Selected Documents*, op. cit., vol.2, p.779
24 King Hussein, *My War with Israel*, as quoted in Eban, *Personal Witness*, p.410
25 As reported by *The Times*, 7 June 1997
26 Dayan, op. cit., and Rabin, op. cit.
27 From Eshkol's letter to President Johnson, 5 June 1967
28 Dayan, op. cit., p.470
29 Shlomo Nakdimon in *Yediot Achronot*, 30 May 1997
30 Dayan talking to Rami Tal on 22 November 1976, in *Yediot Achronot*, 27 April 1997
31 Parker, op. cit., p.230

The Consequences of the Six Day War

1 Dan Horowitz, 'The Israeli Concept of National Security', in *Diplomacy in the Shadow of Confrontation*, Benjamin Newberger
2 Yitzhak Rabin, *Pinkas Sheiruth*, vol.1, p.206
3 Vladimir Jabotinsky, leader of the Revisionist wing in the Zionist movement
4 David Vital, 'The Definition of Aims in Foreign Policy', in Newberger, op. cit.
5 Dayan, op. cit., p.484
6 Statement of Eshkol before the Knesset, 12 June 1967
7 Dayan, op. cit., p.491
8 Moshe Zak, *Hussein the Peace Maker*
9 Ibid.

10 Sachar, op. cit., p.646
11 *Selected Documents*, op. cit., vol.2, p.818
12 Dayan, op. cit., p.510
13 Moshe Dayan, *A New Map – Changed Relations*, p.108
14 Ibid., p.110
15 Mordechai Shalev, *Yigal Allon as Foreign Minister*
16 Shlomo Gazit, *The Stick and the Carrot*
17 Siach Lochamim

THE THIRD DECADE, 1968–78

1 The Palestinian National Covenant was adopted by the First Arab Palestine Congress held in East Jerusalem in May 1964. It specified that 'Palestine with its boundaries at the time of the British mandate is a regional indivisible unit.'
2 Al Fatah policy statement, 19 October 1968, as reported in *The New York Times*, 20 October 1968 and quoted by Henry Kissinger, *White House Years*, p.345
3 *The Jarring Mission, First Phase, Excerpts from Report by the Secretary General of the UN, U Thant*, s/10070, 24 January 1971, as quoted in *Selected Documents*, op. cit., vol.2, p.843
4 *Selected Documents*, op. cit., p.841
5 Mordechai Gazit, *The Peace Process 1969–1973*, p.15
6 Meir, op. cit., pp.315–17
7 Gazit, op. cit., pp.112–13
8 Kissinger, op. cit., p.377
9 Ibid., p.367
10 'The Soviet Role in the Middle East', Alfred L. Atherton in *The Middle East Journal*, vol.39, Autumn 1985; and Rabin, *Rabin Memoirs*
11 Atherton, op. cit.
12 Kissinger, op. cit., p.371
13 Rabin, *Rabin Memoirs*, p.119
14 Atherton, op. cit., p.695
15 Kissinger, op. cit., p.561
16 Dayan, op. cit., p.517
17 Rabin, *Rabin Memoirs*, p.140 (Steimatzky edn), see also Gazit, op. cit., and Atherton, op. cit.
18 Rabin, *Rabin Memoirs*, p.146, Dayan, op. cit., p.541
19 Moshe Zak, *Hussein Makes Peace*, pp.124–30
20 *Selected Documents*, op. cit., p.934
21 Report of the UN Secretary General, 30 November 1971
22 Kissinger, op. cit., p.1285
23 Rabin, *Rabin Memoirs*, p.157
24 See Joseph Kraft, 'Phantom Memorandum' in *Washington Post*, 27.6.1971
25 See the Sadat interview in *Newsweek* 6 Dec. 1971
26 Gazit, op. cit., 'The Failed Suez Canal Agreement'
27 Rabin, *Rabin Memoirs*, p.165
28 Dayan interview to Rami Tal on 22.11.1976, in *Yediot Achronot* on 27 April 1997
29 Ibid.
30 Rabin, *Rabin Memoirs*, p.150

31 Ibid., Dayan Interview
32 Quandt, *Decade of Decision*, p.163
33 Kissinger, op. cit., p.1293

The Yom Kippur War

1 Quandt, op. cit., p.156
2 Dayan, op. cit., p.569
3 Quandt, op. cit., p.166 (Ray S. Cline, Director of Intelligence and Research in the State Department wrote at the end of May: 'Our view is that the resumption of hostilities by autumn will become a better than even bet.')
4 Henry Kissinger, *Year of Upheaval*, pp.461–2
5 Quandt, op. cit., p.159
6 Ibid.
7 Moshe Zak, *Hussein Makes Peace*, p.130
8 Kissinger, *Year of Upheaval*, p.464
9 Dayan, op. cit., p.574. On that day we had all in all 177 tanks on the Golan and 276 tanks on the Egyptian front
10 Meir, op. cit., pp.357–8
11 Nadav Safran, *Israel – The Embattled Ally*, p.277
12 Ibid., p.359
13 Kissinger, *Years of Upheaval*, p.466
14 From Eban, *Autobiography*, pp.486–8; Sharon interview, *Ha'aretz* newspaper, 20 Sept. 1973; Allon to *Yediot Achronot*, 4 June 1973
15 Dayan interview with Rami Tal, 22.11.1976, published in *Yediot Achronot*, 27 April 1997
16 Kissinger, *Years of Upheaval*, p.464
17 Ibid.
18 Dayan, op. cit., p.579
19 Ibid., pp.677–92
20 Kissinger, *Years of Upheaval*, pp.515, 450–544, 'The Middle East War', *Decades of Decision*, Quandt, and Yishai Cordoba, 'The October 1973 War', *The Policy of the United States in the Yom Kippur War*
21 Quandt, p.188
22 WSAG included the Secretary of Defence, James Schlesinger, the Chairman of the Joint Chiefs of Staff, Admiral Thomas Moorer, then Director of central intelligence (CIA), William Colby, the deputy national security adviser, General Brent Scowcroft, the deputy secretary of state, Kenneth Rush, the deputy assistant secretary of state for Near Eastern affairs, Joseph Sisco, and his deputy Alfred Atherton, and William Quandt, a member of the National Security Staff

American–Soviet Confrontation and the Aftermath of the Yom Kippur War

1 Cordoba, op. cit., pp.150–78
2 Quandt, op. cit., p.196
3 Quandt summarized the view from Washington in these words: 'The Israelis were encountering more difficulties than anticipated; the Arabs were both more effective at arms and more skilful at diplomacy.' (ibid., p.202)
4 Kissinger, *Years of Upheaval*, chapter 7

5 Quandt, op. cit., p.245
6 Meir, op. cit., p.378
7 Dayan, op. cit., p.730
8 Rabin, *Rabin Memoirs*, p.191
9 Ibid., p.200
10 See also Quandt, op. cit., 'Beyond Disengagement, Ford's Middle-East Policy'
11 Ibid., p.270
12 Mordechai Shalev, *Yigal Allon as Foreign Minister*, pp.49–50
13 The 28 October 1974 decision of the Rabat summit actually ended King
   Hussein's claim to negotiate the future of the West Bank and of the Palestinians
   living in the territories
14 Cyrus Vance, *Hard Choices*, p.164
15 Rabin, *Rabin Memoirs*, p.232
16 Quandt, op. cit.

Begin Elected Prime Minister
1 Moshe Dayan, *Shall the Sword Devour for Ever*, pp.17–27
2 Vance, op. cit., p.181
3 Ibid., p.183
4 In a joint press conference with Begin in Jerusalem on 21 November 1977,
   Sadat gave a succinct explanation of why he was reluctant to have Soviet
   participation: '… my relations with the Soviets are strained and it appears that
   whatever I do doesn't go to their liking at all. For instance, the visit here also,
   in their comments, doesn't go to their liking at all. I fear that the same attitude
   could be adopted in Geneva, and they are one of the co-sponsors.' (*Selected
   Documents*, op. cit., p.207)
5 Dayan, *Shall the Sword Devour for Ever*
6 *Selected Documents*, op. cit., vol.4, p.162. See also Eric Silver, *Begin*, chapter 18
7 Vance, op. cit., p.194
8 Dayan, *Shall the Sword Devour for Ever*, chapter 6
9 Ibid.
10 Mohamed Heikal, *Secret Channels*, p.259
11 Rabin, *Rabin Memoirs*, p.200
12 *Selected Documents*, op. cit., vol.4
13 Ibid., p.189
14 Ibid., p.190
15 Ibid., p.194
16 Dayan, *Shall the Sword Devour for Ever*, pp.49–50

THE FOURTH DECADE, 1978–88
1 Dayan, *Shall the Sword Devour for Ever*, chapter 9; Vance, op. cit., pp.211–15;
   William B Quandt, *Camp David* (Hebrew edn); Elyakim Rubinstein, *Path of Peace*
2 Kamel, *The Lost Peace*, as quoted by Quandt, *Camp David*
3 Quandt, *Camp David*, p.193
4 Vance, op. cit., p.223
5 Ibid., p.225
6 Dayan, *Shall the Sword Devour for Ever*, p.155
7 Text of *Framework for Peace*, 17 September 1978
8 Begin's agony over the wording 'Palestinian people' and 'Palestinian rights' is

best illustrated in an interview to *Ma'ariv* he gave three days after Camp David: 'We did not use and are not using the term "Palestinian people" even though that is what's in the English version ... these words, in our language, and according to our understanding, will be read "the Arabs of Israel".' (*Selected Documents*, op. cit., vol.5, p.541)

9 Dayan, *Shall the Sword Devour for Ever*, p.158

10 Vance, op. cit., p.229

11 Dayan, *Shall the Sword Devour for Ever*, p.165

12 Joint letter from Sadat and Begin to President Carter, 26 March 1979, in *Selected Documents*, op. cit., vol.5, p.712

13 Quandt, *Camp David*; Vance, op. cit.; Dayan, *Shall the Sword Devour for Ever*; Quandt, *Peace Process*

14 Sachar, op. cit., vol.2; Quandt, *Peace Process*

15 Sachar, op. cit., vol.2; Eric Silver, *Begin*

16 Ned Temko, *To Win or to Die, A Personal Portrait of Menachem Begin*, chapter 26

17 Shamir address before B'nai B'rith Leadership, 15 August 1981, as quoted in *Selected Documents*, op. cit., vol.7, p.120

18 Aryeh Naor, *Cabinet at War*, chapters 1–5; Roni Berman, interviews on the Mossad and Lebanon, in *Ha'aretz*, 3 Jan. 1997

19 Naor, op. cit., quoting Yari and Shiff (Milchemet Sholal)

20 Quandt, *Peace Process*, p.341

21 Naor, op. cit., p.48

22 *Selected Documents*, op. cit., vol.8, p.13

23 *Ha'aretz*, 5 Nov. 1997

24 Naor, op. cit., p.117

25 Yitzhak Shamir, *Summing Up*, p.135

26 George P. Shultz, *Turmoil and Triumph*, p.48

27 Ibid., p.87

28 Shamir, op. cit., p.143

29 Thomas Friedman, *From Beirut to Jerusalem*, p.256

30 Shamir speech to the Knesset, 12 March 1984, in *Selected Documents*, op. cit., vol.8, p.539

31 Shimon Peres, *Battling for Peace*; Shamir, op. cit.

32 Shamir, op. cit., p.170

33 Shultz, op. cit., p.939

34 Quandt, *Peace Process*, 'The Reagan Presidency'

35 Shultz, op. cit., p.453

36 Ibid., p.462

37 Peres, *Battling for Peace*, p.361–2

38 Shultz, op. cit., p.940

39 Ibid., p.948

40 *Selected Documents*, vol.10, p.863

41 Shultz, op. cit., chapter 47

42 Aryeh Shalev, *The Intifada*, p.213

43 *Ministry of Foreign Affairs Bulletin*, 26 July 1986

44 Zeev Shiff and Ehud Yari, *Intifada*, concluding chapter

45 Shalev, op. cit.

46 Aaron S. Klieman, *Israel and the World after Forty Years*, chapter 4

THE FIFTH DECADE, 1988–98

1 Yosef Govrin, *The Relations Between Israel and the Soviet Union*, p.275
2 After the severance of relations between the Soviet Union and Israel in 1967, Holland had represented us in Moscow. See *Envoy to Moscow* by Aryeh Levin for a full description of the resumption of relations with the Soviet Union
3 Interview with Shamir and Rabin, 1 Aug. 1988, in *Selected Documents*, op. cit., vol.10, pp.971–2
4 Quandt, *Peace Process*, pp.371–5
5 Ibid., p.375
6 Statement by President Reagan, 14 Dec. 1988, in *Selected Documents*, op. cit., vol.10, p.1047
7 Mahmoud Abbas (Abu Mazen), *Through Secret Channels*, p.33
8 Rabin interview on Israeli television (Arabic Service), 8 Dec. 1988, in *Selected Documents*, op. cit., vol.10, p.1034
9 David Horowitz ed., *Yitzhak Rabin, Soldier of Peace*; Moshe Arens, *Broken Covenant*, p.48
10 Shamir, op. cit., pp.194–5
11 *New York Times*, 14 Mar. 1989
12 Shamir, op. cit., p.198
13 *Selected Documents*, op. cit., vol.11, p.169
14 Shamir, op. cit.
15 Arens, op. cit., p.126
16 Ibid., p.135
17 James A. Baker, *The Politics of Diplomacy*, op. cit., pp.128–9
18 Baker, op. cit., p.268
19 For Israel and the Gulf War see Shamir, op. cit., pp. 215–25; Arens, op. cit., pp.193–235; Baker, op. cit., pp.385–90
20 Baker, op. cit., pp.436–42
21 Quandt, *Peace Process*, p.495
22 Baker wrote, in *Politics of Diplomacy*, p.513; 'Bentsur was a senior aide to David Levy, who, like his boss, was one of the few members of Shamir's government who I felt wholeheartedly supported the peace process. As early as September of 1990, in fact, in a meeting with Denis Ross as a New York delicatessen, he'd proposed the two-track formula that later became the centerpeace of the US initiative.'
23 Baker, op. cit., p.419
24 Quandt, *Peace Process*, p.497
25 Arens, op. cit., p.242
26 Ibid., p.323
27 *Selected Documents*, op. cit., vol.11, p.153
28 Ibid., p.95
29 *Selected Documents*, op. cit., vol.11, pp.226–8
30 Rabin speech in the Knesset, 14 Sept. 1992
31 Eitan Bentzur, *The Road to Peace Crosses Madrid*, pp.166–7
32 Mazen, op. cit., p.115. The real name of Abu Ala is Ahmad Qurei
33 For full description of the Oslo talks see: Yossi Beilin, *Touching Peace*, Peres, op. cit., and Mazen, op. cit.
34 Letter from Arafat to Rabin, 9 Sept. 1993
35 Mazen, op. cit., p.81

36 Between October 1993 and October 1997, 229 Israelis were killed and 1377 were injured by Palestinian terrorism
37 Horowitz, *Yitzhak Rabin*, pp.124–30
38 Ibid., p.129
39 'The idea of Rabin's appointment [as Ambassador in Washington] first came to me from Moshe Raviv, my trusted adviser in the Foreign Ministry,' Eban, *Personal Witness*, p.478
40 Zeev Shiff, 'Pocket', in *Ha'aretz*, 29 Aug. 1997
41 Rabinovich, *The Brink of Peace, Israel and Syria 1992–1996*, pp.267, 305–327
42 US Information Service, European Wireless File, 12 June 1996
43 'Israel: Towards the Twenty-First Century', address by Ehud Barak at the Steinmetz Centre, Tel Aviv University
44 *Yediot Achtonot*, 4 June 1997

Epilogue

1 I was quite touched when the Prime Minister started his speech with a tribute to me saying: 'Moshe, as you know, is leaving us soon to return to Israel. I believe he has done enormous service for his country and when he leaves, he will leave behind many many good friends. I think that Moshe, throughout my time as opposition leader and now as Prime Minister, has been an absolute stalwart in the relationship between Britain and Israel, so Moshe, on behalf of us all, and on behalf of Britain, thank you.'
2 Report by the Institute for Jewish Policy Research, November 1997

Bibliography

Arens, Moshe, *War and Peace in the Middle East 1988–1992*
Ben-Gurion, David, *Israel*
Ben-Gurion, David, *Towards the End of the Mandate*
Documents on the Foreign Policy of Israel, 1951 and 1952
Eban, Abba, *An Autobiography*
Eban, Abba, *Personal Witness*
Elath, Elyahu, *Through the Mist of the Days*
Eytan, Walter, *Israel among the Nations*
Feldman, Lily Gardner, *The Special Relationship between West Germany and Israel*
Ha'aretz newspaper, ed. Ariyeh Ziv, 'The First Ten Years'
Jenkins, Roy, *Nine Men of Power*
Kohl, Helmut, *History's Inescapable Impact on the Present*
Louis, William Roger, *The British Empire in the Middle East 1945–1951*
Maoz, Moshe, *Syria and Israel*
Medzini, Meron, ed., *Israel's Foreign Relations, Selected Documents 1947–1974*
Peres, Shimon, *David's Sling*
Raphael, Gideon, *Destination Peace*
Sacher, Howard M., *A History of Israel*
Slater, Robert, *Rabin of Israel*
Thatcher, Margaret, *The Downing Street Years*
Weidenfeld, George, *Remembering My Good Friends*

Index